Money Terms

GRAEME PIETERSZ

moneyterms.co.uk

British Library Cataloguing In Publication Data
A Record of this Publication is available
from the British Library

ISBN 978-1-84685-571-9

First Published 2007 by
Exposure Publishing, an imprint of Diggory Press

Diggory Press Ltd, Three Rivers, Minions,
Liskeard, Cornwall, PL14 5LE, UK
Affiliated to:
Diggory Press, Inc. of Goodyear, Arizona, USA
WWW.DIGGORYPRESS.COM

Preface

Much of the material in this book has been suggested by experience. I have tried to cover what I and colleagues have needed to know as analysts. It is not, of course, possible to cover sector specific terminology comprehensively, but I have covered what we have found most important.

Coverage of non-investment topics has been biased to what is useful from an investment viewpoint. Coverage of economics, for example, is selective.

Many parts of financial theory are highly mathematical but covering this is not within the scope of this book. Attempting to cover all the necessary mathematics would considerably lengthen the book. Instead, I have presented useful results (such as the CAPM) without derivation. This is more than adequate for the core area of the book's coverage: the fundamental analysis of equities.

This level of coverage is not sufficient for areas such as the derivatives valuation and risk modelling, so these must be regarded as only covered in outline. I would, in any case, not claim sufficient expertise to be able to write authoritatively on these topics in detail.

This book is primarily written from a British point of view. Most of it is applicable globally. Where I am aware of that different terminology, practices or conventions are used in other countries I have indicated this. Comments on tax, regulation and law should be presumed to only apply to the UK unless otherwise stated. In any case, readers who need reliable guidance on these areas should consult lawyers or other appropriate professionals.

This book was typeset with Latex. The website is generated from the same files using Hyperlatex. I strongly recommend Latex to anyone who writes documents of any length. Its flexibility, the typographically correct end results and the logical structure that comes naturally to Latex documents far outweighs the need to spend a little time learning to use it. It has saved me a great deal of effort.

Conventions and notation

The main part of the book is laid out in simple alphabetic order.

Abbreviations are usually listed separately. Where terms are more commonly used in their abbreviated form the main entry is that for the abbreviation.

Cross referenced terms are set in bold face, followed by a page reference in square brackets, like this: **CAPM** [p. 50].

The word or phrase in bold face may not exactly correspond to the title of the entry to which it refers. It should be sufficient to easily find the entry when used in combination with the page number. This improves readability for those who do not follow the cross reference as it allowed the use of more succinct an natural wording. I apologise if it makes any cross-references harder to follow.

I have not cross-referenced every single occurrence of every term that is defined in the book. In particular, I have omitted many cross-references to basic and commonly occurring terms that most readers are likely to be familiar with. I have cross-referenced even these where they are most relevant.

Mathematics used in this book

The mathematical conventions used are standard. The main exception is the use of words rather than single letters for variables in simple formulae. This is usually self explanatory.

Where words are used for variables, cross referenced words are shown in bold (as opposed to the italic demanded by convention) and are followed by the page reference in italics as usual.

The level of maths used has been kept relatively basic. Some concepts and notation need to be understood. The brief summaries below are meant to help understand ideas presented in this book. They are no substitute for the fuller explanations that may be found in maths textbooks.

Summation

The symbol* Σ is used to compactly represent a series of mathematical expressions that are to be added together.

$$\sum_{i=1}^{n} \frac{1}{x_i}$$

means:

$$\frac{1}{x_1} + \frac{1}{x_2} + \frac{1}{x_3} + \cdots + \frac{1}{x_n}$$

I have usually used the latter form as it is more intuitively understandable.

It is important to understand that an infinite[†] series of such expressions can often add up to a finite total. An example is the **present value** [p. 220] of a series of cash flows that consists of perpetual annual payments that increase by a proportion[‡] g every year, starting with C this year. It is:

$$C + \frac{C(1+g)}{1+r} + \frac{C(1+g)^2}{(1+r)^2} + \frac{C(1+g)^3}{(1+r)^3} + \cdots + = \frac{C}{r-g}$$

---

* actually the Greek letter sigma
† the symbol for infinity is ∞
‡ so that if g is 0.05 the payment increases 5% every year

Averages

The different types of **average** [p. 25] used are explained in the body of the book. The most important in finance are **arithmetic means** [p. 19], **geometric means** [p. 158] and **weighted averages** [p. 344].

Derivatives

Derivatives in the mathematical sense must not be confused with **derivative securities** [p. 96]. As the former are often used in valuing the latter the confusion is not unlikely.

$\frac{dy}{dx}$ means the rate of change of y with x. This is called the derivative of y against x. If x changes by a small amount dx, then y will change by $\frac{dy}{dx} \times dx$.

The notation $\frac{\partial y}{\partial x}$ is used to denote a partial derivative: it is the rate of change of y with x, with all the other factors that y depends on kept constant. Most of the derivatives in this book are partial derivatives. This is because most of the equations in which they occur are related to the prices of derivative securities, which depend on multiple factors.

A full explanation of derivatives is well beyind the scope of this book and is not needed by most investors or analysts.

Integrals

Integrals are not directly used in this book but would be needed to apply some concepts covered. An integral is used to calculate the area under the curve of a function. Some formulae presented in this book can be re-stated using integrals instead of summation. This is necessary when using continuous functions.

Integrals are the opposite of derivatives. If $g(x)$ is** the derivative of $f(x)$, then $f(x)$ (or $f(x)$ plus a constant) is the integral of $g(x)$.

The symbol for an integral is $\int$ and the integral of $f(x)$ between a and b (i.e. the area under its curve from a to b) is written:

$$\int_a^b f(x)dx$$

Probability distributions

A probability distribution is the likelihood of an as yet unknown value (such as the price of a security on a given date in the future) having various values. A probability distribution may be expressed as a function, by the exhaustive listing of the probability of each possible value[§] or depicted as a graph.

**The derivative of $f(x)$ is often written $f'(x)$

[§] this will usually be an approximation

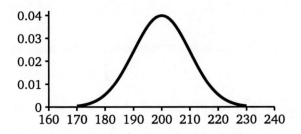

The graph above shows the probability distribution of a share price. The higher the curve at a given price, the more probable that the price at that point will be the actual outcome.

It can be seen from this graph that the expected value (see **expected return** [p. 135]) of the price is 100. The price will probably be between 90 and 110. It is very unlikely that the price will be less than 80 or more than 120.

Variance and correlation

The characteristics of a probability distribution (or of other statistical distributions) can be summed up by a few key characteristics. The most important of these are its **mean** [p. 19] and **standard deviation** [p. 305]. The latter is a measure of how spread out a distribution is.

The relationship between different distributions is also important. For example, if a market index rises, it is likely that the price of a particular share will also rise. The strength of this relationship is measured by the **correlation coefficient** [p. 74] of market returns and returns on the security.

This is a very complex and important topic, and the entries referred to above only cover what is necessary to understand other material in this book.

It is possible, although not always advisable, to do the essential calculations investors need (such as calculating a **beta** [p. 34]) without a full understanding of the mathematics, by using the statistics functions provided by any spreadsheet software.

Learning finance

Many concepts in finance are covered in this book in sufficient depth to allow readers to learn as well as use it as a reference book. Essential topics are listed below in suggested reading order. For other topics it would probably be more interesting to simply find one topic of interest and follow cross-references from there.

1. The **time value of money** [p. 322]

2. **Risk aversion** [p. 281]

3. **Diversification** [p. 103]

4. **Risk free rate of return** [p. 282] and **risk premium** [p. 282]

5. **NPV** [p. 220] and **DCF valuation** [p. 88] (first part)

6. **CAPM** [p. 50] and **beta** [p. 34]

7. **Dividend yield** [p. 107]

8. **Internal rate of return** [p. 183] and **yield to maturity** [p. 350]

9. **Yield spread** [p. 349]

10. **Earnings per share** [p. 122], the **PE ratio** [p. 237] and **earnings yield** [p. 115]

11. **Capital structure** [p. 48] and **capital structure irrelevance** [p. 48]

12. **Enterprise Value** [p. 121], **EBITDA** [p. 116] and **EV/EBITDA** [p. 129]

13. **Depreciation** [p. 95] and **amortisation** [p. 15]

14. **Adjusted EPS** [p. 7] and **prospective PE** [p. 255]

ABC1

A, B and C1 are the highest three **social grades** [p. 298] in the most commonly used classification. Media companies frequently use the proportion of their audience in these grades as a measure of the affluence of their audience – and therefore the attractiveness of the audience to advertisers.

This is in many ways a fairly crude measurement. Its main advantages are that it is widely availability, well understood, generally accepted and it is easy to gather the data. Because it is commonly available, it is useful for comparing different media businesses.

Abnormal return

The abnormal return produced by a portfolio is the excess of the actual return over the return that would be expected given the level of risk taken. For a well **diversified** [p. 103] portfolio it would typically be the outperformance over the market.

More generally, abnormal returns are the excess of the returns given the level of risk of the particular security or portfolio, in other words the size of the **alpha** [p. 14].

Absolute return

An absolute return is the actual amount of money made by an investment; the actual gain as a percentage of the amount invested.

In contrast, **relative returns** [p. 273] are adjusted to show performance compared to a **benchmark** [p. 33].

Investment performance is often measured using relative returns. Relative returns all investors to see how much of their gains were the result of good decisions, and how much merely reflected market movements. Absolute returns nonetheless matter because what matters most to investors is how much money they have, which depends on the absolute return.

Acceptances

Once a takeover bid is formally made shareholders in the target company may choose to accept the offer or not. When shareholders accept the offer, they do not immediately sell their shares to the bidder. This has two main implications:

- The bidder does not have to buy the shares unless the offer becomes unconditional.

- The shareholders accepting the offer will get the benefits of any improvements to the offer after accepting it.

The **City Code's** [p. 58] timetable for bids sets out a timetable that (among other things) limits the time between when the bidder starts being open to acceptances and the latest date for the actual purchase of the shares.

It is usual for a bid to become **unconditional** [p. 330] as to acceptances once the bidder has received sufficient acceptances to give the bidder (and **concert party** [p. 67], if any) a 90% holding. This is because a bidder who succesfully acquires a 90% stake can buy the remaining 10% at the same price through a **compulsory acquisition** [p. 67].

Accounting Rate of Return

The accounting rate of return (ARR) is a very simple (in fact overly simple) rate of return:

$$\frac{average\ profit}{average\ investment}$$

as a percentage.

The profit number used is **operating profit** [p. 227] (usually from a particular project).

The average investment is the **book value** [p. 38] of assets tied up (in the project). This is important as the profit figure used is after **depreciation** [p. 95] and **amortisation** [p. 15]. The means that value of assets used should also be after depreciation and amortisation as well.

ARR is most often used internally when selecting projects. It can also be used to measure the performance of projects and subsidiaries within an organisation. It is rarely used by investors because:

- **Cash flows** [p. 53] are more important to investors, and ARR is based on numbers that include non-cash items.

- ARR does not take into account the time value of money – the value of cashflows does not diminish with time as is the case with **NPV** [p. 220] and **IRR** [p. 183].

- There are better alternatives which are not significantly more difficult to calculate.

Because ARR does not take into account the time value of money, and because it is wholly unadjusted for non-cash items, any method of selecting investments based on it is necessarily seriously flawed. Its only advantage is that it is very easy to calculate. It is fairly easy to construct (realistic) examples where it will lead to different choices from NPV, and the NPV led decision is clearly correct.

Accounting Standards Board

The Accounting Standards Board (ASB) is an arm of the **Financial Reporting Council** [p. 146] that sets accounting standards in the UK.

The role of the ASB is less important than it used to be: all **listed** [p. 190] companies are now required (by EU directive) to use **IFRSs** [p. 166]. The ASB now appears to see its role as lying mainly in influencing the development of IFRSs and European standards.

UK standards (for unlisted companies, which are mostly not bound by the EU directive) are converging with IFRSs and increasingly contain only minor deviations from international standards.

Accrual principle

The principle of accrual (also called matching) is fundamental to accounting. It requires that costs should be matched to the revenues they generate.

This means, for example, that cost of an asset should be **depreciated** [p. 95] over its useful life rather than the entire cost being charged against profits when it is purchased.

It also means that sales are recognised when they are made, rather than when cash is received – so sales and purchases on credit are usually included in **profit and loss account** [p. 234] in the year the sale was invoiced in, rather than when payment is received.

There are more elaborate methods for dealing with issues such as long term projects that are partially completed. See **revenue recognition** [p. 277].

Accruals

Accruals are expenses for which invoices have not been received at the end of an accounting period.

These outstanding amounts are not strictly creditors because invoices have not been received. However, in order to for the accounts to be consistent with the **accrual** [p. 4] principle these costs need to be included on the **P & L** [p. 234] for the period.

Accruals and **deferred income** [p. 92] are often shown as a single balance sheet item.

Including the accrued expenses and excluding the deferred income in the P & L makes it necessary to show the total amounts accrued on the **balance sheet** [p. 28] in order to reconcile the accounts. Then in the next period:

- When accruals are invoiced they are moved from accruals to creditors.

- When the goods or services to which the deferred income relates are supplied, the revenue will be recognised (see **revenue recognition** [p. 277]), and the deferred income on the balance sheet reduced.

Accrued interest

The accrued interest on a bond is the amount of interest that has been deemed to have accumulated on the bond, but which has not yet been paid.

It is the amount of interest that would have been paid if interest was paid daily, but which has not become actually payable yet.

As a simple example, suppose a £100 bond pays 10% interest annually, so a single £10 payment is made each year. Six months after an interest payment would be exactly half way between interest payments, so the accrued interest would be half the annual payment or £5. Three months after an interest payment, we would be a quarter of the way to the next payment, so the accrued interest would be a quarter of the payment or £2.50.

Accrued interest is calculated using a **days convention** [p. 87], which may differ from the actual times elapsed since and between interest payments.

The most common reason for calculating the accrued interest is to calculate one of the **clean price** [p. 59] or the **dirty price** [p. 98], given the other.

Acid test ratio

See **quick assets ratio** [p. 261].

Acquisition

The purchase a company, a business, product lines, or brands is called an acquisition. The purchase, by one company, of another, is also called a takeover.

Buying a listed company requires making a **takeover bid** [p. 317] and going through a heavily regulated process.

Takeover bids may be **agreed** [p. 13] or **hostile** [p. 165].

Takeovers are almost always beneficial for the shareholders of the company being bought (as the share price is pushed up). They are rarely good for the shareholders of the acquiring company. They do tend to benefit the management of the acquiring company who end up running a bigger company.

Organic growth [p. 230] is usually more valuable than growing a business through acquisitions.

Small strategically important acquisitions that fit well with the businesses the company already has ("bolt on" acquisitions) tend to work better than larger ones. Acquisitions can only be justified if the business being bought will be worth a lot more in the hands of its new owners than in the hands of the sellers. The acquiring company should have a clear and convincing explanation of why this is so.

Acquisitions are usually paid for either in cash or with newly issued shares or both. The former leaves the company more highly **geared** [p. 157]. The latter means that the acquirer's original shareholders are left holding a smaller proportion of the enlarged business. The premium they need to pay over the normal share price of the acquired company means that they lose out, to some extent, to the benefit of the original shareholders in the company being bought.

Acquisitive growth

Acquisitive growth is the opposite of **organic growth** [p. 230]. It is the element of growth (including declines) that comes from buying and selling businesses.

It is important to separate organic and **acquisition** [p. 5] driven growth, as organic growth is more valuable. Any company can grow by buying other businesses as long as it has the funds (the fact that it can pay with shares makes this probable).

Organic growth is harder to achieve but usually more sustainable. Acquisitive growth also tends to be more expensive: acquisitions have to be paid for and the previous owners will usually manage to get a fair price or better. This means that acquisitions are rarely of much benefit to the shareholders of the acquiring company.

Several studies have shown that most takeovers destroy shareholder value.

There are some cases where acquisitive growth is good. In some industries companies have grown over the long term by making regular (usually small) acquisitions with strong **synergies** [p. 316].

A good example of sustainable acquisitive growth is the pub sub-sector in the UK from the early 1990s onwards. There were large numbers of small chains and standalone pubs available. By buying these large chains could increase their purchasing power (cutting the cost of supplies) and centralise administration (cutting overheads).

Active investing

Active investing is the opposite of the strategies adopted by **index trackers** [p. 325]. An active investment strategy is an attempt to out-perform the market through picking and trading securities or through **asset allocation** [p. 21].

An active investor therefore expects to be able to find instances of the failure of **efficient markets** [p. 118] to exploit. There are a number of **strategies** [p. 179] that an active investor may use.

Actuary

Actuaries assess the probabilities of certain events occuring and the financial consequences of those events. Their work combines statistics and finance.

In general insurance, actuaries gauge the probability of the insured events occurring and the premiums needed to cover them. They also help devise insurance policies.

The funds of insurance companies and pension schemes require actuarial valuation in order to ensure that they are able to cover future liabilities. This is particularly important, and difficult, in the case of life insurance and pensions. The long term nature of the risk makes assessments very sensitive to the exact assumptions that are made. Assumptions that have to be made include investment returns and life expectancies.

Actuaries usually work either in the insurance industry or for firms of consulting actuaries. The demand in the insurance industry is obvious. Consulting actuaries are needed by clients such as company pension schemes.

Ad driven media

Much of the media sector is dependent on advertising for some, or all, of its revenues. This makes it highly **cyclical** [p. 84] as spending on advertising is easy to cut when savings need to be made, and returns on the same level of advertising are likely to be lower when consumer spending is lower.

The most strongly ad-driven media include free to air broadcasters (both radio and TV), free newspapers and advertising agencies. These are the most cyclical parts of the media sector.

Although trends in overall ad spend are important for the ad driven media, not all advertising is equally cyclical: local and classified advertising tend to be more resilient than display or broadcast advertising.

Business to business advertising is generally more cyclical than advertising aimed at consumers. This may not be true where the advertising is driven by a defensive industry, as might be the case for a trade magazine.

Many media channels have a mixture of revenue streams and the proportions of revenue coming from these streams affects both growth and stability of revenues.

Long term trends are at least as important as the cycles. Currently, new technologies are increasing the number of available TV and radio channels, **fragmenting** [p. 200] the audience. The internet and interactive TV have created new media that are further fragmenting audiences.

Adjusted EPS

It is common to use headline or adjusted EPS rather than **basic EPS** [p. 31] to get a better view of underlying performance and trends. The usual adjustment is reversing the effect on profits of **exceptional items** [p. 132] and other one-offs such as **impairments** [p. 166]. These are excluded because they do not help investors estimate future cashflows.

Companies often **disclose** [p. 98] their adjusted EPS. Analysts forecasts are usually of the headline EPS as well. The exact definition varies and different companies and analysts use different adjustments.

The IIMR (Institute of Investment Management and Research) has set out a widely used definition of headline EPS. This defines certain items that are excluded regardless of whether the company concerned has classified them as exceptionals or not, thus allowing fair comparison of companies that may have different approaches to classifying expenses as exceptional.

Adjusted operating profit

Operating profit adjusted, in much same way as **adjusted EPS** [p. 7], in order to provide a better indication of underlying trends. Like adjusted EPS, the exact definition can vary. It is similar to **trading profit** [p. 327], and can be synonymous with it.

The most important adjustments are the adding back of one-off costs, such as **exceptional items** [p. 132] and **impairments** [p. 166].

Other items that are commonly excluded are changes in the **fair value** [p. 137] of financial instruments and the cost of share based payments. Investors should keep an eye on these. Although neither is a cash cost to the operations of a company, both are real costs to investors. In the case of share based payments, they are usually a recurring cost.

Despite these reservations, adjusted operating profit is a very useful indicator of how a business is performing. It is frequently **disclosed** [p. 98] by companies. If not, investors and analysts may need to calculate it themselves. Even when it is disclosed, it may be necessary to recalculate it if one wishes to use a different definition.

Adjusted present value

Adjusted present value (APV) is similar to **NPV** [p. 220]. The difference is that is uses the cost of equity as the discount rate (rather than **WACC** [p. 342]). Separate adjustments are made for the effects financing (e.g. the tax advantages of debt).

As usual with **DCFs** [p. 88] of this sort, the calculation of adjusted present value is straightforward but tedious.

The first step in calculating an APV is to calculate a base NPV using the cost of equity as the discount rate. This may be the same as the company's cost of equity. In some cases it may be necessary to recalculate it by estimating a **beta** [p. 34] and using **CAPM** [p. 50]. This is most likely when assessing a project or business that is very different from a company's core business.

Once the base NPV has been calculated, the next step is to calculate the NPV of each set of cash flows that results from financing. The most obvious of these are the tax effects of using debt rather than equity. These can be discounted either at the cost of debt or at a higher rate that reflects uncertainties about the tax effects (e.g. future tax rates, whether the company as a whole will be profitable and paying tax). The NPV of the tax effects is then added to the base NPV.

If there are other effects of financing, then these are also added or subtracted, and the end result is the APV.

Given **capital structure irrelevance** [p. 48], the savings from financing should be balanced by changes in the required return on equity with changes in **capital structure** [p. 48]. This usually makes a simple NPV with the WACC as the discount rate preferable.

ADR

See **American Depositary Receipt** [p. 14].

Adverse opinion

If there is a material difference between the financial statements as reported by a company and the auditor's opinion of what the accounts should show, then this should be reflected in the **audit opinion** [p. 25]. The **audit** [p. 25] report should contain a warning that the accounts do not show a true and fair view of the company. This is an adverse opinion.

Adverse opinions are rare, and almost unknown among **listed companies** [p. 190]. If auditors are aware of problems that might cause them to issue an adverse opinion, they will warn the company sufficiently early to allow a solution to be found.

Adverse selection

If insurance is available at the same price to people facing widely varying risks, then those with the greatest risks are more likely to buy insurance. This adverse selection works to the detriment of insurers. Unchecked, it would make **underwriting** [p. 331] unprofitable.

Insurers protect themselves from adverse selection by attempting to measure risk and either charging more from the higher risks, or by refusing to cover them at all. For example, motor insurers charge higher premiums for cars and drivers that are statistically more likely to be involved in accidents. Medical insurers usually exclude pre-existing conditions (i.e. any illness that pre-dates the start of cover) from their cover in order to deter people from buying cover after a problem has been diagnosed.

In part, the problem of adverse selection is dealt with by the insurers' attempts to measure risk, which is anyway necessary to setting premiums. However, this still leaves insurers with a significantly problem in any circumstances where the insured may have more information than they do. This is why, unlike other contracts, insurance contacts are agreed *uberrimae fides* [p. 329] (in utmost good faith). This means that a persons* taking out insurance are required to inform the insurer of all relevant information, not just what they are directly asked for.

---

*This includes corporations and partnerships as well as individuals

In some countries there are restrictions on what information insurers can gather, which can affect their ability to limit adverse selection. In the UK, life insurers cannot require applicants for cover below a threshold level to take genetic tests, even though it is fairly easy for people to have tests performed and conceal the results.

Adverse selection has similarities to **moral hazard** [p. 210]. Both change risks to insurers as a result of customer behaviour.

Advertising elasticity

Advertising elasticity of demand is the change in sales that results from each monetary unit (e.g. each pound or dollar) that is spend on advertising. It is a similar measure to other elasticities such as **price elasticity** [p. 247] and is:

$$\frac{\Delta Q}{Q} \bigg/ \frac{\Delta A}{A}$$

where Q is the quantity sold
A is the advertising expenditure
ΔQ is the change in quantity sold and
ΔA is the change in advertising expenditure

Cross elasticities [p. 80] of advertising will be strong for competing products, some complementary products and other products bearing the same or related (in consumers' perception) branding.

Advisory broking

Advisory stockbroking services offer investors advice from a stockbroker – but the final investment decisions are left to the client. Unlike **discretionary** [p. 99] stockbroking, the client retains control over each and every investment decision. Unlike **execution only** [p. 131] services, the broker does offer advice.

As with discretionary broking services, advisory services usually require a minimum portfolio size from clients. The service is too expensive to provide at reasonable rates for small portfolios. The broker usually charges a commission that is a percentage of the value of each transaction.

The fee structure of advisory broking does create an incentive for brokers to churn (trade more than is beneficial to the client) in order to generate commission. This is very rarely taken to extremes as it becomes apparent to clients and is likely to ultimately draw regulators' (in the UK, the **FSA's** [p. 149]) attention as well.

In terms of cost, the level of control investors have and the amount of work investors need to do themselves, advisory services fall between discretionary and execution only broking services.

The combination of advice and dealing services, and commission based on deal size, makes private client broking superficially similar to the services provided to institutional clients. However:

- A private client is more likely to follow a broker's advice than an institutional client.

- Private clients are likely to be offered more specific advice ("sell A and buy B").

- A private client will almost always use just one broker whereas an institutional client will usually use several.

- The simple advice and research typically offered to private clients is nothing like the detailed research offered to institutional clients.

AER

See **annual effective rate** [p. 16].

Agency cross

A transaction in a security is an agency cross if a broker matches orders between two of its clients directly, rather than through the market.

The broker collects a commission from each client, just as it would if the orders had executed through the market. The broker may be able to save clients the **bid-offer spread** [p. 35] charged by **market makers** [p. 197].

Agency cross trades are regulated in order to ensure brokers do not favour one customer – in particular to ensure that both customers get fair prices.

It is usual for an agency cross to take place at the current **mid-price** [p. 203].

Agency theory

Agency theory is the branch of financial economics that looks at conflicts of interest between people with different interests in the same assets. This most importantly means the conflicts between:

- shareholders and managers of companies

- shareholders and bond holders.

Agency theory explains, among other things, why:

- companies so often make **acquisitions** [p. 5] that are bad for shareholders.

- **convertible bonds** [p. 72] are used and bonds are sometimes sold with **warrants** [p. 343]

- **capital structure** [p. 48] matters.

Agency theory is rarely, if ever, of direct relevance to portfolio investment decisions. It is used to by financial economists to model very important aspects of how capital markets function. However, investors gain a better understanding of markets by being aware of the insights of agency theory.

One particularly important agency issue is the conflict between the interests of shareholders and debt holders. In particular, following a more riskier but higher return strategy benefits the shareholders to the detriment of the debt holders.

It can easily be seen why debt holders lose out: a more risky strategy increases the risk of default on debt, but debt holders, being entitled to a fixed return, will not benefit from higher returns. Shareholders will benefit from the higher returns (if they do improve), however if the risk goes bad, shareholders will, thanks to **limited liability** [p. 189], share a sufficiently bad loss with debt holders.

This conflict can be addressed by the use of **debt covenants** [p. 90], or by providing debt holders with a **hedge** [p. 162] against such action by the shareholders by issuing convertible debt or debt bundled with warrants.

AGM (annual general meeting)

The AGM (annual general meeting) of a company is an annual meeting open to all members (shareholders) of a company.

At an AGM shareholders can vote on a number of resolutions. These are usually proposed by the directors, but shareholders with sufficient voting power (alone or in combination) can put forward their own.

The most important resolutions are usually those appointing (or removing) directors. Other important resolutions may include:

- approving directors' remuneration

- authorising the directors to issue allot unissued shares

- authorising purchases of the company's own shares to create holdings of **treasury shares** [p. 328] or to **return capital** [p. 276].

There are also AGM resolutions that are almost always formalities – such as to receive the accounts.

Unfortunately for shareholders, the appointment of directors is also very often a formality.

An AGM also provides an opportunity for shareholders to question the directors. Most **listed** [p. 190] companies issue most of the information that they intend to **disclose** [p. 98] through other channels (such as **RNS** [p. 282]). This means it is rare for any significant new information to be disclosed at an AGM.

Sometimes, such when there are urgent matters to be dealt with that cannot wait for an AGM, it is necessary to call an **EGM** [p. 119].

Agreed takeover bid

An agreed **takeover bid** [p. 317], as opposed to a **hostile** [p. 165] one, is a bid that is recommended to the shareholders by the directors of the company being bought.

Although it is common for the directors of the target of a bid to go to great lengths to oppose it, there are a number of reasons why they may recommend one:

- They are honestly trying to fulfil their duty to shareholders.

- They will be offered positions on the board of the combined company.

- A takeover is inevitable and the directors prefer this particular one.

- Major shareholders back the bid, so there is little point opposing it.

The recommendation of a bid is usually motivated by several of these motives.

AIM

AIM (alternative investment market) is a market run by the **London Stock Exchange** [p. 192] for trading in companies too small to list on its main market.

The requirements for an AIM listing are much less stringent, and it is far cheaper to list on AIM than on the main market. AIM is designed for smaller companies. Despite having over 2,000 companies listed, it is much smaller than the main market in terms of total **market cap** [p. 196].

AIM does benefit from sharing trading systems and other infrastructure with the main market. Successful AIM companies often go on to list on the main market.

Allotment

Allotment is the allocation of securities to applicants for a **new issue** [p. 215].

The allotment process is trivially simple if an issue is not oversubscribed: each applicant gets whatever they applied for. If an issue is oversubscribed (as happens with popular **IPOs** [p. 182]) then some mechanism has to be used to decide how many shares each applicant gets.

Pro-rata allocation is a very common method of allocation. Every applicant gets the same proportion of what they applied for. Some applicants can be left with so few shares that they would probably prefer not to have applied. Another problem is that applicants can be tempted to apply for more than they really want, in order to get the amount they actually want.

Auction processes are sometimes used and the shares (or other securities) go to the highest bidders. Everyone pays the same price, not the price that they individually bid. The price is set at exactly the level that allows the issue to be fully subscribed.

Alpha

The α (alpha) of a security or fund is its outperformance over the return adjusted for risk, with risk measured by β (beta).

$$\alpha = (r - r_f) - (\beta \times (r_m - r_f))$$

where r_f is the **risk free rate** [p. 282]
r_m is the (forecast) market rate of return
and r_m the return on a fund or security r.

This uses the same risk adjustment as **CAPM** [p. 50]

The advantage of alpha over simply comparing **absolute return** [p. 2] to market (or benchmark index) performance is that it adjusts for the level of risk taken. Investors usually look at returns compared to a **benchmark** [p. 33] (usually the market **index** [p. 169]) which is more visible, receives more publicity, and is not susceptible in any inaccurate estimates.

Alpha is also used as a label by fund management companies to indicate funds that are more aggressive in trying to outperform the market, rather than those that are systematically trying to maximise alpha itself.

American Depositary Receipt

An American Depositary Receipt (ADR) is the most common type of **GDR** [p. 159]. It is a security issued in the USA that bundles together a number of shares in a non-US company. ADRs are also called American depositary shares.

The actual shares are held by a US bank as a trustee. The benefits of the shares belong to the holders of the ADRs. For example, the dividends are passed on to the holders of the ADRs. Each ADR gives **beneficial ownership** [p. 34] of a number of shares.

ADRs are frequently used by non-US companies that want a **secondary listing** [p. 288] in the US. This is becoming somewhat less popular as the cost of listing in the US has increased with more stringent regulatory requirements.

A secondary listing of ADRs in the US may still be worth the expense for very large companies that really do need access to the enlarged pool of investors.

American option

An American option is an **option** [p. 228] that can be exercised at a fixed **exercise price** [p. 135] at any time before the expiry date.

It is fairly easy to demonstrate that an American option is always worth more than the value of the underlying less the exercise price. It is always worth more than the amount that would be raised by exercising it. Therefore investors will always prefer to hold an America option to expiry. This means that it will always generate the same cash flows as a European option on the same security with same expiry date and exercise price. Its value is therefore identical to that of such a **European option** [p. 128].

Amortisation

Amortisation is the equivalent of **depreciation** [p. 95] for intangible assets.

As this is essentially an accounting adjustment that has no effect on future cash flows, investors frequently use profit measures and **valuation rations** [p. 334] that exclude amortisation.

The **balance sheet** [p. 28] value of **intangible assets** [p. 173] is even less related to their economic value than that of **tangible assets** [p. 318]. Intangible assets created within a company (as opposed to bought in) are not even shown in the accounts at all. The case for excluding amortisation from profit numbers is even stronger than that for excluding depreciation.

Under **IFRSs** [p. 166] **goodwill** [p. 159] is no longer amortised. It is revalued very year and the amount of any **impairment** [p. 166] will be written off as a cost.

The rationale and methodology for dealing with the value of tangible assets through depreciation or **depletion** [p. 94] is clearer than that for amortising intangibles.

Angel investor

Many start-up companies cannot raise venture capital investment. This is usually because they are simply too small to interest **venture capitalists** [p. 338], who typically have lower limits on investments of a million pounds or more. They also usually too high risk to be able to borrow.

Angel investors provide an alternative. They are usually individuals rather than funds or financial institutions. Like venture capital companies, they are likely to be involved in the running of businesses they invest in – even more so that venture capitalists.

Angel investors make almost always **equity** [p. 123] investments, as these are able to provide a return that reflects the high risks of investing in small start-ups.

Angel investors are very often individuals with experience relevant to the businesses they invest in. They are often able to make a valuable contribution to the management and running of their investments.

Annual effective rate

An annual effective rate (AER) is an interest rate that takes into account the effects of **compound interest** [p. 66]. It tells an investor or borrower what annually paid rate would be equivalent to the interest being paid – it is adjusted for the effects of differences in the frequency and timing of interest payments.

The calculation is simple:

$$AER = (1 + r/n)^n$$

where r is interest rate and
n = number of times an year interest is paid and compounded (e.g., 12 for monthly interest, 0.5 if interest is paid once every two years).

AER allows straightforward comparison of investments and loans that pay interest at different intervals.

Annual premium equivalent

It is common (in the UK) to use annual premium equivalent (APE) to allow comparisons of the amount of new business (policies written during the period) gained in a period by insurance companies with different proportions of **single premium** [p. 296] and regular premium business.

It is clearly not possible to compare the total amounts of premiums as single premium policies bring in more money up front than equivalent regular premium policies.

Annual premium equivalent is the total amount of regular premiums from new business + 10% of the total amount of single premiums on business written during the year.

PVNBP [p. 258] is a more sophisticated alternative that is part of the **European Embedded Value** [p. 127] standards.

Annual report

A company's annual report is the most important single regular release of information to investors.

Even though companies release a lot of information through other channels, the annual report is unique:

- It is detailed.

- It is **audited** [p. 25].

Listed companies [p. 190] will have **disclosed** [p. 98] most of the information in an annual report well before it becomes available. The annual results announcement will have contained most of the information, and much of the rest is likely to have been in trading statement and other releases.

Although the results announcement is available earlier, the annual report is, once available, preferable. It does have some additional information (both financial and non-financial) and is usually better presented.

Other information released during the course of the year is usually unaudited. These include presentations and trading statements that sometimes give information not in the annual report. The annual results announcement usually is audited, but nothing else usually is.

One opportunity to get more detailed information than is available in the annual arises during IPOs. The **prospectus** [p. 255] issued before an IPO is usually extremely detailed as it needs to contain information that would already have been disclosed over the period of time for a company that is already listed. There is also more pressure for good disclosure when a company with no track record as a listed company is trying to win investor's confidence.

Annuity

An annuity, usually purchased from a life insurance company, pays a regular income until the death of the purchaser in return for a lump sum. The insurance company needs to use the lump sum and the income they get from investing it to meet the annuity payments. As the length of any person's life is uncertain the insurance company bears a risk.

A life **assurance** [p. 23] policy can be thought of as the opposite of an annuity. With a life assurance policy, the insurance company makes a loss when each insured person dies within the term of the policy as it has to make a payment. With an annuity, the insurance company makes a gain when each insured person dies.

The opposing natures of annuities and life insurance means that the annuities an insurance company sells **hedge** [p. 162] certain risks to its life policy payouts and vice-versa. For example, if the death rate rises then the insurance company will have to pay out more on life policies but less on annuities.

API gravity

One of the most important characteristics of crude oil is its density: whether it is light or heavy.

Although it would be possible to quote densities using normal units (such as kg/litre), the oil industry convention is to use API (American Petrochemical Institute) gravity. API gravity is:

$$(141.5 \div s) - 131.5$$

where s is specific gravity at 60 degrees Fahrenheit.

The specific gravity is the ratio of the density of the oil to the density of water.

There is an inverse relationship between API gravity and density; the higher the density the lower the API gravity. Light crudes are generally those with an API gravity over 40. Those with an API gravity below 40 are regarded as heavy.

The density of oil (as measured by API gravity) is one of the key factors used to classify and grade types of **crude oil** [p. 81].

APT

See **arbitrage pricing theory** [p. 19].

APV

See **adjusted present value** [p. 8].

Arbitrage

Arbitrage is the making of a gain through trading without committing any money and without taking a risk of losing money. For example, if it is possible to simultaneously buy a security and sell it at a higher price (for example, in a different market) this is an arbitrage opportunity.

Equivalently, an arbitrage opportunity exists if it is possible to make a gain that is guaranteed to be at least equal to the **risk free rate of return** [p. 282], with a chance of making a greater gain.

Less rigorously, an arbitrage opportunity is a "free lunch", that allows investors to make a gain for no risk. Being less rigorous means that it is not really possible to distinguish between arbitrage and the closely related concepts of **dominant trading strategies** [p. 109] and the **law of one price** [p. 186].

Arbitrage should not be possible as, if an arbitrage opportunity exists, then market forces should eliminate it. Returning to the simple example, if it is possible to buy a security in one market and sell it at a higher price in another market, then no-one would buy it at the more expensive price, and no one would sell it at the cheaper price. The prices in the two markets would converge.

Much of financial theory (and therefore most methods for valuing securities) are ultimately built on the assumption that securities will trade at prices that make arbitrage impossible. In particular, if there is no arbitrage then a risk neutral pricing measure exists and vice versa. Although this result is not something that is used by most investors, it is of great importance in the theory of **financial economics** [p. 139].

Although arbitrage opportunities do exist in real markets, they are usually very small and quickly eliminated, therefore the no arbitrage assumption is a reasonable one to build financial theory on.

When persistent arbitrage opportunities do exist it means that there is something badly wrong with financial markets. For example, there is evidence that during the dotcom boom the value of internet related **tracker stocks** [p. 326] and listed **subsidiaries** [p. 311] was not consistent with the market value of parent companies – an arbitrage opportunity existed and persisted.

Arbitrage pricing theory

Arbitrage pricing theory (APT) is a valuation model. Compared to **CAPM** [p. 50], it uses fewer assumptions but is harder to use.

The basis of arbitrage pricing theory is the idea that the price of a security is driven by a number of factors. These can be divided into two groups: macro factors, and company specific factors. The name of the theory comes from the fact that this division, together with the no **arbitrage** [p. 18] assumption can be used to derive the following formula:

$$r = r_f + \beta_1 f_1 + \beta_2 f_2 + \beta_3 f_3 + \cdots$$

where r is the **expected return** [p. 135] on the security,
r_f is the **risk free rate** [p. 282],
Each f is a separate factor and
each β is a measure of the relationship between the security price and that factor.

This is a recognisably similar formula to CAPM.

The difference between CAPM and arbitrage pricing theory is that CAPM has a single non-company factor and a single beta, whereas arbitrage pricing theory separates out non-company factors into as many as proves necessary. Each of these requires a separate beta. The beta of each factor is the sensitivity of the price of the security to that factor.

Arbitrage pricing theory does not rely on measuring the performance of the market. Instead, APT directly relates the price of the security to the fundamental factors driving it. The problem with this is that the theory in itself provides no indication of what these factors are, so they need to be empirically determined. Obvious factors include economic growth and interest rates. For companies in some sectors other factors are obviously relevant as well – such as consumer spending for retailers.

The potentially large number of factors means more betas to be calculated. There is also no guarantee that all the relevant factors have been identified. This added complexity is the reason arbitrage pricing theory is far less widely used than CAPM.

Arithmetic mean

The arithmetic mean or simple **average** [p. 25] is calculated by adding up all the numbers whose average is needed, and dividing the aggregate by the number of numbers.

For example, the arithmetic mean of 4,8 and 16 is $(4 + 8 + 16) \div 3 = 9.3$.

The arithmetic mean is simple to calculate, and for many purposes it is the most suitable alternative. It is not always appropriate. For example, growth rates should be averaged using the **geometric mean** [p. 158]: see **compound annual growth rate** [p. 65] .

ARPU

See **average revenue per user** [p. 26].

ARR

See **accounting rate of return** [p. 3].

ASB

See **Accounting Standards Board** [p. 4].

Asian option

An Asian option is relatively straightforward. It is an otherwise simple option with an exercise price that is determined by taking the average price of the underlying security over a pre-determined period and applying a fixed discount to it.

The valuation of Asian options is more complex than that of **European** [p. 128] or **American options** [p. 14], but it is nonetheless more straightforward than the valuation of more complex types of **exotic options** [p. 135].

ASK (Available Seat Kilometres)

Available Seat Kilometres (ASK) measures an airline's passenger carrying capacity. It is:

$$seats\ available \times distance\ flown$$

This number should be calculated per plane, but is (at least in an investment context) usually quoted per airline.

A seat-kilometre is available when a seat that is available for carrying a passenger is flown one kilometre. Seats that are not usable for various reasons are excluded.

Asset allocation

Asset allocation is the process of deciding what proportion of an investment portfolio should be invested in:

- different types of investment (shares, bonds, real estate etc.)

- in what markets (what regions and countries, how much abroad, how much in **emerging markets** [p. 121] etc.)

- in what **sectors** [p. 288].

Asset allocation can improve both **diversification** [p. 103] and performance – although these aims do, to an extent, conflict.

The reasons why good asset allocation improves diversification should be fairly obvious. It helps ensure that investments are spread out across a wide range of markets and securities, and the allocations should be chosen to avoid investing too much in markets and securities whose movements are strongly correlated with each other.

Asset allocation can boost performance by identifying markets or sectors that are undervalued as a whole. Correctly identifying these will clearly improve performance. These are also more likely to contain individual securities that are undervalued.

Proponents of asset allocation claim that the main driver of investment returns are at market and sector levels. Proponents of **bottom up investing** [p. 39] tend to argue that the biggest potential gains come from the movements in the best performing individual securities. Both are true, and the choice of approach ultimately tends to depend on how confident and investor is in their ability to pick stocks.

How assets are allocated depends on a number of factors:

- an investor's views on which markets and types of securities will outperform, this depends on views on economic growth and interest rates,

- the need to diversify,

- the aims of the portfolio,

- what assets an investor owns outside investment portfolios.

Investors who rely heavily on asset allocation are using a **top down** [p. 324] approach.

Asset backed securities

Asset backed securities are debt instruments (i.e. a type of **bond** [p. 37]) secured against specific assets or against specific cash flows.

Asset backed securities may be used to remove assets from the issuers balance sheet or to manage risk by limiting lenders' recourse other than to the specific assets concerned.

The creation of an asset backed security requires the **securitisation** [p. 290] of a pool of assets or a series of future cash flows.

In some cases the assets may themselves be backed by other assets belonging to the issuer's borrowers. For example, a bank might finance a large chunk of its mortgage lending with an asset backed security.

Asset turnover

Asset turnover measures how effectively a business is using assets to generate sales. It is:

$$sales \div assets$$

There are a few variations on this, depending on what measure of assets is used. The most obvious is total assets, i.e., **fixed assets** [p. 142] + **current assets** [p. 83]. This measures how many pounds in sales is generated for each pound invested in assets.

From an investor's point of view, it can be argued that current liabilities should be deducted from the amount of assets used. Investors are concerned with returns on their investment, Therefore the funding of current assets from **current liabilities** [p. 84] can be ignored.

Taking this further; what investors care about is the sales generated by their investment, i.e. *equity + debt*. This leaves us using the same denominator as **ROCE** [p. 283]. Using this definition thereby gives us a nice decomposition:

$$ROCE = \textbf{EBIT}[\text{p. 115}]\ \textbf{margin}[\text{p. 253}] \times asset\ turnover$$

This appears to be the most widely used definition of asset turnover.

Assets under management

Assets under management is the amount of clients' funds that a financial sector company such as a fund manager is responsible for managing.

This is a measure of the size of the business. It is often used to value fund managers, particularly when assessing **takeovers** [p. 317], or the possibility of takeovers.

The value of a fund manager is also affected by other factors, most importantly the type of funds as this affects the level of fees. Active funds charge far more than **index trackers** [p. 325] (charges in both cases are usually a percentage of the assets managed). **Hedge funds** [p. 162] have more complex fee structures and it is usual for them to charge a (high) percentage of any gains.

Changes in assets under management can reflect both inflows and outflows of funds (i.e. clients investing or withdrawing investments) and gains and losses in the value of the assets. In order to understand underlying trends it is important to break down the changes in order to see whether the changes are due to gains or loss of clients funds (fund inflows and outflows) or investment gains and losses.

Investment gains or losses are, in themselves, not much of an indication of an underlying trend. The loss of client business probably is. Poor fund performance can do reputational damage, and thus affect the flow of business, potentially severely.

Associate company

An associate is a company in which a group of companies has a substantial stake, but not outright control. This usually means more than 20% but less than 50%. More than 50% would give the group control and make it a **subsidiary** [p. 311].

Associates are not fully **consolidated** [p. 68]. Revenue and profits from associates (and **joint ventures** [p. 184]) are shown on the group **P & L** [p. 234] but they are shown separately.

The group **balance sheet** [p. 28] shows the value of the shares owned in the associates. Although shown separately, they are treated like any other investment.

When calculating an **EV** [p. 121] the value of the holdings in associates should be deducted. Alternatively, the cost of completely buying out the associate should be added – but this approach makes more sense for subsidiaries. When calculating an **EV/EBITDA** [p. 129], the **EBITDA** [p. 116] should be adjusted in line with the EV.

Assurance

Assurance is insurance against events that will inevitably occur.

The common example of assurance is life assurance.

There is no real difference between assurance and insurance, although the long term over which life assurance is taken complicates all the **actuarial** [p. 6] calculations linked to it.

At the money

An option is said to be at-the-money if the price of the **underlying** [p. 331] equals its **exercise price** [p. 135]. In other words its **intrinsic value** [p. 179] is zero.

The value of an at-the-money option is its **option value** [p. 229].

ATK (Available Tonne Kilometres)

Available Tonne Kilometres (ATK) is a measure of an airline's total capacity (both passenger and cargo). It is:

$$capacity\ in\ tonnes \times km\ flown$$

This is a similar measure to **ASK** [p. 20]. It provides a combined measure, but is more suited to being a measure of freight capacity.

ATK should be calculated per plane, and these numbers summed to get an ATK number for the airline.

ATS (automated trading system)

An automated trading system (ATS) is a computerised system for matching orders in securities. The main function of an ATS is to accept orders and match these according to the trading rules. Trading rules vary between exchanges, and even more between countries.

This means that an ATS typically has to:

- Accept orders of whatever types are allowed.

- Reject orders that are not allowed.

- Match orders according to quite complex rules.

- Determine the prices at which certain orders match (for example, if a limit buy at 100p matches a limit sell at 90p) according to trading rules.

- Expire orders that reach built-in time limits.

- Pass details of trades to clearing and settlement systems.

- Provide market information.

- Provide information and tools to market regulators.

- Enforce automatic trading halts and other restrictions.

The replacement of trading floors with electronic systems has hugely lowered trading prices. It has had few real drawbacks.

Not all ATSs are operated by stock exchanges. Some are operated by **inter-dealer brokers** [p. 176] and similar financial institutions.

Some ATSs are developed internally by stock exchanges. Others are available from a number of software vendors.

Audit

An audit is a verification of a company's accounts. Internal audits are checks carried out as part of the company's own controls. When used unqualified the word audit is usually taken to mean external audit: the examination of accounts by external accountants (auditors) that is required by law.

There are legal restrictions on who can carry out an audit. In the UK the auditor must be a member of (or, more commonly, a partnership of members of) one of a small number of professional institutes. They must also be authorised by their institute to act as auditors. The institutes are the three British institutes of chartered accountants (in England & Wales, Scotland and Ireland), and the Association of Chartered Certified Accountants.

The annual report of a company must be audited. The audited accounts include an **auditor's opinion** [p. 25] on the accounts.

The National Audit Office audits most public sector bodies in Britain. It is answerable to Parliament and independent of the government. The Audit Commission appoints auditors for NHS and local government bodies. Both bodies have a wider role in examining the effectiveness and efficiency of public services.

Audit has traditionally been regarded as a somewhat boring profession. Its profile has been significantly increased following accounting scandals such as Enron.

Auditors' opinion

The auditors opinion is the most important part of the **audit** [p. 25] report that is provided with company accounts.

The auditor will give an opinion that is **unqualified** [p. 333], **qualified** [p. 260], or **adverse** [p. 9].

The auditor may additionally state that there is a fundamental uncertainty.

Average

Generally when one refers to an average, one means an **arithmetic mean** [p. 19].

However, average is a generic term that can also mean a **geometric mean** [p. 158], a **median** [p. 201], a **mode** [p. 205] or a even **weighted average** [p. 344].

In any context where being rigorous is important the term "average" should not be used without qualification.

Average down

Averaging down is buying more of a security an investor has already bought at a higher price.

Because of the **unit cost averaging** [p. 332] effect, averaging down leads to an average price closer to the current (lower) price rather than the original (higher) price.

The effect of this is that it greatly improves the chances that the holding of the security in question will be profitable. However, it does this by diluting the impact of the original holding. It cannot actually create gains where there were none. It obscures the loss made so far by mixing it in with new purchases that will, hopefully, be bought cheap enough to make gains.

Averaging down is an approach that makes an interesting contrast to **stop loss** [p. 308] sales.

Average Revenue Per User

Average Revenue Per User (ARPU) is a measure most often used by telecommunications companies, although it is also sometimes used by others in similar industries. It states how much money the company makes from the average user. This is the revenue from the services provided divided by the number of users buying those services.

ARPU is important because it provides a breakdown of what is driving revenue growth, and it also gives some indications of what is driving margins. Growing by increasing revenues from users tends to be better for margins than increasing revenues by increasing the user base, as the latter incurs additional costs.

ARPU growth can also indicate how successful a company is being in moving users to new services (e.g. pictures messaging, data connections etc.) that are regarded as strategically important and an indicator of how **margins** [p. 253] will fare (newer services tend to be higher margin). However, companies often disclose the composition of their revenues streams separately in any case.

Back-testing

To test a **financial model** [p. 140] that makes any kind of predictions, it is clearly impractical to enter the currently available data and then wait to see how well forecasts are met – particularly as it will be necessary to do this many times in order to obtain a statistically meaningful measure of the accuracy of forecasts.

The solution is to test the model by using it on only the data available at some past date, and then comparing the predictions to what happened subsequently. This is back testing.

For example, suppose we estimate the **volatility** [p. 340] of securities based only on their past price movements (this type of model is often used for risk management). The way we would test this would be, in outline, something like this:

1. Decide on a time period, a pool of securities, the length of time (call it t) over which to take data over.

2. Pick a time at random (call it t_1), within the time period.

3. Pick a security at random from the pool.

4. Feed the price data for the security for the period t_1 to $t_1 + t$ into the model.

5. Compare the resulting estimate with the actual volatility over a period after $t_1 + t$.

6. Go back to step two.

The errors in the estimates can then be used, using standard statistical techniques, to estimate the reliability of the estimates.

Back testing will usually be computerised rather than carried out entirely by hand.

Backward integration

Backward integration is vertical integration that combines a core business with its suppliers.

The advantages of backward integration may include assurance of the pricing, quality and availability of supplies, and efficiencies gained from coordinating production of supplies with their consumption. There are other means to these ends: for example, **derivatives** [p. 96] can **hedge** [p. 162] changes in the price of supplies, while working closely with suppliers can deliver the other gains.

Backwardation

Backwardation is the opposite of **forwardation** [p. 145]. It is a state in which the price of a future is less than the **spot price** [p. 303] of the underlying **commodity** [p. 64].

As forwardation is the usual condition of futures, backwardation occurs when prices are moved by factors such as predictable cycles in supply and demand. This is why backwardation is seen in agricultural commodities but is fairly unlikely to occur in most hard commodity markets.

Bad debt

Bad debt is debt that is unlikely to be paid. It is particularly important for banks and financial institutions that make their profits by lending money, but a high or rising level of bad debt can be an indicator of problems in any organisation.

When debts are classified as bad, they are charged as a cost on the **P & L** [p. 234]. Because a certain level of bad debt is expected, it is common practice for companies to make a **provision** [p. 256] for the amount of debt that is expected to become bad.

For banks (and other financial institutions), the level of **non-performing assets** [p. 216] is a leading indicator of bad debt.

Balance sheet

The balance sheet is one of the most important statements in a company's accounts. It shows what assets and liabilities a company has, and how the business is funded (by shareholders and by debt: the **capital structure** [p. 48] of the company).

The balance sheet provides information that is useful when assessing the financial stability of a company. A number of financial ratios use numbers from the balance sheet including **gearing** [p. 157], the **current assets ratio** [p. 83] and the **quick assets ratio** [p. 261]. However, ratios based on profits and cash flow are at least as important for assessing financial stability: the most important of these are **interest cover** [p. 176] and **cash interest cover** [p. 53].

A balance sheet is usually presented in two sections that must reach to same total – this requirement that the two sections balance is the reason it is called a balance sheet.

The typical format of a balance sheet is:

- Assets

    o **Fixed assets/Non-current assets** [p. 142]

    – Property, plant & equipment
    – **Intangible assets** [p. 173] (**goodwill** [p. 159] is often shown separately)
    – Investments in **subsidiaries** [p. 311] (not in **consolidated accounts** [p. 68]), **associates** [p. 23] and **joint ventures** [p. 184]

    o **Current assets** [p. 83]

    – **Stocks** [p. 307]
    – Receivables
    – Cash

- Total Assets

- Liabilities

    - Current liabilities

        - Short term debt
        - Payables
        - Tax
        - **Provisions** [p. 256]

    - Non-current liabilities

        - Long term debt
        - Pensions
        - Provisions

- Total Liabilities

- Net assets (total assets less total liabilities)

And in the second section:

- **Equity** [p. 123]

    - **Share capital** [p. 293]

    - Share premium account

- Other reserves

- Retained earnings

- Total shareholder's equity

- **Minority interests** [p. 204] (only in consolidated accounts)

- Total equity

There are a number of common variations on this. The most common moves liabilities from the first section to the second. In this case the two "sides" of the balance sheet show the assets on the first side and the way they are funded on the second.

Another common variation is showing current liabilities as a deduction from current assets.

Bancassurance

Bancassurance is the selling of insurance and banking products through the same channel, most commonly through bank branches selling insurance. The sales **synergies** [p. 316] available have been sufficient to be used to justify **mergers** [p. 201] and **acquisitions** [p. 5].

Some of the sales synergies come through the extensive customer base that banks have. Some come from opportunities to sell insurance together with some banking products. For example, banks generally insist on life insurance for mortgage borrowers. Although borrowers are not obliged to buy insurance from the lender, many do (despite it often being very over-priced) as it is an easy option.

Credit cards and personal loans create opportunities for banks to sell protection insurance (another high **margin** [p. 253] business) and the knowledge a bank has of its customers' finances creates opportunities to sell other products.

Bancassurance has become significant. Banks are now a major distribution channel for insurers, and insurance sales a significant source of profits for banks. The latter partly being because banks can often sell insurance at better prices (i.e., higher premiums) than many other channels, and they have low costs as they use the infrastructure (branches and systems) that they use for banking.

What has not happened to any great extent, at least in Britain, is the merger of banks and insurers to form integrated bancassurance companies.

Barrel of oil

A barrel of oil is 42 US gallons or 159 litres.

The term comes from the size of the old wooden whiskey barrels used to transport oil in the mid nineteenth century. This unit of measurement has remained unchanged despite the replacement of wooden barrels by larger steel barrels, and the replacement of the latter by pipelines.

Barrels of oil per day (bpd) is a standard unit of oil production.

As oil and gas are often produced from the same fields, it is common to measure reserves and production in **boe** [p. 37].

Barrier options

A type of exotic option, the value of which depends on the underlying passing (or not) a particular price point.

Knock-out and knock-in options are the commonest types of barrier option. See **exotic options** [p. 135].

Barriers to entry

Barriers to entry are anything that makes it difficult for a new entrant to break into a market. They make companies already in the market more valuable as they reduce the risk of new competition.

Capital costs are often a key barrier to entry in industries (such as telecoms) where the investment that needs to be made in **fixed assets** [p. 142] by a start-up is high relative to the sales and profits those assets will generate.

In many such industries the cost of the fixed assets is a **sunk cost** [p. 312] as far as the existing suppliers are concerned. This means that they will accept lower prices rather than scale back volumes, meaning that new entrants are likely to find that they drive prices down too much for the market to be worth entering.

Network effects [p. 214] are often a powerful barrier to entry and, by their very nature, reinforce **first mover advantages** [p. 140] and create barriers to entry that get stronger with time.

Branding, distribution and customer relationships can also create strong barriers to entry.

Basic EPS

The basic **EPS** [p. 122] is calculated with no adjustments to profits or the number of shares.

The most common adjustments are the exclusion of non-cash and one-off items (**adjusted EPS** [p. 7]) and including shares that have not yet been issued but are expected to be issued (**diluted EPS** [p. 97])

Basis points

A basis point is one hundredth of a percentage point (0.01%). Basis points are often used to measure changes and differentials in interest rates and **margins** [p. 253]. For example, if a **floating interest rate** [p. 144] is set at 25 basis points more than **Libor** [p. 187], and Libor is 3.5%, the floating rate will be 3.75%.

Basis points are also convenient in discussing margins, because percentage changes are often small. It is important to discuss such small changes as **operational gearing** [p. 227] or **financial gearing** [p. 157] often means they have big effects on the bottom line.

bboe

See **boe** [p. 37].

Bear

A bear is an investor who is pessimistic about the prospects for a market, a sector or a particular security. The expectation of a fall in a security or an index is described as "bearish". The opposite of a bear is a **bull** [p. 42].

A bearish view (if it eventually proves to be correct) is as much a source of profitable trading opportunities as a bullish view. An investor can exploit expected declines by using **derivatives** [p. 96] (for example by buying **put options** [p. 258]) or **short selling** [p. 296].

Many bearish strategies can be risky. Short selling and writing (see **option writer** [p. 229]) **call options** [p. 45] are particular dangerous as they can lead to losses linked to the extent of a price rise. There is therefore no ceiling on the possible loss.

Bear raid

A **bear** [p. 31] raid is an attempt by traders to drive down price of a security by heavy **short selling** [p. 296]. The selling may be accompanied by the spreading of (negative) rumours.

Once the price falls, the traders can cover short positions cheaply.

Once they have built **long positions** [p. 192], they then wait for the price to recover and sell at a profit.

A bear raid is usually carried out by a group of traders working together – a single trader is unlikely to be able to sell enough to drive the price down. Even if a single trader could force the price down, the manipulation is likely to be more apparent to regulators who could trace the selling to a single source.

Bear raids are (obviously) a form of market manipulation and illegal in most of the world.

Bear squeeze

If a security has been heavily **short sold** [p. 296] (relative to its liquidity), or had other types of bearish positions taken on it (e.g. derivatives positions) then, if the price rises, there can be heavy demand from **bears** [p. 31] seeking to cover their positions and limit losses.

The result of this is that the demand from bears increases prices still further, increasing the bears' losses. This is a bear squeeze.

Bear trap

A bear trap is a short term fall in the price of a security, which then returns to a long term upward trend.

Bears [p. 31] who interpreted the fall as the start of a longer term decline, and used strategies such as **short-selling** [p. 296], then make a loss.

When the price rises bears are forced to buy at higher prices and make a loss. This may well lead to a **bear squeeze** [p. 32].

Bearer securities

A security is in bearer form if possession of the security confers ownership. No register of ownership is maintained.

Ordinary shares are not usually bearer securities and the main record of ownership is not the certificates that are issued, but the company's register of shareholders. Certain types of **bonds** [p. 37] are commonly issued as bearer bonds, the most important being **Eurobonds** [p. 126]. Bearer shares and **ADRs** [p. 14] exist, but bearer shares are a rarity.

There are obvious security problems associated with the handling of bearer securities. Some types of bearer securities (including Eurobonds) are traded through systems that minimise physical movements of the securities by depositing quantities of the bearer security securely in banks. The registered ownership of the deposited securities can then be traded.

Bearer securities are also regarded, by governments, as making tax evasion and money laundering easier. This has lead to some types of bearer security becoming rarer.

Behavioural finance

Behavioural finance is a branch of financial economics that deals with the the behaviour of investors. In common with other branches of economics, financial theory tends to make fairly simplistic assumptions about the behaviour of people – that investors act rationally to maximise their wealth (strictly speaking, their **utility** [p. 334]).

Phenomena such as **investment bubbles** [p. 41] demonstrate that investors are far from uniformly rational, and that the behaviour of markets in general shows that behavioural factors are important.

In recent years both the broader discipline of economics and the theory of finance have developed theories that do take behavioural factors into account. At the moment these studies, although interesting, do little to help investors, except to warn them against known common mistakes.

Benchmark index

Then most important type of benchmarking from the point of view of investors, is the benchmarking of the performance of funds and portfolios.

Funds usually choose an **index** [p. 169] to be their performance benchmark. The index will match the region or sector the fund invests in. A British technology fund might choose one of the **Techmark** [p. 319] indices, whereas an **emerging markets** [p. 121] fund may choose one of the **MSCI** [p. 210] indices.

The use of indices as benchmarks is one of the reasons why so many different indices exist: they need to match the variety of funds. Even so, some funds and portfolios are better served by using a composite of several indices.

One danger this brings is that it tempts managers to track their benchmark index (and thus avoid the risk of under-performing) rather than genuinely trying to beat it: supposedly actively managed funds thus become **closet trackers** [p. 61].

Benchmark price

Particular prices are sometimes regarded as benchmarks for a wider range of prices, this is most common with **commodities** [p. 64].

This is usually because a single commodity exists in many forms that can be distinguished by different properties or quality. This means that investors need to be clear what price they are following, and this usually means the price of the commodity in a form that is closely specified and traded on an exchange.

For example, the price of **crude oil** [p. 81] generally means the price on one or another of certain crude oils that are regarded as benchmarks or a composite of them.

Beneficial ownership

The beneficial owner of an asset is the person for whose benefit it is being held. Beneficial ownership arises when an asset is owned by one person (the "legal owner") who has a duty to use it on behalf of another; one person holds assets as trustee for another.

Securities, especially those held by private investors, are often held by brokers' **nominee** [p. 216] companies. Like other property, securities may also be held by trustees, and it is sometimes necessary to trace ownership through a long line of holding companies and trustees to find the ultimate beneficial owner.

The difficulties involved in tracing ultimate beneficial owners can make it more difficult to enforce regulations, such as those regarding takeovers. Mechanisms exist in the UK to help uncover them. For example, the Companies Act gives companies the power to demand that legal owners (whose names are shown in the register of shareholders) disclose information about beneficial owners.

Beta

The β (beta) of a security is essentially a measure of the strength of the relationship between the price of a security and the market. It is used to calculate **discount rates** [p. 88] for **CAPM** [p. 50].

A high beta security will tend to move more than the market, and a low beta security less. This is sometimes presented as a definition of beta. This correct to an extent, but is so vague as to be misleading.

The beta is defined using two relatively straightforward statistical measures.

$$\beta = \frac{cov_{s,m}}{var_m}$$

where $cov_{s,m}$ is the **covariance** [p. 74] of the security price with the market and var_m is the variance (see **standard deviation** [p. 305]) of the market.

Market, here, strictly speaking means a market portfolio: all of every available security. In practice an **index** [p. 169] is used rather than calculating this directly.

Bid price

A bid price is the highest price at which a buyer is willing to buy a particular security. The buyer may be a **market maker** [p. 197] or an ordinary investor. Which it is depends on the trading system used. This, in turn, depends on the market, and sometimes (as in London) on the particular security.

The best price at which a seller is willing to sell is the **offer price** [p. 222]. The difference between the bid price and the offer price is the **bid-offer spread** [p. 35].

In general, the bid price is also the best price at which it is possible to sell a particular security – however there will be a limit on the quantity that is available at the bid price.

If trading is with a market maker, then trading a larger quantity may require contacting the market maker (or several) by telephone and asking for a price for a larger quantity. Special arrangements may also allow better prices to be obtained even on smaller quantities.

If trading is matched bargain, then the seller has a choice of accepting whatever lower prices are available for the excess quantity, or placing a limit order and hoping it will be matched.

Bid-offer spread

The bid-offer spread is the difference between the **bid price** [p. 35] and **offer price** [p. 222].

This difference is, in effect, part of the costs of investing in much the same way that brokers commissions are. Bid-offer spreads are also where **market makers** [p. 197] make their profits, which is the reward they get in return for improving the liquidity of the securities in which they make a market.

From an investor's point of view, the spread is an extra cost, like the broker's commission. It needs to be regarded as such, especially when considering the costs of very active trading strategies.

Black-Scholes

The Black-Scholes formula values **options** [p. 228]. It is the most widely used method of valuing options but others do exist. These more complex alternatives are used when the assumptions made by Black-Scholes may not be accurate.

The Black-Scholes formula for the price of a call option is:

$$sN(d_1) - e^{-r(T-t)}XN(d_2)$$

where s is the price of the **underlying security** [p. 331]
$N(x)$ is the cumulative standard **normal distribution** [p. 218] of x
e is the mathematical constant
r is the **risk free rate of return** [p. 282]
X is the **exercise price** [p. 135] of the option
T is the time of expiry of the option
t is the time at which the option is being valued
σ is the **volatility** [p. 340] of the option
d_1 is $(1/(\sigma\sqrt{T-t})(ln(s/X) + (r + \sigma^2/2)(T-t))$ and
d_2 is $d_1 - \sigma\sqrt{T-t}$.

There is more than one way of deriving Black-Scholes. Even the easiest is a little too mathematical to cover here, but is well described in a number of textbooks. The derivation starts from the construction of a portfolio that uses **delta hedging** [p. 93] to generate the same cash flows as an option. By the **law of one price** [p. 186] this must have the same value as the option.

The Black-Scholes formula has some weaknesses: for example, it assumes that the probabilities of future prices of the underlying security follow a **normal distribution** [p. 218]. This is an approximation that is good enough most of the time – but the wide use of Black-Scholes creates some opportunities for traders and **arbitragers** [p. 18] who can model something more complex when necessary.

As well as being used in the valuation of traded options, Black-Scholes is also used when there is **option value** [p. 229] in **embedded** [p. 120] or **real options** [p. 265].

It can also be used to calculate share prices by regarding shares as an option to own a business outright by paying off the debt. If a business becomes worth less than its debt then a company can default leaving shareholders with nothing and debt holders with the business. This is not usually of much practical use but does explain why shares have a positive value even if a company's **EV** [p. 121] is less than its outstanding debt.

Blue chip

A blue chip is a large and well established company, or its shares. The key criteria is that these are large companies, primarily in terms of **market capitalisation** [p. 196]. The term also implies financial strength and stability.

Blue chip shares are often regarded as less risky that those of smaller companies, but there are plenty of examples of blue chips performing extremely badly. Investors should rely on **diversification** [p. 103] and proper assessments to control risks, rather than simply equating blue chip with safe.

It is perfectly possible for large cap stocks to perform badly, as investors in GEC (renamed, first Marconi, and then Telent) discovered: someone buying the share at its peak would have lost almost their entire investment. Investors in large telecoms companies during the dot com boom also made substantial losses during the bust.

The origin of the term appears to lie in gambling, with blue counters in casinos being the most valuable.

While the definition of blue chip is a little vague, it is often used of companies that are constituents of large cap **indices** [p. 169] such as the the **FTSE 100** [p. 150] in the UK or the **Dow Jones Industrial Average** [p. 109] in the US.

Boe

The basic unit used to measure oil and gas production is barrels of oil equivalent (boe). It is often necessary to use millions or billions of barrels of oil equivalent (mboe or bboe) when discussing oil reserves. Production volumes are measured in boed (barrels of oil equivalent a day) or mboed (millions of barrels of oil equivalent a day).

A boe is the amount of energy contained in a **barrel of oil** [p. 30]. Approximately 6,000 cubic feet of natural gas is considered equivalent to one barrel of oil, but the exact rate varies depending on the type of gas.

This measure is used to quantify the output of an oil company in way that:

- allows output of oil (measured in barrels) and gas (measured by its volume) to be added together to form one figure

- measures production volumes rather than values.

Investors do also have another single figure that measures output of both oil and gas: the value of production. As this is dependent on the volatile prices of both **commodities** [p. 64] it does not tell us much the actual level of production.

Bonds

A bond is a financial security that pays interest. Most bonds have a fixed life, and the **principal** [p. 251] is returned on maturity. A debenture is similar to a bond from the point of view of investors, but is legally different.

The interest rate is most often a **fixed rate** [p. 177], but it may be a **floating rate** [p. 144]. In either case, it is expressed as a percentage of the nominal value (**face value** [p. 137]) of the bond.

Some bonds are issued at a discount to their face value so the payment at maturity is greater than the purchase cost. **Zero coupon bonds** [p. 350] pay no interest, and are therefore issued at a deep discount.

Bond prices change if interest rates or the market's perception of the **credit risk** [p. 79] changes. The interst rate sensitivity of a bond may be measured by its **duration** [p. 113] or (more accurately) its **modified duration** [p. 205].

Bonds are issued by companies, governments (see **government bonds** [p. 160]) and other organisations. The credit worthiness of an organisation is reflected in the **risk premium** [p. 282] on the bond.

The rates on bonds issued by governments in their own currency (on which default is virtually impossible) are used to measure the **risk free rate** [p. 282] of return.

The real value of bonds may also be eroded by inflation – whereas shares give partial ownership of a real business, which provides a **hedge** [p. 162] against inflation. An exception to this are the index linked bonds issued by some governments that have interest payments and a return of principal that are adjusted for inflation.

A company may have several classes of bonds, and some may take priority over others for repayment (in the case of liquidation). Those with a lower priority (junior or **subordinated** [p. 310] bonds) are higher risk and therefore should have a higher yield. A company may also issue bonds with extra or different characteristics – the most common example are **convertible bonds** [p. 72]. **Preference shares** [p. 244] are legally shares but are economically (from an investors point of view) little different from very junior bonds.

Bonus issue

See **scrip issue** [p. 287].

Book value

The book value of an asset is the value of the asset as shown in the accounts – specifically in the **balance sheet** [p. 28].

The book value of assets can be very different from their real economic value to a company which (depending on circumstances) can be more accurately gauged by estimating replacement cost or resale value.

The book value shown in the accounts is usually the cost of an asset less accumulated **depreciation** [p. 95]. This is sometimes called the net book value or the written down value. It may also include other adjustments: **impairment** [p. 166] and revaluation.

When a company sells such an asset, if the price at which it is sold is more than the book value, the difference is shown as a profit on disposal in the **P & L** [p. 234]. If an asset is sold for less than the book value, a loss is shown.

The book value of an entire company (or a business within one) is its **net asset value** [p. 213].

Book to bill ratio

The book to bill ratio is most commonly used in the **semiconductor** [p. 292] industry, although it is applicable to any industry that takes orders significantly in advance of invoicing. It is the ratio of the orders taken in a period to the amount invoiced over the same period. Invoicing is usually done shortly after shipping.

The amount invoiced is significant as it is usually what is recognised as revenues by most companies, although **revenue recognition** [p. 277] policies do vary: they can be much more complex than simply adding up the invoices sent out in a period.

The difference between the amount ordered and the amount invoiced is an indicator of whether demand is rising or falling. A book to bill ratio of one shows stability, more than one indicates growth and less than one indicates decline. However this is true only after correcting for seasonal variations.

Although book to bill is an important leading indicator of sales, it should not be looked at in isolation, particularly in the semiconductor industry where demand can change quite rapidly.

Bottom fishing

Bottom fishing is simply buying the cheapest investments (in terms of **valuation ratios** [p. 334]) available. Bottom fishing is **value investing** [p. 337] concentrated on the very cheapest companies. The term can be derogatory as it can imply a lack of attention to the quality of the investments selected.

Bottom fishing strategies can generate very good returns because the low valuations mean there is a lot of room for **re-rating** [p. 264]. There are usually good reasons why shares have low valuations and picking very cheap shares can be dangerous as many of them are cheap to reflect high risk.

Bottom-up stock selection

Approaching investment decisions by focusing on individual securities and picking those that are undervalued is a bottom-up approach. A bottom-up stock picker would start by analysing potentially interesting companies (preferably as many as possible) to find those that are undervalued.

Using such an approach implies that an investor is attempting to outperform the market by picking shares (or other securities) that are undervalued, whether in absolute terms or relative to their **sector** [p. 288].

A bottom up approach does not mean neglecting **diversification** [p. 103], but it does require discipline to ensure that a bottom up portfolio is well diversified.

The opposite of a bottom-up strategy is a **top down** [p. 324] strategy.

Brand

A brand is a rather nebulous concept because it can be extended to cover a lot of quite intangible and hard to assess benefits, that are nonetheless genuine.

In its narrowest sense, a brand is the identifying name and symbols of a product or a related group of products. This may be a company name, a trading name used by the company, or a name or symbol used to mark its products. The distinguishing names and symbols of a brand may be trademarked, and usually are.

The narrow definition of a brand can be extended to cover the public perception of a business and its products or services, it. This is where the definition becomes harder to pin down.

Even more difficult is the valuation of brands with a view to showing them as an asset on the **balance sheet** [p. 28]. This relies on techniques such estimating how much a brand will add to future **cash flows** [p. 53] and calculating a present value of these. The value of approaches such as this is questionable as they are on a wholly different basis to other assets shown on the balance sheet, and forecasting of cash flows is probably better left to analysts and investors.

Under **IFRSs** [p. 166] only acquired brands can be shown on the balance sheet. At least for these a price has been paid therefore a more certain valuation can be attached to them. In any case these are often amounts that would otherwise appear on the balance sheet in some other guise such as **goodwill** [p. 159].

Brand dilution

Brand dilution is the weakening of a **brand** [p. 40] though its overuse. This frequently happens as a result of ill-judged **brand extension** [p. 41]. Price cutting that increases volumes but moves a brand down-market can be similarly damage a brand.

Brand dilution is an ever present risk for companies that rely on a strong brand for high margins. A company that owns a strong brand obviously wants to leverage it to sell as much as possible, but the very strategies used to purse this end often also bring the danger of brand dilution.

Investors need to look at strategies designed to exploit brands by extension (or through otherwise increasing the market served by a brand) in order to be warned of dangers of brand dilution.

Brand extension

Brand [p. 40] extension is the widening of the range of products (or services) sold using a particular brand.

By extending a brand to more products, a business can make maximum use of the additional sales a strong brand can generate. Brand extension is most commonly done by adding products closely related to those already sold using a particular brand

Brand extension may be less obvious. A common example is adding products that appeal to the same market segment, exploiting the (presumably) good image a brand has in the minds of target customers.

Brand extension, if overdone, can risk **brand dilution** [p. 40]. It may also make a business more dependent on that brand – and brands can weaken.

Break-even

A break-even point is the level of sales (in terms of either value of volume) needed to cover the fixed costs; the level at which a company (or business unit or product) does not make either a profit or a loss.

Break-even analysis is useful because it helps analyse the chances of a new venture succeeding. The concept is also closely related to **operational gearing** [p. 227]. The closer to break-even, the higher the operational gearing.

The break-even point in number of units sold is:

$$\frac{fixed\ cost}{\textbf{contribution}[\text{p. 72}]\ per\ unit}.$$

or in revenue terms:

$$\frac{fixed\ costs}{1 - \textbf{contribution margin}[\text{p. 72}]}$$

Brent crude

Brent crude is one of the most important **benchmark** [p. 34] crude oils. Two thirds of the world's internationally traded crude oil supplies are priced relative to it. The benchmark oil is a combination of **crude oil** [p. 81] from 15 different oil fields in the Brent and Ninian areas of the North Sea.

The **API gravity** [p. 17] of Brent is 38.3 degrees and it contains little sulphur making it a "light sweet" crude oil.

Bubble

When a particular investment (or class of investments) performs particularly well this tends to draw the attention of investors. This in turn leads to more money being put into the investment which causes further price rises which makes still investors more confident.

This leads to an upward spiral that takes prices far above the levels which can be justified by any rational assessment of the real value of the future cash flows an investment may generate. This is an investment bubble.

Even investors who are aware that there is a bubble, and that prices are too high to justify on fundamentals, frequently buy into bubbles. One reason is the **greater fool** [p. 160] theory, which, unfortunately, is often correct during bubbles.

Another reason is that investors may not wish to miss opportunities that others are taking. For private investors this is likely to be merely the fear of being left out. In the case of professionals, such as fund managers, those who stay out of a bubble will be seen to be under-performing. During the dot com bubble some fund managers who stayed out of overpriced internet stocks lost their jobs as a result of the poor **relative returns** [p. 273] of their funds.

During bubbles investors (and analysts) tend to try to rationalise high valuations. For example, during the dot com bubble some analysts were valuing internet companies using **market cap** [p. 196] per user as a valuation ratio. They compared internet companies against each other without taking into consideration the ability of any of them to convert popularity with users into cash flows.

Part of the problem is the focus **sell-side analysts** [p. 291] have on narrow sectors, and therefore on sector relative valuations. This is much less serious than the more fundamental problem of the power of herd instinct and the fear of being left out – and the fear of publicly making a controversial wrong call.

As a result of this the explanation of bubbles is largely a matter of **behavioural finance** [p. 33] rather than valuation theory.

Bubbles inevitable ultimately lead to a price crash. These often mirror the characteristics of a bubble and can be a valuable buying opportunity.

Bull

A bull is an investor who expects a market, sector or security to rise in price. The adjective "bullish" is also used. The opposite of a bull is a **bear** [p. 31].

Bullish strategies can be fairly obvious (buying). Bulls may nonetheless use **derivatives** [p. 96] and other instruments to gear the rise they expect or to gain broad exposure. A bull may buy a index derivative (see **contract for difference** [p. 71]) as a result of being bullish about a market as a whole.

A very bullish strategy may need to be **hedged** [p. 162] in order to control risks.

Being bullish on one investment may mean being bearish on others. For example, being bullish on the prices of a **commodity** [p. 64] implies being bullish on the companies that produce it, but bearish on the companies that use it as a raw material.

Bulldog bond

A bulldog bond is a sterling **bond** [p. 37] whose issuer is not British.

Bulldog bonds are a type of **eurobond** [p. 126] and the types of security issued, the methods of issue and trading mechanisms will be the same as for other eurobonds.

A bulldog bond would usually be issued because the issuer has (or intends to acquire) a revenue stream or assets in sterling. Matching these to sterling debt reduces **exchange rate risk** [p. 133].

Bundling

Bundling is the practice of supplying two separate products together so that consumers who only want one must buy both.

A more subtle form of bundling is to give buyers who buy products together a discount.

Usually, if a supplier bundles its products, then consumers have the choice of simply going to another supplier who does not bundle. However, if a **monopolist** [p. 207] bundles, it can be a way of leveraging a monopoly in one market into another.

Examples of bundling include 3M's offers of discounts on its very strong Scotch Tape and Post-it Note products to buyers who also bought other products, and Microsoft's inclusion of its web browser and media player "free" with its Windows operating system.

Of course, less controversial examples of bundling happen all the time. The commonest familiar example is the inclusion by consumer goods and food manufacturers of a new product with an already established one, in order to encourage consumers to try the new product.

Business to business

The term business to business simply means sales made to another business as opposed to consumers.

Although the term is applicable to a wide range of industries, it is most often used in the media sector. It is the media sector that most often supplies otherwise similar products to both consumers and businesses. For example, a magazine publisher is likely to publish both consumer magazines and trade magazines.

It is important to distinguish between consumer and business revenue streams because they follow slightly different **cycles** [p. 84].

During the dot com boom, the abbreviation b2b was often used for business to business. It has become less popular, probably because of its association with the bursting of the bubble (after which it was sometimes said to stand for "back to banking").

Buy-side analyst

A buy-side analyst is one who works for an institutional investor such as a fund management company. Most of a buy-side analyst's work is intended primarily for internal use, although some of it may be shown to clients.

Employing buy-side analysts, rather than relying on the work of **sell-side analysts** [p. 291], has a number of advantages:

- The independence of buy side analysts from the companies they cover is more certain.

- They can be asked to concentrate on the companies and sectors of the greatest interest to the money manager, and in the context of specific strategies, goals and portfolios. For example, they can consider not just is "X a buy?", but "is X a buy for the growth portfolio we run for client Y which already has a lot of stocks from X's sector?".

- Buy side analysis is exclusive and therefore can be a source of advantage both in improving performance and in **differentiating** [p. 253] a fund manager to clients, This is why some fund managers advertise the strength of their buy side teams.

CAGR

See **compound annual growth rate** [p. 65].

Call auction

A call auction is an alternative to the continuous matching of orders usual in securities markets.

Limit orders are collected over a (fixed) period. At the end of this time the orders are processed in the auction. The price that enables the largest number of orders to be executed is chosen: if the price were higher the trade volume would fall through lack of buys, if the price were lower the trade volume would fall through lack of sells.

Call auctions concentrate liquidity, but have a number of obvious disadvantages:

- Investors have to wait until the next auction is held to find out if their orders have executed.

- The market reacts more slowly to news.

Call auctions are used by some stock exchanges to fix opening or closing prices – trading starts or ends with a call auction. Their use as a main trading mechanism is now rare.

Call option

A call option is an **option** [p. 228] that gives the holder the right to buy the **underlying security** [p. 331].

A call option can simply be a way of speculating on a rise in the price of security. Call options are also used to implement more complex strategies.

Cannibalisation

Cannibalisation is what happens if one part of a company grows by taking sales from another. For example, if a retailer opens a new shop close to an existing one, then the existing shop is likely to lose some sales to the new one.

Cannibalisation is most commonly a concern where a company is selling the same products though different channels or in different locations. An example of the former would be a retailer's web site competing with its shops.

Cannibalisation reduces sales growth (as the benefits of growth in one place will be offset by a reduction elsewhere). It may also reduce **margins** [p. 253] if customers switch to a lower cost (for them) and lower margin (for the seller) sales channel.

Conversely, obviously, cannibalisation may encourage a switch to a higher margin channel (e.g. internet sales may cut out a middle man) or it may be a price worth paying to develop a new business.

Cannibalisation is often a problem. Its effect is often less significant than might be expected because most companies are already in a competitive environment: they compete with others, so the extra impact of also competing with themselves is often limited.

Competing with oneself may even be turned to a company's advantage by inducing customers to look at the same produce twice in different guises. This is why some companies (such as car manufacturers and food producers) often sell very similar products with different branding.

Capex

See **capital expenditure** [p. 46].

Capital adequacy

Regulators try to ensure that banks and other financial institutions have sufficient capital to keep them out of difficulty. This not only protects depositors, but also the wider economy, because the failure of a big bank has extensive knock-on effects.

The risk of knock-on effects that have repercussions at the level of the entire financial sector is called **systemic risk** [p. 316].

Capital adequacy requirements have existed for a long time, but the two most important are those specified by the Basel committee of the Bank for International Settlements.

Basel 1 defined capital adequacy as a single number that was the ratio of a banks capital to its assets. There are two types of capital, tier one and tier two. The first is primarily share capital, the second other types such as preference shares and subordinated debt. The key requirement was that tier one capital was at least 8% of assets.

Each class of asset has a weight of between zero and 1 (or 100%). Very safe assets such as government debt have a zero weighting, high risk assets (such as unsecured loans) have a rating of one. Other assets have weightings somewhere in between. The weighted value of an asset is its value multiplied by the weight for that type of asset.

The Basel 1 accord is to be replaced, in stages, by new rules (Basel 2). Basel 2 is based on three "pillars": minimum capital requirements, supervisory review process and market forces.

The first "pillar" is similar to the Basel 1 requirement, the second is the use of sophisticated risk models (see **financial model** [p. 140]) to ascertain whether additional capital (i.e. more than required by pillar 1) is necessary.

The third pillar requires more **disclosure** [p. 98] of risks, capital and risk management policies. This encourages the markets to react to the taking of high risks.

In addition to specifying levels of capital adequacy, most countries (including the UK) have regulator run guarantee funds that will pay depositors at least part of what they are owed. It is also usual for regulators to intervene to prevent outright bank defaults.

Capital asset pricing model

See **CAPM** [p. 50].

Capital expenditure

Capital expenditure (capex), is the amount a company spends on buying fixed assets, other than as part of **acquisitions** [p. 5].

As this expenditure is an investment it is not immediately shown in the **P & L** [p. 234]. The amount of cash expenditure is shown in the **cash flow statement** [p. 54] and the effects of capex obviously show on the **balance sheet** [p. 28]. Most companies also comment on capex in their results.

It can be difficult to distinguish between maintenance capex (to keep existing operations going at their current levels) and investment made to drive future growth. Investors may be able to infer a certain amount from comments and by looking at a company's circumstances and track record. Capex that is continuously high which has not lead to high growth is likely to be maintenance capex.

Apparent profits or **operating cash flows** [p. 225] are not actually making shareholders wealthier if high maintenance capex requirements soak up the money. This is why investors should look at measures such as **free cash flow** [p. 146].

Capital gains

Capital gains are the gains made by the increase in the value of an asset, especially a financial instrument. For example, the holder of a share gains from any increase in the share price after purchase.

The other source of gains made from ownership of an asset is any income it generates: for example, the dividends paid to a shareholder. The combination capital gains and income is the **total return** [p. 325].

The best known **equity** [p. 123] **indices** [p. 169] track only the capital gains made by their constituents, although total return indices also exist.

Capital gains are taxed differently from income and generally more favourably. UK tax law contains some provisions to prevent this being exploited for tax avoidance.

Capital intensive

A business is capital intensive if it requires heavy capital investment in buying assets relative to the level of sales or profits that those assets can generate.

This means that a capital intensive business will typically have some mixture of the following characteristics:

- high **depreciation** [p. 95] costs

- high **operational gearing** [p. 227] on **operating profit** [p. 227], but much less on pre-depreciation measures such as **EBITDA** [p. 116]

- high operational gearing on free cash flows if high **capex** [p. 46] is continuous rather than a one off "entry fee".

- high **barriers to entry** [p. 30]

- large amounts of **fixed assets** [p. 142] on the **balance sheet** [p. 28].

Measures of how effectively assets are used, such as **ROCE** [p. 283], **ROIC** [p. 284] and **asset turnover** [p. 22], are therefore particularly important measures of efficiency.

In addition, because capital intensive companies have a lot of assets to fund relative to their size, they are likely to borrow more heavily (especially as the assets also provide security for lenders). This means more attention may need to be paid to balance sheet ratios such as **gearing** [p. 157] and **interest cover** [p. 176].

Capital intensive companies may reduce the amount of capital the business needs by leasing or renting assets rather than purchasing them. For example, it is common for airlines to lease rather than buy aircraft. Retailers and hoteliers frequently enter into sale and leaseback arrangements of existing properties.

Arrangements like the above mean that a business needs to raise less capital, or can return capital released to shareholders. Using less capital increases returns on capital (using measures such as **ROE** [p. 283]). There is a price to be paid for this. Either financial or operational gearing also increases. Which increases depends on the accounting treatment required for the particular arrangement entered into.

Capital structure

The capital structure of a company is the particular combination of debt, **equity** [p. 123] and other sources of finance that it uses to fund its long term financing.

The key division in capital structure is between debt and equity. The proportion of debt funding is measured by **gearing** [p. 157].

This simple division is somewhat complicated by the existence of other types of capital that blur the lines between debt and equity, as they are hybrids of the two. **Preference shares** [p. 244] are legally shares, but have a fixed return that makes them closer to debt than equity in their economic effect. **Convertible bonds** [p. 72] may be likely to become equity in the future.

Considering the division between debt and equity is sufficient to understand the issues involved.

Simple financial theory models show that capital structure does not affect the total value (*debt + equity*) of a company. This is not completely true, as more sophisticated models show. It is, nonetheless, an important result, know as **capital structure irrelevance** [p. 48].

Capital structure irrelevance

Simple financial theory shows that the total value of a company should not change if its **capital structure** [p. 48] does. This is known as capital structure irrelevance or (Modigliani-Miller (MM) theory. Total value is the value of all its sources of funding, this is similar to a simple (*debt + equity*) **enterprise value** [p. 121].

The MM argument is simple, the total **cash flows** [p. 53] a company makes for all investors (debt holders and shareholders) are the same regardless of capital structure. Changing the capital structure does not change the total cash flows. Therefore the total value of the assets that give ownership of these cash flows should not change. The cash flows will be divided up differently so the total value of each class of security (e.g. shares and bonds) will change, but not the total of both added together.

Looking at this another way, if you wanted to buy a company free of its debt, you would have to buy the equity and buy, or pay off, the debt. Regardless of the capital structure you would end up owning the same streams of cash flows. Therefore the cost of acquiring the company free of debt should be the same regardless of capital structure.

Furthermore, it is possible for investors to mimic the effect of the company having a different capital structure. For example, if an investor would prefer a company to be more highly geared this can be simulated by buying shares and borrowing against them. An who investor would prefer the company to be less highly geared can simulate this by buying a combination of its debt and equity.

MM theory depends on simplifying assumptions such as ignoring the effects of taxes. However, it does provide a starting point that helps understand what is, and is not, relevant to why capital structure does seem to matter to an extent. The different tax treatments of debt and equity are part of the answer, as are **agency** [p. 11] problems (conflicts of interest between shareholders, debt holders and management).

There are extensions to MM theory which suggest that the actions of market forces, together with the tax treatment of debt and equity income in the hands of investors, means that for most companies the gains that can be made by adjusting capital structure will be fairly small.

Given that companies would not deliberately adopt inefficient capital structures, we can assume that all companies have roughly equivalently good capital structures – so from a valuation point of view we can reasonably assume that capital structure is irrelevant.

Using enterprise value based valuation ratios such as **EV/EBITDA** [p. 129] and **EV/Sales** [p. 130] implicitly assumes that capital structure is irrelevant.

Capital structure irrelevance is closely related to **dividend irrelevance** [p. 105].

Capitalisation

Capitalisation is the addition to the balance sheet as an asset of an amount that could otherwise have been treated as an expense.

For example, if a part of **R & D** [p. 261] expenditure is capitalised it will be added to the balance sheet as an **intangible asset** [p. 173], and then **amortised** [p. 15]. If it is not capitalised, then it will simply be shown as a cost on the **P & L** [p. 234].

Capitalisation is a result of the accrual principle. Although accounting standards contain more detailed rules, the fundamental purpose of capitalisation is to allow the **accrual** [p. 4] of expenses in the current period to sales in future periods.

Expenses that may be capitalised include:

- development expenditure,

- computer software (but not all internal development costs)

- other intangible assets provided future benefits are probable and costs are reliably measureable,

- interest paid while while acquiring an asset or preparing it for use.

Investors may sometimes find it useful to adjust the accounts by capitalising expenses that a company does not capitalise. For example, capitalising all R & D.

Capitalisation issue

See **scrip issue** [p. 287].

CAPM

The capital asset pricing model (CAPM) is a method of valuing not just securities, but any investment, using a **DCF** [p. 88] with a risk adjusted discount rate.

The method used to calculate an appropriate discount rate uses the investment's **beta** [p. 34]. This is a measure of the amount of risk that the investment would have in the context of a diversified portfolio. Beta is denoted by the Greek letter β. Estimates of the beta of the shares of most **listed** [p. 190] companies can be obtained from many financial data providers.

The discount rate used in a CAPM DCF is:

$$r = r_f + (\beta \times (r_m - r_f))$$

where r_f is the **risk free rate** [p. 282]
r_m is the expected return on the market and
β is the beta of the cash flows or security being valued.

The term $r_m - r_f$ is the market **risk premium** [p. 282]. The term $\beta \times (r_m - r_f)$ is the risk premium on the cash flows (or security) being valued.

If the securities being valued are shares it is usual to use the **equity risk premium** [p. 123] and the beta of the share against the stock market. It is possible to use the wider securities market but there is no real reason to do so.

The beta adjusts the discount rate for the **correlation** [p. 74] between the cash flows being valued and the volatility of the market. This an important measure of risk because this element of risk cannot be diluted by diversification.

The cash flows should the be the expected values (see **expected return** [p. 135]) of the future cash flows.

The CAPM is the mostly widely used single valuation model as it can easily be applied to the most common types of investment. Other important valuation models include **arbitrage pricing theory** [p. 19] (which is harder to apply) and **Black-Scholes** [p. 36] (primarily useful for **options** [p. 228]).

Carrier pre-select

Carrier pre-select is a regulator imposed system that compels telecoms networks to allow customers to route all their calls through another (a competitor's) network.

The importance of carrier pre-select is that it allows competitors to use an **incumbent's** [p. 168] infrastructure.

The call is carried by the telecoms company that controls the local loop as far as its exchange, but is rerouted to the customer's chosen carrier there.

Although this is superficially similar to **local loop unbundling** [p. 191], it is far more limited in its effects. As it does not require the installation of another network's equipment in telephone exchanges (but merely a connection from each exchange to the other network) it is far cheaper and simpler to roll-out. This also means that the incumbent teleco retains line-rental revenues and control over the provision of the line.

Cartel

A cartel is a group of firms acting together to restrict prices. Most commonly, a group of producers agree not to sell below a given price. By acting together the firms in a cartel are able to give themselves the same, or similar, pricing power to a **monopoly** [p. 207].

In general, cartels are illegal. They are precisely what competition laws (called anti-trust laws in the US) are designed to prevent. However there are, and have been, various exemptions for particular industries. Some cartels in international markets are operated by national governments; the best example of this the oil cartel OPEC. OPEC sets output quotas rather than selling prices, but as price depends on supply the effect is the same.

It is difficult to enforce the competition laws designed to prevent cartels from controlling prices. One of the problems is actually proving collusion. Any discussion between the operators of an illegal cartel is likely to be carried out covertly. They may sell at similar prices, purely as a result of the operation of a normal competitive market. Even suspiciously high **profit margins** [p. 253] may be explained away by an **oligopolistic** [p. 223] market.

There are also many things that companies within a particular industry may do, that are capable of legitimate explanation, but which may have the effect of setting minimum prices or of locking out other competitors or of erecting barriers to entry. Any cooperation between companies within an industry should be regarded with suspicion by consumers.

Cartels are sometimes ended by competition regulators. They may also collapse because a member of a cartel sees an opportunity to gain an advantage by breaking whatever agreements bind the cartel. For example, by suddenly cutting prices a company may be able to capture enough market share to more than compensate for the lower margins that result.

Cash conversion

The cash conversion rate (or simply cash conversion) measures the proportion of profits that are converted to **cash flow** [p. 53]. It is therefore:

$$\frac{cashflow}{profits}$$

This can be measured at several levels, but the profit and cash flow measures should match for this to be meaningful. It is usual to use post tax profit and **free cash flow** [p. 146] before dividends as they both measure profits available to share holders. One could also look at the conversion of **operating profit** [p. 227] into **operating cashflow** [p. 225].

Cash cost

Cash costs, in mining, are the costs of production, at site level, per unit of output. Cash costs include operational cash costs at site level. This:

- includes transport, refining and administration costs and royalties
- excludes non-cash costs such as **depreciation** [p. 95] and **amortisation** [p. 15]
- excludes costs not at site level (such as head office costs).

The value of the by-products is deducted from the final cash cost of the metal. For example, if a copper mine produces gold as a by-product, then the value of the gold produced will be deducted from the cash cost of the copper. This is the usual accounting treatment for by-products in most industries.

Cash cycle

The cash cycle, also called the cash conversion cycle, is a measure of the length of time it takes to get from paying cash for **stock** [p. 307] to getting cash after selling it. It is equal to:

$$stock\ days + debtor\ days - creditor\ days$$

See **stock days** [p. 308], **debtor days** [p. 91] and **creditor days** [p. 79].

The length of the cash cycle dictates the amount of money that needs to be tied up in **working capital** [p. 347] for a given level of sales.

A shorter cash conversion cycle is better, other things being equal. It is possible for the cash conversion cycle to be negative, this is most likely for certain retailers who buy on credit, sell for cash and have a high **stock turnover** [p. 308].

Cash flow

Cash flows are what ultimately matter to investors – how much money actually comes in, and when it comes in, are more important to investors than accounting profits.

There are a number of different definitions of cash flow. Some are shown on the cash flow statement. Others need to be calculated from it, or from other accounting statements.

Free cash flow [p. 146] is often used as a basis for **DCF** [p. 88] valuations. **Operating cash flow** [p. 225] is used as a measure of how good a company is at converting profits into cash-flow. **EBITDA** [p. 116] is closely related to operating cash flow and is often used as a cash flow measure

Cash flow per share

Cash flow per share is simply **cash flow** [p. 53] divided by the number of shares in issue.

As there are many different cash flow measures, calculating a cash flow per share requires choosing one. It would be logical to use a measure of cash flow after interest as this is a per share measure and therefore want something related to returns to shareholders.

Free cash flow [p. 146] after interest would be a good choice that meets the above requirements, but it is not the only possible choice.

The most common reason for calculating cash flow per share is to calculate **price/cash flow** [p. 250]

Cash interest cover

A company's ability to pay interest due to its creditors is often measured using **interest cover** [p. 176]. However interest cover is calculated using accounting profits, which may not accurately reflect the actual amount of cash inflows a company makes its interest payments out of.

Cash interest cover uses **operating cash flow** [p. 225] rather than EBIT, and net interest paid (interest paid minus interest received) as shown by the cash flow statement instead of interest payable. It is:

$$\frac{operating\ cash\ flow}{interest\ paid}$$

Cash interest cover avoids some of the weaknesses of the **P & L** [p. 234] based interest cover, but has its own.

For example, if interest is incurred but the actual payment is delayed, then the cash interest cover may appear much better or worse than the real picture due to this lumpiness. Cash interest cover is probably best used as a supplement to interest cover rather than a substitute.

Cash return on invested capital

See **CROIC** [p. 80].

Cash shell

A cash shell is a company that does not quite meet the definition of a **shell company** [p. 295], but whose main value nonetheless lies in its **listing** [p. 190] rather than its assets or its business.

Cash shells may be literally just that: a shell company with a bit of cash or investments added.

More commonly, shell companies have a rump of their former business. The normal fate of these businesses is to be sold once the shell successfully completes a **reverse takeover** [p. 278].

As with shells, some exchanges dislike having too many listed cash shells, and may make it difficult or impossible for their listing to be maintained indefinitely.

Cashflow statement

Unlike the **profit and loss** [p. 234] account, which follows the **accruals** [p. 4] principal, the cashflow statement records the actual movements in cash in an accounting period. All cash received (inflows) by the company, and spent (outflows) by the company will be shown in this statement.

As determining cash amounts involves less use of judgement and discretion than determining profits or asset value, the cashflow statement is harder to manipulate than the other main accounting statements (the **profit & loss account** [p. 234] and the **balance sheet** [p. 28]).

The cashflow statement shows cash coming into a company (from sales, income from investments, asset sales) and going out (payments to suppliers, investment), the raising of capital (money borrowed or raised from shareholders) and the payment of returns of capital (interest and dividends) and tax.

Like profit, cash flow can be measured at a number of levels. For example, **operating cash flow** [p. 225] roughly corresponds to **operating profit** [p. 227] with the effects on non-cash items stripped out.

The main items in a typical cash flow statement are (in order):

- cash flow from operating activities

- returns on investments and servicing of finance

- taxation

- **capital expenditure** [p. 46] and financial investments

- **acquisitions** [p. 5] and disposals

- equity dividends paid

- management of liquid resources

- financing

The returns on investments and servicing of finance includes dividends received (e.g. from subsidiaries) and interest from fixed interest securities and bank deposits. It will also show payments to lenders: both banks and holders of a company's fixed interest securities.

Capital investments and financial investments will show the cashflow relating to the purchase and disposal of **fixed assets** [p. 142]. Liquid resources are cash and **liquid** [p. 190], short term, investments.

All items in the cash flow statement can be significantly different from equivalent items on the P & L. This is what makes the cash flow so valuable (it is not susceptible to manipulation), but it can also make it less meaningful (there are good reasons for accruing in the other accounting statements).

Operating cash flow is very often looked at by investors. The capital expenditure item is a quicker way of finding out how heavily the company is investing than looking at the balance sheet (and then correcting for **depreciation** [p. 95] etc.) but it has two weaknesses: it does not record purchases not yet paid for and it does not allow one to separate capital expenditure on operating assets from long term financial investments.

A more complex use of the cashflow statement is the calculation of **free cash flow** [p. 146], which can be used in valuation ratios and **DCF** [p. 88] valuations. All the items in the cashflow statement provide a useful check on items in the other accounting statements and are a vital input to the financial models used for forecasting.

Catastrophe bonds

Catastrophe bonds (cat bonds) are a form of insurance **securitisation** [p. 290]. They are an alternative to insurance that transfers risk to investors rather than insurers.

Catastrophe bonds may be issued by an insurer to spread risk, in order to protect their own balance sheets in the event of large scale payouts such as those caused by natural disasters. They therefore also reassure policy holders.

They may also be issued an entity that requires insurance against a single large risk. In this case they can be regarded as a form of insurance **disintermediation** [p. 100]. A good example of was FIFA's issue of $260m worth of catastrophe bonds against cancellation of the 2002 football world cup.

Catastrophe bonds are usually issued by an **SPV** [p. 304]. The SPV will keep bondholders' money and pay them interest. It will also usually receive a premium from the insured. In the event of the "catastrophe" occurring the bondholders lose their money as it is used to pay the "insured".

In return for a low risk of losing all their money cat bondholders get a better yield and an otherwise reasonably safe investment. The risk is also usually an easily **diversifiable** [p. 102] one.

Cathode metal

Miners often disclose production of cathode metal. This is metal that has been electro-refined.

This is done by electrolysis (passing an electrical current though a liquid). One terminal, the anode, is made of impure metal. The metal is removed from this and deposited on the other terminal, the cathode.

This process is typically used to improve the purity of the already refined metal, after **concentration** [p. 67], smelting and initial refining.

Electro-refining is commonly used in copper production. 99.5% pure refined copper is electro-refined to produce 99.99% pure copper cathode. This is sufficiently pure for most uses such as electrical cables.

Central counterparty

A central counterparty is a financial institution that acts as an intermediary between security market participants. This reduces the amount of **counterparty** [p. 76] risk that market participants are exposed to.

Most major stock exchanges (including London) have trading systems that make use of a central counterparty.

The seller of a security sells to the central counter party. The central counterparty simultaneously sells to the buyer. This means that if one party defaults then the central counterparty will absorb the loss.

This eliminates both the risk of direct financial loss though a default and the risk of indirect loss through having to unwind a trade. This is a much more complete control of counterparty risk than alternatives such as simple **DVP** [p. 113].

CER

See **constant exchange rates** [p. 69].

CFD

See **contract for difference** [p. 71].

Chartist

See **technical analysis** [p. 319].

Chinese wall

A Chinese wall is a system (that may consist of rules, physical separation, software, etc.) designed to prevent confidential information leaking from one department of a financial institution to another.

Chinese walls are necessary because financial institutions such as large investment banks have departments that serve clients with conflicting interests, and even clients whose interests conflict with those of other departments of the same bank.

For example, the corporate finance department of an investment bank may know of **takeover bids** [p. 317] that are being considered, but for the bank's trading or fund management operations to act on this information would constitute **insider trading** [p. 171]. This makes it necessary that such information is restricted to the departments actually involved, so that other departments can function normally.

The effectiveness of Chinese walls has often been questioned, particularly where where the incentives to cooperate are clearly very strong.

Churn

Churn is the proportion of subscribers to a service who cancel it but are replaced by new subscribers over a given period of time. It is most often **disclosed** [p. 98] by media and telecoms companies.

Suppose a pay TV broadcaster has a million subscribers. Of these 50,000 (5%) cancel their subscriptions over the course of an year. Over the same year it gains 70,000 new subscribers. It ends the year with 20,000 more subscribers than at the beginning of the year.

This means that its subscriber numbers grew by 20,000 or 2% and it had a subscriber churn of 50,000 or 5%.

As churn is the number of customers who have unsubscribed but been replaced, if there has been a net loss of customers then churn will be equal to the number of new customers. So if the same company had lost 50,000 customers and gained 30,000 new ones it would have a net subscriber loss of 20,000 (2%) and a churn of 30,000 (3%).

Calculating churn for mobile telecoms companies is further complicated by inactive accounts. Many pre-pay customers will simply cease using a connection when they get a new one. Therefore customers who have not used their phones for some months should not be regarded as current customers (when calculating churn, or for most other purposes). Including inactive accounts will understate churn.

Churn is important as it is a measure of customer loyalty, and therefore how stable a company's **subscription revenues** [p. 311] are likely to be if sales growth flags.

City Code on Takeovers and Mergers

The City Code on Takeovers and Mergers governs how **takeover bids** [p. 317] in the UK are carried out. It is drawn up by, and is primarily enforced by, the **Takeover Panel** [p. 318].

The key requirements of the City Code are:

- All shareholders must be offered equally good terms, as defined by the code.

- All shareholders must be given equal access to information.

- A time table is adhered to that sets time limits for each phase of the bid.

- Bidders and members of a **concert party** [p. 67] must disclose their dealings.

- The bidder must set an acceptance level (of over 50%) at which the bid becomes unconditional.

- There are limits on the conditions attached to a bid.

- A **mandatory offer** [p. 195] must be made if a shareholder's or concert party's holdings exceed 30%.

- The board of the target company may not use **poison pills** [p. 240] and other actions to frustrate a *bona fide* bid, unless they have shareholder approval.

In addition to these the Companies Act imposes its own requirements: all shareholdings of above 3% must be disclosed, and any changes of more than 1% in such shareholding must also be disclosed, whether or not they are related to a bid.

The City Code is also now required to follow the rules laid down by the EU directive on takeovers. It directly incorporates part of the directive.

Claims equalisation reserve

The claims equalisation reserve is a **balance sheet** [p. 28] item showing funds an insurance company has (nominally) set aside in order to smooth fluctuations in the cost of claims. The claims equalisation reserve is not required and is used at a company's discretion.

It produces more consistent revenues, but it is obviously something that lends itself to abuse.

There is a certain irony in there being a recognised balance sheet item that allows insurance companies to use a (limited) form of profit smoothing – something that accounting standards are designed to make as difficult as possible in any other industry. There is, of course, a reason for this: the availability of **actuarial** [p. 6] estimates of the "normal" level of claims provides a sounder basis for smoothing.

Claims ratio

Claims payable as a percentage of premium income. This is the equivalent of **gross margin** [p. 160] for an insurance business. An insurer's investment income is also part of its core business so the comparison with gross profit is not exact.

The claims ratio can be combined with the **expense ratio** [p. 136] to produce the **combined ratio** [p. 62].

Clean price

Bond prices are normally quoted as clean prices. The clean price of a bond is the actual price that will be paid (the **dirty price** [p. 98]) less the **accrued interest** [p. 5].

The reason markets use clean prices is that the dirty prices fluctuate with interest payments. This means that clean prices show the underlying trend in prices more clearly.

Consider a £100 bond with a 10% **coupon** [p. 77] rate and the interest payment about to be made. If the dirty price is £105 and the clean price £95, it is easier to think of this as a bond trading at £95 with £10 interest due, than as a bond worth £105, the value of which will go down to £95 once the coupon is paid.

The dirty price will fall by £10 when the interest is paid (other things being equal). This is a regular occurrence for most bonds. This means that the price of a bond will show a pattern of sudden drops, followed by gradual recoveries (a "sawtooth" pattern), that will obscure underlying trends.

The clean price will be unchanged by the interest payment, because the fall in the dirty price will be balanced by the equal fall in the accrued interest.

Clearing house

A clearing house provides settlement services for trades that take place through an exchange. The exchange matches buyers with sellers, the clearing house then has to deal with the transfer of ownership.

The clearing house used by the London Stock Exchange is LCH Clearnet. In the US the Depositary Trust & Clearing Corporation (DTCC) has a monopoly on clearing services.

It is common for a clearing house to guarantee trades by acting as a **central counterparty** [p. 56] (as happens for most securities trading in the UK). It is also common for a clearing house to provide **depositary** [p. 95] services, recording ownership of **dematerialised securities** [p. 94] as DTCC does.

Clinical trials

Clinical trials are the core of the process of testing through which new drugs (and other treatments such as vaccines) go in order to demonstrate their safety and effectiveness to regulators. They are the parts of the testing process that involve administering a drug (or other treatment) to humans. Clinical trials are conducted by the developers of a drug and the data is passed on to regulators.

Clinical trials are a long and complex process that needs to determine not only how safe a drug is, but also how effective it is. It not only important that a drug be approved, but what it is approved for. Regulators restrict the marketing of a drug, and in particular the labelling – the information a pharmaceutical company may distribute about the usage of a drug.

Labelling matters because a drug may be approved only for certain variants of a disease, or for certain types of patients. Some drugs are approved as treatments for more than one disease or condition. The wider the approval, the bigger the market that the drug may be promoted to. Regulators may also require that drugs carry certain warnings.

The labelling does not directly restrict how doctor may prescribe a drug, but it does limit how a pharmaceutical company markets the drug, and marketing to prescribers is obviously a crucial (and expensive) part of selling a drug.

Clinical trials are carried out in three phases. The amount of information gathered and the number of people participating grows at each stage.

Pre-clinical testing

This precedes clinical testing and involves laboratory and animal testing of a drug. Pre-clinical trials need to provide enough information on safety to allow regulators to decide whether to permit clinical trials – whether the drug is safe enough to try on people.

Phase I clinical trials

These are the first trials with human beings. They typically involve a comparatively small number of people (a few tens of people) and are completed in a few months. The main purpose of phase I trials is to establish that a drug is safe enough to more on to phase II trials and to establish safe dosages. About 70% of drugs pass this phase.

Phase II clinical trials

Phase II trials involve more people, typically hundreds of people, and usually take longer (at least a few months, sometimes a year or two). The emphasis shifts from purely safety to looking for evidence of effectiveness, although safety continues to be studied. If no new safety issues emerge and the treatment appears effective in a significant proportion of patients then the drug can move to the next stage. About half the drugs that go into Phase II trials fail; only a third of the drugs that enter clinical testing will make it past this phase to go into Phase III.

Phase III clinical trials

Phase III trials involve hundreds or thousands of people and take at least a year, often several years. A phase III trial studies all aspects of safety, effectiveness and dosage. A control group of patients on standard medication (or none) is used to provide a yardstick for comparisons. This phase of clinical trials is clearly expensive but the majority of drugs that phase II also pass phase III. A drug entering Phase I typically has around a quarter to a third chance of making to to the end of Phase III.

Approval

Once a drug has passed through clinical trials it will take at least a few months (or even years), before it receives approval and can be marketed. About 20% of drugs that enter Phase I trials will eventually be marketed. After reaching the market the drug continues to be monitored for problems and risk of problems that could prompt withdrawal or narrowing of approval always remains, but slowly diminishes.

Close period

A close period is a period, usually of two months, prior to the release of re- sults during which directors and other insiders are not allowed to trade in a company's shares.

It is also usual for companies to refrain from making other price sensitive announcements (e.g. trading statements) during the close period. This is not required, but it is usually regarded as good practice.

Many companies issue a trading statement immediately before the start of the close period so that investors have information that is as up to date as pos- sible during the close period.

It is always possible for a company to be overtaken by events and put in a position that makes it necessary to make an announcement during the close period.

Closet tracker

A closet tracker is a fund that is supposedly actively managed, but that is nonetheless run in a very conservative manner that makes it little different from a **tracker fund** [p. 325].

Investors are generally better off investing in a genuine tracker fund for two reasons:

1. A real tracker fund will charge (lower) tracker fund level fees.

2. A real tracker fund will track its chosen index very accurately.

A closet tracker is not just a tracker fund, it is usually an expensive and sloppily run tracker fund.

Many supposed active funds are also in fact run as a combination of a closet tracker with a (often smaller) real active fund. Again, investors pay over the odds as they pay active management fees on their whole investment, but only part of it is really actively managed.

Collective investment vehicle

A collective investment vehicle is any entity that allows investors to pool their money and invest the pooled funds, rather than buying securities directly as individuals.

Collective investment vehicles are usually managed by a fund management company which is paid a fee for doing so. The fee is usually a percentage of **assets under management** [p. 22] but it may also be linked to performance. The latter is a common arrangement for **hedge funds** [p. 162].

Other costs that investors in various collective investment vehicles may face are initial or exit charges, spreads, broker's commission and stamp duty.

Single priced [p. 296] vehicles have no spread but the savings on this are usually more than offset by initial or exit charges.

The commonest types of collective investment vehicle are **unit trusts** [p. 333] (called mutual funds in the US and most other countries), **investment trusts** [p. 180] (more accurately called investment companies outside the UK), **exchange traded funds** [p. 124] and **OEICs** [p. 221].

The British government plans to introduce **REITs** [p. 272], which are already popular in many other countries.

Combined ratio

In general (non-life) insurance, the combined ratio is claims and operating expenses as a percentage of premium income.

If it is less than 100% the company is making an **operating profit** [p. 227] on investment underwriting. A company may still make a profit despite a combined ratio of over a 100% as insurance companies normally have substantial investment income.

It is may include or exclude amounts reimbursed by **reinsurers** [p. 271]. It is important to be clear which of these variants is being used in any instance.

The combined ratio combines two types of costs: claims and operational expenses. It can be decomposed into two ratios, the **claims ratio** [p. 59] and the **expense ratio** [p. 136] to give a more detailed breakdown.

Commercial paper

Commercial paper is a short term debt instrument issued by a company. The main characteristics of commercial paper are:

- It is unsecured.

- It is short term (maturity and full repayment usually within an year of issue).

- It is usually less liquid than bonds – there is no real **secondary market** [p. 288].

Commercial paper is usually issued in order to meet short term requirements rather than fund long term investments. Given that it needs to be repaid after a comparatively short time it would be very risky to tie the money up.

The savings made by issuing commercial paper over raising money by simpler means such as borrowing from a bank are fairly small in terms of the difference in interest rates. This means that commercial paper is usually useful only for raising fairly large amounts. This combined with its short term nature means its use restricted to large borrowers.

Commoditisation

A **commodity** [p. 64] is a product that is completely undifferentiated. If a product becomes less differentiated, so that buyers care less about who they buy from, this change is called commoditisation.

The key effect of commoditisation is that it reduces the pricing power of the producer: if products become more alike from a buyer's point of view they will tend to buy the cheapest.

Commoditisation is a key reason why many growth markets disappoint investors. Sales volumes grow as expected but, as the market matures, prices come under pressure and margins shrink. This is a key issue to consider when picking growth stocks.

In order to avoid commoditisation companies need to be able to differentiate their products with something unique, that is not easily copied by competitors, and which is valued by customers. This may take the form of a strong brand, a technology lead, good design, good retail locations, or anything else that will convince customers not buy the cheapest product. The alternative to avoiding commoditisation is, of course, to compete on price.

The personal computer market and certain other types of computer hardware provide a perfect example of this. When this was a fast growing industry each computer manufacturer would sell a computers together with a built in operating system, both of which were unique. Different manufacturers' products looked different, ran different software and had very different capabilities. At this point the market attracted many growth investors at it was obvious that demand for the new technology was exploding.

As the market matured two vital changes happened. The product became standardised, and therefore largely commoditised. In addition personal computer manufacturers largely ceased being significant producers of software – which **is** highly differentiated and commands huge margins.

Commodity

A commodity is a product that is **fungible** [p. 153]; any supplier's product is interchangeable with any other's and buyers do not care who they buy from.

Commodities are most commonly products whose properties can be precisely described and measured, and whose production does not involve anything that allows it to be differentiated.

The interchangeability of commodities means that they can be traded on exchanges in a similar manner to financial securities. This also means that financial products based on commodity prices can be created, most importantly **futures** [p. 154] and **options** [p. 228].

A product being a commodity is necessary for perfect competition to exist, which is important as it is this type of competition which guarantees (this can be mathematically prove starting from some reasonable assumptions) economic efficiency.

Important commodities include:

- **crude oil** [p. 81]

- metals

- certain agricultural products.

Futures markets exist for a wide range of commodities (oil, copper, orange juice, pork bellies etc.) and are used by suppliers (to **hedge** [p. 162] against price falls), buyers (to hedge against price rises) and speculators.

Non-perishable commodities such as metals are called hard commodities. Perishable commodities such as agricultural commodities are called soft commodities.

Products that are not commodities can gradually lose their differentiation and become more **commoditised** [p. 63].

Company secretary

A company secretary is the officer of a company responsible for administrative matters such as maintaining registers of holders of **registered securities** [p. 270], carrying out **corporate actions** [p. 73] and filing documents with the registrar of companies. A company secretary should also try to ensure that high standards of **corporate governance** [p. 74] are followed.

A company secretary may be an individual or a corporate body (i.e. a company). There may be a single company secretary or several joint secretaries. The company secretary of a public company (one that may sell its shares to the public) in the UK must be appropriately qualified. This means that they should be an accountant, a lawyer, a member of the Institute of Chartered Secretaries and Administrators or have other appropriate experience or qualifications.

It is not uncommon for a company secretary to be a director of the company. Given that nature of the job it is not surprising that it is common for it to be combined with other duties in the areas of law, finance and administration.

It is fairly common for companies to **outsource** [p. 232] either the entire role (small companies often appoint an external secretary) or significant parts of it (for example, by using an external **registrar** [p. 270]).

Compound Annual Growth Rate

Compound annual growth rate (CAGR) is an **average** [p. 25] growth rate over a period of several years. It is a **geometric average** [p. 158] of annual growth rates:

$$CAGR = \left(\frac{ending\ value}{starting\ value} \right)^{1/number\ of\ years} - 1$$

If a company had sales of £10m in 2000 and £15m in 2005 then the CAGR of its sales is: $(15 \div 10)^{1/5} - 1 = .084 = 8.4\%$

If percentage growth rates are used it is important to remember to add one to each of them before calculating the geometric average. For example, the CAGR over two years of 10% one year and 20% the next is $(1.1 \times 1.2)^{1/2} - 1$.

Although no historical data is a substitute for a forecast, the CAGR over a number of years (typically the last five) is a better indication of a trend than a single year's growth which may be atypically good or bad.

CAGR should be used because arithmetic averaging (see **arithmetic mean** [p. 19]) of growth numbers gives incorrect results. For example, if a company's sales rose from £10m in year one to £15m in year two and then fell back to £10m in year three, then there has been a 50% increase (year-on-year) followed by a 33% decrease (year-on-year). Adding these up would give 17% and therefore an arithmetic mean of 8.5%, whereas it is obvious that the average growth has been 0%. A geometric average gives the correct answer.

Compound interest

Interest payments can be added to the principal. This means higher interest in the next period for which interest is paid. This compounding of interest can, over a period of time, mean that the total amount of interest paid is far higher than the simple interest.

Suppose £100 is invested in an account that pays 10%, which is paid annually. Assume that interest is paid out of the account. Then the total interest paid over the ten years will be £100.

If the interest is allowed to accumulate in the account, then there will be a total of £259.37 in the account after 10 years – the total interest payment will be £159.37.

The longer the time period the greater the effect of compounding. Suppose the same scenario as above but with a 20 year time period. Then the interest paid, if it is withdrawn as soon as it is paid, will be £200. If it is allowed to accumulate over 20 years the account will contain £672.75 – total interest payments will be £572.75.

The effect of compounding will also be stronger if the frequency of payment is greater. Interest of 10% paid quarterly will compound over the period of an year, so the annual rate of compounded interest will be 10.4%, and the total interest paid over a ten year period will be £280.

The total amount (principal plus interest) arising from compounded interest is:

$$p \times (1 + i)^t$$

where p is the amount of the principal
i is the interest rate per period (typically an year) and
t is the number of periods.

Continuously compounded interest

As the period over which interest is paid becomes smaller the amount given by the formula above converges to the value given by the formula below. This is continuous compounding which can be useful for some calculations. This amount is:

$$pe^{it}$$

where p is the principal,
i is the interest rate,
t is the time and
e is the constant.

The time and the interest rate must use consistent periods of time: if i is an annual interest rate, then t must be the time in years.

Compulsory acquisition

In order to prevent a small number of people from blocking a **takeover bid** [p. 317], a bidder who buys more than 90% of a company can compel the remaining shareholders to sell.

The terms on which the sale is compelled are regulated by the **City Code** [p. 58], which essentially requires that the terms are as good as those offered to other shareholders who sold during the bid.

While this often feels unfair to the shareholders who are compelled to sell, the intent is to allow shareholders to, in effect, agree to sell a company *in toto* without being blocked by a small minority.

Concentrate

In mining, concentrate is partially purified ore. It is produced by mixing ground ore with water and blowing air bubbles through the water. These carry mineral particles to the surface.

Concert party

A concert party is a group of people acting in concert in order to take over a target company. Regulators such as the **Takeover Panel** [p. 318] apply rules applicable to takeover bids to all members of a concert party.

Of particular importance is that the 30% threshold at which a **mandatory offer** [p. 195] must be made is considered to be reached when a concert party jointly hold 30% of the shares in a company, not when one of them does.

Some entities are presumed to be acting in concert unless shown otherwise. These include the directors, **subsidiaries** [p. 311], **associate companies** [p. 23] and the **parent company** [p. 236] of the bidder.

Even entities that are not part of a concert party may find that some rules apply to them: they are required to disclose dealings in the share of the bidder or the target. These "associates" are people who have an interest in the outcome of the bid (other than simply as shareholders) but who are not deliberately acting in concert with the bidder, An example of associates are the directors the target company even when they are not acting in concert with either the bidder or a potential counter-bidder.

Conglomerate

A conglomerate is a company that has many **subsidiaries** [p. 311] and **associates** [p. 23] that operate in a wide range of businesses.

There are several problems with conglomerates:

- There are few **synergies** [p. 316] between unrelated businesses.

- The extra layers of management needed, compared to standalone businesses, increases costs.

- A conglomerate is likely to **disclose** [p. 98] less information than standalone businesses; many numbers are disclosed **consolidated** [p. 68], rather than separately for each business.

- The complexity of a conglomerates' accounts can make them harder to analyse – and makes it easier for management to hide things.

- Management are very unlikely have real expertise in all areas of the business.

For these reasons conglomerates have become much less common in developed markets than they once were. Most have chosen an area of business to focus on and sold or **demerged** [p. 94] non-core businesses.

Conglomerates are still common in some **emerging markets** [p. 121]. A number of explanations have been put forward. Most explanations for this revolve around the lack of well developed capital markets in developing economies. So the conglomerates take on the role of allocating capital to individual businesses, whereas in developed economies this is done by the market.

Lack of regulation and ineffective legal systems also make investors in emerging markets more suspicious of smaller companies (because if you are cheated you are less likely to be able to sue successfully or to expect regulators to act). This means that large companies, especially those that have a track record of treating **minorities** [p. 204] well (at least by emerging market standards!) have an advantage in raising capital. They can also fund investment in growth businesses from more mature cash generative businesses, avoiding the need to raise capital in the market altogether.

Consolidated accounts

A group of companies is required to prepare accounts for the group as a whole as well as the company. These consolidated accounts are almost always what matter to investors.

Initial announcements of results usually contain consolidated results and annual reports always have both company and consolidated accounts. The consolidated accounts are often called group accounts.

The consolidated **P & L** [p. 234] includes the profits of **subsidiaries** [p. 311] and the company's share of profits made by **associates** [p. 23] and **joint ventures** [p. 184]. If any subsidiaries are not fully owned then a deduction will be made further down the P & L for the profits attributable to **minority interests** [p. 204].

The consolidated **balance sheet** [p. 28] similarly shows the amounts of assets and liabilities of the company and all its subsidiaries. It also shows The value of holdings in associates and joint ventures.

In contrast the company balance sheet and P & L only shows only shows the value of assets, liabilities and profits of the company itself. The impact of subsidiaries, associates and joint ventures is limited to the value of shares in them and dividends paid by them.

Consolidation

A share consolidation is the opposite of a **share split** [p. 294].

Each shareholder's shares are replaced with a smaller number of shares with a higher par value. If a shareholder has a 1,000 shares with a par value of 10p, then after a 1 for 2 consolidation the shareholder will have 500 shares with a **par value** [p. 235] of 20p.

Constant currencies

See **constant exchange rates** [p. 69].

Constant exchange rates

If a company sells in a foreign currency that means that underlying trends in its sales and profits can be obscured by foreign currency movements. The result is that growth in turnover or profits in the company's reporting currency (the currency its accounts are in) will not give investors a full view of how the business performed.

Consider a very common situation: a British company sells largely abroad and sets its prices (and is paid) in dollars. Suppose sales increased in dollar terms by 10%, but that the dollar fell against the pound and was on average five percent lower during the year than it was the previous year. The result is that the sales growth shown in the accounts will only be about 5%.

Most companies that are significantly affected by exchange rate fluctuations **disclose** [p. 98] sales, and sometimes profits, in a way that strips out the effects of exchange rate changes.

This can be done in a number of ways including:

- Translating the current year's turnover and operating profit using the previous year's exchange rate. This is what we mean by constant exchange rates.

- Stating the sales and profits in the appropriate foreign currencies.

- Stating how much sales or profits were reduced or increased as a result of exchange rate changes.

Constant exchange rates are not always better indicators of performance. Some countries have high inflation and currencies that depreciate persistently (the two are linked, see **interest rate parity** [p. 177]). This means that adjusting for the fall in such a currency **gives** an overoptimistic view of growth. This most often happens when looking at companies with significant **emerging markets** [p. 121] operations.

The ideal solution would be to look at inflation adjusted growth numbers but this requires a considerable amount of analysis.

Contango

See **forwardation** [p. 145].

Contingent liabilities

Contingent liabilities are possible future liabilities that will only become certain on the occurrence of some future event. A contingent liability is less certain than a **provision** [p. 256]: the latter is expected to occur, a contingent liability might occur.

Contingent liabilities are not shown in the balance sheet, but must be **disclosed** [p. 98] in the **notes to the accounts** [p. 219].

Common types of contingent liabilities include guarantees and the results of legal disputes. Guarantees may be given on behalf of an associate company, or as part of a larger deal (banks frequently give guarantees of various sorts as part of their business).

Contingent liabilities often do not ever become actual liabilities. If they are large they may nonetheless be enough of a risk to have a significant impact on valuation.

Investors should look out for large, unusual or potentially problematic contingent liabilities such as:

- guarantees given without apparent or sufficient reason

- contingent liabilities that do not fit in with the usual course of the business.

Continuing operations

When companies disclose numbers for "continuing operations", it means that they have stripped out the effects of disposals but not of **acquisitions** [p. 5]. They have done the favourable part of the adjustments needed to calculate **organic growth** [p. 230], but not the unfavourable part.

The implied justification for this is that acquisitive growth is part of how the continuing businesses grow and is to some extent sustainable, whereas disposals are no longer part of the company and their performance is irrelevant.

Continuing business numbers are not as useful for investors as organic growth numbers, and **pro-forma** [p. 252] organic numbers are generally preferable. If the acquisitions are part of a continuing pattern why not the disposals?

The two may well be tied together as substantial disposals may be helping to pay for acquisitions.

Organic numbers, when compared to the reported numbers, allow investors to see what the effects of acquisitions disposals are – such as what effect they have on **margins** [p. 253]. Pro-forma numbers allow investors to see exactly how the business as it now is has performed.

Contract for difference

A contract for difference (CFD) is similar to a **future** [p. 154]. The difference is that a CFD cannot be settled by delivery. It an agreement to pay an amount based on the change in some number. This also means that a CFD can exist where the **underlying asset** [p. 331] is not deliverable.

For example, a CFD may pay £1 for every point an index gains (and charge £1 for every point the index loses). This means that it is possible to have CFDs on **indices** [p. 169], natural phenomena (such as the weather) and anything else that is measurable.

It is common practice to call many CFDs futures – e.g., an index future. Where the underlying is not deliverable the "future" is in fact a CFD. CFDs sold to private investors also sometimes called spread bets.

Options [p. 228] with a non-deliverable underlying asset are also closely related to CFDs.

These contracts can resemble insurance contracts (in that they can transfer the risk of an event occurring) and **catastrophe bonds** [p. 55]. A good example would be the purchase of CFDs or options on weather by a company that has a business that depends on weather conditions.

Contrarian Investing

Following a strategy of consistently going against the current views of the market is called contrarian investing.

For example, contrarian investors are likely to sell shares that are currently favoured, and buy shares that are out of favour. They are also likely to prefer sectors, markets or types of investments that other investors avoid and sell whatever is generally well regarded.

Contrarian investing can be very successful during bubbles and busts as contrarian investors are likely to sell during a bubble and buy when the investors are unduly pessimistic about shares. The problem is that the market is right most of the time and therefore contrarians will find it hard to do well most of the time.

Out-performing the market (assuming that it is not due to pure luck) must involve spotting investments that the market has failed to price correctly. Thus far contrarians are right. However, they go further and assume that the way to spot opportunities to outperform is to assume that most investors are wrong.

This is sometimes true (as during bubbles), what is questionable is whether it is true enough of the time to be a good strategy.

Few investors are likely to be simple contrarians who automatically do the opposite of what the majority thinks. Many contrarians are likely to follow the more sensible strategy of looking at what market prices assume and looking for the occasions where the opposite is likely to be true. Most contrarians, when it comes to specific decisions, make much the same arguments as would a **growth** [p. 161] or **value** [p. 337] investor who favours the same investments.

Contribution

The contribution of a sale is the amount it adds to profits. The term reflects the contribution a sale makes towards covering **fixed** [p. 143] costs. Contribution is:

$$amount\ of\ a\ sale - associated\ \textbf{variable costs}[\text{p. }338]$$

or, more commonly, on a per unit basis

$$price - variable\ cost\ per\ unit$$

Contribution margin

Contribution margin is a measure of **profit margin** [p. 253] that focuses on what proportion of sales revenue is left over after paying associated variable costs. This is the amount that is left over to cover fixed costs, or to add to profits. It is:

$$\frac{contribution}{sales}$$

where *contribution* is the total**contribution** [p. 72] from all units sold.

It can also be usefully expressed in a way very different from other types of margin, on a per unit basis:

$$\frac{contribution}{price}$$

where *contribution* is the contribution per unit.

Convertible bonds

A convertible bond (convertible) is a bond that can be exchanged for shares on or before maturity. A convertible bond is equivalent to a straight bond plus a **warrant** [p. 343].

Convertibles give bond holders a hedge against the risks arising from **agency issues** [p. 11]. If a company follows a risky strategy that increases the value of shares but decreases that of debt then holders of convertibles can choose to convert. **Debt covenants** [p. 90] are also used to control this risk but warrants and convertibles are simpler.

Another way of looking at convertibles is as shares with a long term **put option** [p. 258]. The holders of convertibles get all the benefits of shares (except for the dividends and voting rights before conversion), but they get interest payments until conversion (more than making up for dividends). In addition, if the shares under-perform, they can choose to keep the bonds. The equivalence is not exact (as it is to a bond plus warrant) but it does reflect a possible reason for buying convertibles.

Core business

The core business of a company is the business that it is primarily in.

It is generally considered good for a company to focus on its core business and get rid of other businesses unless it has strong **synergies** [p. 316] or strategic reasons to justify operating other businesses.

Companies are usually run by managers who understand the core business best (because that is what is most important) so they can generally run the core business better than non-core businesses. The latter are therefore better run as standalone businesses.

Running non-core businesses also means more a complicated management structure and distracts management from the core business.

When companies get rid of non-core businesses they may do so by selling them to a trade buyer (another company in the same industry) or by **demerging** [p. 94] them.

The problem of running non-core businesses is most acute in companies with so many diverse businesses they have no clearly identifiable core business. See **conglomerates.** [p. 67]

Corporate actions

Corporate actions are anything that a company does that has a direct impact on shareholdings or that involves payments to or from shareholders.

Examples of corporate actions include **rights issues** [p. 280], **scrip issues** [p. 287], **splits** [p. 294], **consolidations** [p. 69], **demergers** [p. 94] and dividend payments.

Handling corporate actions easily and efficiently is one of the biggest advantages to a company of using an external **registrar** [p. 270]. It is also equally an advantage to large investors of using a **custodian** [p. 84].

The use of automated paperless **clearing houses** [p. 59] and **depositary systems** [p. 95] has greatly reduced the administrative costs of corporate actions.

Corporate governance

Corporate governance is a term used to describe the systems used to control corporations. It is often an issue because there are clear **agency conflicts** [p. 11] between the interests of shareholders and management.

Attempts to enforce good corporate governance come from a variety of sources. There are statutory measures, such as the clear legal duties that directors have to act in shareholder's interests. There are also corporate governance codes and recommendations that are not compulsory, but which **listed companies** [p. 190] are under very strong pressure to adopt; they give shareholders minimum standards that they can demand from management.

Current provisions recommended in the UK to ensure good corporate governance include:

- separation of the roles of chairman and managing director

- a minimum proportion of non-executive directors

- committees of non-executive directors to supervise sensitive issues such as directors' remuneration and **audit** [p. 25].

Standards of corporate governance have become more formalised and transparent over the years because of pressure, from both shareholders and regulators, in response to visible abuses by directors.

Correlation coefficient

A coefficient of correlation is a mathematical measure of how much one number (such as a share price) can expected to be influenced by changes in another (such as an **index** [p. 169]). It is closely related to covariance (see below).

A correlation coefficient of 1 means that the two numbers are perfectly correlated: if one grows so does the other, and the change in one is a multiple of the change in the other.

A correlation coefficient of -1 means that the numbers are perfectly inversely correlated. If one grows the other falls. The growth in one is a negative multiple of the growth in the other.

A correlation coefficient of zero means that the two numbers are not related.

A non-zero correlation coefficient means that the numbers are related, but unless the coefficient is either 1 or -1 there are other influences and the relationship between the two numbers is not fixed. So if you know one number you can estimate the other, but not with certainty. The closer the correlation coefficient is to zero the greater the uncertainty, and low correlation coefficients means that the relationship is not certain enough to be useful.

The description above is of is a relationship between two variables. It is also possible to calculate correlations between many variables. Adding more variables should increase the correlation; any variables that do not significantly improve the correlation should be excluded.

Covariance

The covariance of two variables (numbers measuring something) is a measure of the relationship between them. It closely related to the correlation and calculated as an intermediate step in calculating the correlation.

The covariance of two numbers is the arithmetic mean, over all values of x_1, and the corresponding values of x_2, of:

$$(x_1 - \mu_1)(x_2 - \mu_2)$$

where x_1 is the value of one variable
x_2 is the value of the other variable
μ_1 is the arithmetic mean of of x_1 and
μ_2 is the arithmetic mean of of x_2.

The correlation of x_1 and x_2 is:

$$\frac{cov(x_1, x_2)}{\sigma_1 \sigma_2}$$

where $cov(x_1, x_2)$ is the covariance of x_1 and x_2
σ_1 is the **standard deviation** [p. 305] of x_1 and
σ_2 is the standard deviation of x_2.

Cost of sales

Cost of sales, or cost of goods sold, measures the cost of goods or services supplied in a period. The cost of what a company sells is **accrued** [p. 4] with the cost of producing or supplying it. The cost of sales is the difference between sales and **gross profit** [p. 161].

The cost of goods sold is one of two costs deducted in arriving at the operating profit. The other is **sales, general and administrative costs** [p. 286].

Because stocks may be revalued, the cost of sales in a particular period reflects both any revaluation of stocks and the methods of allocating the cost of stocks [p. 307] (such as the use of **FIFO** [p. 138] or **LIFO** [p. 188] and methods of allocating overhead costs to particular products).

As the cost of sales excludes overheads, it has a higher proportion of **variable costs** [p. 338] than the operating costs as a whole. It does contain some fixed costs such as labour costs. Nonetheless, in many cases the cost of goods sold does consist almost entirely of variable costs.

Cost/assets ratio

The cost/assets ratio measures costs in relation to the size of a deposit taker (e.g. a bank). It is:

$$\frac{operating\ expenses}{average\ assets\ over\ the\ period}$$

It is a similar efficiency measure to the **cost/income ratio** [p. 76], but it is less directly related to profitability. It is not affected by interest rate changes so it can give a better picture of gains or deterioration in efficiency at times when rates or spreads have changed significantly.

Cost/income ratio

The cost/income ratio is

$$\frac{operating\ expenses}{operating\ income}$$

The cost/income ratio is an efficiency measure similar to **operating margin** [p. 226]. Unlike the operating margin, lower is better. The cost income ratio is most commonly used in the financial sector.

It is useful to measure how costs are changing compared to income – for example, if a bank's interest income is rising but costs are rising at a higher rate looking at changes in this ratio will highlight the fact.

The cost/income ratio reflects changes in the **cost/assets** [p. 76] ratio and in **interest margin** [p. 176]

Counterparty risk

A counterparty is a party with which a transaction is done. If A sells something to B, then B is a counter-party from A's point of view and vice-versa.

The risk that the counterparty will fail to fulfil their obligations – usually either by failing to pay or by failing to deliver **securities** [p. 291] – is called counterparty risk.

There are a number of ways of controlling counterparty risk. Some are trading mechanisms such as **DVP** [p. 113] or the use of a **central counterparty** [p. 56].

Financial institutions should track and manage counterpart risk in much the same way as any other **credit risk** [p. 79], and this should be integrated into institutions' overall risk management system.

The counterparty risks from securities trading are either simple credit risks (where the risk is that the other party will not pay) or a combination of credit risk with the risk of a position in a derivative (where the risk is that the other part will not deliver securities).

Counterparty risk tends to be at least as much of a concern to regulators as to the institutions exposed to it. This is because a large financial institution will be a counterparty to many others, and therefore the knock-on effects of its failure pose a **systemic risk** [p. 316].

Coupon

A coupon is a payment on an **bond** [p. 37]. The term comes from detachable coupons that are in effect mini-certificates that were cashed to claim interest payments: the holder would cut the coupon off the certificate and exchange it for the cash payment.

The actual use of physical coupons is now rare, as are the **bearer bonds** [p. 33] on which they used. The term has remained in use.

The coupon rate is the nominal interest rate (the annual coupon divided by the **face value** [p. 137]). Coupon payments on certain securities (usually government bonds) may be separated from the bond to create **strips** [p. 309].

Covariance

See **correlation** [p. 74].

Covered

A trading position is considered to be covered if it is offset by another position. In other words it is a synonym for **hedged** [p. 162] but usually only in the the context of trading and arbitrage.

The opposite of covered is "uncovered" or "naked".

Covered interest arbitrage

Covered interest arbitrage is a trade in a foreign currency fixed interest security (usually a government bond) together with a matching **forward** [p. 145] agreement to **hedge** [p. 162] the currency risk.

The trade make use of a inconsistencies between interest rates and forward rates to make a riskless profit.

The possibility of interest rate arbitrage together with the no **arbitrage** [p. 18] requirement can be used to deduce a relationship between currency depreciation and inflation. For a description of this and a simple example of an arbitrage trade see **interest rate parity** [p. 177].

Covered interest arbitrage is a true arbitrage strategy. This is not true of **uncovered interest arbitrage** [p. 331] which leaves the trader exposed to currency risk.

Covered warrants

Covered warrants are **derivatives** [p. 96] very similar to **options** [p. 228]. They are different from company issued **warrants** [p. 343] in two very important ways:

1. Like options they exist in both call and put varieties whereas company issued warrants only have a call variety.

2. They are settled for cash (more usual) or by delivery of existing shares, whereas company issued warrants are settled by issuing new shares.

From the point of view of an investor there is very little difference between the essential characteristics of options and covered warrants. The choice of which to buy tends to depend on what underlying securities are available for each, what exchanges they trade on, and the cost of trading.

CPI

See **HICP** [p. 164].

Credit rating

Credit ratings are issued by a number of rating agencies that assess the quality of debt securities and the financial soundness of organisations as a whole. Credit rating agencies usually have access to unpublished and usually confidential details of company accounts, which is the main reason their ratings are more influential than those of other credit analysts. They issue ratings for **sovereign debt** [p. 300] (that of countries), local government bodies and other organisations as well as companies.

The credit rating agencies each uses a scale of ratings. These start with a top rating such as AAA (very low risk of default), with lower ratings reflecting increasing levels of risk and actual default. The highest few grades are regarded as investment grade and those below them as junk bond grades. Many funds are restricted to investing in investment grade debt instruments. The agencies use "+" and "-" modifiers on the basic ratings to provide a finely graded scale. They also indicate when they are considering changing a rating, and the direction of the likely change.

As ratings are a measure of default risk they should be roughly in line with the **risk premium** [p. 282] on the securities concerned. This is the case but the market does seem to react faster (by changing prices) to changes in risk than the rating agencies do (by changing ratings).

The credit rating agencies make their money by charging the organisations they rate. The ratings are then freely available but the agencies also charge for detailed reports. The market is dominated by a small number of agencies:

Standard & Poors and Moodys are the two largest and significantly bigger than Fitch (the third largest). Other agencies are much smaller and only significant in specialist areas, such as AM Best in insurance.

The credit rating agencies have attracted considerable criticism in recent years. Concerns have included the **oligopolistic** [p. 223] nature of the market, the slow reactions of the agencies to changes in circumstances and their lack of independence from the companies they rate (their clients).

Credit risk

Credit risk is the risk that the issuer of a debt security such as a bond will default on the payments due.

Credit risk is one of the main determinants of the price of a **bond** [p. 37]. The price of a debt security can be explained as the **present value** [p. 220] of the payments (of interest and repayment of principal) that will be made. This leaves the question of what determines the discount rate.

This can be decomposed into two elements:

- **the risk free rate** [p. 282]

- the **risk premium** [p. 282] or **yield spread** [p. 349].

The risk free rate depends only on the currency and the timing of payments.

The risk premium depends on the level of credit risk and the **correlation** [p. 74] of the the credit risk with the risk of holding other investments (in accordance with the **CAPM** [p. 50]).

Credit risk is also an issue for lenders such as banks. In this context the key is the risk of losses to the bank so correlation with the bank's other lending is what matters – not correlation with debt available in the market.

Creditor days

Creditor days, a similar measure to **debtor days** [p. 91]. It is the average time that a company takes to pay its creditors. It is:

$$\frac{trade\ creditors}{annual\ purchases} \times 365$$

The problem is that the amount of annual purchases is rarely **disclosed** [p. 98] and does not form part of any of the mandatory financial statements (a value added statement would disclose this but these are rare). This means that it is usually necessary to use a proxy for the amount of annual purchases. The **cost of goods sold** [p. 75] is often used. This is completely accurate where a company is purely a trading operation, as the cost of goods sold is purely the cost of purchasing. For companies such as manufacturers it is likely to be inaccurate (far too pessimistic).

Where companies do not disclose the cost of goods sold, provided the company has a low **gross margin** [p. 160], then sales can be used as a proxy. This still requires all the conditions for using cost of sales as a proxy to be true *as well* in order to be used as a proxy for purchases and it will always be the less accurate of the two.

Lengthening creditor days may mean that a company is heading for financial problems as it is failing to pay creditors, on the other hand it may mean that a company is simply getting better at getting good credit terms out of its suppliers (improving its **working capital management** [p. 347]), or that its pattern of purchasing has changed. Looking at other measures of financial health such as **gearing** [p. 157], **interest cover** [p. 176] and **cash flow** [p. 53] will help investors assess which is more likely.

CRM

Customer relationship management (CRM) is the way in which a company manages its relationships with customers.

This covers a range of strategic and operational issues that can affect customer loyalty and maximise sales to individual customers.

Because of the large amount of data involved and the complexity with which it has to be manipulated, this is very different from the management of transactions. CRM software has become a sizable part of the enterprise software industry.

CROIC

Cash return on invested capital (CROIC) is similar to **ROIC** [p. 284], except that it looks at cash investment and returns.

This means using cash returns rather than a profit measure for the denominator. The line between CROIC and ROIC is rather blurred as **EBITDA** [p. 116] is arguably a cash flow measure, and therefore using it gives a CROIC rather than a ROIC.

CROIC may be calculated using one of many cash flow measure such as **free cash flow** [p. 146] or **operating cash flow** [p. 225]. Free cash flow has the advantage of being the most most accurate measure of the returns to providers of capital.

Like ROIC and **ROCE** [p. 283], CROIC measures returns before the effects of **capital structure** [p. 48].

Cross elasticity

A cross elasticity is the effect on the change in demand or supply of one good as a result of a change in something related to another product. Unqualified, it means a cross **price elasticity** [p. 247]: how much the change in price of one product will change sales volumes of another.

The cross price elasticity of product A with product B is:

$$\frac{\Delta Q_A}{Q_A} \bigg/ \frac{\Delta P_B}{P_B}$$

where Q_A is the quantity sold of A
ΔQ_A is the change in the quantity of A sold
P_B is the price of B
and ΔP_B is the change in the price of B.

A cross elasticity may be positive or negative. If the two goods are complementary then an increase in the price of one will reduce demand for both. If they are substitutes (e.g., natural and synthetic rubber) an increase in the price of one will increase demand for the other.

Cross selling

Cross selling is the sale of a product to customers who already purchase a different product from the supplier.

Cross selling is often cited as a source of competitive advantage to an existing business and as a source of **synergies** [p. 316] that justify an **acquisition** [p. 5].

For cross selling to be effective it demands some relationship between the products concerned: for example, the buyer of one may have an obvious need for the other at the same time (so estate agents can cross sell mortgages to house buyers) or the products involved may sell to the same general market. It is also possible to cross sell products that appeal to the same demographic groups (e.g. same age groups, income levels, **social grades** [p. 298] etc.).

As cross selling can lead to savings on very significant overheads such as advertising, sales forces and retail space it can be a significant source of saving. Where the potential from cross selling is not proven (as in a proposed acquisition), investors do well to be sceptical. Points to consider include the existence or not of examples of the successful cross selling of similar product combinations and whether the target markets for two products are really the same.

Crude oil

Crude oil is a mixture of liquid hydrocarbons, often found together with natural gas. The main characteristics of crude oil are:

- its density; in the oil industry this is usually measured by its **API Gravity** [p. 17].

- its sulphur content.

Crude oil is normally described as sweet (low sulphur) or sour (high sulphur) and light or heavy (depending on its density). Heavier oils may also be described as medium (self explanatory) and bitumen (so heavy it is solid).

A light crude oil is generally one with an API gravity of less than about 40. **Brent crude** [p. 41], an important **benchmark** [p. 34] crude, has an API gravity of 38 to 39. Heavy crudes will typically have an API gravity of 20 or less – the higher the API gravity, the lower the density.

Sweet crude oil has a sulphur content less than 0.5%, anything more is sour. Heavy crude is:

- harder to handle (it is two thick to pump easily through pipelines unless diluted with light crude)

- more expensive to refine to produce the most valuable petroleum products such as petrol, diesel and aviation fuel.

Sweet crude is preferable to sour because it is also (like light crude) more suited to the production of the most valuable refined products.

Almost every oil field produces crude with a unique mixture of characteristics. It is therefore easiest to follow the prices of key benchmark varieties. The more important benchmark prices include **Brent** [p. 41], **West Texas Intermediate** [p. 345], The **OPEC basket price** [p. 224], Dubai crude, Tapis (Malaysian) and Minas (Indonesian).

Cum-dividend

A share is said to be trading cum-dividend when the payment of a dividend is due in the near future and investors who buy the share now will receive the dividend. Once the security goes ex-dividend buyers will not receive the dividend; it will go to the seller who held the shares immediately prior to their going ex-dividend.

When a dividend is paid, it is paid to holders who are on the register (the company's register of shareholders in the case of shares) on a particular date, called the record date. In order to be on the register of shareholders on the record date a buyer needs to purchase the shares early enough that the trade will be settled (i.e. the shares transferred to the buyer) by the record date.

When a share goes ex-dividend, the price will drop (other things being equal) by the amount of the dividend.

Cum-rights

A share is trading cum-rights as long as buyers will be entitled to a forthcoming **rights issue** [p. 280]. Once the share goes ex-rights, buyers will no longer be entitled to receive the rights.

The mechanism is similar to the process by which shares go from being being **cum-dividend** [p. 82] to ex-dividend. In both cases the data is freely available and published to ensure buyers and sellers know what they are getting.

As with shares going ex-dividend, the price of shares will fall when shares go ex-rights. The calculation of the correction needed to compare cum with ex prices is slightly different.

Cumulative preference shares

Cumulative **preference shares** [p. 244] will accumulate any dividend that is not paid when due.

Any unpaid dividend is added to the amount payable the following year and no dividends can be paid on ordinary shares until the entire backlog of unpaid dividends on cumulative prefs is cleared.

Unless a company is in a very poor financial condition, holders of cumulative prefs can be fairly sure of getting the due pseudo-interest, although the timing is somewhat more uncertain than would be the case with **bonds** [p. 37].

Current assets

Current assets are those assets that are expected to be used (sold or consumed) within a year, unlike **fixed assets** [p. 142]. Current assets are shown on the **balance sheet** [p. 28], and are listed in order of increasing liquidity (i.e. how easy they are to convert to cash). Usually stocks will be listed first, followed by debtors, with cash last.

The current asset position of a company is important, both for assessing its financial strength financial position (see **current assets ratio** [p. 83]) and for gauging its operational efficiency.

Current assets ratio

The current assets ratio measures a company's ability to pay the liabilities that it is most likely to have to pay soon with that assets that should yield cash the quickest. It is

$$\frac{\textbf{current assets}[\text{p. 83}]}{\textbf{current liabilities}[\text{p. 84}]}$$

As a rule of thumb, a current assets ratio of more than two is generally considered adequate, but this should be considered in the context of the company: the nature of the assets in question, the company's ability to borrow further to meet liabilities and the stability of its cash flows.

An alternative that takes account of the fact that **stocks** [p. 306] cannot necessarily be sold quickly is the **quick assets ratio** [p. 261].

Current liabilities

Liabilities that are to be settled in less than a year are called current liabilities. These include trade creditors and debt due within an year (including debt repayable on demand such as overdrafts). Current liabilities are one of the major groups of items on the **balance sheet** [p. 28].

Current liabilities are very important in gauging a company's financial health as the company needs to have the money to meet these commitments in the short term – see **current asset ratio** [p. 83] and **quick assets ratio** [p. 261].

Custodian

A custodian bank holds securities on behalf of an institutional investors.

The main reason for custodian banks to hold assets, rather than the institution that owns or manages the assets are cost cost savings. The cost economies come from that fact that custodian banks usually act as custodians for many institutional investors. As a result of this, they are able to invest more in systems that provide lower costs and to exploit **economies of scale** [p. 117] in general.

The cost savings are particularly large where investors invest in markets in which they themselves do not have local operations. In these markets, custodians have the systems and expertise to deal with issues such as local withholding taxes.

Because large investors invest globally, many large banks offer global custody services that, as the name suggests, allow fund mangers to use a single custodian across all (or nearly all) the markets they invest in. They usually use sub-custodians in for at least some markets.

In addition to the traditional safekeeping and administrative services, many custodians now offer higher margin value added services such as performance and risk measurement and reporting to regulators.

The benefits of using custodians are similar to those of other forms of **outsourcing** [p. 232].

Cyclical

Cyclical businesses are those that are sensitive to the broader economy; the opposite of **defensive** [p. 92] businesses.

The profits of a cyclical business would normally be expected to be much higher during economic booms than during recessions. The share prices of cyclicals are heavily influenced by the outlook for the economy. Cyclical business include most media companies (especially those that depend on advertising revenues), most leisure business, and most non-food retailers.

Investors will choose to buy into cyclical businesses if they believe that the economy will do better than the market expects.

Some sectors may follow cycles that lead or lag general economic growth. An important example of this is that consumer and business demand are rarely perfectly synchronised, so it is possible to have recovery in one while the other is in cyclical decline.

Businesses that are sensitive to **interest rates** [p. 177] are also regarded as cyclical. This is because changes in interest rates are closely linked to the performance of the economy as a whole.

Some industries follow cycles of their own that may or may not depend on the economy as a whole. A good example of this are sales of games consoles (and video games to play on them) which follow a technological cycle driven by the introduction of new generations of consoles.

Dark fibre

Dark fibre is fibre optic cable that has been laid for use by telecoms networks, but which is not used. There are a number of reasons why fibre may remain dark:

- ill-judged over-investment in capacity (this was particularly bad during the dotcom boom)

- deliberate planing for future growth.

Deliberate building of excess capacity happens because of the difficulties involved in laying fibre optic cables: digging up the ground (or even worse, running cables through oceans) is very expensive, so there is every reason to lay more than you need immediately, in order not to have to do it again in the near future.

Dark fibre is sometimes sold, the buyers presumably having plans to make it "lit".

Data revenues

Telecoms companies, and the mobile networks in particular, frequently **disclose** [p. 98] the proportion of their revenues that come from carrying data rather than voice traffic. This does have an impact on margins and growth prospects, but the impact is not straightforward and extrapolating from this data is not easy.

Different types of data revenues have very different characteristics. Bandwith (amount of data transferred over time) usage varies enormously. The margin on different data revenue streams tends to fall over time as they mature.

Data revenues cover everything that comes from non-voice services, this includes:

- SMS: text messages use very little network capacity so the price per unit of data transferred is very high, but the amount of data transferred is very low.

- MMS: picture messages use substantially more data than text messages.

- web browsing: still more data traffic needed.

- VOIP: still larger amounts of data, but **cannibalises** [p. 45] voice revenues.

- other services such as music quality audio produce still more demand for data and can allow telecoms companies to sell content as well as connectivity as well as the connection: as long as they can persuade customers to stay in their **walled garden** [p. 343].

- video: Needs by far the most data transferred.

Which revenue sources have most room to grow depends on current market conditions which currently vary quite widely form country to country. Voice is clearly the most mature and volume growth will largely be driven by price cuts (inevitable in the competitive environment) so revenues are not likely to grow very much, and are likely to decline in the long term.

SMS is fairly mature in some countries (in Europe in particular), MMS less so. Other services are very new and have room to grow but there are uncertainties about demand.

In addition, all these services other than SMS and MMS can be delivered over any internet connections and internet connectivity in general is becoming increasingly **commoditised** [p. 63]. Even SMS and MMS could be replaced by instant messaging services if they gain enough traction.

Any move towards more general internet carried services would make services like **wi-fi** [p. 345] more of a threat. The cost of wi-fi is much lower, so much so that some cities are planning to build free wi-fi networks.

Dawn raid

A dawn raid is the purchase of a large shareholding in a target company in a very short time, prior to the announcement of a **hostile takeover bid** [p. 165].

These are called dawn raids because they are often carried out at the start of a trading day. The aim is to build as big a stake as possible without the market or the management of the target noticing.

The substantial acquisition rules formerly imposed by the **Takeover Panel** [p. 318] have now been dropped so substantial dawn raids are once again permitted. A bidder can now purchase up to 30% of the shares in a company as fast as shares can be bought. Once the bidder (or **concert party** [p. 67]) has a 30% stake they must announce the bid.

The problem with allowing a bidder to build up such a large stake (and the reason lower limits were formerly imposed) is that it may put a bidder in a position to block rival bids before its own bid is made public.

However, allowing substantial stakes may encourage more hostile bids, which will be good for shareholders. One big advantage is that, with a 30% stake, the would be bidder can block attempts at **poison pills** [p. 240] and other tactics that try to make a bid unpalatable.

Day trading

Day trading involves trading securities during the trading day but closing all positions by the end of the day. The trader, a more accurate description than investor, will not have any holdings or short positions to carry forward to the next day.

The proprietary trading operations of investment banks do often day trade, but the term is most commonly associated with individual investors. Compared to traders at investment banks, individual investors have much less access to information, much less sophisticated systems and much less support in terms of research and trading systems. These are all crucial to short term trading. The banks can also deal far more cheaply than private investors.

The biggest problem for private investors who day trade is the cost of trading. The returns that are needed to cover trading costs are huge if one considers that the profit has to be made in a matter of hours.

Day trading is a very high risk approach, and requires the expenditure of considerable time. Some investors make spectacular returns from day trading – but at least as many make spectacular losses. The two are often the same people, as it is not uncommon for investors to be lucky for a while and then, confident in the ability to make money by day trading, to keep putting their money back into day trading, and eventually make large losses.

Day trading tends to be popular during booms, when the general upward movement in share prices makes it more likely that day traders will make money. It is very whether most day traders can make sustained positive returns even in these circumstances.

Days convention

A days convention is used to calculate **accrued interest** [p. 5]. In order to simplify the calculation the accrued interest is calculated as though the number of days elapsed and/or the number of days in a year are different from reality.

For example, if the 30/360 days convention is used the accrued interest is calculated as though there are 30 days in each complete month that has passed since the last interest payment and that there are 360 days in the year.

Days conventions include:

- 30/360

- 30/365

- actual/360

- actual/actual

The origin of days conventions lies in the need to simplify calculations before computers were widely used. They remain in use through sheer inertia. The use of days conventions causes very small inaccuracies. Their continue use, while it may be strictly incorrect, is harmless.

DCF valuation

A discounted cash flow (DCF) is the most fundamentally correct way of valuing an investment. Most other methods of valuation can, to a large extent, be seen as simplified approximations of a DCF. A DCF valuation requires making many estimates and assumptions which introduce a lot of uncertainty and it is therefore often simply not worth doing.

The value of an asset is the value of the future benefits it brings. The value of an investment is that cash flows that it will generate for the investor: interest payments, dividends, repayments etc.

These cash flows need to be adjusted for two things:

- the **time value of money** [p. 322]

- the risk that the amount of money will not be what is expected.

In a DCF valuation, a discount rate is chosen which reflects the risk (the higher the risk the higher the discount rate) and this is used to discount all forecast future cash flows to calculate a **present value** [p. 220]:

$$PV = \frac{CF_1}{1+r} + \frac{CF_2}{(1+r)^2} + \frac{CF_3}{(1+r)^3} \cdots$$

where PV is the present value of the stream of cashflows
CF_1 is the cashflow the investor receives in the first year, CF_2 the cashflow the investor receives in the second year etc. and
r is the discount rate.

In the case of bonds, the cash flows would be interest payments and repayments. In the case of shares, the actual cashflows investors receive are dividends, but there are other cash flows that can be meaningfully discounted instead.

CAPM [p. 50] can be used to calculate the discount rate r, used in the calculation above. Unless the series of cash flows has a known finite endpoint a **terminal value** [p. 321] will need to be assumed.

DCF valuation methods for shares

As mentioned in passing above, the actual cash flows shareholders receive, and therefore the obvious cash flows to discount are the dividends (see **dividend discount model** [p. 104]). This is also theoretically the most correct thing to do. The problem with discounting dividends is that not only do you have to forecast the performance of the company, you also need to guess its future dividend policy.

As the money made by a company belongs to its shareholders regardless of whether it is paid to them or not, we can avoid having to guess at dividend policies by instead discounting the company's earnings. So can we discount the **EPS** [p. 122]? We cannot, because retained earnings are invented and boost future earnings. Simply discounting future EPS would lead to double counting.

Profits do no necessarily bring in cash to the company (as profits are calculated using the **accrual** [p. 4] principle). Therefore it makes sense to discount cash flows instead. If we discount **free cash flows** [p. 146] we also get rid of the double counting problem. Financial theory would also suggest that unless a company has very high return opportunities for expansion (or is investing very badly) then the difference in valuation between a dividend discount valuation and a free cash flow discount valuation will be comparatively small.

Relationship with valuation ratios

Two companies with the same growth prospects, similar profitability, similar debt levels (relative to profits) and trading at a price which reflects the same discount rate, would then be on similar **PE ratios** [p. 237]. Even if debt levels were different they would have similar **EV/EBITDAs** [p. 129].

This is why companies in the same sector should have similar valuation ratios unless there are differences in the risks they face or their growth prospects. Investors should look for the reasons for the differences in "rating" between a company and its nearest peers and decide whether there are sufficient reasons to justify the difference – or if the difference should be be bigger.

Differences in valuation ratios should ultimately reflect differences in growth or risk that would also be reflected the same way by a DCF. Even investors who do not use DCF valuations should keep them in mind. For all their faults, they are fundamentally correct.

Dead cat bounce

A dead cat bounce is a recovery in the price of a security (usually a share) that does not indicate any sustained recovery or a significant **re-rating** [p. 264]. It is a recovery from a very low level to a higher level that is still low by historical standards. The bounce looks significant only because it is from such low levels.

Dead cat bounce is a fairly derogatory term and its use implies a negative opinion of the fundamental valuation of a share and the prospects for a sustained recovery.

Debenture

Although there are legal and other differences between **bonds** [p. 37] and debentures, the terms are loosely used and in practice investors can ignore the difference. It is usually more important to look at the terms on which a particular security is issued.

Debt covenants

Debt covenants are agreements between a company and its creditors that the company should operate within certain limits. Debt covenants are agreed as a condition of borrowing. They may be changed if debt is restructured.

The conditions agreed to vary. A company may, for example, agree to limit other borrowing or to maintain a certain level of **gearing** [p. 157]. Other common limits include levels of **interest cover** [p. 176], **working capital** [p. 347] and **cash flow** [p. 53].

Debt covenants can impose quite heavy obligations – a company may well be forced to sell assets in order to stay within a debt covenant on gearing.

In theory, breach of a debt covenant usually allows creditors to demand immediate repayment. This rarely happens in practice. The debtor is not usually in a position to make an immediate repayment. A breach of covenants therefore usually leads to a renegotiation of the terms of debt. The debt is likely to be re-negotiated on worse terms as a *quid pro quo* for not demanding immediate repayment.

In order to prevent companies from meeting the requirements by adjusting their accounting practices rather than by genuinely maintaining the required level of financial health, debt covenants not only specify the numbers that should be met, but also exactly how they should be calculated for the purposes of the debt covenant.

This means that if a company breaches, or is in danger of breaching its debt covenants, not only does this indicate that the company is not financially strong, but the problems are likely to become worse as lenders react.

Debt/equity ratio

Debt to equity is the commonest type of **gearing ratio** [p. 157]. There are three basic variations on this ratio:

$$\frac{long\ term\ debt}{equity} \text{ or } \frac{total\ debt}{equity} \text{ or } \frac{net\ debt}{equity}$$

All these numbers should be on the **balance sheet** [p. 28]. It may be necessary to look at the **notes** [p. 219] to separate debt from other liabilities.

Each of these can be further adjusted by including or excluding particular assets that it may not be prudent to include, most commonly goodwill.

Long term debt/equity is the most correct measurement if:

- What you are interested in is a company's capital structure

- All short term debt is genuine short term debt

The second qualification is necessary because it is possible for a company to have what is technically short term debt that is effectively long term debt: for example, an overdraft which, although it is payable on demand, is not paid off for several years. In this case it may be preferable to use total debt over equity.

As companies can use their cash (and short term investments) to pay off debt at short notice, it is common to subtract these from the amount of debt to give a better idea of solvency. This gives us the last definition.

Debtor days

Most businesses make a large proportion (or even all) of their sales on credit. Debtor days is a measure of the average time payment takes. Increases in debtor days may be a sign that the quality of a company's debtors is decreasing. This could mean a greater risk of defaults (so it does not get paid at all). It could also be an indicator that **cash flow** [p. 225] is likely to weaken or that more **working capital** [p. 347] will be required.

This ratio is commonly expressed in one of two forms. One is debtor collection days, the number of days debtors take to pay:

$$\frac{trade\ debtors}{sales} \times 365$$

The other is the percetage of sales still unpaid:

$$\frac{trade\ debtors}{sales} \times 100$$

Generally lower debtor days numbers are better. Comparisons for the same business over different periods of time are the most often used. Comparison of companies in different sectors are rarely meaningful as the differences are usually largely the result of the nature of different businesses.

Even within sectors different companies with different types of business will have different business models that naturally lead very different debtor days. For example, retailers selling only for cash have no trade debtors, but within the same sector there are retailers who specialise in selling on credit, who therefore have high debtor days and working capital.

Investors should be aware of why changes in debtor days are happening, especially if there is a very large increase or a clear long term increasing trend. It may reflect a change in how the business operates, or its environment. This is not necessarily bad, but it can be an indication of a potentially serious problem.

Defensive

A defensive business is one whose profits are not particularly sensitive to economic conditions; the opposite of a **cyclical** [p. 84] business.

Examples of defensive business include tobacco, pharmaceuticals and food retailers. Defensives tend to be those companies that sell essentials that people (or companies) cannot easily cut back on when money is tight.

Investing in defensives reduces (or even avoids) losses if the economy does worse than the market expects. It misses opportunities if the economy does better than expected.

Deferred income

Deferred income is similar to **accruals** [p. 4]. It is income received during an accounting period, but for which the company has not yet supplied the goods and services as at the end of the period. These amounts should not be included in the **P & L** [p. 234] for the period.

An item that gives rise to deferred income is the other side of a **prepayment** [p. 246]. Where a buyer has a prepayment, its supplier will have deferred income.

Accruals [p. 4] and deferred income are often shown as a single balance sheet item. Some companies **disclose** [p. 98] them separately, which is useful for financial modelling, because it makes future recvenues more visible.

Deflation

Deflation is simply negative **inflation** [p. 171].

In general, inflation is positive at the level of an economy as a whole. Deflation at that level is most likely during **recessions** [p. 267], and does not always occur even then.

There are a number of reasons why deflation is rare. One of the most important is that it is difficult to reduce wages. This means that suppliers cannot easily reduce the prices of **labour intensive** [p. 186] products and services, even in response to low demand.

Deflation is not common in certain industries. In certainly technology sectors it is usual.

Delivery vs payment

See **DVP** [p. 113].

Delta

The delta (the Greek letter Δ) of a derivative is the rate of change in the price of a **derivative** [p. 96] with the price of the underlying. A delta may also be the rate of change in the price of a portfolio with the price of the security.

This is roughly the same as the change in the price of derivative (or portfolio) that would result from a one unit change in the price of the underlying security.

A more accurate (if more mathematical) definition is that the delta is the derivative of the price of the derivative against the price of the underlying, i.e.:

$$\Delta = \frac{\partial P}{\partial S}$$

where P is the price of the derivative or the value of the portfolio
and S is the price of the underlying.

The delta, along with a group of other similar numbers known as the **greeks** [p. 160], is of great importance in derivatives valuation and trading. The delta is best known in the context of **delta hedging** [p. 93], but it also used by more complex techniques.

The delta is not a fixed value, it depends on the price of the underlying security. The relationship between the two depends on the characteristics of both the derivative and the underlying.

Delta hedging

The **delta** [p. 93] of a derivative can be used to hedge a holding of the derivative with a position in the underlying security or vice-versa.

The number of units in the underlying security needed to **hedge** [p. 162] (or which can be hedged by) a derivative is equal to the delta of the derivative.

Delta hedging is used to cover trading positions, and to **arbitrage** [p. 18] differences between the cost of the derivative and the cost of buying enough of the underlying to delta hedge it.

The delta changes with the price of the underlying, so a delta hedge must be continuously rebalanced.

As a delta hedge can be used to hedge a position in a derivative, by reversing the hedge, and combining this with cash or debt, one can replicate the cash flows of the derivative. By the **law of one price** [p. 186] the value of the derivative must be equal to the value of the portfolio that replicates it. This is used to derive the **Black-Scholes** [p. 36] formula.

Dematerialised securities

Dematerialised securities are those that can be held without evidence of ownership in the form of certificates. Ownership is usually instead recorded in a **depositary** [p. 95]. Shareholders usually receive regular paper statements of their holdings (not dissimilar to bank statements).

The advantage of dematerialised holdings is that they are far cheaper to administer. The elimination of paperwork and the automation that makes it cheaper also makes it faster. Some modern systems can transfer both payment and ownership immediately. All dematerialised systems are faster and cheaper than dealing with paper certificates.

Demerger

A demerger is the opposite of an **acquisition** [p. 5] – a company spins off some business it owns into a completely separate company.

A demerger is usually carried out by distributing shares in the business to be spun off to shareholders of the company carrying out the demerger, in proportion to their shareholding in the original company.

Demergers can have beneficial effects on the quality of management as they allow the management of demerged companies to concentrate on their core business, they make companies easier for investors to analyse (by simplifying the business) and they often demonstrate a management focus on increasing shareholder value.

A demerger may be full, or partial. A partial demerger means that the parent company retains a stake (sometimes a majority stake) in the demerged business.

The motive for a partial demerger is sometimes to force the market to separately value the business that is demerged, in the expectation that this will lead to a higher **sum of parts valuation** [p. 311] of the parent company.

Depletion

Depletion is a similar to **depreciation** [p. 95], but is applied to assets that are used up in a measurable way. The most important examples of these are oil reserves and mines.

The value of an oil reserve is reduced, not by the passage of time, but by the extraction of oil. Therefore the cost charged in the accounts each year is proportionate to the amount of oil extracted during that year. Depletion would be calculated in a similar way for other assets, the calculation basically being:

$$D = \frac{U}{O} \times (C - R)$$

where U is the amount used in the accounting period
O is the amount that was available when the asset was bought

C is the cost of the asset and
R is the residual value that the asset is expected to have after it is fully depleted.

Depositary System (Central Depositary/CDS)

A depositary system for securities records ownership of **dematerialised securities** [p. 94].

In some countries, the same institutions to combine the functions of a securities depositary and a **clearing house** [p. 59]. This is not the case in the UK. The main depositary system in the UK is Crest, operated by Crestco which relies on information from the clearer to update holdings.

Depreciation

When a company purchases assets that will produce benefits (in some way make money for the company) over a long period they should be regarded as investments. This means that their cost can not fairly simply be charged immediately to the **P & L** [p. 234].

Many assets a company buys as investments firstly are meant to produce a return over a period of time, but have a limited useful life. In order to follow the **accrual** [p. 4] principle, the cost shown on the P & L should be spread out over the years of an assets useful life.

The solution is to depreciate the cost over a number of years and take each year's depreciation as that year's cost. The most commonly used method is straight line depreciation which charges a fixed amount of depreciation every year. The depreciation for each year is:

$$\frac{cost - residual\ value}{expected\ life}$$

If a company spends £100,000 on a machine that is expected to last 10 years and have negligible value after 10 years then, using straight line depreciation, each year the company would:

- reduce its value as shown on the **balance sheet** [p. 28] by £10,000

- show that £10,000 as a cost in the profit and loss account

This is by far the commonest method used in the accounts, but it is not the method used for tax purposes. This is one reason why taxable profits are often very different from accounting profits. The **reducing balance** [p. 269] method is often used for tax, but infrequently for reporting.

Intangible assets are **amortised** [p. 15] rather than depreciated, but the principle is much the same.

Certain assets such as land and investments are not depreciated.

It is important to understand that depreciation is not directly related to the replacement costs of assets, which investors may need to consider separately.

Depletion [p. 94] is a similar to depreciation but applied to assets that are used up in a directly measurable way.

Depression

A depression is a severe sustained **recession** [p. 267]. There is no clear dividing line between a recession and a depression, the term depression is used for a recession that is sufficiently deep and goes on for long enough.

Derivatives

A derivative is a security, the value of which depends on the value of another asset. The asset in which its value depends is called the **underlying asset** [p. 331]. Derivatives are used for both **hedging** [p. 162] risk and as high risk investments.

There is a wide range of different types of derivatives available. The commonest are **futures** [p. 154], **options** [p. 228] and **warrants** [p. 343]. **Swaps** [p. 313] are also important.

Contracts for difference [p. 71] are also common. They are widely used to provide derivatives of an underlying number that can not itself be directly traded (**index** [p. 169] values, weather etc.) and to provide access to derivatives for retail investors.

Derivatives are used for hedging by buying a derivative with a value that moves against that of another investment that an investor holds. For example, shares in a given company can be hedged by buying **put options** [p. 258] in the same company.

As speculative investments, derivatives allow investors to:

- Make a greater gain (or loss!) from the same price movement than would result from buying the underlying.

- Make a gain from a fall in the price of the underlying.

- Arbitrage certain inconsistencies between the prices of other investments

The common types of derivatives (e.g. futures and options) are sometimes described as vanilla, while more complex types are described as **exotic** [p. 135].

Derivatives can be **embedded** [p. 120] in other financial instruments to create securities such as **structured notes** [p. 310].

The valuation of derivatives on **balance sheets** [p. 28] has often been a concern for investors. This has only been partially addressed by improvements to accounting standards.

Diluted EPS

A **basic EPS** [p. 31] is calculated using the weighted average number of shares in issue during the period. A diluted EPS is calculated using all shares in issue and those due to be issued (e.g. under share option schemes).

A fully diluted EPS is calculated using all shares issued, due to be issued and which could be issued if all existing **warrants** [p. 343] are exercised, convertible bonds are converted to equity etc. This tends to be less commonly used because of the complexity and uncertainties involved.

Directors dealing

In the UK (and most other countries) directors of a **listed** [p. 190] company are required to disclose their trades in the company's shares (and its other securities).

Dealing by directors and other people who know a company well is sometimes confusingly described as insider dealing. To avoid confusion with **insider trading** [p. 171] it is preferable to use the term directors' dealing.

Directors are obviously in an excellent position to assess the value of a company, however the value of their investment decisions as an indicator is reduced because:

- Directors may choose to sell for a variety of reasons; to raise money for personal reasons or to **diversify** [p. 103] their portfolio.

- Directors may buy as a deliberate gesture of confidence, or hold back from selling so as not to damage investor's confidence.

- If they have specific **price sensitive** [p. 248] information, insider trading law forbids them from trading until the information is disclosed to the market.

For these reasons, when looking at directors' dealings, it is important to look not just at the most recent directors' dealings, but at the overall pattern and the amounts involved. The more directors have bought or sold, and the larger the deals, the more likely it is that the dealing means something from an investor's point of view. While directors are likely to buy small amounts as a gesture, they are less likely to invest significant amounts of their personal wealth just to make shareholders a little more confident. A consistent pattern of buying or selling by several directors is the most likely indicator from which something can be usefully inferred.

Directors' dealings should not be the only reason for making an investment decision, however they may be useful in conjunction with other information.

Dirty price

The dirty price of a bond is the actual price paid for it. It contrasts with the **clean price** [p. 59] which is adjusted for **accrued interest** [p. 5].

Whenever a **coupon** [p. 77] payment is made, the dirty price immediately falls by the amount of the coupon. These sudden movements unrelated to valuation issues are what makes it easier for investors to think in terms of the clean price.

Obviously, even though the clean prices are what is quoted, buyers and sellers need to know the dirty prices as well.

Disclosure

The meaning of the word "disclosure" is not greatly different in the context of investment from its usual meaning in ordinary English. Because companies have a great deal of leeway in choosing what to disclose, it is an important issue for investors.

The numbers and facts the companies have discretion over disclosing are often useful to investors. Most of the examples below give extra detail on underlying trends and are therefore very useful for **modelling** [p. 140] and forecasting. When a company fails to disclose numbers that its peers do investors should be suspicious: the company may have something to hide.

Obviously there is a great deal that companies are compelled to disclose, however there is a great deal of useful information that companies may or may not choose to disclose. Common examples include the disclosure of divisional profits and **organic growth** [p. 230] rates.

Some of the extra disclosure is only relevant to, or is only widely used in, certain industries. Examples of these are **like-for-like** [p. 188] growth rates (for retailers) and **proportionate** [p. 254] numbers (for mobile telecoms).

Disclosure of liabilities has been a problem in the past, particularly the use of **off-balance sheet financing** [p. 221]. However improvements to accounting standards designed to address this *should* mean that it will be less of a problem in the future. There is, in any case, little investors can do about this type of problem, as the omission is not usually apparent from the published accounts.

One thing investors can do is to read the notes to accounts very carefully, as companies sometimes attempt to bury awkward numbers deep in the notes. This is not a matter of disclosure but presentation, but the intent and end result are often the same.

Although one would expect **sell-side analysts** [p. 291] to find and draw attention to such trickery in presentation, experience shows that it can be a surprisingly effective tactic. There have been many instances of the market reacting strongly to "bad news" that was disclosed in the notes to the last set of accounts. So much for **efficient markets** [p. 118]!

In general, greater disclosure is good from investors point of view. It means they can assess companies more accurately. It also makes it less likely that the numbers they have are in some way misleading. Like any form of transparency, it engenders greater trust.

Discount broking

See **execution only** [p. 131].

Discount rate

See **DCF** [p. 88].

Discounted cash flow

See **DCF** [p. 88].

Discretionary broking

A discretionary stock broking service is one that offers portfolio management as well as dealing. Clients can simply had over their money to the broker and the broker will make all investment decisions. Clients can impose constraints such as ethical investing requirements and retain some involvement in the process if they wish.

Brokers usually charge a percentage of the value of the portfolio annually for discretionary portfolio management. However, they do not usually charge commission for each trade made on a discretionary account. This means that brokers are not tempted to churn (trade more frequently than necessary) clients' investments in order to generate more commission. It does however mean there is some temptation for brokers to invest conservatively and then do little actual work on a discretionary portfolio.

Discretionary broking is usually the most expensive way of investing, and it offers the investor the lowest level of control over their investments. It does mean the least work for the investor and should mean the most work put into portfolio management by the broker. The amount of work required to provide a discretionary service means that most brokers are only willing to offer discretionary broking to clients who have portfolios of a reasonable size (typically £50,000+, often considerably more).

Diseconomies of scale

A diseconomy of scale is the opposite of an **economy of scale** [p. 117]. If some cost of a business rises with an increase in size, by a greater proportion than the increase in size, it is a diseconomy of scale.

A more precise definition is that long run average cost per unit rises with an increase in output.

Diseconomies of scale are rarer than economies of scale and they are often offset by economies of scale that exist in the same business. This can make it hard to decide which will have more effect.

For example, there is evidence that diseconomies of scale exist in pharmaceutical companies' **R & D** [p. 261]. There are undoubtedly economies of scale in manufacturing and marketing. The latter are also important costs. They will usually outweigh R & D combined, and often alone, but R & D is a growth driver and its efficiency has a strategic importance they lack.

Causes of diseconomies of scale usually relate to the difficulties of managing a larger organisation. A larger organisation is harder to monitor, it is more complex and therefore co-ordination between different departments and divisions becomes more difficult. As well as making management less effective, and therefore indirectly imposing costs, the systems designed to cope with the extra complexity may also directly impose costs (that is usually less important as it can be quantified and managed). People working within a larger organisation may also feel less committed to it.

Diseconomies of scale can also occur for reasons external to a firm. For example, as a business becomes larger it may put pressure on its supplies of raw materials and labour, raising input prices.

In certain industries, regulation can be tighter on large firms as a result of competition law or industry specific regulation. Usually, however, there are economies of scale in dealing with regulation – this is one of the advantages large pub chains have over small chains and (even more) independent pubs.

In general economies of scale are more significant and important for investors, but diseconomies of scale can occur and are worth considering especially when dramatic expansion or **acquisitions** [p. 5] are being considered.

Disintermediation

Disintermediation is the removal of intermediaries from a process, supply chain or market. The disintermediation of capital markets is particularly important in an investment context.

Disintermediation of capital markets

Disintermediation has become increasingly important in financial markets, largely as a result of the increasing use of securities to raise capital from capital markets, rather than from banks.

Banks usually act as financial intermediaries for debt, borrowing from depositors and lending to borrowers. By selling securities such as bonds, instead of borrowing, a borrower can borrow directly from investors, by-passing the banks. The greater use of a wider range of financial instruments such as **asset backed securities** [p. 21] and **convertibles** [p. 72] (in addition to the traditional types of security such as **bonds** [p. 37] and **debentures** [p. 90]) has encouraged this.

More disintermediation reduces the amount of business available for commercial banks. It also increases the size of capital markets and generates more business for investment banks (advising on the issue of securities) and, indirectly, for other investment businesses (brokers, fund managers, stock exchanges etc.).

Borrowers can hope to borrow at lower cost as a result of disintermediation. Investors lose the safety of bank deposits but the they also should get better rates of return. Investors take on some extra risk which can be controlled through the usual mechanisms of **diversification** [p. 103] and the selection of appropriate investments. At the same time disintermediation eliminates the banks' **interest margin** [p. 176] and this benefit is shared by investors, borrowers and investment market intermediaries and advisors.

Supply chain disintermediation

An example of supply chain disintermediation is a manufacturer selling directly to retailers, rather than indirectly through wholesalers.

The advantage of disintermediation is obviously the greater efficiency and lower cost achieved by reducing the number of transactions and processes involved, however disintermediation may not always be easy to achieve as there is often a reason why the intermediaries existed in the first place, for example, wholesalers who sell the products of many manufacturers may achieve **economies of scale** [p. 117] that a single manufacturer's distribution system can not replicate.

New technology has had a significant impact on supply chain disintermediation by opening new sales channels (internet sales for example) and by allowing better tracking of **stocks** [p. 307].

Disruptive technology

A disruptive technology is one that, when introduced, either radically transforms markets, creates wholly new markets or destroys existing markets for other technologies.

For an investor, disruptive technologies represent both opportunities and threats. A disruptive technology will be an opportunity for at least those who bring it to market. It may also boost related markets. On the other hand change is usually bad for some – especially the dominant suppliers to the market being disrupted.

Examples of disruptive technology (current and historical) include:

- **VOIP** [p. 340], which is destroying voice telecoms revenues while increasing **data revenues** [p. 85]. The internet in general has both created and destroyed many markets.

- Digital cameras, which are destroying the market for photographic film, but at the same time creating markets for storage devices and photo printers.

- Railways, which displaced many forms of transport such as canals while creating demand for fuel, steel and other materials they needed. They also encouraged the emergence of new services.

- Video recorders and television hugely reduced the cinema industry, but the film industry benefited from new income streams.

There are many other obvious examples such as electricity, telephones etc.

It can be very difficult to foresee the impact of a disruptive technology. Investors in the 1990s rightly thought that the internet was a disruptive technology that would have a huge impact. Investors over-estimated how much money could be made from the change and how quickly. At the same time investors misjudged who would make money. For example, many bought media stocks, such as recorded music companies, that now look likely to lose revenues as a result of lower **barriers to entry** [p. 30] from the introduction of new channels of distribution.

Investors who do successfully call the impact of a disruptive technology can make extremely good returns and save themselves losses on the losers.

Distributable reserves

A company is not allowed, by law, to pay as much money out in dividends as directors or shareholders may wish. It may only pay out a certain part of the shareholder's **equity** [p. 123].

In a company's accounts the shareholder's equity is divided into several categories. These are shown on the **balance sheet** [p. 28]. It may only pay dividends out of its retained earnings – dividends have to come from profits.

This provides a limited amount of protection for creditors. They are assured that a company cannot pay dividends that will reduce its capital below a certain level. Of course its capital may nonetheless shrink through losses.

Diversifiable risk

Diversifiable risk is simply risk that is specific to a particular security or sector so its impact on a **diversified** [p. 103] portfolio is limited.

An example of a diversifiable risk is the risk that a particular company will lose market share. It will not have any impact on other companies in a diversified portfolio, so the only loss to an investor holding shares in the company will be the decline in that one share.

On the other hand a rise in **interest rates** [p. 177] will reduce the value of all shares and bonds. This means that it is not possible to diversify **interest rate risk** [p. 178] away.

Of course, non-diversifiable risks can be controlled by **hedging** [p. 162]. It is also possible to choose securities that are less exposed to non-diversifiable risks: for example, a portfolio that is overweight on **defensives** [p. 92] is less vulnerable to an economic slowdown, but at the cost of lower **expected returns** [p. 135].

Diversification

Investors can reduce risk, and improve the level of risk relative to return, by diversifying their portfolios. Diversifying portfolios moves them closer to the **efficient frontier** [p. 118]

The key to diversification is to choose investments whose prices are not strongly **correlated** [p. 74].. Although some financial institutions use sophisticated financial models to calculate and control risks, a private investor can achieve good diversification with little more than reasonable common sense.

Firstly, investing in different **sectors** [p. 288], geographical regions and classes of security improves diversification: the values of shares, **bonds** [p. 37] and pieces of real estate will be more correlated with each other than with investments of completely different types.

In a globalised economy investors in shares will find it hard not to have geographically diverse exposure, as so many **listed companies** [p. 190] have substantial sales or operations around the world.

Within a **equity** [p. 123] portfolio an investor does not need to buy lots of different shares to be well diversified: eight or ten is enough provided their returns are not too highly correlated.

Dividend cover

This shows how many times over the profits could have paid the dividend. For example, if the dividend cover is 3, this means that the firm's profit attributable to shareholders was three times the amount of dividend paid out.

$$dividend\ cover = \frac{\textbf{EPS}[\text{p. }122]}{\textbf{DPS}[\text{p. }106]}$$

Dividend cover is a measure of the ability of a company to maintain the level of dividend paid out. The higher the cover, the better the ability to maintain dividends if profits drop. This needs to be looked at in the context of how stable a company's earnings are: a low level of dividend cover might be acceptable in a company with very stable profits, but the same level of cover at company with volatile profits would indicate that dividends are at risk.

Because buyers of high yield shares tend to want a stable income, dividend cover is an important number for income investors. Dividend cover is the inverse of the **dividend payout ratio** [p. 237]

Cash dividend cover

Cash dividend cover is similar to dividend cover. It is simply how many times dividends could have been paid out of cashflow rather than profits

Dividend discount model

A dividend discount model is a financial model that values shares at the discounted value of future dividend payments. A share is worth the **present value** [p. 220] of all future dividends. As it values shares on the actual cash flows received by investors, it is theoretically the most correct valuation model.

A dividend discount model would typically be a discounted cash flow (DCF) using dividend forecasts over several stages.

1. If there are any dividends that have been announced but for which the share has not yet gone **ex-dividend** [p. 82], these are known amounts in the near future and do not require forecasts.

2. There are likely to be forecasts based on detailed **financial models** [p. 140] for the near future (the next two to five years)

3. Beyond that, forecasts based on less detailed models (for example, assuming a gradual reduction in profit growth and a fixed **payout ratio** [p. 237]) can be used

4. Assuming a fixed growth rate (typically equal to the long term growth rate of the economy) beyond some point (say after five or ten years) allows a **terminal value** [p. 321] to be calculated at that point

The problem with dividend discount models is that long term forecasting is difficult, and the valuation is very sensitive to the inputs used: the discount rate and any growth rates in particular. This much is true for any DCF, but a dividend discount model adds an extra layer of difficulty to the forecasts by requiring forecasts of dividends, which means anticipating the dividend policy a company will adopt. As with other DCF models, the discount rate is most likely to be calculated using **CAPM** [p. 50].

It can be argued that changes to the dividend policy do not matter, as the money belongs to shareholders however it is used. However, in this case, one might as well use a **free cash flow** [p. 146] discount valuation.

Dividend irrelevance

If a company makes money, in the form of cash inflows, that money belongs to shareholders. It should not matter whether a company keeps money and invests it. or returns the money to shareholders. This is what is assumed, correctly, by most valuation methods such as **free cash flow** [p. 146] **DCFs** [p. 88].

It is also possible to show that it should make little difference to investors whether dividends are paid or not as investors they can reproduce the cashflows of different dividend policies. For example, if a company pays out dividends, but an investor would prefer the money to be re-invested, then the investor can simply use the dividends to buy more shares.

Conversely, if a company retains too much (from a shareholder's point of view), then the share price will be boosted by the company's stronger cash position, and the shareholder can offset that by selling a few shares.

These arguments for dividend irrelevance are closely related to the Modigliani-Miller arguments for **capital structure irrelevance** [p. 48].

However investors do often react to changes in **dividend policy** [p. 106] for a number of reasons.

One reason for paying or not paying dividends are the tax consequences. What a companies can do to minimise the ultimate tax bill (its own and shareholders' combined) will vary with tax rules and its shareholder base (different types of shareholders, such as individuals and pension funds, face different tax rules).

Tax undoubtedly has an important effect but it is far from being the whole story: companies pay dividends even under tax laws which make it always better, from that point of view, to retain the money. The simple version of dividend irrelevance also ignores transaction costs (the costs of buying and selling shares). If a company follows a dividend policy that suits them, shareholders are saved the transactions costs incurred by mimicking a different policy.

Finally, and most importantly, paying dividends sends signals to the market. Most companies' management do not like cutting dividends. This is why **special dividends** [p. 301] are used for one-off payments. Therefore, when a company pays a dividend it is showing that the management are confident that the company's earnings will always be sufficient to pay that dividend.

Returning money to investors, whether through dividends or **returns of capital** [p. 276], also shows investors that a company is willing to return money it can not invest profitably enough to benefit shareholders. This is, of course, what companies should do but, given that many companies have wasted shareholder's money on empire building (i.e. over-expansion and **acquisitions** [p. 5]), a willingness to return money is reassuring for investors.

Although dividend irrelevance is not completely correct, it a good enough approximation to reality that fundmental valuation should usually ignore dividend policy. The signalling aspect of the more complete theory suggests that **dividend yield** [p. 107] is an important measure of management confidence, and therefore can be taken as an indicator of the stability of earnings.

Dividend per share

Dividend per share (DPS) is a simple and intuitive number. It is the amount of the dividend that shareholders have (or will) receive, over an year, for each share they own.

$$DPS = \frac{total\ dividends\ paid}{number\ of\ shares\ in\ issue}$$

Dividends are paid to holders of shares on the "record date" which will be announced beforehand by the company. More important from an investor's point of view is the ex-dividend date on, and after, which shares bought or sold on a stock exchange under normal terms will be sold without the dividend (so that the seller will get the dividend).

Companies may pay interim dividends during the year as well as a final dividend. These should all be added together to get the total annual amount in order to calculate DPS, **dividend yield** [p. 107] and other ratios.

Special dividends [p. 301] may also be declared. They main significance of a dividend being declared a special dividend is that this is a signal to investors that it is not part of a company's normal **dividend policy** [p. 106] and therefore does not indicate that future similar dividends will be paid annually, as is otherwise the case. These should not be included in the DPS or when calculating dividend yield, but should be looked at separately.

Most companies avoid dividend cuts unless their financial condition demands it or there has been some other change in the business or its **capital structure** [p. 48]. As a result of this, increases in the dividend are taken to be a sign that the management is confident that the new level can be maintained or improved on.

Dividend policy

A company's dividend policy is the company's usual practice when deciding how big a dividend payment to make.

Dividend policy may be explicitly stated, or investors may infer it from the dividend payments a company has made in the past. If a company states a dividend policy it usually takes the form of a target **pay-out ratio** [p. 237].

If a company has not stated a dividend policy then investors will infer it. Assumptions that investors are likely to make are:

- The **DPS** [p. 106] will be maintained at at least the previous year's level (excluding **special dividends** [p. 301]) – unless **dividend cover** [p. 103] is very low or the company has warned that a dividend cut is possible

- If the payout ratio has been maintained at a roughly constant level in the past, the same will be done in the future

- Any other pattern of dividend growth will continue as long as the **cover** [p. 103] does not fall too low.

Companies do not normally increase dividends unless they are confident that the increase is sustainable. This means that increasing the dividend is a way in which the management of a company can signal investors that they are confident.

Conversely, dividend cuts are often an acknowledgement of some permanent deterioration in a company's business. Sometimes it only reflects a need to keep cash for **capex** [p. 46]. It is usually clear which it is.

Dividend yield

Dividend yield is often referred to simply as yield. It is the rate of return investors get from holding the share. It is calculated by taking the total dividends paid per share over the course of a year and dividing by the share price.

For example, if a share pays out 20p in dividends over the course of a year and trades at 500p, then it has a dividend yield of 4%.

The dividend yield usually means the historical dividend yield: the current price divided by the dividend declared in the last financial year. Forward looking numbers are used as well, but should be specifically identified as such.

Special dividends [p. 301] should be excluded when calculating the yield. So if the company in the example above had also paid a 100p special dividend during the year, its yield would still be 4%.

Mature, well-established companies tend to have higher dividend yields, while young, growth-oriented companies tend to have lower yield. Many fast growing companies do not have a dividend yield at all because they do not pay out dividends.

Simple financial theory suggests that **dividends are irrelevant** [p. 105] for valuation.

Divisia money supply index

A Divisia index (or aggregate) is a measure of **money supply** [p. 206] that, rather than simply adding up the various components of money supply, attaches a weight to each component.

The justification for doing this is that not all money is held purely to make transactions with. Some types of money are clearly held primarily to use for transactions (e.g. physical cash, deposits in current accounts) while others are held primarily as a store of wealth (e.g. long term bonds).

A Divisia monetary aggregate assigns a weight to each type of money depending on the extent to which it is held for transactions.

Thus notes and coins would receive a high weighting (1 or *very* close to 1) whereas long term deposits would get a much lower weighting, and instant access savings accounts something in between.

The Bank of England Divisia index is based on components of **M4** [p. 195]. It uses interest rates to calculate weights: the higher the interest rate, the lower the weight.

The assumption is that interest rates are a good measure of why a particular type of money is held: the higher the interest rate, the more likely it is to be held because of an investment motive rather than to fund transactions. This appears to be a sound assumption as the main reason for accepting lower rates is to keep money more readily available for transactions.

While Divisia indices seem to be theoretically more correct than simple aggregates, they are a comparatively new development and have not yet as widely used.

Divisia indices are named after their originator, Francois Divisia.

Dogs of the Dow

The Dogs of the Dow is a fairly simple **mechanical investment strategy** [p. 199].

It can be described fairly briefly: pick the 10 highest yield shares in the **Dow Jones Industrial Average** [p. 109] and put an equal amount of money into each of them. Adjust the portfolio once a year so that it once again has equal amounts in the top ten shares by yield.

The **strategy** [p. 179] has become so popular that there are even two special Dow Jones indices (the Dow 5 and the Dow 10) that track the performance of Dogs of the Dow type strategies.

The track record of this type of **value investing** [p. 337] is fairly good, and it is certainly a strategy worth considering.

It also has the advantage of requiring a portfolio re-balancing only once a year which means that trading costs are low. Using an **execution only** [p. 131] broker who charges a flat rate per trade, the maximum possible commission paid per year is just twenty times the commission per trade. It is likely to be much lower.

Dominance

A strategy dominates another if it is guaranteed to lead to a better results.

In financial economics, the assumption that a **dominant trading strategy** [p. 109] cannot exist leads to several important results. It is closely related to the **no arbitrage** [p. 18] assumption.

The concept of dominance also occurs in other areas, such as **game theory** [p. 154]. In game theory dominance can be used to analyse games and identify which strategies would be used.

Dominant trading strategy

A dominant trading strategy is a portfolio that costs the same as another one, but which is always guaranteed to out-perform it.

Equivalently, a dominant trading strategy exists if it is possible to start with no money and make a guaranteed trading profit. The difference between this and **arbitrage** [p. 18] is that an arbitrage opportunity does not guarantee making money, it is merely a chance to make money with no risk of a loss.

The concept is similar to those of no arbitrage and the **law of one price** [p. 186], and it is similarly useful in proving much of financial theory.

It can be proved that:

- If there is no arbitrage there is no dominant trading strategy, but there may be arbitrage opportunities even if there are no dominant trading strategies.

- If there is no dominant trading strategy then the law of one price holds, but the law of one price may hold even when trading strategies exist.

- If there are no dominant trading strategies then it can be shown that there must exist a linear pricing measure.

The last of these cannot be fully explained here. In essence it is a weighting for each possible "state of the universe"; each possible combination of securities prices. The value of a security can be calculated by multiplying its price in each possible state by the value of the pricing measure for that state. The existence of a linear pricing measure can be used to prove a number of important results in **financial economics** [p. 139].

Dow Jones Averages

The Dow Jones Averages are a series of **indices** [p. 169] that are the most closely followed in US markets (and probably globally).

This is unfortunate as these indices are seriously flawed. Given these flaws in the index, it may be preferable to use alternatives such as the S & P 500.

The best known of the Down Jones Averages indices is the Dow Jones Industrial Average, often abbreviated to DJIA. It is often referred to as the Dow Jones or simply "the Dow". The other two Averages are the Transportation and Utility averages. They are obviously **sector** [p. 288] indices.

The publisher of the DJIA, Dow Jones Indexes, also publishes a number of other indices.

The most serious flaw of the Averages is that they are not **market cap** [p. 196] weighted (see **weighted average** [p. 344]) but price weighted. The method used to calculate the index consists of little more than adding share prices together and dividing by factor that is adjusted to reflect changes in the constituents of the index and certain corporate actions such as **scrip issues** [p. 287] and **demergers** [p. 94].

The problem with this is that a movement of the same proportionate size (e.g. a 10% fall) in the price of a company with a higher share price will have a greater impact on the index. This contrasts with more modern equity indices that weight the impact companies have on the market by their market cap.

The other flaw in the index is that there is no consistent method for choosing and reviewing the constituents of the index: they are selected by the editors of the *Wall Street Journal* and rarely changed.

This leads to the question of why such a flawed index as the DJIA is so widely followed and distributed.

The minor part of the answer is the length of time over which the Dow provides data. It provides a continuous series of index values from 1896 onwards. However, while this is very useful for purposes such as academic studies of long term returns, it has little relevance to most investors.

The main reason for its dominance is simple inertia. The Dow has enormous mind share: it is the one US index that almost everyone has heard of. There is a whole branch of **technical analysis** [p. 319] known as "Dow Theory", the name appears in the titles of books and Dow index levels are widely reported by the media.

Downstream

Downstream operations, in the oil and gas industries, include refining and distribution, as opposed to **upstream** [p. 333] (exploration and production).

The major oil companies tend to be integrated (have both upstream and downstream operations) whereas the smaller ones tend to specialise.

DPS

See **dividend per share** [p. 106].

DRIP

A dividend re-investment plan (DRIP) is a means of allowing shareholders to cheaply reinvest their dividends in the purchase of more shares in a company. The operator of the DRIP (typically the company's **registrar** [p. 270]) pools the cash dividends payable to shareholders who have chosen to use the DRIP, purchases shares in the market and allocates them to the shareholders.

From the point of view of a shareholder it is similar to receiving a **scrip dividend** [p. 287], but there are important differences:

1. A DRIP does not retain cash within the company.

2. There are (small) dealing costs.

3. The number of shares a shareholder gets depends on the price on the day on which the DRIP operator purchases the shares.

Drug pipeline

In the pharmaceuticals sector, a drugs pipeline consists of the drugs that a company has under development or is testing. This includes completely new drugs, variants of existing drugs and new applications of existing drugs.

The pipeline starts with new drug discoveries and it is important to assess companies' ability to discover new drugs as well as drugs that are currently in the pipeline. The early stage of the pipeline needs to be refilled as drugs move up. Good **R & D** [p. 261] is crucial.

New drugs require extensive development, pre-clinical testing, three stages of **clinical trials** [p. 60] and then have to approved in each country the company wishes to sell the drug in. This means that many uncertainties lie between discovering a new drug and selling it. The uncertainties lessen as a drug moves along the pipeline .

It is not uncommon for companies to buy and sell drugs that are in various stages of development, or to enter into agreements to jointly develop or market drugs. In these circumstances one company may receive milestone payments from another for completing particular stages of development, trials and approval, as well as royalties on the drug once it is marketed.

Major pharmaceutical companies always have pipelines with many drugs in them. This may appear to spread the risk, but it is often the case that most of the value of the pipeline lies in a small number of drugs, or even in a single "blockbuster" drug

Assessing the pipeline is often the most important part of valuing a pharmaceutical company, and the most difficult. The value of a pipeline is the sum of the values of each drug in the pipeline. To assess the value of a drug in the pipeline one needs to consider:

- the size of potential market for the drug

- how much market share the drug will be able to gain

- the risk that it will not be approved.

The size of the potential market may be clear. If the drug is to treat a specific disease, recognised disease for which the need for treatment is accepted it may be easy. However if the diagnosis or treatment is a matter of controversy, if existing treatments are effective or if treatment is so expensive that health services or insurers may not pay for it, then the market size is less clear.

How much market share a drug gains will depend on its cost and effectiveness compared to competitors. This includes not just the drugs already on the market, but others that are in development.

The risk of failure to gain approval is the hardest thing to assess. It requires evidence of both effectiveness and safety. Effectiveness is generally demonstrated fairly early on (but not always). Safety problems may show up at any point in the clinical trials, although the risk diminishes in the later stages.

Companies largely dependent on established products are easier to assess, and there are fewer uncertainties in the valuation. The best growth opportunities in the sector are small companies with a platform for developing new drugs. The valuations of these are, of course, very uncertain.

Dry natural gas

Dry natural gas is what remains in **natural gas** [p. 212] after:

- the liquefiable hydrocarbons have been removed

- any significant amounts of non-hydrocarbon gases have been removed.

Dry natural gas is also called consumer grade natural gas.

Due diligence

Due diligence is what is done in order to check that everything is as it appears. In an investment context it usually refers to the checks carried out before a major transaction. For example:

- by a bidder before making a **takeover bid** [p. 317].

- by an **underwriter** [p. 331] prior to an **IPO** [p. 182] or other issue

- by a **venture capitalist** [p. 338] before making an investment.

Due diligence often implies gaining greater access to a company's accounts than is available in the published accounts. This is one reason why, when possible, an **agreed takeover** [p. 13] is preferable to a **hostile takeover** [p. 165] – the target company is under no obligation to allow special access to its accounts, but may be persuaded to.

This is also a good reason for investors to be cautious about any company that has received a takeover approach that has failed to materialise after the would be bidder started due diligence. The bidder may have found problems that are not evident in publicly available information.

Duopoly

A duopoly is superficially similar to a **monopoly** [p. 207]. A duopoly is a market that has only two suppliers, or a market that is dominated by two suppliers to the extent that they jointly control prices.

Unless the two suppliers act in concert (which would be illegal in most countries) there is likely to be competition in a duopolistic market. Rather than being similar to a monopoly, it is the simplest case of an **oligopoly** [p. 223].

However, this competition is likely to be limited, leading to higher prices, and a worse deal for consumers in other ways, than in a truly competitive market.

Duration

The Macaulay duration, often simply called the duration, of a **bond** [p. 37] is a measure of the average time it takes an investor to get their money (**principal** [p. 251] and interest).

$$duration = \frac{1}{P} \times \left(\frac{C_1}{(1+r)} + 2\frac{C_2}{(1+r)^2} + 3\frac{C_3}{(1+r)^3} + \cdots + n\frac{C_n}{(1+r)^n} \right)$$

where P is the market price of the bond,
C_x is one of n payments (of interest and principal) and
r is the **yield to maturity** [p. 350].

This formula assumes that payments are made at regular intervals.

The value of a bond is the **present value** [p. 220] of the interest payments and the repayment of the principal. As with any present value, increasing the time before a cashflow is received reduces its value. This means that the duration is a measure of the sensitivity of a bond price to interest rates. The **modified duration** [p. 205] is a more accurate measure.

DVP

Delivery vs payment (DVP) is a way of controlling the risk to which securities market participants are exposed.

Delivery of securities (i.e. the change in their ownership) is done simultaneously with payment. This means that neither the buyer or the seller is exposed to the risk that the other will default.

It directly protects security market participants (such as brokers) rather than investors. This indirectly reduces the cost and risks of trading for everyone.

DVP is far from being a perfect system. Unless settlement is real time (done immediately on the trade being agreed) it means that, if there is a trade failure, trades will have to be unwound. If buyers are allowed to sell before settlement (as is usual), multiple trades may have to be unwound for a single failure. Being forced to unwind a trade can mean investors make a loss.

Major markets either use DVP with real time settlement, or a **central counterparty** [p. 56] to eliminate the risk of having to unwind trades.

Earnings accretive

Acquisitions [p. 5] are said to be earnings accretive or earnings enhancing if they increase **EPS** [p. 122] and earnings dilutive if they decrease EPS.

An accretive acquisition is not necessarily good any more than a dilutive acquisition is necessarily bad.

- Acquisitions paid for with cash tend to be accretive because they reduce cash or increase debt, swapping interest payments for returns on an actual business. The effect of many acquisitions is to reduce PEs but also to increase risk thanks to higher **gearing** [p. 157].

- The acquired business may have a lower PE because it is slower growing or is higher risk.

- The improvement expected may assume synergies (most often cost savings) that may not actually be delivered.

- **Operational gearing** [p. 227] may be increased by deferred consideration or other continuing agreements with the seller of the acquired business.

- The increase in earnings may result from, or be exaggerated by, the accounting treatment of the acquisition. For example, by writing down the value of assets on acquisition (to **fair value** [p. 137]) and thus reducing future **depreciation** [p. 95].

In general, companies will try to spin an accretive acquisition as necessarily good and work hard to justify a dilutive acquisition. Investors should be sceptical and look at the nature of the combined business and at a full range of valuation measures (**EV/EBITDA** [p. 129], **price/cashflow** [p. 250], etc.)

Earnings dilutive

Acquisitions [p. 5] are said to be **earnings accretive** [p. 114] if they increase **EPS** [p. 122] and earnings dilutive if they decrease EPS.

Dilutive acquisitions clearly need justifying. There are a number of reasons why a company may be right to make a dilutive acquisition:

- An acquisition may boost growth through sales or cost **synergies** [p. 316]; it may be accretive in the long term

- The acquired business may deserve a higher **PE** [p. 237] if it is lower risk than the acquirer. It would therefore be dilutive, but nonetheless worth buying.

- The acquisition may have strategic advantages (such as new technology or brands) that will boost growth in the long term.

- The combined business may be more stable or allow better coordination: for example, by increasing **vertical integration** [p. 339].

Earnings enhancing

See **earnings accretive** [p. 114].

Earnings yield

Earnings yield is the inverse of the **PE** [p. 237] ratio, and is used in much the same way. It tells an investor the same thing. It is:

$$\frac{EPS[\text{p. 122}]}{share\ price}$$

So a share that cost 200p and had an EPS of 10p would be on a PE of 20 and would have an earnings yield of 5%.

PE is more widely used and discussed and it is therefore what most investors prefer to use out of sheer familiarity. Earnings yield is more consistent with other measures that are used such as **dividend yield** [p. 107], bond yields and interest rates.

It can also be illuminating to invert (divide one by the ratio) other valuation ratios such as **EV/EBITDA** [p. 129] and **price/cash flow** [p. 250]. Inverting price/**free cash flow** [p. 146] is particularly interesting as it tells you what the yield would be if the company paid out as much as it could in dividends without affecting existing operations. It gives the cash return the company makes for shareholders, including what it retains as well as what is actually paid out.

EBIT

Earnings before interest and tax (EBIT) is very closely related to **operating profit** [p. 227] and often the same. It may include some profits or losses that are excluded from operating profit.

EBIT is used in similar ways to other profit measures such as **EBITDA** [p. 116]. The valuation ratio that most commonly uses EBIT is EV/EBIT which is similar to **EV/EBITDA** [p. 129] – apart from the inclusion of depreciation and amortisation as costs. **EBITA** [p. 116] and EBITDA are generally preferable to EBIT, especially when used as a denominator for **EV** [p. 121].

Trading profit [p. 327] is similar to operating profit and EBIT but excludes items that although do not arise from the regular trading actives of a business – certain asset sales for example.

EBITA

Earnings before interest, tax and amortisation (EBITA) is similar to **EBIT** [p. 115] but strips out **amortisation** [p. 15]. Amortisation is always a non-cash item and therefore of limited interest to investors.

Amortisation is of less interest than depreciation (itself excluded from many measures) because it relates to **intangible assets** [p. 173], and it cannot be used as even a rough proxy for replacement cost.

EBITA is used in similar ways to other profit measures such as **EBITDA** [p. 116]. The commonest valuation ratio that uses EBITA is **EV/EBITA** [p. 128]. This is similar to **EV/EBITDA** [p. 129] apart from the inclusion of depreciation as a cost. EV/EBITDA is usually preferable.

EBITDA

Earnings before interest, tax, depreciation, and amortisation (EBITDA) has two main uses:

- as a comparison over time of the profitability of a company's operations without the potentially distorting effects of changes in **depreciation** [p. 95], **amortisation** [p. 15], interest and tax
- to calculate **EV/EBITDA** [p. 129], a valuation ratio free of these distortions, allowing fair comparisons of companies with different **capital structures** [p. 48].

Interest and tax are excluded because they include the effect of factors other than the profitability of operations. Interest is a result of the company's financial structure. Depreciation and amortisation reflect the accounting treatment of past purchases and are unrelated to future cash flows, and future cash flows are what ultimately matter to investors.

As EBITDA is an adjusted profit number it is usual to state it before **exceptional** [p. 132] items.

EBITDA can also be regarded as a measure of underlying cashflow. It is closely related to **operating cash flow** [p. 225]. The difference is that operating cash flow includes the effects of changes in **working capital** [p. 347]). EBITDA can therefore be used as a measure of underlying cash flow (i.e. stripping out the volatile effects of changes in working capital).

EBITDA margin

EBITDA margin is **EBITDA** [p. 116] as a percentage of sales.

EBITDA margin is often more useful than **operating margin** [p. 226] for the same reasons that EBITDA is more useful than **operating profit** [p. 227] – it excludes non-cash items such as **depreciation** [p. 95].

It is one of several types of **profit margin** [p. 253].

Econometrics

Econometrics is a branch of statistics that is applied to economics and financial economics. The key distinguishing feature of econometrics is that it deals specifically with time series data.

The problem with time series data is that it introduces many spurious correlations. If two data series both show a consistent trend over time they may appear correlated when they are not. They will may have a positive **correlation coefficient** [p. 74] although there is no causal link between them. This can also make it harder to find the true correlations.

Another problem with economic and financial data is that the data available may be limited, and it is not possible to perform experiments (as a physicist or a chemist would) to test hypotheses. Hypotheses usually have to be tested against existing historical data. This also makes the statistical techniques used to analyse the available data are more important.

Econometrics is hugely important to economics in general, and to financial economics in particular. It is largely the development of econometrics that has made economics a much more mathematical subject than it was a few decades ago.

Econometrics is used to both verify theories and to construct the **models** [p. 140] that are used to apply theories in many practical applications.

Economies of scale

A larger business is often able to do things more cheaply than a smaller one, other things being equal. Anything that helps save costs if the scale of operations increases is an economy of scale.

There are many sources of economies of scale, which ones are important depend on the industry (and company) in question. Common economies of scale include:

- spreading administrative overheads over a bigger operation

- purchasing power to get better deals from suppliers

- lower costs in manufacturing – e.g., if a bigger factory has lower costs per unit produced

- better logistics leading to lower distribution costs

- **cross selling** [p. 81]

Economies of scale are often the claimed justification for **mergers** [p. 201] and **acquisitions** [p. 5] but it is very difficult for investors to assess the potential savings and the actual savings often disappoint.

In some cases economies of scale may be offset by **diseconomies of scale** [p. 100] that exist in the same business. Economies of scale are *usually* more significant.

It is important to remember that economies of scale do not necessarily happen because a business is bigger. For example, combining two completely unrelated businesses is likely to lead to higher costs (by adding an extra layer of management) and worse management (by reducing focus on each business and adding bureaucracy). This is why conglomerates usually trade at a discount to their **sum of parts** [p. 311] valuation.

EEV

See **European embedded value** [p. 127].

Efficient frontier

The efficient frontier describes the relationship between the return that can be expected from a portfolio and the riskiness (**volatility** [p. 340]) of the portfolio. It can be drawn as a curve on a graph of risk against **expected return** [p. 135] of a portfolio. The efficient frontier gives the best return that can be expected for a given level of risk or the lowest level of risk needed to achieve a given expected rate of return.

The efficient frontier is usually used to describe the curve that is drawn in the absence of a risk free asset. With a risk free asset available it becomes a straight line: the **securities market line** [p. 290].

The efficient frontier is extremely important to the theory of portfolio construction and valuation.

The concept of an efficient frontier can be used to illustrate the benefits of **diversification** [p. 103]. An undiversified portfolio can be moved closer to the efficient frontier by diversifying it. Diversification can, therefore, increase returns without increasing risk, or reduce risk without reducing expected returns.

Efficient markets

An efficient market is one in which securities prices reflect all available information. This means that every security traded in the market is correctly valued given the available information.

There are a number of different definitions of what constitutes an efficient market depending on the what information is deemed to be available.

The weakest form of efficient markets is that securities prices reflect all information contained in historical prices. This is the easiest to prove, by showing that share prices follow a **random walk** [p. 263].

The strongest form of efficient markets is that prices incorporate all information that any investor can acquire. This seems unlikely given that **insider traders** [p. 171] can undoubtedly make money fairly consistently.

The semi-strong form of efficient markets is that securities prices incorporate all publicly available information. Given how difficult it is to find groups of "smart" investors who consistently outperform the market, this seems likely. There do seem to be some investors with very impressive records. The semi-strong efficient markets hypothesis is probably very close to being true, but not always true.

The most glaring exceptions to efficient markets seem to occur during investment bubbles and collapses when prices reach levels that can not be explained by reasonable valuation methods. As a result, there are often great inconsistencies in how different investments are valued and these violations of the **law of one price** [p. 186] are, in themselves, evidence that markets are inefficient.

Efficient portfolio

An efficient portfolio is one that lies on the **efficient frontier** [p. 118].

An efficient portfolio provides the lowest level of risk possible for a given level of **expected return** [p. 135]. If a portfolio is efficient, then it is not possible to construct a portfolio with the same, or a better level, of expected return and a lower **volatility** [p. 340].

An efficient portfolio also provides the best returns achievable for a given level of risk. If a portfolio is efficient it is not possible to construct a portfolio with a higher expected return and the same or a lower level of volatility.

EGM

An extraordinary general meeting (EGM) of a company is a general meeting of all members of a company (this usually means shareholders) other than the **AGM** [p. 12].

Like an AGM, an EGM gives shareholders a chance to vote on important decisions. An EGM may be called at any time. An EGM is therefore called when a decision needs to be made that cannot wait for the next AGM. There are also some decisions that, by law or by a company's articles, require an EGM: in this case the EGM may take place immediately before or after the next AGM.

An EGM is called by the directors of a company. Shareholders with a stake of over 10% (in combination) may force an EGM.

Reasons for calling an EGM include:

- approving a major **acquisition** [p. 5]

- allowing major shareholders to arrange the removal directors with whom they have disagreed

- changing the name of the company

- approving major changes to a company's **capital structure** [p. 48] that require a reduction or increase in share capital.

Electronic point of sale

See **EPOS** [p. 122].

Embedded option

An embedded option is an **option** [p. 228] that is part of another security. It therefore does not trade by itself, but it does affect the value of the security of which forms a part.

Analysing embedded options is essential to valuing securities that contain them. For example, the value of a **convertible bond** [p. 72] is the value of an equivalent bond that is not convertible plus a **call option** [p. 45] on a share. The embedded call option is on the issuer's share with a strike price of the maturity value of the bond and an expiry date that is the date on which the bond matures.

More subtly, the value of a bond that is **redeemable** [p. 268] at the option of the issuer, has an embedded **short position** [p. 295] in a **call option** [p. 45]. The holder has effectively **written** [p. 229] a call option to the issuer. The value of the bond is the value of an equivalent bond that cannot be redeemed early, less the value of a call option over the bond.

Even ordinary shares in a company that has debt may be viewed as options to purchase the company free of debt by paying off the debt. This is not an approach that is often used, but it is theoretically correct.

Embedded Value

The embedded value of a life insurance business is an estimate of the value of both its net assets and the income stream expected from policies already in force.

$$E = PV + NAV$$

where E is the embedded value,
PV is the present value of future cash flows on policies already in force and
NAV is the company's **NAV** [p. 213] with investments valued at market value.

The future profits do *not* include the value of policies that the company will sell in the future, only those already sold. Policies that the company can expect to sell in the future are an important component of the difference between the embedded value and the actual value of the business to investors.

Emerging markets

Emerging markets are capital markets in non-developed economies. The characteristics of an emerging market vary from country to country but the following are common:

- high economic growth

- high **exchange rate risk** [p. 133]

- high political risk

- lack of effective regulation and weak legal systems

- weak protection for **minority shareholders** [p. 204]

- large numbers of companies that are controlled by a single majority shareholder, or a group of connected shareholders (e.g. a family)

- the existence of large **conglomerates** [p. 67].

Exchange rate risks are often over-estimated by investors as they are usually offset by the inflation (and therefore profit growth) that tends to follow on depreciation. The other risks that are attached to investing in emerging markets are largely **diversifiable** [p. 102].

The weak protection of minorities is often reflected in prices, but some of the other risks that result from weak regulatory environments are not so easy to dismiss. In particular, investors can rely less on brokers and other advisers in emerging markets than they generally can in developed economies.

The existence of (often, the dominance of markets by) conglomerates is the result of several other aspects of emerging markets and developing economies – the lack of liquid capital markets, and poor regulation, in particular.

Enterprise resource planning

See **ERP** [p. 124].

Enterprise value

Enterprise value (EV), attempts to measure the value of a company's business rather than the company. It answers the question "what would it cost to buy this business free of its debt and other liabilities?"

EV is calculated by adding together:

1. the **market capitalisation** [p. 196] of the company

2. the value of its debt financing (bonds and bank loans, not items such as trade creditors)

3. the value of other liabilities such as a deficit in the company pension fund

and subtracting the value of liquid assets such as cash and investments.

The calculation is made more complex where there are **minority** [p. 204] stakes in **associates** [p. 23] and **subsidiaries** [p. 311]: see **EV/EBITDA** [p. 129]. These adjustments also apply to other valuation measures using EV such as EV/**EBIT** [p. 115] and EV/**EBITA** [p. 116].

EPIC code

Epic codes are now called **TIDMs** [p. 322].

EPOS

Electronic point of sale systems (EPOS) are the computerised systems that are used by retailers: modern tills and associated systems. Their basic functions include scanning bar codes or radio frequency ID (RFID) tags to identify products, scanning credit cards, and cash handling.

EPOS systems do not only handle transactions. They can also connect to networks making information on sales instantly available. This is useful for providing management with information for decision making, and for improving logistics and **stock** [p. 307] control.

Stock control improves because with exact sales data a retailer knows exactly how much of any given item is available at any given locations as well as how fsat items are selling at each location. This means less **working capital** [p. 347] is required, while at the same time the chances of running out of any item can be reduced.

Large retailers tend to have very sophisticated logistics systems and the data from EPOS systems is a vital to these.

EPS

Earnings per share (EPS) is the profit attributable to shareholders (after interest, tax, **minority interests** [p. 204] and everything else) divided by the number of shares in issue. It is the amount of a company's profits that belong to a single ordinary share.

Companies are required to publish the statutory (also called "basic") EPS but there are a number of adjusted EPS numbers that are more useful to investors.

The most common alternative EPS numbers used are **adjusted EPS** [p. 7] and **diluted EPS** [p. 97].

Equity

Equity is the stake its owners have in a company. The word can be used to refer to balance sheet quantities, or as an adjective to describe securities that give their holders a share of ownership of the issuer.

On a **balance sheet** [p. 28], the equity is the amount that belongs to the shareholders; a company's assets less its liabilities.

Equity one of the two main sources of funding (see **capital structure** [p. 48]) for companies, the other being debt.

Companies raise equity capital by issuing equity **securities** [p. 291]. This is most commonly in the form of ordinary shares. Ordinary shares usually have equal voting rights to all other ordinary shares (one share, one vote), and are entitled to equal dividends.

Some companies may have special classes of shares that have more rights than ordinary shares. This has become uncommon.

Some companies also have classes of share that have fewer rights than ordinary shares, most commonly non-voting shares. These are typically entitled to the same share of profits as ordinary shares, but do not give the shareholder who holds one any voting rights. Again, these are becoming less common.

Investors are generally (quite rightly) very wary of companies that voting rights structured to distribute control differently from economic interests in the company. This usually means that a particular group of shareholders can run the company (or very strongly influence its running) to suit themselves.

The other common type of shares are **preference shares** [p. 244], which have some characteristics that make them more akin to **bonds** [p. 37], although they are legally (and therefore for tax purposes) shares.

A company's articles define the rights of different classes of shareholders and endless variations on the above are possible. Changes to the rights of different classes of shareholders usually require the agreement of the majority of shareholders of each class of shares affected, even if these are non-voting shares.

Equity risk premium

The equity risk premium is the difference between the **expected rate of return** [p. 135] on shares (collectively) and the **risk free rate of return** [p. 282]. It is the amount of extra return investors demand for taking the extra risk involved in investing in shares.

The concept of the equity risk premium is central to the valuation of shares, and to using **CAPM** [p. 50] in particular.

Estimating the equity risk premium is fairly tedious and uncertain. It involves working backwards from market profit growth forecasts and current share prices to the equity risk premium this implies. This is sufficient for valuing shares against the market.

It is also worth comparing the current equity risk premium to historical values and considering whether it may be too high or low, implying that the market as a whole is under-valued or over-valued respectively. In estimating historic values of the equity risk premium it is usual to assume that the actual market returns (up to now) are the returns that were expected.

ERP

The term enterprise resource planning (ERP) is almost always used to refer to ERP software.

The aim of ERP systems is to integrate systems related to a company's operations, covering areas as diverse as manufacturing, logistics and finance.

The advantages of ERP systems include:

- elimination of manual re-entry of data

- reduced paperwork

- easier tracking of the progress of order fulfilment and other processes.

- improved coordination between functions.

Commonly cited disadvantages of ERP systems are:

- cost: these are complex systems that are notoriously very expensive to deploy

- execution risk: as with any complex system the expensive implementation may not go as planned or deliver the benefits expected

- disruption to existing systems while ERP systems are being deployed

- inflexibility which can force organisations using ERP to adapt their *modus operandi* to the software rather than vice-versa.

There are a number of vendors of ERP software. The best known is SAP.

ERP systems usually provide systems for back office functions. An similar level of sophistication and integration of customer facing functions is provided by **CRM systems** [p. 80].

ETF

An exchange traded fund (ETF) is an investment fund, units of which can be bought and sold on a stock exchange. They are usually used by **tracker funds** [p. 325].

The key difference between ETFs and **unit trusts** [p. 333] is that they are tradeable on an exchange, which means that the **bid-offer spread** [p. 35] is usually much smaller (because it is set by the market rather than the fund manager).

However, unlike **single priced** [p. 296] **OEICS** [p. 221], ETFs do have a bid-offer spread. Like OEICS and unit trusts, and, unlike investment trusts, ETFs are open-ended (money can be added to or withdraw from the fund). This means that ETFs will trade at close to their **NAV** [p. 213], investment trusts often do not.

Ethical drug

See **prescription drug** [p. 246].

Ethical investing

Ethical investing appears simple enough: not investing in companies that do not meet certain ethical standards. Ethical investors typically do not invest in companies that that supply certain products or services, of that operate in or supply certain countries.

A simple example of an ethical investor's limits would be something like: no investments in tobacco or armaments and no investments in companies with links to certain countries.

At first glance this would appear to be reasonably straightforward. One simply invests in companies outside those sectors, and looks at where a company's turnover originates (which is disclosed in its accounts) and where it has operations (usually disclosed elsewhere in its annual report).

However things are not really that easy. A paper manufacturer may make paper for cigarette manufacture. An electronics company may sell components to arms manufacturers.

Geographical constraints are even harder to check. The geographical breakdown of turnover is usually done at the level of regions rather than countries so it is likely not to be specific enough. Looking at where a company operates is definitely not enough: may companies sell to countries they do not operate in.

There is also the question of how much exposure to something inethical a particular investor is prepared to tolerate: it may not be reasonable to not buy shares in an electronics company purely because 1% of its sales are to arms manufacturers.

For this reason investors sometimes use services that provide research that can be used to filter investments against an investor's ethical criteria.

Investors can also do their own research. In addition to the disclosure of geographical breakdowns and where a company operates, companies often **disclose** [p. 98] a lot of additional information that can be useful. For example, many companies disclose major contracts and other deals. The commentary on results can also be useful, for example, if a company says that high defence expenditure boosted revenues, you can be fairly certain that military customers are significant.

A clear advantage of investors doing their own research is that they can balance different facts against each other. A particular individual investor may decide to invest in a company that fails one ethical criterion because it has an outstanding performance elsewhere.

Investors doing their own research may find useful information available from many sources. For example environmentalist websites may have information on a company's environmental record.

Another alternative is to invest in ethical investment funds. These have become more common and investors now have a good choice of ethical funds, many of them good performers.

In spite of the range of ethical funds available, investors may not find funds that exactly match their criteria. It may be difficult to find a fund that meets an unusual criterion. Investors may also find many funds too strict; for example in order to avoid investing in tobacco, it may also be necessary to avoid investing in alcohol, arms etc., even if the investor concerned does not object to them.

One obvious disadvantage of ethical investing is that it can (depending on the criteria used) make it more difficult to **diversify** [p. 103]. This is rarely a serious issue given that there are ethical investments available in most major sectors.

Apart from investing in corporate securities, it is sometimes possible to take ethical criteria into account when considering other investments. For example the Co-operative Bank not only has ethical criteria for lending, but it also regularly carries out surveys to find out what ethical criteria its depositors want applied.

Eurobonds

Eurobonds are bonds issued in a currency other than the issuer's home currency outside the issuer's home country.

Eurobonds are usually **bearer bonds** [p. 33] that pay interest annually without deduction of tax. They are often issued by an off-shore **subsidiary** [p. 311] of the ultimate borrower in order to ensure the latter.

Eurobonds may vary in the ways bonds usually do: they may pay fixed or **floating rates** [p. 144], and they may be **convertible** [p. 72].

Eurobonds usually trade off exchange and are aimed at institutional rather than retail (private) investors.

Eurocurrency

Eurocurrency is money in the form of bank deposits of a currency outside the country that issued the currency.

The use of the prefix "euro" is somewhat misleading. It is used for historical reasons. Eurocurrency deposits may be of any currency in any country.

The most common currency deposited as eurocurrency is the US dollar, and the term **eurodollar** [p. 127] is often used to refer to dollar deposits.

One advantage of eurocurrency from a bank's point of view is that it allows a bank to operate outside the regulation of the country issuing the currency in question. One particular advantage is that most countries do impose a **reserve requirement** [p. 274] on foreign currency operations: a bank can therefore lend a higher proportion of its eurocurrency deposits, improving its **interest margin** [p. 176].

It also makes sense for a bank that has customers who wish to hold or borrow foreign currency the convenience of doing so in their own country.

Sufficiently large borrowers often issue **eurobonds** [p. 126] instead of borrowing from banks' eurocurrency operations.

Eurodollar

Eurodollars are the most common form of **eurocurrency** [p. 126]; they are US dollar deposits held outside the US.

There is no difference between eurodollars and other eurocurrency, except that the US dollar is the currency most commonly held outside its country of issue.

Historically, eurocurrency markets started with US dollars. During the cold war the Soviet Union did not wish to take the risk of holding dollar deposits in the US that could be seized or frozen. Soviet banks instead deposited dollars with banks in London and Paris.

European embedded value

European Embedded Value (EEV) is a standardised calculation of **embedded value** [p. 120] and related numbers that is being adopted by European insurance companies to make their results more meaningfully comparable.

The EEV principles provide consistent definitions, actuarial assumptions and **disclosure** [p. 98] requirements for EEV.

Although EEV provides a tighter set of rules and more consistency between companies, it still leaves a number of important decisions (such as risk premiums to be used) to individual companies. Given the complex nature of insurance accounts, investors should not expect this to mean that comparisons are now easy.

A key part of EEV is a uniform method of comparing new business premiums: **PVNBP** [p. 258].

European option

A European **option** [p. 228] can only be exercised at a pre-determined price (written into the option contract) on the expiry date of the option.

Although European options may appear to be significantly different from **American options** [p. 14], it can be shown that investors will hold American options to expiry. Therefore, American and European options on the same security with the same strike price and expiry date will have the same value.

EV

See **enterprise value** [p. 121].

EV/EBIT

This valuation ratio is similar to, but a little simpler than **EV/EBITDA** [p. 129], with which it shares the advantage of valuing a company regardless of its . [p. 48] It is:

$$\frac{EV}{EBIT}$$

where EV is **enterprise value** [p. 121] and
$EBIT$ is **earnings before interest and tax** [p. 115].

EV/EBIT is not much used in practice. It is almost has hard to calculate as EV/EBITDA because it requires calculating an enterprise value. Having done this one might as well go on and do the comparatively simple addition of **depreciation** [p. 95] and **amortisation** [p. 15] to EBIT. We can then use EV/EBITDA with its other advantages.

EV/EBITDA is generally preferable, but sometimes the information needed is not available: for example, when doing a **sum-of-parts valuation** [p. 311] and divisional/**subsidiary** [p. 311] depreciation and amortisation numbers are not available.

EV/EBITA

This valuation ratio is very closely related to **EV/EBITDA** [p. 129] and **EV/EBIT** [p. 128]. It is:

$$\frac{EV}{EBITA}$$

where EV is **enterprise value** [p. 121] and
$EBITA$ is **earnings before interest tax and amortisation** [p. 116].

It is usually preferable to use EV/EBITDA rather than EV/EBITA. The calculation is barely more complicated (the extra work needed is to add **depreciation** [p. 95] to the denominator) and it has the advantage of correcting for both major non-cash items.

EV/EBITA may sometimes be useful when insufficient information available to calculate an EV/EBITDA.

EV/EBITDA

This is one of the most widely used valuation ratios. It is:

$$\frac{EV}{EBITDA}$$

where *EV* is **enterprise value** [p. 121]

and *EBITDA* is **earnings before interest tax depreciation and amortisation** [p. 116]

Its main advantage over the **PE ratio** [p. 237] ratio is that it is unaffected by a company's **capital structure** [p. 48]. It compares the value of a business, free of debt, to earnings before interest.

If a business has debt, then a buyer of that business (which is what a potential shareholder is) clearly needs to take account of that in valuing the business. EV includes the cost of paying off debt. EBITDA measures profits before interest and before the non-cash costs of depreciation and amortisation.

EV/EBITDA is harder to calculate than PE. It does not take into account the cost of assets or the effects of tax. As it is used to look at the value of the business in EV terms it does not break this value down into the value of the debt and the value of the equity.

As EV/EBITDA is generally used to value shares it is assumed that debt (such as **bonds** [p. 37]) that has a verifiable market value is worth its market value. Other debt may be assumed to be worth its book value (the amount shown in the accounts). Alternatively, it is valued in line with the company's traded debt (for example, with the same risk premium as the most similar traded debt).

Equity can then be assumed to be worth EV less the value of the debt.

The first advantage of EV/EBITDA is that it is not affected by the capital structure of a company, in accordance with **capital structure irrelevance** [p. 48]. This is something that it shares with EV/**EBIT** [p. 115] and EV/**EBITA** [p. 116]

Consider what happens if a company issues shares and uses the money it raises to pay off its debt. This usually means that the **EPS** [p. 122] falls and the PE looks higher (i.e. the shares look more expensive). The EV/EBITDA should be unchanged. What the "before" and "after" cases here show is that it allows fair comparison of companies with different capital structures.

EV/EBITDA also strips out the effect of depreciation and amortisation. These are non-cash items, and it is ultimately cash flows that matter to investors.

When using EV/EBITDA it is important to ensure that both the EV and the EBITDA used are calculated for the same business. If a company has **subsidiaries** [p. 311] that are not fully owned, the **P & L** [p. 234] shows the full amount of profits from but is adjusted lower down by subtracting **minority interests** [p. 204]. So the EBITDA calculated by starting from company's operating profits will be the EBITDA for the group, not the company. There are two common ways of adjusting for this:

- Adjust the EV by adding the value of the shares of subsidiaries not owned by the company. The end result is an EV/EBITDA for the group. This becomes complicated if there are a lot of subsidiaries.

- Include only the proportion of EBITDA in a subsidiary that belongs to the company. So if the company has a 75% stake in a subsidiary, only include 75% of the subsidiary's EBITDA in your calculation. This is simple for companies (such as many telecoms companies) that disclose **proportionate** [p. 254] EBITDA. Otherwise, it can become difficult if the subsidiaries' results are not separately available. It also needs the corresponding adjustment to EV. In the example above, only 75% of the subsidiary's debt would be included in the group EV.

Given these complications, **a sum of parts valuation** [p. 311] may be considered as an alternative for complex groups. EV/EBITDA could still be used to value each individual part of the group.

EV/EBITDA is usually inappropriate for comparisons of companies in different industries, as their capital expenditure requirements are different. Ideally one would substitute EBITDA minus maintenance capex (capital expenditure required if the business does not expand) for EBITDA. This is difficult. Alternatively, depreciation could be used as an inaccurate but easy proxy for maintenance capex which would mean using EV/**EBITA** [p. 116]

As with **PE** [p. 237] it is common to look at EV/EBITDA using forecast profits rather than historical, and similar terminology is then used.

EV/sales

EV/sales is the most commonly used and the most meaningful of the valuation ratios based on sales. **Price/sales** [p. 250] is also sometimes used. EV/sales is:

$$\frac{EV}{sales}$$

where *EV* is **enterprise value** [p. 121]

As with price/sales, comparisons are only be meaningful with similar companies as margins vary a lot between sectors, and even between companies with different business models in the same sector.

Valuations based on sales rather than profits implicitly assume that a company will be able to return to "normal" margins, or that it will be **taken-over** [p. 317] by someone who can restore normal margins. Therefore it needs to be treated with caution and investors need to asses the real odds of a return to "business as usual": e.g., achieving the same margins as the peers against whom its EV/sales is being measured. Using EV/sales implicitly assumes that margins are not normal, as otherwise a profit based ratio would be preferable.

EVA (Economic value added)

Economic value added (EVA) is a measure of by how much a company's returns exceed those required by suppliers of capital. It therefore tells one how much wealth the company has created for providers of capital (meaning shareholders). The exact definition used varies, but, in essence it is:

$$EVA = P - WACC \times (D + S)$$

where P is **NOPAT** [p. 218]
WACC is **weighted average cost of capital** [p. 342]
D is the amount of debt funding and
S is the amount of **shareholder's equity** [p. 293].

The operating profit number used is adjusted in a number of ways, including for **amortisation** [p. 15]. The amount of capital used is also subject to various adjsutments including **capitalising** [p. 49] **R & D** [p. 261] and operating leases.

The aim of EVA is to provide management with a measure of their success in increasing shareholder's wealth: a better measure than profit of how much the company had made for shareholders.

It is not of much direct use for valuation, but that is not what it is intended for. However, even in its intended role, the lack of risk adjustment for taking on debt means that it has an in-built bias in favour of high gearing.

EVA is a trademark of Stern Stewart & Co. It is not the only such term to be trademarked, but is the best known.

Ex-dividend

See **cum-dividend** [p. 82].

Execution only

Discount or execution only broking is a simple dealing service. The broker does not offer any advice or portfolio management services.

Many brokers offer execution only services as one of several alternatives. The other commonly offered types of broking service are **advisory** [p. 10] (the investors makes the final decisions, but the broker offers advice) and **discretionary** [p. 99] (the broker manages the portfolio). There are also many stockbrokers who specialise in execution only services.

Execution only broking is the the cheapest way in which to buy and sell shares and other securities, hence the use of the term discount broking. Discount brokers also often a good way to buy funds.

The reason execution only services are cheaper is simple: they are cheaper to provide. The reason for this is that orders can be taken by call centre staff who are paid far less than stockbrokers and the time taken to process orders is little compared to the time required to assess a portfolio and a client's needs to provide advice or (especially) discretionary portfolio management. In addition, because the broker does not take any responsibility for the investment decisions there is no potential liability for bad decisions and far lower compliance costs (the costs of ensuring compliance to laws and regulations).

Internet based execution only services cut costs further by feeding orders directly into automated systems. Although a broker may have to make significant investments to set up and maintain such systems, they can handle large volumes and the costs directly associated with each order are very low (A high proportion of the commission charged on each order is **contribution** [p. 72].

This cost structure also means that the broker's commission on trades for execution only broking are usually fixed per order, rather than being a percentage of the cost of the order (usual for advisory services) or of the value of the portfolio (usual for discretionary broking). Depending on the broker, there may also be periodic charges, but these are also usually fairly low.

The low costs also mean, that unlike for many advisory and discretionary broking services, there is rarely a large (or any) minimum portfolio size for execution only broking services, which makes them far more accessible to small investors.

Ex-rights

See **cum-rights** [p. 82].

Exceptional items

Special items, or exceptional items, are costs or profits that need to be separately **disclosed** [p. 98] in order to provide a better view of the accounts. Companies usually go further and disclose profit numbers without special numbers. These should provide a better view of underlying trends and sustainable performance.

Special items arise from outside the usual course of a company's business, they are very often one-off items that will not recur.

Examples of special items include profits on disposals, restructuring costs and other unusual profits or losses. Some may recur (for example reorganisations may last several years) but they should clearly not be things that keep recurring.

There is obvious room for manipulation in what is classified as a special item and what is not.

There is little real difference between special items under **IFRS** [p. 166] and **exceptional items** [p. 132] under UK **GAAP** [p. 154].

Excess return

An excess return is the amount by which the return on an investment is greater than the **risk free rate of return** [p. 282] over a period.

This is not the same as the **abnormal return** [p. 2], which is the out-performance over the risk adjusted return.

Exchange rate risk

Exchange rate risk is simply the **risk** [p. 281] to which investors are exposed because changes in exchange rates may have an effect on investments that they have made.

The most obvious exchange rate risks are those that result from buying foreign currency denominated investments. The commonest of these are shares **listed** [p. 190] in another country or foreign currency **bonds** [p. 37].

Investors in companies that have operations in another country, or that export, are also exposed to exchange rate risk. A company with operations abroad will find the value in domestic currency of its overseas profits changes with exchange rates.

Similarly an exporter is likely to find that an appreciation in its domestic currency will mean that either sales fall (because its prices rise in terms of its customers currency) or that its **gross margin** [p. 160] shrinks, or both. A depreciation of its domestic currency would have the opposite effect.

However the two risks can often **hedge** [p. 162] each other. Suppose an investor in the US buys shares in a British company. There will be a risk that the value of the investment in dollar terms may decline if the pound falls against the dollar.

Now suppose that the British company makes a substantial proportion of its sales in the US and most of the rest of its sales are dollar denominated exports. This situation is not uncommon in sectors like pharmaceuticals or IT, or any which sell into truly global product markets.

In these circumstances a fall in the value of sterling is likely to reduce the value of the shares of the British company in dollar terms, for a given share price in sterling terms. However if the pound depreciates, the share price is likely to rise as the value in pounds of its dollar denominated sales rises.

The end result is that the two types of exchange rate risk neatly hedge each other.

This type of offsetting of risks can also be important when dealing with investments in **emerging markets** [p. 121] (especially small emerging markets) that often combine a volatile currency with high dependence on imports and exports*.

---

*An economy that lacks technology must import many things or do without. An economy that produces a small range of goods or service in quantities that far exceed domestic demand, must depend on exporting them.

Exchange rate transaction effects

Unlike **translation effects** [p. 134], transaction effects show actual changes in the profits produced by a company in terms of its working currencies.

Transaction effects result from the exposure a company has to foreign currency if it when it has debtors or creditors in a foreign currency. Transaction effects can affect a company that does not have operations that operate in a different currency if it either buys or sells in a currency other than its reporting currency.

Companies commonly use **options** [p. 228], **futures** [p. 154] and other derivatives to **hedge** [p. 162] transaction risks.

Exchange rate translation effects

Translation effects are the effects of changes in exchange rates on the **consolidated accounts** [p. 68] of a company that has businesses that report in different currencies. For example, a British company that has a US operations that makes a profit of $1m two years running is likely to find that the profit in pounds sterling is different in the two years.

The main problem from and investor's point of view is that translation effects can obscure the underlying improvements or deteriorations in performance. Many companies publish **CER** [p. 69] numbers to separate the effects of currency fluctuations.

Although transaction effects can be stripped out to show the underlying performance of businesses that report in a different currency, this does not mean that they are wholly unimportant. Clearly the company is making more or less money in terms of its reporting currency as a result of fluctuations and this affects its valuation in its reporting currency.

Exchange traded fund

See ETF [p. 124].

Execution risk

The risk that a company's plans will not work is called execution risk. This usually applies at a time of change, for example when introducing new systems or entering a new market.

A good example of this is when a company is rolling out complex new systems that are difficult to implement – such as **ERP systems** [p. 124]. There is a very good chance that something will go wrong somewhere, and that it will cost money to fix, and, possibly, that there will be loss of business while it is being fixed.

Similarly, new product introductions might fail because a product does not live up to promises or because it hits manufacturing difficulties. These are also execution risks. It may also fail because it does not appeal to consumers, which would not be regarded as execution risk – execution risk is internal, not related to market conditions.

Mergers [p. 201] and **acquisitions** [p. 5] are another common source of execution risk as (in order to gain whatever **synergies** [p. 316] are expected) it is necessary re-structure businesses and integrate businesses.

Exercise price

The exercise price, also called the strike price, of a **future** [p. 154] or **option** [p. 228], is the price at which a **derivative** [p. 96] gives the right or obligation to buy or sell the **underlying asset** [p. 331].

In most cases, the exercise price is simply a property of the security that is known from the outset and remains unchanged. **Asian options** [p. 20] and some **exotic options** [p. 135] have exercise prices that depend on the price of the underlying or its price history.

Traded options [p. 327] usually have a standardised set of exercise prices: an investor cannot find or **write** [p. 229] traded options at an arbitrary exercise price, but only at certain exercise prices (as well as expiry dates).

Exotic options

The more complex types of **option** [p. 228] are regarded as exotic, as opposed to the relatively straightforward **European** [p. 128], **American** [p. 14] and **Asian** [p. 20] types of option.

Examples include:

- Knock-out options: these lapse if the price goes above or below a certain level. They can be much cheaper than vanilla options as much of the value of options greatly dependent on the chances of extreme circumstances.

- Knock-in options: These are the converse of a knock-out option. They can only be exercised if the price of the underlying has crossed a particular level. Knock-out option and knock-in options are both types of barrier options.

- Options on options: These are very high volatile securities whose nature is fairly obvious.

Expected return

The expected return of an investment is exactly what it says. The return on most investments is uncertain, however it is possible to describe the future returns statistically as a probability distribution. The **mean** [p. 25] of this distribution is the expected return.

Take a very simplified example. Suppose we know that a particular security will, over the next year, either:

- rise 25%, with a 50% probability that this will happen, or

- fall 20% with a 50% probability

Then:

$$Expected\ return = (25\% \times 50\%) - (20\% \times 50\%) = 2.5\%$$

For a real security the possible returns are more numerous. The above example is also unrealistic in that the expected return can not actually occur itself. In most real cases not only can the expected return occur, but it is likely to be fairly close to the most likely level of return.

While there is a risk to expected returns, what matters to investors is not the risk to returns on the security (i.e. the **volatility** [p. 340] of that security) but the part of that volatility that **correlates** [p. 74] with movements in the market. This is because the impact on a portfolio of volatility that is not correlated with movements in the market can be diluted to insignificant levels by **diversification** [p. 103]. Volatility that correlates with the market cannot be. This risk is measured by a security's **beta** [p. 34].

Expense ratio

A general insurer's expense ratio is its operating expenses as a percentage of its premium income.

It is analogous to the **overhead cost ratio** [p. 233] but in the context (and suited to the very particular requirements) of insurance.

It, together with the **claims ratio** [p. 59], is part of the decomposition of the **combined ratio** [p. 62].

Extraordinary general meeting

See **EGM** [p. 119].

Fabless semiconductor company

A fabless semiconductor company is one that designs and markets **semiconductors** [p. 292], but does not manufacture them.

This has become a common business model because setting up a fab (a semiconductor factory) is enormously expensive, and has become more so as the technology has become more complex. Apart from the sheer cost, there are other **barriers to entry** [p. 30] such as the patents held by the major semiconductor companies.

This means that, for many companies, manufacturing themselves requires too big an investment to be justifiable. These companies contract out their manufacturing and concentrate on other aspects of their business.

The major semiconductor companies (Intel, IBM, etc.) have their own fabs. Some of these do contract work for fabless manufacturers. There are also companies that are specialist manufacturers, that do not design or market their own products (such as TSMC). These tend to be well known within the industry but not outside it.

Face value

The face value of a security is the amount that is shown on certificates (if issued) or on legal documents.

The face value of a share is also called its **par value** [p. 235] and it has little importance. For ordinary shares it represents little more than an arbitrary value chosen the company.

The face value of a **bond** [p. 37] is more important because it is the amount payable on maturity: the face value of bonds has an effect on their value that the face value of shares does not.

Fair value

Fair value is the value of an asset or liability in an arms length transaction between unrelated willing and knowledgeable parties. The concept of fair value is used in many accounting standards including the **IFRSs** [p. 166] covering **acquisitions** [p. 5], and the valuation of securities, but is not limited to these.

Fair value is used when there is some reason why the actual cost cannot be used. Assets may need to be revalued (such as when the market value of securities changes), or their purchase price may not be separable from a larger transaction (as happens in an acquisition).

Some methods of determining fair value are preferred to others as they are more accurate when they can be used. The methods used are, in IFRS order of preference:

- If there are identical transactions in the market, assets and liabilities should be valued with reference to such transactions

- If identical transactions do not exist, but similar transactions exist, fair value should be estimated making the necessary adjustments and using market based assumptions

- If either of the above methods cannot be used, other valuation methods (such as **present value** [p. 220]) may be used.

Fair value often has a subjective element as so many valuations are likely to use the latter two methods.

Fair value of intangible assets

The value of **intangible assets** [p. 173], especially **goodwill** [p. 159] has a significant effect on reported profits and **balance sheets** [p. 28]. The common exclusion of goodwill for valuation purposes makes this less important for investors. After the initial recognition of goodwill, it should be tested for **impairment** [p. 166] annually.

The methods used for valuing intangible assets are categorised (by an IFRS) into market methods (the first two above) and the income method (the third of the above).

Fair value of securities

IFRSs require use of the following methods, in order of preference:

- Quoted market prices should be used if available.

- The price should be estimated using market data and with reference to the current market value of a similar instrument.

- Where the above methods cannot be used, a company should use cost less impairment.

FCF

See **free cash flow** [p. 146].

FIFO

First In First Out (FIFO) is a method of valuing **stocks (inventory)** [p. 307] for accounting purposes. Stocks issued (such as for sale or further processing) are assumed (for calculating the cost of sales) to be issued from the oldest available stocks.

This is the opposite of the assumption made for **LIFO** [p. 188] valuation.

An advantage of valuing stocks using FIFO is that the value of the the remaining stocks will be closer to the current market prices, therefore the balance sheet value or stocks will be more accurate.

Assuming positive inflation, FIFO increases profits by recording lower costs (old prices). It also increases the value of stocks recorded in the balance sheet. Given deflation, FIFO would have the opposite effect. While not the usual case, deflation of the value of stocks is normal in some industries.

Financial economics

Financial economics is the study of the valuation of **securities** [p. 291], **risk** [p. 281] and returns, the financing of companies and the making of investment decisions.

It is a branch of economics and uses many of the same concepts and tools. Like the rest of economics, modern financial economics is a very quantitative discipline and makes extensive use of **econometrics** [p. 117] as well as a range of other mathematical methods.

Important subject areas within financial economics include the valuation of securities and corporate finance (the financing and behaviour of companies).

Particularly important results and models include:

- **CAPM** [p. 50]

- **arbitrage pricing theory** [p. 19]

- the **Black-Scholes** [p. 36] formula

- **capital structure irrelevance** [p. 48]

- **dividend irrelevance** [p. 105].

Key concepts include:

- the **time value of money** [p. 322]

- **arbitrage** [p. 18], the **law of one price** [p. 186], and **dominant trading strategies** [p. 109]

- **risk premiums** [p. 282].

Areas of overlap with other branches of economics and with other disciplines include:

- econometrics

- **agency theory** [p. 11]

- **behavioural finance** [p. 33].

Econometrics is the most important* of the areas of overlap with other disciplines. It is central to the application and testing of financial economics. Agency theory is an important part of corporate finance while behavioural finance is a newer and somewhat peripheral, but interesting, field.

---

*Apart from fundamental concepts such as price determination by the matching of supply and demand.

Financial gearing

See **gearing** [p. 157].

Financial model

A financial model is anything that is used to calculate, forecast or estimate financial numbers. Models can therefore range from simple formulae to complex computer programs that may take hours to run.

At the simple end a valuation ratio, such as the PE, is a simple valuation model. Although the term model is rarely used for something quite as simple as a straightforward, commonly used ratio, it is commonly used for slightly more complex formulae of a similar nature.

Specific methods of calculating numbers are often called models: for example, application of a **DCF** [p. 88] to dividends to value a share would be called a dividend discount model.

Spreadsheets used for budgeting and for forecasting profit and cashflow are also financial models.

More specialist computer software is used for more complex models, especially those that require a more complex application of statistics and financial mathematics.

In areas such as risk management and economic forecasting, the models used are extremely complex. Models such as **value at risk** [p. 336] are implemented using specially written computer programs. Investment banks employ **quantitative analysts** [p. 260] and computer programmers who specialise in devising and implementing financial models.

First mover advantage

The first company to launch a new type of product should have a competitive advantage over those that start later. Before competitors get started it should have been able to:

- build a customer base

- build a strong brand

- develop **economies of scale** [p. 117]

- develop distribution channels.

This should mean that a first mover should have a very good chance of remaining the market leader, however it is not uncommon for a first mover (or other market leader) to be overtaken. An new entrant may have:

- a better product, especially if they learn from the mistakes the first mover made

- better distribution

- a strong existing brand, especially if it already sells related products.

If the first mover is comparatively small its may well find that larger late entrants already have strong brands (developed for other products), better distribution channels (also developed for other products) and the resources to start on a large scale, or to absorb losses while building market share.

The usefulness of first mover advantage needs to be judged in the context of the product, the industry concerned and the actual and potential competition are. Points to consider include:

- whether there are **network effects** [p. 214]

- how much of an advantage is conferred by having an established customer base

- whether there are any advantages in distribution or economies of scale that competitors will find hard to replicate.

Fisher hypothesis

The Fisher hypothesis is that, in the long run, inflation and **nominal interest rates** [p. 216] move together, meaning that **real interest rates** [p. 265] are stable in the long term. This is also called the Fisher effect.It was formulated by Irving Fisher.

The Fisher equation is:

$$n = i + r$$

where i is the rate of **inflation** [p. 171]
n is the nominal interest rate and
r is the real interest rate.

This is an approximation. The difference between this and the absolutely correct equation is very small unless either interest rates or inflation is very high. The perfectly correct equation is:

$$1 + n = (1 + i)(1 + r)$$

If the Fisher hypothesis is correct (the Fisher effect is real), then n and i move together, which means that r (the real interest rate) is stable in the long term.

Fisher separation

Fisher separation is fundamental to the theory of finance.

It was shown by Irving Fisher that given **efficient capital markets** [p. 118], firms (in effect, profit making companies) should concentrate on maximising their **NPV** [p. 220] rather than taking into account the cash flows that investors (shareholders) need.

This is because an investor who needs cash can sell an investment, or part of it, and an investor to whom an investment pays more cash than needed can re-invest it.

This means that maximising investor's **utility** [p. 334] means maximising the NPV of their investments.

This simplifies investment decisions because we can value investments without regard to investors' need for cash. Therefore we can use valuation models such as **CAPM** [p. 50] and **APT** [p. 19] to make investment decisions.

Fixed asset

Fixed assets, as opposed to **current assets** [p. 83], are those assets with a remaining useful life of over an year. Following the **accruals** [p. 4] principal, these assets are shown on the balance sheet but their value is **depreciated** [p. 95], and treated as an expense in the **P & L** [p. 234] account for each year of their life.

There are two types of fixed assets:

- **Tangible** [p. 318] fixed assets

- **Intangible** [p. 173] fixed assets

Tangible fixed assets include physical assets such as land and buildings and equipment. Long term financial investments are also considered tangible.

The most important intangible fixed asset is **goodwill** [p. 159]. Other intangibles includes patents, copyrights and trademarks.

Fixed asset turnover

Fixed asset turnover is similar to **asset turnover** [p. 22]. It is a narrower measure and measures how effectively sales are generated by fixed asset investments and ignores current assets. It is most likely to be useful in a capital intensive industry. It is:

$$\frac{sales}{fixed\ assets}$$

Tangible asset turnover narrows this down further by using only tangible fixed assets. This is reasonable for the same reasons that **intangible assets** [p.

173], especially **goodwill** [p. 159], are ignored in calculating many valuation ratios. The same end could be achieved with other asset ratios by deducting either goodwill or the total value of all intangible assets from the assets figure.

Fixed costs

Fixed costs are those that do not change with the level of sales. If sales increase or decrease but nothing else changes then fixed costs remain the same. Common examples of fixed costs include rents, salaries of permanent employees and **depreciation** [p. 95].

A high level of fixed costs increases **operational gearing** [p. 227].

Costs that are not fixed are **variable** [p. 338] or **semi-variable** [p. 292].

Fixed interest

Fixed income (or fixed interest) securities pay interest at a rate that does not change with any external variable; the **coupon** [p. 77] payments are known in advance. Coupons are almost always all for the same amount and paid at regular intervals.

There are two risks with fixed income securities:

- **credit risk** [p. 79]

- **interest rate risk** [p. 178].

The usual alternative to fixed interest is a **floating interest rates** [p. 144], which changes the nature of the interest rate risk. A change in interest rate will change the value of a fixed income security but not the income stream it pays. With a floating rate security the value will change less but the income stream will change.

The sensitivity of a fixed interest security to interest rates is measured by **duration** [p. 113] or, more accurately, **modified duration** [p. 205].

Fixed odds betting terminals

Fixed odds betting terminals are electronic gambling machines that play a variety of games. Each machine accepts bets for amounts up to a pre-set maximum and pays out according at fixed odds on a simulated outcome of the game. The games offered are varied single player versions of a range of gambling games including roulette.

Fixed odds betting terminals are increasingly common in bookmakers but the amounts betted, maximum payouts and the number of machines allowed are subject to regulation.

They bring betting shops' offerings closer to that of the bottom end casinos. Casinos still have much bigger potential payouts and some marketing advantages.

Flat yield

The flat yield of a **bond** [p. 37] is simply the annual **coupon payment** [p. 77] divided by the current price.

The only virtue of the flat yield for valuation is that it is extremely simple to calculate. It can be a reasonable approximation of the **YTM** [p. 350] for a bond that has a long remaining life, and is equal to the YTM for a perpetual bond (one that will never mature and be repaid, but carry on paying interest indefinitely).

There is little reason to use to flat yield, except perhaps when constructing a portfolio to yield a target income. Computers automate the calculation of YTM, and many trading systems and information services display the YTM of publicly traded bonds.

Floating interest rates

A floating rate is an interest rate that will change over time in line with a benchmark rate.

A floating rate is usually fixed at a fixed premium in percentage points (or **basis points** [p. 31]) above a market rate such as **LIBOR** [p. 187], a particular bank's declared base rate or a central bank's official base rate.

A wide variety of debt instruments pay floating rates.

In contrast, **fixed income** [p. 143] interest rates do not change over time. If a £100 bond pays 10% fixed interest it will pay £10 every year.

Footfall

The number of people visiting a shop or a chain of shops in a period of time is called its footfall.

Footfall is an important indicator of how successfully a company's marketing, brand and format are bring people into its shops.

Footfall is an indicator of the reach a retailer has, but footfall needs to be converted into sales and this is not guaranteed to happen. Many retailers have struggled to turn high footfall into sales.

Trends in footfall do tell investors something useful. They may be an indicator of growth and help investors to understand why a retailer's sales growth (or decline) is happening. Investors may want to know whether sales growth due to an increase in the number of people entering the shops (footfall) or more success at turning visitors into buyers (which can be seen by comparing footfall to the number of transactions).

Sales growth may also come from selling more items to each buyer (compare number of transactions to sales volumes), selling more expensive items (an improvement in the **sales mix** [p. 286]), or increasing prices. Which of these numbers is **disclosed** [p. 98] varies from company to company. Investors should look at whatever is available.

Forward integration

Forward integration is **vertical integration** [p. 339] through combining a core business with its buyers.

The advantages of forward integration include excluding competing suppliers, greater ability to reach end customers and better access to information about end customers.

Forwardation

The price of a **futures** [p. 154] contract is usually greater than the **spot price** [p. 303] of the underlying (usually a **commodity** [p. 64]). This state is called forwardation or contango.

The reason is simple if one considers a typical hard (non-perishable) commodity such as gold. It is preferable to enter into a forward contract than to invest in buying the commodity itself.

The holder of a future or forward will benefit from any gains in the price of the underlying. That gain can be realised either by selling the commodity after delivery of the future, or by selling the (now more valuable) future in the meantime. At the same time, the holder of a future has not put down money to buy the commodity, and can therefore can receive interest on the money thus saved (compared to buying the commodity).

The situation is slightly more complex for futures on financial assets. Futures on securities (uncommon, as options are usually preferred) are affected by dividend payments and similar benefits. In the case of currency forwards, both parties continue to receive interest so the relationship between the spot and forward prices is related to the interest rate differential (see **interest rate parity** [p. 177]). In neither case can forwardation be assumed.

Forwardation does not always hold for soft (perishable) commodities due to factors such a seasonal demand and supply cycles.

Forwards

Forward contracts and **futures** [p. 154] are very similar. A forward is an agreement to buy or sell:

- a given quantity of a particular asset

- at a specified future date

- at a pre-agreed price.

FRC (Financial Reporting Council)

The Financial Reporting Council regulates financial reporting in the UK. Its roles include:

- Investigating cases of accounts that may not adhere to the requirements of accounting standards and the Companies Act.

- Acting as a disciplinary body for accountants, although it only investigates cases of "public interest" referred to it by the accountancy bodies.

- Authorising accountants' professional bodies to act as supervisory bodies for the profession and to offer professional qualifications. It also overseas these bodies.

- Setting accounting standards

- The oversight of **actuaries** [p. 6] and setting actuarial standards.

The standards setting part of the FRC's responsibilities are limited in scope because of the adoption of **IFRSs** [p. 166]. The FRC's standard setting arm, the **ASB** [p. 4], now sees its main role as influencing the development of IFRSs.

Free asset ratio

A solvency measure used by British life insurance companies, the free asset ratio is:

$$\frac{available\ assets - required\ minimum\ margin\ of\ solvency}{admissible\ assets}$$

The exact definition varies and the numbers disclosed by different companies as headline free asset ratios may not be comparable. For example, some companies include future profits. The ratio will also depend on the assumptions made in valuing liabilities.

In general, the higher the ratio, the more surplus capital a company has available.

Free cash flow

Free cash flow (FCF) measures how much money a company makes after deducting maintenance **capex** [p. 46], but before capex on expansion.

This is important as it allows valuation of the existing business without the harder to asses value of investment in expansion and new ventures. The latter should be worth more than the money that is being invested in them. How much more is hard to assess and valuing companies using their free cash flow sidesteps the question.

This means that using free cash flow based valuations will undervalue companies which have particularly good opportunities to invest. It will also mean that it will overvalue companies which are sufficiently badly run to make investments that destroy shareholder value. The latter is not as uncommon as it should be because managers usually benefit by expanding more than is in the best interests of shareholders.

The free cash flow is the same as what the dividends would be if a company decided to pay out as much as it could in dividends without either running down its operations or increasing debt.

Free cash flow (FCF) is often used in **discounted cash flow** [p. 88] valuations.

A rough free cash flow can be calculated from the **cash flow statement** [p. 54]:

$$FCF = O - T - C$$

where O is **operating cash flow** [p. 225]
T is tax
and C is **capex** [p. 46]

This free cash flow number would be used in a **DCF** [p. 88]. Free cash flow can also be used in valuation ratios. Comparing it to **EV** [p. 121] is probably the most generally useful: EV/FCF. An equity investor may prefer to also subtract net interest paid and use that number in a DCF, or to calculate **cashflow per share** [p. 53].

The problem with this rough free cash flow is that it includes all **capital expenditure** [p. 46], not just maintenance capex (the amount required to keep existing operations going). This is not serious problem when using a DCF provided that the forecasts used in the DCF reflect the benefits of the extra investment. It can badly distort EV/FCF and cashflow/share for companies that are investing heavily. It is usually a reasonable approach as maintenance and expansionary capex are not easily separable and expansion may be a necessity in order to stay in business, rather than being genuinely discretionary.

Free float

The free float of a company is the proportion of shares that are held by investors who are likely to be willing trade. It is a measure of how many shares are reasonably **liquid** [p. 190]. It therefore excludes those shares held by strategic shareholders.

Strategic shareholdings typically include those of directors and those connected to them as well as shares held by parent companies and others who have links with the company that go beyond those of a portfolio investor.

Indices [p. 169] such the **FTSE 100** [p. 150] are adjusted for the free float, so that companies are weighted by the total value of shares that are actually available to portfolio investors (i.e. **market cap**[p. 196] × *free float* or a similar weighting) rather than the total market cap.

This is useful for performance measurement as it provides a benchmark more closely related to what money managers can actually buy.

Free float tends to be a much more important issue for smaller companies which commonly have several strategic shareholders and where directors shareholdings can be a significant part of the total share capital.

It is unusual for director's shareholdings in large companies to be large (in proportion to market cap), and there are fewer other strategic shareholders (other large shareholders tend to be fund managers) than in smaller companies.

Free float is rarely an issue for private investors except for companies that are both very small and closely held. It can be very important to institutional investors.

How to calculate free float

Calculating a company's free float to reasonable accuracy is not intrinsically at all difficult, but can require some care.

A company's annual report will contain a list of its largest shareholders and of director's shareholdings. Significant changes to these are also reported through announcements.

It is therefore possible to calculate a reasonably accurate free float estimate simply by:

1. Going through the annual report and identifying the strategic shareholders.

2. Collating their shareholdings and updating the totals by looking at relevant company announcements.

3. Summing the resulting updated shareholdings.

4. This total divided by total shares in issue is the percentage that is not free float. Subtracting this from 100% gives us the free float.

Although this can be a little tedious, the only real difficulty lies in identifying which of the major shareholders we should regard as strategic. Clearly another company in the same industry, a director, or a parent company will not sell their shares as lightly as a normal portfolio investor.

Fund mangers are usually portfolio investors. Some financial institutions have both fund management arms and **private equity** [p. 252] arms. It is usually clear which is the shareholder, but it is easy to make a mistake here.

A similar problem can arise with individuals with large shareholdings. Unless the individual is a director it may be difficult to tell what the nature of their interest is.

FRN

A floating rate note, often called an FRN or "floater", is a **debt instrument** [p. 37] that pays a **floating interest rate** [p. 144]. The interest rate is usually based on an accepted market benchmark rate such as **LIBOR** [p. 187]. Maturities at issue are usually in the three to five year range.

The value of FRNs is not as sensitive to interest rates as that of debt securities that pay fixed interest. This makes them less risky for an investor who may which to sell them.

From the point of view of an investor who wishes to secure a stable income and is willing to hold to maturity, FRNs are more risky.

As interest rates change in line with the **risk free rate** [p. 282] the **present value** [p. 220] of an FRN is fairly stable providing that its risk does not change (provided the issuer remains equally financially stable).

FSA

The Financial Services Authority is the regulator of all financial services in the UK.

Firms providing certain financial services are required to register with the FSA. The FSA can refuse to register firms, and can ban firms from providing certain services. It frequently investigates allegations of violations of its rules by registered firms.

The FSA also sets requirements for individuals to do certain jobs. Among other things, it requires those in certain roles (such as giving financial advice to retail investors) to pass exams it sets.

This means that investors can usually rely on those selling them services or advice having a certain minimum level of competence and conduct. However this is a minimal acceptable level, not a high one.

FTK (Freight Tonne Kilometres)

Freight Tonne Kilometres (FTK) measures actual freight traffic

It is the equivalent of **RPK** [p. 285] for freight.

One FTK is one metric tonne of revenue load carried one kilometre. The sum of FTKs for every flight stage flown by every aircraft over a period is the FTK of an airline over the period.

FTSE

FTSE is a publisher of indices and the name of the family of **indices** [p. 169] it publishes.

The most widely followed of these indices is the **FTSE 100** [p. 150], often referred to simply as "the Footsie".

FTSE, the company, is a joint venture between the Financial Times and the London Stock Exchange. The name was originally an abbreviation of Financial Times Stock Exchange Index.

The most important FTSE indices and their constituents are:

- FTSE 100: The 100 largest UK **listed companies** [p. 190], covering about 80% of UK **market cap** [p. 196]

- **FTSE 250** [p. 151]: The next 250 largest companies

- FTSE 350: A combination of the above two: about 90% of total UK market cap

- FTSE **Techmark** [p. 319] indices: three indices that cover London listed technology companies.

- FTSE Eurotrack: a family of indices at cover European markets as a whole.

There are many more FTSE indices available covering different regions, sectors, **investment styles** [p. 179] and **ethical investment** [p. 125] requirements.

FTSE indices are market cap weighted, with an additional adjustment for the availability of shares to investors (based on **free float** [p. 147]).

To keep the indices meaningful, adjustments are made when necessary. For example, when companies issue new shares and when companies are added to or deleted from an index.

FTSE 100

The **FTSE** [p. 150] 100 is easily the most widely followed **index** [p. 169] in Britain.

It is an index of the 100 largest London **listed companies** [p. 190]. This includes many foreign companies but it does not include companies that only have **secondary listings** [p. 288] in London.

It is popular partly because it is familiar to investors. The fact that it has been available for many years means that there is sufficient historical data for most purposes.

Because the FTSE 100 covers about 80% of UK **market cap** [p. 196] there is rarely much difference between it and a wider index such as the FTSE-All share.

It is also easily available through many sources and published in **real time** [p. 266].

FTSE 250

A **FTSE** [p. 150] **index** [p. 169] that covers the 250 UK **listed** [p. 190] companies that are the next largest after those in the **FTSE 100** [p. 150].

Companies in the FTSE 250 are generally considered **mid-caps** [p. 202].

The calculation of the FTSE 250, and the selection of its constituents (the companies whose shares are included in it) are almost the same as the FTSE 100.

The FTSE 250 is not as widely followed as the FTSE 100 as the companies it covers, although greater in number, only jointly account for about 10% of UK **market cap** [p. 196]. However, it can often be interesting to look at any divergences in performance between the **blue-chips** [p. 36] and mid-caps.

The FTSE 250 is the obvious **benchmark** [p. 33] for anyone investing specifically in mid-cap shares. The FTSE 250 is also not as dominated by a the four largest **sectors** [p. 288] as the FTSE 100 is.

FTSE 350

The **FTSE** [p. 150] 350 **index** [p. 169] tracks UK **blue-chips** [p. 36] and **mid-caps** [p. 202]. It's constituents are the shares of companies in the **FTSE 100** [p. 150] and the **FTSE 250** [p. 151].

It is a wider index than the FTSE 100 and is a slightly better indicator of the market as a whole but it is not as widely followed or as well publicised. With about 90% of the **market cap** [p. 196] of the 350 coming from FTSE 100 companies there is rarely much difference between the two indices.

The index value is calculated using the same methodology as the FTSE 100 and 250, and the selection of constituents is obviously the same.

Fund mandate

The mandate of a **collective investment vehicle** [p. 62] is a statement of its aims, the limits within which it is supposed to invest, and the investment policy it should follow.

A fund (or portfolio) will typically define:

- the aim of the fund (e.g., to generate dividend income or long term growth)

- the type of **investment strategy** [p. 179] it will follow (which will tend to follow from the above)

- what regions it will invest in (UK, Europe, **emerging markets** [p. 121], etc.)

- what sectors it will invest in.

- what types of securities it will invest in (**equities** [p. 123], **bonds** [p. 37], **convertibles** [p. 72], **derivatives** [p. 96], etc.)

- whether the fund will **short sell** [p. 296] and whether it will be **hedged** [p. 162]

- whether it will be **geared** [p. 157] and to what extent

- a benchmark **index** [p. 169] that the fund aims to beat (or match if it is a **tracker fund** [p. 325]).

Fund mandates are set by the fund management company, but publicised so that investors can choose a fund that suits their requirements.

There are also legal limits on how some types of investment vehicle can invest.

Fund of funds

A fund of funds is a **collective investment vehicle** [p. 62] that invests in other funds. Funds of funds (also called multi-manager funds) have become increasingly popular in recent years.

Advantages to investors

The main advantage to investors is that they have access to investments that are not directly available to retail investors. This is why funds of **hedge funds** [p. 162] have been particularly successful.

Advocates of funds of funds often claim they offer better **diversification** [p. 103]. This is largely illusory. The difference between a fund of funds and any well diversified fund with the same geographical and sector mandate is very unlikely to be significant.

Funds of funds add an extra layer of costs. This is not as bad as it would appear as funds of funds can often invest more cheaply than a retail investors would be able to do directly. However, retail investors are still picking, and paying for, a fund manager whose only real role is to pick other fund managers. There is a saving to be made cutting out the middleman.

Advantages to fund managers

Probably more important to the popularity of funds of funds are their advantages to fund managers.

Funds of funds allow fund managers to expand the range of products they have to sell, without incurring too much in the way of costs.

They also allow less highly regarded (or less well performing) fund management companies to claim that they offer funds that are being managed by managers with better reputations. A fund of funds can be marketed on the track records of the funds it is investing in, rather than that of the managers running it.

Fundamental analysis

Fundamental analysis is the most common way in which investors analyse securities.

It means exactly what it says: the valuation of securities on the basis of their fundamental financial characteristics. It therefore covers a broad range of techniques (including most of what is covered by this site). It is ultimately based on the scientific and testable theories of financial economics.

The most widely used alternative to fundamental analysis is **technical analysis** [p. 319]. Somewhat better founded alternatives include:

- complex **quantitative models** [p. 140] based on market data – these are used by hedge funds and index trackers

- pure trading strategies such as **arbitraging** [p. 18] – this is an essential part of the functioning of markets

- the use of **behavioural finance** [p. 33] to predict share prices – this is closest to technical analysis in spirit, has a better foundation, but remains rarely used.

The ultimately correct tools of fundamental analysis are very careful modelling and forecasting, and the use of theoretically correct valuation methods such **CAPM** [p. 50] based **DCF** [p. 88]s.

Given the difficulties of using methods that are absolutely theoretically correct, other techniques such as valuation ratios (such as **PE** [p. 237]) have their place.

At the heart of fundamental analysis are the models it uses for forecasting future profits and (most importantly) cash flows.

Fundamental analysis is the main subject of this book.

Fungible

A security or commodity is fungible if it is perfectly interchangeable with any other of the same type and class.

Most financial securities are fungible: a share in a particular company is exactly the same as another share in the same company (of the same class if the company has more than one class of share).

Financial markets for **commodities** [p. 64] usually specify the nature of the commodity (e.g the purity of a metal being traded) sufficiently tightly for it to be treated as fungible.

Futures

Futures contracts are like **forwards** [p. 145], but they are standardised and often publicly traded on exchanges. Futures are used both to **hedge** [p. 162] and as (fairly speculative) investments in themselves.

Futures are most often used in **commodity** [p. 64] and currency markets where both producers and buyers gain security from fixing their buying or selling prices, but have little to gain by paying the extra for an option as their possession of, or foreseeable future need for, the underlying commodity or currency is hedged by the future.

As with options, almost all futures traded on exchanges are settled by payment of their value on the day they expire rather than by delivery of the **underlying asset** [p. 331].

GAAP

Generally accepted accounting principles (GAAP) are a set of rules, accounting principles and standards that are used in a particular region or country.

GAAP are drawn from several sources. Standards (such as **IFRSs** [p. 166]) are the most obvious source, however there are others. Company law (specifically, the Companies Act) is also very important in the UK.

The Accounting Standards Board sets UK accounting standards, which are now based on IFRSs. Company law changes less frequently.

US GAAP is set by the Financial Accounting Standards Board (FASB).

Game Theory

Game theory is a branch of mathematics that provides a framework for analysing what choices rational individuals will make, when the outcome ("payoff") depends on both their choice and the choices of other "players".

Game theory has many applications in economics and and some in finance – it has uses in exchange rate theory, for example.

A simple example of how game theory works is given by the prisoners' dilemma game. This is a hypothetical situation in which two criminals caught by the police may each confess and give evidence against the other. The possibilities are:

1. If neither confesses both will face a minor charge that carries a one year prison sentence.

2. If one confesses and the other does not, the one who confesses will go free, the other can expect to be convicted and get a 10 year prison sentence.

3. If both confess, both will go to prison, but will receive more lenient (say 5 year) sentences.

A game theorist will represent the possibilities as a strategic form game:

		Player A	
		Co-operate	Defect
Player B	Co-operate	-1,-1	0,-10
	Defect	-10, 0	-5,-5

The players are the two criminals, "cooperate" means helping the other player (e.g. by not confessing), "defect" means the opposite, the payoffs are shown in the table, first the payoff for player A, then that for player B.

It is obvious that the two players (the prisoners) will be best off if they both "cooperate" (try to help each other), as they will then both receive light sentences.

However, from the point of view of each player, he or she is better off if he or she defects regardless of what the other player does. The strategy of defecting dominates (see **dominance** [p. 108]) the alternative.

The result is that, assuming rational and non-altruistic players, they both defect.

There are game theory analyses that take account of cooperation. These are cooperative game theory, the use of which is less common that non-cooperative game theory.

Simple dominance is only one possibility. Another common outcome in economics and financial economics is a **Nash equilibrium** [p. 211].

Gamma

The gamma of a **derivative** [p. 96] (or portfolio) is the rate of change of its delta with the price of the underlying security.

It is approximately the change in the **delta** [p. 93] that results from a one unit change in the price of the underlying.

More accurately (and more mathematically rigorously) it is the second derivative of the price of a derivative security against the price of the underlying security, i.e.:

$$\Gamma = \frac{\partial^2 P}{\partial S^2}$$

where P is the price of the derivative
and S is the price of the underlying

The gamma of a derivative is used in constructing portfolios that are **gamma hedged** [p. 156], which require less frequent re-balancing than a **delta hedged** [p. 93] portfolio.

It can also be used as an indication of whether delta hedging is a sufficiently good strategy. If gamma is low, then delta hedging will be workable. If gamma is high the delta may change so fast that delta hedging requires more frequent re-balancing than is practical.

Gamma hedging

The main shortcoming of **delta hedging** [p. 93] is that a **delta** [p. 93] hedge requires frequent re-balancing. When ever the price of a security changes, so does the delta of any **derivative** [p. 96] based on it. When the delta changes significantly, the composition of any delta hedged portfolio will need to be changed.

The greater the change in the delta, the greater the change that is needed in a delta hedged portfolio. Therefore the amount of re-balancing needed can be reduced by reducing the amount by which the delta changes for a price movement – in other words by reducing the rate of change of the delta, which we call the **gamma** [p. 155].

A gamma hedged, or gamma neutral, portfolio will need to be re-balanced less than one what is only delta hedged. It will still need re-balancing, especially if there are large price movements, because the gamma, like the delta, changes with underlying price.

Gamma hedging is also more complex because it requires holding two derivatives to hedge a each holding of a single security.

GDP (Gross Domestic Product)

Gross Domestic Product (GDP) is the total value of all goods and services produced in an economy. It can also be looked at as the total **value added** [p. 335] of every business in an economy.

The usual textbook definition) is:

$$GDP = C + I + G + X - Z$$

where C is consumer expenditure
I is investment
G is government expenditure
X is exports
and Z is imports

An advantage of this definition is that the data needed to calculate GDP this way is comparatively readily available.

GDP growth generally considered to be very important. It is the key measure of economic growth and is often used in financial modelling. It is the most widely used measure of the size of the economy and:

- Many financial models assume a relationship between demand for particular goods and services and GDP – strong correlation indicating **cyclical** [p. 84] goods/services.

- The last period of many **DCF** [p. 88] models assumes long term growth in line with long term GDP growth.

GDP is usually stated in real terms (i.e. corrected for **inflation** [p. 171]) by adjusting it with a special inflation measure, the **GDP deflater** [p. 157].

GDP deflater

The GDP deflater is the **inflation** [p. 171] measure that is used to adjust economic growth statistics, primarily **GDP** [p. 156]. Its calculation is not greatly different from other measures of inflation, but it must measure a fuller range of costs, than, for example, a consumer price index.

GDR

See **global depositary receipt** [p. 159].

Gearing

Gearing, called leverage in the US and some other countries, measures the extent to which a company is funded by debt. One common definition is:

$$\frac{debt}{shareholders\ funds}$$

Shareholders' funds is the amount also called shareholders' **equity** [p. 123]

Unfortunately, there are other definitions, and the other that is widely used (which many people find easier to understand intuitively) is:

$$\frac{debt}{capital\ employed} = \frac{debt}{debt + shareholders'\ funds}$$

Regardless of the definition, and there are variations even on **debt/equity** [p. 90], it is usual to show gearing as a percentage rather than a fraction.

Debt includes only borrowing, not other debt such as trade creditors. It is not unusual to subtract **goodwill** [p. 159] from the value of shareholders' funds when calculating gearing. Although this is not universally done, it is logical as goodwill reflects a company's history rather than its current financial strength.

As a general rule debt/equity of more than 100% or debt/capital employed of more than 50% is "high", but there is no cut-off point that is too high. As debt gets higher, profits for shareholders become more volatile for the same reasons as with **operational gearing** [p. 227].

A high level of debt is a cause for concern, but it does accelerate profit growth as well as declines. Companies with more stable operating profits can safely take on higher levels of debt, so what is acceptable depends on the business.

Interest cover [p. 176] is a more direct measure of the effect of gearing on the volatility of profits.

Generic drug

A generic drug is one that is made other than by the original developer of a drug or under its authority. Generic drugs become available when a drug goes out of patent.

Due to the increasing pressure on the budgets of both state and private health care providers there has been increasing pressure on prescribers to use generic drugs whenever possible and the result has been that the original versions lose market share very quickly once generics become available.

Generic versions can receive approval quite quickly as regulators do not require them to go through the full process including **clinical trials** [p. 60] and so on. Instead, generics manufacturers need to be able to show that the drug is equivalent to the original version. This is reasonable as the drug will have the same active ingredient and as similar a formulation as the generic manufacturer can make.

In some countries (most importantly the US) the first generic manufacturer to reach market can receive an addition reward, such as a period of exclusivity before regulators approve any more generic versions of the same drugs.

Patent holders clearly have a lot to lose from the launch of generics and often go to great lengths to delay them. One common tactic is to separately patent the formulation of a drug (at a later date from the patenting of the active ingredient itself) in order to, in effect, lengthen the life of the patent. This frequently leads to litigation as, at the same time, generic manufacturers have, in recent years, become more aggressive about launching quickly and more willing to go to court.

Another common response to the launch of generics is to launch improved formulations (again covered by new patents) as patents expire.

Geometric mean

The geometric mean is an **average** [p. 25] calculated by multiplying a set of numbers and taking the nth root, where n is the number of numbers.

For example, the geometric mean of 4, 8, 16 is:

$$(4 \times 8 \times 16)^{1/3} = 8$$

A common example of when the geometric mean is the correct choice average is when averaging growth rates, see **compound annual growth rate** [p. 65].

Gilts

Gilts are simply British **government bonds** [p. 160].

A very wide range of gilts are in issue at any given time, with remaining times till maturity of up to 50 years. There are still some irredeemable gilts (ones that will never mature, but pay a perpetual fixed income stream) in issue, but no more are being issued.

One particularly interesting type of gilts are index linked gilts, which are the ultimate in safe securities for British investors. Not only are they government backed (enough, in itself, to classify investments as risk free) but all payments are linked to inflation, which means that even the risk of inflation eating away at the real value of the investment is eliminated. This is an investment that is well suited to investors who need to guarantee their income and do not need high returns.

The **yields to maturity** [p. 350] (also called redemption yields) on gilts are the **risk free rates** [p. 282], over various periods of time, for valuation **models** [p. 140] for British securities and sterling denominated **eurobonds** [p. 126].

Global depositary receipt

A Global Depositary Receipt (GDR) is a security issued in one country that bundles together a number of shares in a company in another country.

GDRs are mostly frequently used by companies that already have a main listing in one country, and want a **secondary listing** [p. 288] in another.

The most common depositary receipts are those issued by non-US companies with a US secondary listing. These are called **ADRs** [p. 14].

Goodwill

Goodwill arises when a company buys another business at a price greater than the value of its assets. The excess of the amount paid over the **NAV** [p. 213] of the acquired business, is shown in the **balance sheet** [p. 28] of the acquiring company.

As goodwill does not have any relationship to future cash flows, but only the past, it is often ignored by investors. The use of profit measures such as **EBITDA** [p. 116] and **EBITA** [p. 116] is widespread. Measures of financial strength such as **gearing** [p. 157] should also exclude goodwill.

The value used in calculating goodwill on acquisition (under **IFRS** [p. 166]) is not the amount shown in the acquired businesses accounts before it is bought but the **fair value** [p. 137]. This is also (necessarily) the value at which assets themselves are shown in the acquirers' accounts.

In the past, companies **amortised** [p. 15] goodwill if it was positive, even adding it to the **profit and loss account (P & L)** [p. 234] over several years if it was negative – either way, the impact was evenly spread over several years.

IFRS [p. 166] 3 now requires companies to add negative goodwill to profits in whole and immediately. Positive goodwill (which is usual) is shown as an asset but is not amortised every year. Companies that have goodwill on their balance sheets are required to review the value of the goodwill annually and, if its value has been impaired, take the amount of the **impairment** [p. 166] as a cost in the P & L. If the value of goodwill is not impaired its can be shown in the balance sheet indefinitely.

Government bonds

Government bonds are **bonds** [p. 37] issued by a government in its own currency.

A government is always able to print more of its own currency with which to pay debt in its own currency. This means that there is no risk that a government will be unable to meet payment on government bonds, and the yield on government bonds is used to determine the **risk free rate** [p. 282] of return.

While there may be some **sovereign risk** [p. 301] that a government may choose to default, this is so unlikely that it can safely be disregarded under *normal* circumstances. Government short term **zero coupon bonds** [p. 350] are called **treasury bills** [p. 328].

British government bonds are called **gilts** [p. 158].

Greater fool

The greater fool principle for buying an over-priced investment is that investors are being sufficiently irrational to justify expecting that it will be possible to sell at a profit to a "greater fool".

The greater fool principle is most often true during **investment bubbles** [p. 41].

Regrettably, the greater fool theory can frequently be right and a good strategy, although a risky one as the foolishness can evaporate (during bubbles this leads to a crash), and prices rapidly fall to more rational levels.

Greeks

The greeks are a series of measures of the rate of change (in mathematical terms, the derivative) of the price of a portfolio or a security with another quantity. They are often used for **hedging** [p. 162].

They are: **delta** [p. 93], **gamma** [p. 155], **rho** [p. 279], **theta** [p. 322] and **vega** [p. 338].

All but vega are Greek letters, which are the symbols used to represent them.

Gross margin

Gross profit [p. 161] divided by sales. It is usually expressed as a percentage.

Gross margin is one of several **profit margin** [p. 253] measures. It shows how much of a mark-up a company is achieving between the cost of what it sells and the selling price.

Because **fixed costs** [p. 143] have to paid out of gross profit, a change in gross margin usually causes a larger change in operating margin and an even larger change in pre-tax profit and **EPS** [p. 122].

Gross premium written

See **premium written** [p. 246].

Gross profit

Gross profit is a very simple measure of profit. It is:

$$sales - \textbf{cost of sales}[\text{p. 75}]$$

Given that it excludes many costs, including all overheads and all financing costs, it is not a good measure of how profitable a company is as a whole, but rather of how much of a mark up it can make on sales.

Changes and trends in gross profit **margin** [p. 253] often give investors useful information.

Gross win

The gross win of a gambling business is the amount it has won (and its customers have lost) over a given period.

As a high proportion of the total amount paid by customers as stakes is returned to them (and never becomes the bookmaker's or casino operator's money as such) the amount of gross win is an important measure of how much money is coming in. Investors should also look at the total amount staked. The latter is a better indicator of the size of an operation and its market share.

The gross win can fluctuate randomly as a result of wins and losses. In case of casinos even a single individual may have a significant effect. Bookmakers can also be badly hit by a few wrong outcomes: events like a string of favourites winning races would be quite damaging to a bookmaker. This can make underlying trends harder to discern.

Growth investing

Growth strategies imply focusing on future rather than current profit. This implies that an investor following the strategy is looking for capital gains rather than income, but the converse is not necessarily true. It can be reasonable to follow a value strategy for capital gains.

Growth investing is one of the two most common **strategies** [p. 179], the other being **value investing** [p. 337]. However, not all growth investors follow similar strategies: the aggressiveness of the risks they take, the type of growth (expansion of existing operations vs new technology) they favour and what indicators they will look at (sales growth or profit growth for example) will vary.

H-share

See **red chip** [p. 268].

Haircut

A haircut is the percentage deducted from the value of a security (usually debt) to determine the maximum amount against which it can be used as collateral.

For example, if a debt security with a market value of £100 has a 5% haircut, it can be used as collateral to raise up to £95.

The amount of the haircut reflects the riskiness of the security. This is not just the risk that the issuer may fail to meet payments, but also the **volatility** [p. 340] of the security over the lifetime of the loan. A security with a high **modified duration** [p. 205] will need a larger haircut.

Some trading systems allow **repos** [p. 274] and similar deals to be matched on criteria that include the size of the haircut required.

Headline EPS

See **adjusted EPS** [p. 7].

Harmonised index of consumer prices

See **HICP** [p. 164].

Hedge

A hedge is a financial strategy that reduces the risks from one security (or other investment) by buying or selling others. A common example is the use of **options** [p. 228] and **futures** [p. 154] to reduce the risks of holding a portfolio of investments.

Foreign exchange futures are also very commonly used by importers and exporters who would otherwise be faced with a very high level of short term **risk from exchange rate fluctuations** [p. 133].

More complex hedges are used and can involve the use of complex financial instruments and large numbers of transactions to provide effective hedges at the lowest cost. See **delta hedging** [p. 93] and **gamma hedging** [p. 156].

Hedge fund

Hedge funds are high risk **collective investment vehicles** [p. 62] that use a variety of techniques including complex **arbitrage** [p. 18] and **short selling** [p. 296]. They are often highly **geared** [p. 157]. They often **hedge** [p. 162] against market movements so their performance depends on their strategies and not market movements.

Hedge fund managers' fees (and individual mangers remuneration) is usually strongly tied to performance. Typical fees are a (fairly high) proportion of the gain.

The growth in both hedge funds and **index trackers** [p. 325], taken together, shows a change in how investors invest. Rather than putting money in moderately **active investments** [p. 6], some investors have switched to favouring a mixture of passive and extremely active investments.

This makes the high fees (compared to ordinary active funds) charged by hedge funds look more reasonable. They are offset by the low fees (compared to active funds) paid on index trackers.

Hedonic price index

A price index adjusted for changes in factors such as the quality of goods using a **hedonic pricing model** [p. 163]. This allows **inflation** [p. 171] to be measured more accurately.

Many indices use hedonic adjustments on some components (e.g. prices of the products of fast changing technology), other quality adjustments on other components, and no adjustment at all to components that are not deemed to require it.

Adjustments for quality are made to a number of widely used indices including the UK's **CPI** [p. 164], its equivalent in other EU countries, and the US CPI.

Hedonic pricing model

A hedonic model of prices is one that decomposes the price of an item into separate components that determine the price.

A simple, and common, example is that the price of a house may depend on its size, its location and other factors. It possible to construct a better **model** [p. 140] (especially when trying to construct a predictive model) by separating these factors.

A hedonic model does not necessarily separate all the factors that could be separated, only those that affect the usefulness to a buyer of what is being sold. A good model should also separate out other factors: for example, a model of house prices should also separate out interest rates.

One use of hedonic models is to adjust measures of inflation. The difference this makes is most significant for products that are not directly comparable with those that were sold in the past because technology has improved. Consider an entry level personal computer bought today compared with one bought ten years ago: the price is not greatly different, but it is much cheaper than the price of a similar computer bought ten years ago.

The adjustment that is needed is more complex than it may appear, as it should reflect the increase in usefulness (strictly speaking **utility** [p. 334]) of a product to customers. A computer that is ten times more faster with ten times as much memory etc. is not necessarily ten times more useful to a customer, and it is the increase in usefulness that is being measured.

Hedonic price factors are not usually of much importance to investors except when doing detailed modelling of product prices. This will only occur when doing very detailed models or when looking at prices that can naturally be decomposed into hedonic elements (such as house prices).

HICP

The Harmonised Index of Consumer Prices (HICP) is an **inflation** [p. 171] measure required by the EU. The HICP for the UK is called the Consumer Price Index (CPI). It is an important measure because the UK's inflation target is based on it. The Bank of England is required to set **interest rates** [p. 177] so as to keep inflation, as measured by the CPI, within a target range.

Historically, the CPI was calculated by the UK's Office of National Statistics (ONS) using a different methodology. The new CPI/HICP replaced the old CPI.

The differences between the CPI and other inflation measures such as the retail price index (RPI) can be important.

- The CPI/HICP excludes costs related to home ownership such as mortgage interest, estate agents' fees and building insurance.

- The RPI excludes costs paid by the highest income (top 4%) households, pensioners dependent on benefits, foreign visitors and students.

These differences reflect the different purposes of the measures. The CPI measures inflation for the purpose of setting economic policy. The primary users of HICP measures are the European Central Bank, the ank of England and other EU central banks. RPI measures the cost of living for ordinary households, and its uses include the index linking of social security payments and index linked **gilts** [p. 158].

Historical PE

A historical **PE** [p. 237] is based on past data (usually published accounts) rather than forecast data. This usually means the last available annual results, or the **trailing twelve months** [p. 328] results.

A historical PE may be (and is most likely to be useful if it is) based on **adjusted EPS** [p. 7].

Although future performance is what matters for valuation, and investors would normally look at **prospective PE** [p. 255] or other forward PE ratios, the historical PE does have the advantage of being usually known with certainty.

It can therefore make a useful starting point for investors; something they can look at before considering growth.

Horizontal integration

Horizontal integration is the widening of a business at the same point in the supply chain. For example, supermarkets that are moving towards selling a larger variety of non-food items are increasing their level of horizontal integration.

The advantages of horizontal integration can lie in reaching the customers (if you are already selling them one thing, use the opportunity to sell more) but can include **economies of scale** [p. 117] in purchasing, logistics and operations.

Businesses can also **integrate vertically** [p. 339].

Hostile takeover bid

A hostile **takeover bid** [p. 317] is one that is made despite the opposition to it expressed by the directors of the target (the company that would be taken over).

There are a number of ways in which the directors of the target may attempt to block the takeover (beyond simply advising shareholders against it) including:

- a **poison pill** [p. 240] to make the takeover more expensive

- Finding a **white knight** [p. 345] (a bidder the directors prefer)

- increasing the target's **market cap** [p. 196] by making acquisitions of its own, paid for by issuing new shares.

Hostile bids often reveal a serious conflict of interest between shareholders and directors. Shareholders are offered a chance to sell their shares, usually at substantially above the market price prior to the bid. Directors stand to lose their jobs.

In theory, directors should recommend a bid unless they have a good chance of getting a better offer, or have very good reason to believe that the market is undervaluing their company. How impartial a decision directors will realistically make is obviously questionable.

Some financial economists have suggested that one of the key reasons for the occurrence of hostile bids is that they offer a way in which to replace incompetent but well entrenched management. This is because institutional shareholders rarely vote against incumbent management, making it hard to replace the directors even if they underperform.

IFRS

An International Financial Reporting Standard (IFRS) is an accounting standard set by the International Accounting Standards Board. IFRS has replaced the older term International Accounting Standard (IAS).

IFRSs are compulsory for **listed companies** [p. 190] in the EU, and most national accounting standards globally are also converging on IFRSs.

IFRSs have been adopted by many other national accounting standards bodies. In the US, the Financial Accounting Standards Board is working towards converging US **GAAP** [p. 154] with IFRSs. Japanese accounting standards have been extensively revised to bring them into line with IFRSs. In the rest of the world IFRSs are either being incorporated into national standards or national standards are being gradually converged with IFRSs.

The advantages to investors is clear. IFRSs make it easier to compare the accounts of companies in different countries. They also incorporate many improvements on most current standards. As things stand, the problem of differences in accounting standards will continue to exist for some time.

US standards will take some years to fully converge with IFRSs and some other countries will take even longer. IFRSs currently allow a number of choices (alternative standards) that will need to be gradually eliminated to provide true uniformity.

Major changes in the UK that resulted from the adoption of IFRSs include:

- the treatment of **goodwill** [p. 159]

- the value of options issued as remuneration being shown as a cost on the face of the **P & L** [p. 234]

- the use of **fair value** [p. 137] rather than **book value** [p. 38] for assets acquired in a **takeover** [p. 317]

- valuation of **embedded options** [p. 120].

Impairment

If the value of an asset, as shown in the balance sheet, exceeds its actual value to a company, then the amount shown in the balance sheet needs to be reduced. This reduction is shown as a cost in the **P & L** [p. 234]. This is impairment.

The treatment of impairment under **IFRSs** [p. 166] is significantly different from the previous treatment under UK **GAAP** [p. 154].

For most assets the test is that the balance sheet value exceeds both the amount for which the asset could be sold *and* the **present value** [p. 220] of the future cashflows it will generate.

In general, the possibility that an asset has been impaired will be examined if the asset has in some way become less useful since it was acquired. There are exceptions to this:

- The value of **goodwill** [p. 159] is subject to an annual review.

- The value of other **intangible assets** [p. 173] that have an indefinite life or are not yet in use is also subject to annual review.

- The value of **stocks** [p. 307] (inventories) must always be stated at the lower of cost and net realisable value (the price at which they could be sold minus the cost of selling).

- Investment properties and certain agricultural assets may be valued at **fair value** [p. 137], in which case the value must always be stated at a current fair value and changes taken through the P & L.

- Financial assets, pension funds and assets held for sale are subject to separate, sometimes quite complex, rules.

From an investor's point of view, impairments are usually one off events and should be treated as **exceptionals** [p. 132]. Goodwill reflects the history of a company and has very little relationship to future cash flows so it should be ignored anyway.

Implied volatility

In order to estimate **volatilities** [p. 340], one approach is to use purely historical data. The alternative is to use the volatility implied by current securities prices.

To see how this works, consider the **Black-Scholes** [p. 36] equation. In order to price an **option** [p. 228] one would simply plug in the time till expiry, the **exercise price** [p. 135], the **price** [p. 331] of the underlying security, the volatility of the underlying, etc. into the equation and calculate a price.

However, as there will usually be a market price for a publicly traded option we can take the price as known, take the volatility as the unknown and then solve the equation for the volatility.

The result is the implied volatility.

This is an estimate based on market prices and is therefore the volatility expected by the market. If the security is correctly priced, as implied by the **efficient markets hypothesis** [p. 118], this should be a good estimate.

However, as with other market price derived data, there are periods during which market prices may be badly wrong (for example, during **investment bubbles** [p. 41]).

In the money

An **option** [p. 228] is said to be in the money (often written"in-the-money") if its **intrinsic value** [p. 179] is positive.

A **call option** [p. 45] is in-the-money if current price of the **underlying asset** [p. 331] is greater than the **exercise price** [p. 135], vice versa for a **put option** [p. 258].

Option value declines as an option goes more deeply into the money, and the intrinsic value becomes comparatively more important.

Income investing

An income investor is one who invests in order to generate an income, rather than for capital gains as a **growth investor** [p. 161] would. An income investor would usually invest in **bonds** [p. 37], high **yield** [p. 107] shares and bond like securities such as **prefs** [p. 244].

The typical income investor is someone who depends on their investments for income, and therefore they generally tend to be conservative and buy low risk investments. However, most investors who are willing to take some risk for a higher income – otherwise they would not invest in anything other than index linked **gilts** [p. 158]!

In the case of shares, income investors will often pick the same investments as **value investors** [p. 337]. This is because dividend levels are usually set at levels a company feels confident it can maintain. So dividends are related to conservative expectations about short term profitability. This means that high yields are a positive signal for value investors.

Valuation measures that income investors are likely to use include **dividend yield** [p. 107] and **dividend cover** [p. 103] for shares, and both **flat yield** [p. 144] and **YTM** [p. 350] for bonds.

However, income investors should not only look at these measures. They will usually need to at least preserve their capital, and they should therefore also look at the measures a growth investor would use.

Income statement

See **P & L** [p. 234].

Incumbent telco

An incumbent telecommunications company is a former monopoly that still has a dominant market share. For example,the incumbent telco in Britain is BT, the former British Telecom.

Incumbent telecoms companies are in a very strong position. Even though their legal **monopolies** [p. 207] have been removed in almost all countries, they still continue to have considerable monopoly power because the infrastructure they have built over the years results in high **barriers to entry** [p. 30]. Without regulation there would also be very strong **network effects** [p. 214].

The result of this is that incumbent telecoms companies are usually very tightly regulated. This means tighter controls on the prices they can charge customers and other networks (e.g. for incoming calls). Because of the monopoly power incumbents have, many regulators (such as **Ofcom** [p. 221] in the UK) also require them to provide access to their network to other telcos as regulated wholesale prices. For example, BT is required to:

- allow others to act as resellers of its telephone lines

- provide ADSL lines to customers of other internet service providers, who pay BT's wholesale arm the same rate as other divisions of BT itself.

- allow **local loop unbundling** [p. 191]

- operate parts of its business on an arms length basis to ensure they do not favour other BT businesses.

All these are done at regulated prices and terms that aim to allow other operators to compete with the incumbent.

Index

A stock market index (such as the **FTSE 100** [p. 150], **Dow Jones** [p. 109], Nikkei, Hang Seng, etc.) tracks the movement of a market as a whole. Other indices track the performance of **sectors** [p. 288], regions and different classes of security.

The basic data used to calculate an index are securities prices, but the calculation of an index means weighting price changes appropriately to reflect company size and the availability of securities to investors.

Indices are often used as **benchmarks** [p. 33] of fund and portfolio performance. This can encourage cautious money managers to **closet track** [p. 61] the indices. As well as providing an indicator of markets, indices are used as the basis for constructing **tracker funds** [p. 325]. There are also **derivatives** [p. 96] whose value depends on indices (see **CFD** [p. 71]).

Index calculation

Most **equity** [p. 123] **indices** [p. 169] track the change in aggregate **market cap** [p. 196] of the shares included in that index. The number is arrived at by dividing the total market cap by a divisor. This divisor is a number that was set (to provide a convenient index level such as a 100 or 1000) when the index was started and which is periodically adjusted.

Another way of looking at this is that the change in the index is the **weighted average** [p. 25] of the changes in the share prices of companies in the index, the weights used being the market caps of the companies.

Most indices, including almost all the **FTSE indices** [p. 150], are calculated this way.

Older indices were calculated more simply by adding share prices together and then dividing by a fixed factor. The effect of this is that the index is weighted by share price. A movement in a higher priced share will have a greater impact than a movement of the same proportionate size in a lower priced share, regardless of the relative size of the companies.

The obvious incorrectness of this compared to market cap weighting means that it is now rarely used. The only index of any importance calculated this way is the **Dow Jones Industrial Average** [p. 109]. This is a very good reason to use another index (such as the S & P 500) instead of the Dow.

To keep the indices meaningful, adjustments are made when a company issues new shares or purchases shares and when companies are added or deleted from an index.

Important indices

- FTSE 100: an index that includes the 100 largest UK **listed companies** [p. 190] which covers about 80% of UK market cap.

- **FTSE 250** [p. 151]: the next 250 largest companies

- FTSE 350: includes all companies in the above two indices: covers about 90% of total UK market cap

- FTSE **Techmark** [p. 319]: a technology index in which companies are included based on a broad definition of technology that includes pharmaceutical and medical device manufacturers as well as IT, electronics and engineering companies

- FTSE Eurotrack: a family of indices at cover European markets as a whole

- CAC-40: the main (most widely used) index for the Paris borse

- DAX: the most widely used German index

- **Dow Jones** [p. 109]: the most widely used US index, but badly flawed

- S & P 500: constituents are the 500 largest US listed companies

- Russell 2000: a broad US index

- Nikkei:the main index for the Tokyo stock exchange

- Hang Seng: the main index for Hong Kong

- **MSCI** [p. 210]: a family of indices most widely used for **emerging markets** [p. 121]

Index tracker

See **tracker fund** [p. 325].

Inflation

Inflation is a deceptively simple concept: as everyone already knows, it is the rate at which prices rise. However the accurate definition and measurement of inflation is not that easy.

There are far too many goods and services produced in and imported by an economy for it to be feasible to gather data on the prices and sales volumes of every single one. Inflation is therefore usually measured as the percentage change in a representative basket of goods.

It are also difficulties in deciding how to treat financial services. For example, higher mortgage interest payments would be an extra expenditure for many people. However, strictly speaking, they represent economic rents (transfers of wealth) rather than payments for services, and therefore should be excluded from inflation measures.

In the UK, a number of different inflation measures are published by the Office of National Statistics. These include the consumer price index (which excludes mortgage interest payments and certain other housing related costs) and the retail price index (which includes them).

Another difficulty is that the products available at different times may be different in ways that make direct price comparisons less meaningful. The most common problem is that the quality of products is often improved by advancing technology: consider a comparison of the cost of a song on CD with that of a vinyl recording from thirty years previously. The (partial and rather difficult) solution is the use of **hedonic price indices** [p. 163].

Negative inflation is called **deflation** [p. 92].

Insider trading

Making investment decisions using information that should be confidential is called insider trading. It is a criminal offence in most countries, although the effectiveness of enforcement varies from country to country. The reason it is regarded as sufficiently harmful to merit strong deterrents are:

- It is unfair on investors who do not have access to the information.

- It may deter investors from participating in the market at all, undermining the basic purpose of markets, which is to allow companies to raise capital.

- It may destabilise markets by encouraging rumours.

Not all information that is not publicly available is likely to be defined as insider trading, but anything that can reasonably be expected to have a significant effect on a company's share price is. The source of the information and the way in which is was acquired also affects the legality of trading on it.

Investors should be cautious about using any information that is not publicly available: not only may it put them in jail, but rumours and "tips" are often fabricated by those trying to manipulate the markets.

Investors can sometimes, perfectly legally, get an edge over others by ensuring that they make use of all possible sources of information.

- Not all published information is necessarily used by all investors.

- Information that is not technically **price sensitive** [p. 248] may be useful but not well circulated. A frequently useful example is information of a technical nature rather than related to finances or sales.

- Information related to other companies (other than the one whose shares are being dealt in) may be useful but would not be inside information.

This means that investors may be able to legally gain an edge by doing more research than others and digging up information that is not generally known. In particular doing research on, and understanding, sectors and industries as well as companies can tell investors a lot.

Investors who do have access to confidential information are well advised to be cautious and to get appropriate professional advice when in doubt.

Institutional broking

Institutional stock broking is the provision of stock broking services to fund managers and other financial institutions.

Clients usually get access to **sell side research** [p. 291] **bundled** [p. 43] with broking services, with the level of access dependent on how much business they give the broker.

Clients who give brokers any significant level of business will get:

- access to research published on paper and in electronic form

- contact with sell side analysts

- invitations to investor conferences which offer chances to meet many companies in a particular sector in at one event

- updates from institutional sales people (brokers) who will sometimes be sector specialists very familiar with their firm's research

- in some cases, various forms of **soft commission** [p. 299]

- increasingly, access to systems that interface with the client's own systems to enable **straight through processing** [p. 309] etc.

Institutional clients are in a significantly stronger position in dealing with a broker than are private clients. Not only do they have more business to offer, they are also rarely as dependent on the broker. They will use several brokers, who are thus constantly competing to for their business.

Fund managers will often use a mixture of major brokers (those owned by the big investment banks) and smaller "boutique" brokers who are niche specialists (such as smaller companies or a particular sector).

There is a significant risk that institutional broking will be changed by regulators and clients pushing to unbundle broking and research. This may also open the way for independent research houses to take market share in research, while broking becomes more **commoditised** [p. 63] and therefore lower **margin** [p. 253]. That said, the biggest brokers are very well established as providers of research and will not be easily dislodged.

Intangible assets

Assets that do not have a definite existence are called intangible assets. They have neither a physical form nor give their owner definite financial rights.

Intangible fixed assets are shown separately on the **balance sheet** [p. 28] from **tangible** [p. 318] **fixed assets** [p. 142].

Securities, financial instruments, bank deposits and debt are tangible assets *not* intangible, although, as they are often current assets, the distinction may not need to be made anyway.

Under **IFRS** [p. 166], IAS 38 requires that an intangible asset, should:

- be identifiable

- be controlled by the company

- increase future profits

Different rules apply to **goodwill** [p. 159]. Although it is an intangible asset it has unique characteristics. It is covered in separate standard (IFRS 3).

In more detail:

An intangible asset should be separately identifiable (the company can sell it, licence it, etc).

Intangible assets can arise from a purchase (for example, through the purchase of a patent) or be generated within the organisation (for example, through expenditure on **R & D** [p. 261]). Something that can be purchased can obviously be identified. If a profit making enterprise purchases something it should be in the expectation that it will generate cash flows.

If an intangible is created within a company rather than purchased, the requirements are slightly more complicated. There are few intangibles than justify their cost being **capitalised** [p. 49] and shown on the balance sheet. Although companies talk of "investing" in brands, advertising and marketing expenditure go straight to the P & L for good reasons. The role such expenditure plays in generating cash flows is too indirect and uncertain to justify treating what it creates as an asset.

There are special rules for R & D costs.

It is usual to either **amortise** [p. 15] the cost of an intangible asset over each year of its life, or to carry our regular reviews and show **impairment** [p. 166] as and when necessary. The latter is the required treatment for goodwill. Amortisation is the required treatment for assets (such as patents) that have a limited life.

Intellectual property

A broad range of **intangible assets** [p. 173] are lumped together by the rather nebulous term intellectual property. It always covers patents, copyrights and trademarks. It is sometimes expanded further to include any know-how and trade secrets over which a company has some sort of legal claim.

The term is much beloved of lawyers specialising the area, and of companies that claim to have a lot of it. From an investor's point of view the important things are:

- how much cash these generate

- whether they can reduce risk by raising **barriers to entry** [p. 30].

The three main types of intellectual property granted by law (patents, copyright and trademarks) have very different characteristics.

Certainty

The ownership and validity of copyrights is usually clear. Trademarks are a little less certain because they can be lose through becoming generic terms in common use, however most financially important trademarks are safe enough for this to be a minor concern.

Patents are highly uncertain. Apparently valuable patents are frequently found to be invalid by the courts. There is also a positive uncertainty about patents and a patent portfolio may be more valuable than is realised. Companies frequently fail to enforce valuable patents. This may happen accidentally or deliberately. A company may simply fail to realise that an idea it has patented has, either through independent re-invention or through copying, been put to use elsewhere.

A company may also deliberately "submarine" a patent. This means not enforcing a patent (or even drawing attention to its existence) in the hope that the idea it covers will become widely used. Once it is in wide use the patent holder is in a much stronger position to demand royalties, especially if **network effects** [p. 214] have entrenched a particular technology covered by the patent.

Although patents are a matter of public record, the volume of current patents means checking these is extremely difficult.

These uncertainties are one of the reasons the cross-licensing* of patent portfolios is important in certain industries. They protect participants from the consequences of accidental breaches of others patents, and also erect **barriers to entry** [p. 30].

Life span

Patents have a limited life. Many patented products, such as drugs, may take years to reach the market. This means that many cash flow streams derived from patents last for less than twenty years, and a high proportion of these cash flows have only a few years to run. This is a particularly important in the pharmaceutical sector.

Copyright on recent works (created in the last few decades) lasts long enough to be safely regarded as perpetual from a financial point of view. However, a few companies have "libraries" of older material whose limited remaining time in copyright may need to be considered.

The life span of trademarks is more complex. They potentially last perpetually, but, as mentioned above, they can be lost.

Cost

Copyright is automatic on the creation of a copyrightable work and it does not require registration. Trademarks and patents are expensive to register. Patent litigation can also be very expensive, and the effects on the loser's business can be disastrous.

International variations

Copyright and trademark law are fairly similar in most developed economies. Patent law varies more – the US allows patents on business methods, and a far wider range of patents on software than other countries.

Economic effects

It is interesting, if not particularly relevant to investment decisions, that patent and copyright laws are the subject of considerable controversy, largely because there is little actual evidence what economic effect they have. What all involved do agree on is that the effects are large and far-reaching!

---

*In their simplest form, cross-licensing agreements can be summarised as "you get a license on all my patents in return for giving me a license on all your patents".

Inter-dealer broker

An inter-dealer broker acts as an intermediary between other participants in capital markets (brokers and **market makers** [p. 197]) who wish to buy or sell large quantities without revealing their identities.

Large inter-dealer brokers deal in huge volumes of securities (albeit at low commission rates). They have trading systems similar in scale and functionality to those used by stock exchanges, but inter-dealer brokers serve a more restricted market of professional investors.

Inter-dealer brokers may also be able to deal in securities and **derivatives** [p. 96] that are not traded on exchanges.

Interest cover

Interest cover is a measure of the adequacy of a company's profits relative to interest payments on its debt. The lower the interest cover, the greater the risk that profit (before interest) will become insufficient to cover interest payments. It is:

$$\frac{\text{EBIT}[\text{p. } 115]}{net\ interest\ paid}$$

It is a better measure of the gearing effect of debt on profits than **gearing** [p. 157] itself.

A value of more than 2 is normally considered reasonably safe, but companies with very volatile earnings may require an even higher level, whereas companies that have very stable earnings, such as utilities, may well be very safe at a lower level. Similarly, cyclical companies at the bottom of their cycle may well have a low interest cover but investors who are confident of recovery may not be overly concerned by the apparent risk.

If a company has **capitalised** [p. 49] interest, then it will not show the capitalised interest as interest paid in the **profit and loss** [p. 234] account (P &L).

When calculating interest cover capitalised interest should be included. The number used should be net interest paid as shown on the P & L plus interest capitalised. This is one of the problems avoided by using **cash interest cover** [p. 53].

Interest margin

Interest margin is:

$$\frac{interest\ income - interest\ expense}{average\ interest\ earning\ assets}$$

as a percentage.

The interest earning assets are essentially various forms of lending.

This is essentially the **gross profit** [p. 161] that is earned by a bank on its lending.

Interest margin is very similar to **interest spread** [p. 179].

Interest rate

Although interest rates may appear to be straightforward, they may be quoted and calculated in a number of different ways. This is why regulators have required the use of some standards, such as **AER** [p. 16], and financial markets have evolved others (such as **YTM** [p. 350]).

The **risk-free rate** [p. 282] is important to investors as it is used for valuation.

It is often useful for investors to think in terms of **real** [p. 265] rather than **nominal interest rates** [p. 216].

Some investments pay **floating interest rates** [p. 144] rather than fixed interest.

Interest rate parity

According to interest rate parity the difference between the (risk free) interest rates paid on two currencies should be equal to the differences between the **spot** [p. 303] and **forward** [p. 145] rates.

For example, the relationship for US dollars and pounds sterling is:

$$\frac{1 + r_{\pounds}}{1 + r_{\$}} = \frac{\pounds/\$_f}{\pounds/\$_s}$$

where $r_{\pounds}$ is the sterling interest rate (till the date of the forward),
$r_{\$}$ is the dollar interest rate,
$\pounds/\$_f$ is the forward sterling to dollar rate,
$\pounds/\$_s$ is the spot sterling to dollar rate

Unless interest rates are very high or the period considered is long, this is a very good approximation:

$$r_{\pounds} = r_{\$} + f$$

where f is the forward premium: $\frac{\pounds/\$_f}{\pounds/\$_s} - 1$

The above relationship is derived from assuming that **covered interest arbitrage** [p. 77] opportunities should not last.

Assuming **uncovered interest arbitrage** [p. 331] leads us to a slightly different relationship:

$$r = r_2 + E[\Delta S]$$

where $E[\Delta S]$ is the expected change is exchange rates.

As the forward rate will be the market expectation of the change in rates, the two equations are equivalent – unless one is speculating on market expectations being wrong.

If interest rate parity is violated, then an **arbitrage opportunity** [p. 18] exists. The simplest example of this is what would happen if the forward rate was the same as the spot rate but the interest rates were different, then investors would:

1. borrow in the currency with the lower rate

2. convert the cash at spot rates

3. enter into a forward contract to convert the cash plus the expected interest at the same rate

4. invest the money at the higher rate

5. convert back through the forward contract

6. repay the principal and the interest, knowing the latter will be less than the interest received.

Therefore, we can expect interest rate parity to apply.

Interest rate risk

Interest rate risk is simply the **risk** [p. 281] to which a portfolio or institution is exposed because future **interest rates** [p. 177] are uncertain.

Bond prices are obviously interest rate sensitive. If rates rise, then the **present value** [p. 88] of a bond will fall sharply. This can also be thought of in terms of market rates: if interest rates rise, then the price of a bond will have to fall for the **yield to maturity** [p. 350] to match the new market rates.

The longer the **duration of a bond** [p. 113] the more sensitive it will be to movements in interest rates.

Shares are also sensitive to interest rates, again it is obvious that if interest rates change (and other things remain equal, which the **Fisher effect** [p. 141] suggests may not be the case) then **DCF** [p. 88] valuations will fall. In addition, the profits of highly **geared** [p. 157] companies will be significantly affected by the level of their interest payments.

Banks can also have significant interest rate risk: for example they may have depositors locked into fixed rates and borrowers on **floating rates** [p. 144] or vice versa.

Interest rate risk can be hedged using **swaps** [p. 313] and interest rate based **derivatives** [p. 96].

Ways in which interest rate risk can be controlled include:

- investment in **floating rate** [p. 144] rather than **fixed rate** [p. 143] securities

- investing only in securities due to mature in the short term

- buying interest rate **derivatives** [p. 96].

Interest spread

Interest spread is the difference between the average lending rate and the average borrowing rate for a bank or other financial institution. It is:

$$\frac{interest\ income}{interest\ earning\ assets} - \frac{interest\ expense}{interest\ bearing\ liabilities}$$

This is very similar to **interest margin** [p. 176]. If a bank's lending was exactly equal to its borrowings (i.e. deposits plus other borrowing) the two numbers would be identical. In reality, bank also has its shareholder's funds available to lend, but at the same time its lending is constrained by **reserve requirements** [p. 274].

Changes in the spread are an indicator of profitability as the spread is where a bank makes its money.

Intrinsic value

The intrinsic value of an **option** [p. 228] is the current price of the **underlying security** [p. 331] minus the **exercise price** [p. 135]. It is the amount of money a holder of the derivative would make if the option was exercised immediately (even if the option is not actually exerciseable immediately).

The value of an option is likely to be different from the intrinsic value, the difference is the called the **option value** [p. 229].

In general, the higher the intrinsic value of an option the lower the option value as it becomes less likely that the option will not be exercised.

Inventory

See **stock** [p. 307].

Investment strategy

An investment strategy is an approach to choosing investments. This can also be called an investment style. Different investment strategies reflect investors' varying objectives, timescales and risk tolerance.

In some financial economics contexts "investment strategy" is used to mean a choice of investments. This usage is synonymous with the word portfolio.

The commonest strategies are **growth** [p. 161] and **value investing** [p. 337]. The former focuses on picking companies with opportunities to grow in the long term, whereas the latter prefers companies that are undervalued relative to their present profits or cash flows.

Because companies with strong cash flows are also those able to pay high dividends, investors looking for an immediate income tend to use some form of value investing.

Another common strategy, often used unwittingly, is **momentum investing** [p. 205]: buying whatever is going up, selling whatever is going down. The danger is that it leads investors into buying already overvalued shares and selling bargains. Momentum investors drive bubbles and crashes. It can be useful in conjunction with another strategy as it help investors time decisions, so that they buy or sell when the market is moving in their direction.

Contrarian [p. 71] investing is the opposite of momentum investing, doing the opposite of what other investors do. A contrarian would buy on a slump and sell in a boom, and would look to buy out of favour stocks and sell those that have risen sharply. It is also worth considering being contrarian on strategy: at times when everyone wants growth stocks you are more likely to be able to find opportunities in value stocks and vice-versa.

There are also many mechanical stock picking strategies, and elaborate techniques based on price charts. There is no evidence that **"technical analysis"** [p. 319] works. If it does work it should be possible to show statistical evidence for it.

Other mechanical strategies range from the very simple to the very complex. Again there is very little evidence that these strategies can allow you to perform better than the market (or an index fund) would have done, but for those with large portfolios it may be cheaper.

One of the most interesting mechanical strategies is the **Dogs of the Dow** [p. 108] (together with variants of it). It is also one of the simplest and cheapest.

There are also many short-term trading strategies. These tend to be high risk require a lot of work. Aggressive trading, and **day trading** [p. 87] in particular has made many people rich – it has also ruined many people. For the vast majority of people one or another buy and hold strategy is best.

Investment style

See **investment strategy** [p. 179].

Investment trust

An investment trust is a company whose sole business is to manage the investments it owns. The management of an investment trust may be employees of the trust (in which case it is called a self-managed trust) or, more commonly, may be an external fund management company.

The use of the term trust is slightly misleading (and largely confined to Britain and the Commonwealth) as there is no trustee involved. It reflects the historical origins of investment trusts.

The shares of investment trusts are **listed** [p. 190] and therefore they are bought and sold through a broker, like the shares of any listed company. There is usually an annual management charge that is paid out of the investment trust's assets.

Unlike **OEICs** [p. 221], investment trusts are closed ended so the amount of money in the fund does not change; investors cannot withdraw money from an investment trust, or add to the money in the trust: they buy or sell its shares.

This means that investment trusts usually trade a discount to the value of their assets. A particularly well regarded trust may trade at a premium, one about which the market is very pessimistic is likely to trade at a large discount. The discounts can lead to an extra gain if the trust is wound up.

More information (obviously not from a particularly disinterested perspective) can be obtained from the Association of Investment Trust Companies.

Investor relations

Investor relations is the sum of a company's activities aimed at providing investors with information about the company.

The most important part of investor relations is the provision of published information that is available to all investors. This is important because companies must ensure that **price sensitive** [p. 248] information is made available to all investor at the same time.

This means that whenever any price sensitive information is to be revealed it must be publicly announced. This usually means through **RNS** [p. 282] or its equivalent on other exchanges.

Companies also release a lot of other information publicly. Company websites, in particular, can have a huge range of useful information, although they vary.

Companies also have presentations (made either by management or investor relations staff) to which **analysts** [p. 291] are invited. These are most frequent after results announcements.

Presentations are also commonly made at investor conferences organised by brokerages. Again, these are attended by analysts and fund managers. Some companies make a practice of visiting brokerages and making presentations in order to reach the widest possible audience.

Many companies also arrange guided visits to their operations for analysts. This gives the company a chance to explain their operations more clearly to investors – for example, a retailer can show analysts their **format** [p. 275] in operation and explain why they do things the way they do.

Clearly access to presentations and company visits is only available to a small number of people. While no price sensitive information is disclosed, the accumulation of a lot of non-price sensitive information, and the chance to get an insight into how a company's management are thinking, can make a significant difference to how an analyst views a company.

The issue has been partially addressed by technology: for example, most companies now make presentations available on their websites. However this still leaves private investors at a disadvantage to analysts. The latter get a chance to meet management, visit operations and ask questions.

The most privileged group of investors are those who already have substantial shareholdings in a company. They can hold the management to account and directors are well aware of this.

Even if large shareholders are able to get price sensitive information (for example, because a large shareholder is on the board of directors) **insider trading** [p. 171] rules restrict their use of it.

IPO

An Initial Public Offer (IPO) is the sale of shares to the public as a precursor to the shares trading on an exchange for the first time.

An IPO is not the only way in which a company can start trading in its securities, but it is the most common for shares. The shares offered in an IPO are usually a new issue, but they may also be shares held by major shareholders, or a mixture of both.

The process of the IPO can vary but it will involve some sort of application process for shares. The price at which the shares are sold will either be pre-determined or determined by an auction process. An IPO also usually needs a mechanism for deciding how to distribute shares when there are too many applications (the offer is "over-subscribed"). This **allotment** [p. 13] may be done by pro-rata allocation or by using an auction process.

The terms of any particular IPO are described in detail in the offer document. In fact the level of **disclosure** [p. 98] available during an IPO tends to be extremely good, and can be better than that of similar listed companies (or the company's own disclosure post-IPO). This results from the need to compensate for the lack of a track record as a listed company.

An IPO would usually be priced low enough to ensure that the entire offer is taken, and they are also usually **underwritten** [p. 331].

The fees paid to advisers and underwriters for an IPO are substantial and, along with **mergers and acquisition** [p. 5], they are a major source of revenue for investment banks, especially when **bullish markets** [p. 42] and high valuations tempt private companies to list.

Another major expense of an IPO, especially for smaller companies, arises from the need to publish a **prospectus** [p. 255].

IRR

Internal rate of return (IRR) is a rate of return on an investment. The IRR of an investment is the interest rate that will give it a **net present value** [p. 220] of zero.

The IRR is calculated by a trial and error process

Starting with a guess at the IRR, r, the process is as follows:

1. The NPV is calculated using r.

2. If the NPV is close to zero then r is the IRR.

3. If the NPV is positive r is increased.

4. If the NPV is negative r is decreased.

5. Go back to step 1.

It is generally preferable to use **NPV** [p. 220] to IRR to make investment decisions. A smaller investment with a better rate of return will have a higher IRR, but investors' total wealth would be increased more by making a larger investment with a lower IRR but a higher total gain.

This is only a problem where investments are limited in size (not scalable) and mutually exclusive, so it is not a concern for securities valuation. However, the only common use of IRR for securities valuation is the use of **yield to maturity** [p. 350] for bonds.

IRR has even worse failings. If the investment has negative cash flows following positive cash flows, then there may be more than one IRR, or even none at all. While it is possible to use more complex procedures to work around this, the best thing to do is to simply not use IRR. If used, it should not be used for any pattern of cash flows that ever changes from positive to negative.

Some of the failings of IRR are addressed by **MIRR** [p. 204].

Islamic banking

Some of the principles of Islamic banking are similar to more general **ethical investment** [p. 125]. Others are related to avoiding the use of interest payments and speculation.

Banking without the payment of interest creates complexities and requires a range of products designed with this ban in mind. The ban on interest is linked to the disapproval of usury. This is something Islam shares with many other religions, including Christianity and Judaism. However the strict Islamic prohibition is stronger, in that it bans all interest, not just usurious (exploitative or unfair) interest rates.

Islamic banks replace interest payments with profit shares. Depositors get a share of the profits earned by their deposits.

The profits come from hire-purchase and leasing, sale and buy-back arrangements, service charges, purchases on behalf of a customer who later pays the bank back with a agreed mark-up.

There are other restrictions, very similar to those in any type of ethical investing. This means not investing in non-Islamic businesses such as alcohol, pork, non-Islamic banking etc.

As well as specialist Islamic banks, many major banks have Islamic banking operations.

ISIN

An International Securities Identification Number (ISIN) is an alphanumeric code that uniquely identifies a security.

An ISIN consists of a two character country code, a nine digit number and one check digit.

Each country where ISIN numbers are used has a single national numbering agency to assign numbers using that country code. This guarantees that the same ISIN cannot be issued to two different securities.

ISINs are not the only codes used to identify securities. They are not even always the most useful. One problem is that nine digit numbers are not very memorable. For this reason, most exchanges have other coding systems that are easier for human beings to use (to call up quotes or enter trades) while the computers that handle clearing and settlement are more likely to use ISIN codes.

Other important codes are **TIDM** [p. 322] (used for UK **listed securities** [p. 190]), **SEDOL** [p. 291] (London Stock Exchange Codes), CUISIP (the US and Canadian equivalent of a SEDOL code), Reuters codes, and Bloomberg codes.

For example Marks and Spencer's **ordinary shares** [p. 123] have the TIDM MKS, Reuters code MKS.L, Bloomberg code MKS LN, SEDOL 3127489 and ISIN GB0031274896. It also has an **ADR** [p. 14] with a CUISIP of 570912105.

It can be seen from this example that Reuters and Bloomberg codes are based on the EPIC together with an extension to identify the London market, and that the ISIN for UK companies is based on the SEDOL together with a country code (GB) and a check digit (the 6 at the end in the example above).

Joint venture

A joint venture (JV) is a business that is jointly controlled by two (usually) or more parties by explicit agreement.

Companies that have stakes in joint ventures will usually **consolidate** [p. 68] them by showing a proportionate share of the profits and assets of the joint ventures in the consolidated accounts.

IFRSs also allow joint ventures to be consolidated in the same way as **associates** [p. 23].

The joint ventures of **listed companies** [p. 190] will almost always be incorporated themselves.

The classification of a business as a joint venture requires that there be an explicit agreement to share control. This means that joint ventures will almost always be clearly labelled as such from the start.

If one company has outright control of a business, then it is a **subsidiary** [p. 311], not a JV.

If no one company has outright control, several parties have significant stakes and there is no agreement over control then it is likely to be an associate.

Junk bond

A junk bond is a bond that has a **credit rating** [p. 78] that falls below the investment grades.

Many funds are restricted to investment grade debt instruments and cannot invest in junk bonds. Junk bonds are obviously higher risk but offer correspondingly better returns. Many junk bonds, despite the name, are not hugely high risk investments. At the bottom end are very high risk bonds that trade at a fraction of their **face value** [p. 137] – with correspondingly spectacular gains to be made in the unlikely event that payments are made.

The highest risk bonds are obviously those in the lowest grades, which indicate that payments have actually been defaulted on.

Despite the name junk bonds can be a reasonable investment to make in the context of a **diversified portfolio** [p. 103], as well as for speculators.

KPI (Key performance indicators)

Key performance indicators (KPIs) are a set of critical measures of the performance of a business. The term is most commonly disclosed by mobile telecoms companies who regularly (in the UK, usually quarterly) release KPI numbers.

The KPIs used of the UK mobile operators include measures of both customer base and financial performance. The numbers relating to customer base are usually:

1. number of active customers (excluding pre-pay connections that have been unused for some time)

2. number of new customers

3. **churn** [p. 57]

4. **SAC** [p. 310]

5. **ARPU** [p. 26]

6. total revenues.

Breakdowns of some numbers (usually revenues and ARPU) by voice and data are given in KPI announcements, as are breakdowns by types of customer (contract and pre-pay) and by country or region.

KPIs are extremely useful and often disclose numbers that have more impact on the value of a company than the final results do.

Labour intensive

A labour intensive business is one in which the main cost is that of labour, and it is high compared to sales or value added. The obvious contrast is with a **capital intensive** [p. 47] business where the cost of capital assets is the main cost.

A labour intensive business is likely to have a high level of **fixed costs** [p. 143], although this can vary considerably. Labour costs are never completely fixed, but reducing the size of a workforce is usually expensive, as is hiring people when (if!) sales increase again. This, at the very least, means that the salaries of permanent employees are not a variable cost in the short term.

A labour intensive business will obviously be exposed to wage increases. This can also be tricky to forecast as wage bills are influenced by both economic and industry specific factors. The extent to which any company is exposed to this risk, and the extend to which costs are fixed

Just a capital intensive business may attempt to reduce **operational gearing** [p. 227] by, for example, leasing or renting assets, a labour intensive one may try to reduce operational gearing by **outsourcing** [p. 232] or automation.

Law of one price

The law of one price states that two portfolios that will produce exactly the same cash flows in the future must have the same value to start with.

This is a less demanding requirement than the non-existence of **dominant trading strategies** [p. 109] or no **arbitrage** [p. 18]. It is nonetheless useful in developing some parts of financial theory.

If there are no dominant trading strategies the law of one price holds but it is possible for dominant trading strategies to exist despite the law of one price holding.

As with arbitrage and dominant trading strategies we would expect the law of one one price to hold. If it did not hold, then market forces should bring prices back into line. No one would buy the more expensive portfolio if the cheaper one would produce the same cash flows, therefore the price of the constituents of the more expensive portfolio would come down.

However, there are occasional examples of failures of the law of one price and the existence of persistent **arbitrage** [p. 18] opportunities.

Leveraged buy-out (LBO)

A leveraged buy-out (LBO) is an **acquisition** [p. 5] that is largely funded by debt. LBOs are often used by **private equity firms** [p. 252] as a way in which to make large acquisitions that they would not otherwise have the resources for.

The type of debt depends on the circumstances in which the money is raised. One method is the issue of **bonds** [p. 37] by a company set up especially to carry out the acquisition. The aim will be to repay the bonds with the cash flows of the target.

If the bid fails the acquisition vehicle may not enough money to repay the bonds. The default rate on LBO bonds is high: these are very much **junk bonds** [p. 185].

LBOs also frequently use bank debt, borrowings form other financial institutions, and **mezzanine** [p. 201] finance. A single LBO (especially a large one) may use several types of debt.

Once an LBO is completed, the result is a highly **geared** [p. 157] business. This means that a good target for an LBO would have strong stable cashflows, low levels of existing debt and a strong **balance sheet** [p. 28] (assets to back the new debt).

A successful LBO also usually requires an exit strategy. Many LBO acquisitions have been broken up and sold, so a large part of the impact of those LBOs was creating shareholder value by breaking up a conglomerate. This was particularly true at the time LBOs first became common in the 1980s. Although LBOs occurred before then, the technique was popularised in the 70s and 80s by American private equity firms such as Kohlberg Kravis Roberts.

Other possible exit strategies include an **IPO** [p. 182] or a trade sale (a sale to another company in the industry). An intermediate step, especially if the acquirer is able to improve the operations of the acquired company, may be to further increase gearing to **return capital** [p. 276].

LFL

See **like-for-like** [p. 188].

Libor

The London interbank offered rate (Libor) and is the rate of interest at which banks in London are willing to lend to other banks.

Banking in London takes place in a huge range of currencies. Libor rates are available for many of them. Libor is often used as a benchmark to fix **floating interest rates** [p. 144].

The Libor rate most commonly used as a benchmark is that calculated by the British Bankers Association (BBA). A number of banks report their rates to the BBA and a number based on these is released to the market daily.

The BBA publishes daily Libor rates, but the latest rates are only available through subscription information services.

LIFO

Last in first out (LIFO) is a method of valuing **stocks (inventory)** [p. 307] for accounting purposes. Stocks issued (for sale or further processing) are assumed to be the most recent purchases, the opposite assumption to that made by **FIFO** [p. 138].

The advantage of using LIFO is that the prices used to calculated the cost of sales, and therefore the **gross profit** [p. 161] number, are more recent: and therefore more closely reflect their economic value.

Given positive inflation, LIFO reduces profits (as the most recent cost goes to the profit and loss account) and it tends to understate the value of stocks in the balance sheet. Under deflation the opposite is true.

Like-for-like

The term like-for-like (LFL) growth has a fairly well defined meaning in retail and similar sectors. It has a less well defined meaning in some other sectors

Retailers

In the context of retailers, the term like-for-like growth, means growth after to the stripping out of the effects of expansion and shop closures. Most companies in the **FTSE** [p. 150] general retailers and food & drug retailers sectors **disclose** [p. 98] like-for-like numbers – at least like-for-like sales growth.

Like-for-like growth is usually calculated by measuring the increase or decrease at stores that have been open for at least two years.

It is not uncommon for the definition of like-for-like to vary: for example, to exclude shops that have been significantly expanded or refitted, or excluding new openings over different time scales. The phrase "same store sales" has a similar meaning but it definition tends to vary more.

Other sectors

The term LFL is also used in other sectors. With pubs and restaurants the meaning is the same. In other sectors it may refer to stripping out the effects of other distorting factors such as exchange rate fluctuations and acquisitions or disposals or whole businesses. In some cases it may have a similar meaning to **organic growth** [p. 230].

One common adjustment is the exclusion of sales of newly launched products or services. Like-for-like means a measure of growth from the business as it was. For example, a media company may exclude newly launched publications or channels, or a manufacturer may exclude new products.

Limit order

A limit order is one that is given with a price limit.

An investor wishing to buy or sell securities places a limit order for a certain number of shares at a certain price. If an investor is selling it will be a minimum price, if an investor is buying it will be a maximum price.

A limit order is valid for a certain lifetime, after which it expires.

If a limit order is matched against another limit order at a different price (e.g. a buy at 100p can match a sell at 99p), then the market's trading rules will determine which price the trade takes place at.

In most markets a limit order may be partly filled, if there are insufficient shares available/asked for within the price limit. There are other (less commonly used) order types for investors who wish to trade only certain minimum quantities etc.

Limit orders are widely used for dealing in shares that trade through **matched bargain** [p. 198] systems. They are less useful for share that trade through **market makers** [p. 197] although they are still useful for investors who want to buy only if the price falls or sell only if the price rises.

Private investors investing in reasonably liquid securities will usually find the convenience of a **market order** [p. 197] preferable.

Limited liability

Shareholders are not liable for the debts of a company they own shares in (with certain very limited exceptions which are not relevant to shareholders in **listed companies** [p. 190]). This is limited liability.

Apart from the obvious consequence (shareholders cannot lose more than what they actually put into buying shares), limited liability greatly affects the valuation of both **equity** [p. 123] and **debt** [p. 37].

Limited liability means that debt holders have no recourse other than to a company's own assets (except where explicit guarantees have been given, or other special circumstances exist). This simplifies the valuation of debt, although it reduces its actual value.

Limited liability also creates an **agency** [p. 11] problem by creating a conflict of interest between shareholders and debt holders. Shareholders can, in effect, walk away from a failed company, leaving creditors with its assets. This means that by following a more profitable but riskier business strategy shareholders can benefit at the expense of debt holders.

For the same reason, limited liability also means that shares can (although they rarely are) be valued as options – shareholders can pay debt and keep the profits, or they can walk away (in effect, exercise a **put option** [p. 228]) leaving the assets and business of a company (the **underlying security** [p. 331]) to its creditors.

Liquidity

Liquidity is the extent to which a security is easily tradeable.

If a security is constantly trading in large quantities it is liquid. A liquid security can be sold easily and quickly, so investors have the assurance that if they wish to sell a holding they will be able to find a buyer at a reasonable price without problems.

Other things being equal, the price of a liquid security is less volatile because, with a constant stream of purchase and sales being offered, each investor has less influence on the price.

Selling an illiquid security is more difficult and the price more volatile. For some securities the effect can be ameliorated by the use of suitable trading systems, for example by requiring **market makers** [p. 197] to always maintain offers to buy and sell minimum quantities, as is done for **mid-cap** [p. 202] shares in London.

The problem is more difficult to solve for **small cap** [p. 297] shares and more obscure securities, not least due to the lack of willing market makers.

Listed company

A company is said to be "listed", "quoted" or "have a listing" if its shares can be traded on a stock exchange.

To be more accurate, it is the securities that are listed, not the company. The phrase "listed company" is widely used to mean a company that has listed shares.

It is possible (although not common) for a company to have listed debt securities but not listed shares.

In the UK inclusion, on the **Official List** [p. 222] is a pre-requisite for trading on an exchange. It is inclusion on the official list that defines a listed company.

The Official List is published by the **UK Listing Authority** [p. 330].

Lloyd's of London

Lloyd's is an insurance market. It provides a framework in which buyers of insurance can be matched with sellers. It is *not* an insurance company;

Lloyd's is particularly popular for risks that are hard to place elsewhere.

As with any market it has its brokers, and there are many insurance brokers that bring business to Lloyd's.

On the other side are investors who underwrite risks through Lloyd's syndicates that are run by managing agents.

Each syndicate is, in essence, an insurance company. The syndicates pay claims, not Lloyds itself. This is why Lloyd's can be described as a market: its function is to match the syndicates with their clients.

Load factor

In the electricity industry, load factor is a measure of the output of a power plant compared to the maximum output it could produce.

The two commonest definitions are:

- the ratio of average load to capacity

- the ratio of average load to peak load in a period.

Assuming the first definition, a higher load factor is better:

- A power plant may be less efficient at low load factors.

- A high load factor means fixed costs are spread over more kWh of output.

- A high load factor means greater total output.

Therefore a higher load factor usually means more output and a lower cost per unit, which means an electricity generator can sell more electricity at a higher **spark spread** [p. 301].

Many companies **disclose** [p. 98] load factors for their major plants. When comparing load factors over time it is important to remember that there are likely to be large seasonal changes quarter-on-quarter, so year-on-year changes are more likely to be significant.

Local loop

The local loop, also called the "last mile", is the connection from a telephone exchange to a subscriber's premises.

The local loop is enormously expensive for new entrants to replicate and gives **incumbent** [p. 168] operators a huge advantage. The incumbent operators had lines already laid to every fixed line subscriber before the competition started building their infrastructure.

Regulators have imposed **local loop unbundling** [p. 191] and **carrier pre-select** [p. 51] to provide more equal competitive access to local loops.

The problem has also been significantly reduced by new technology. Cable TV companies have an alternative network that is capable of carrying both voice and data. In some countries fixed radio links are used to reduce the cost of installing local loops. Mobile phones also now cost little enough to provide alternative networks.

Local loop unbundling

Control of the **local loop** [p. 191] gives **incumbent telecoms companies** [p. 168] an enormous advantage in fixed line and data communications. Incumbents still control the cheapest technology for voice calls and for high speed internet access.

In order to counter this, **Ofcom** [p. 221] and other European regulators require that incumbents allow other operators direct access to local loops. This has also means that incumbents are required to allow these other operators to install equipment at their exchanges – to handle connections from that point on. This is called local loop unbundling.

Local loop unbundling has been slow to take off as incumbents have, unsurprisingly, dragged their feet. It is greatly strengthening the position of smaller telcos.

Carrier pre-select [p. 51] is a simpler and less expensive, but also less effective solution.

London Stock Exchange

London Stock Exchange (LSE) is the world's third largest stock exchange; only the New York Stock Exchange and the Tokyo Stock Exchange are bigger. In addition to its main market it operates the **AIM** [p. 13] and trading systems for overseas securities.

Although some other exchanges, such as Virt-X, list many of the same securities, the LSE has far more liquidity than other British and European exchanges which helps it maintain its dominant position.

The **liquidity** [p. 190] created by the large pool of investors using the LSE attracts more companies to list on the LSE. This not only makes it the dominant exchange in the UK and helps it maintain its leading position in Europe, but attracts listings from further afield.

Very many large overseas companies have **secondary listings** [p. 288] in London, and a fair number have primary listings in London.

London's main competitor for overseas listings is the US (the NYSE and the NASDAQ). The high and increasing cost of complying with US regulations is attracting more companies to London.

Long position

An investor who has a holding of a particular security has a long position in it.

An investor with who has **sold a security short** [p. 296] has a short position in it.

More generally, a long position is one that will produce a profit from a rise in the price of a security, a short position is one that will produce a profit from a fall in the price of a security. This means that it is possible to have a long or short position indirectly by holding **derivatives** [p. 96].

A long position in a **call option** [p. 45] implies a short position in the **underlying asset** [p. 331].

Long term liabilities

Long term liabilities are those that are due to be paid in more than an year. Those due in less than a year or on demand are **current liabilities** [p. 84].

The most important type of long term liability is debt. **Preference shares** [p. 244] are not debt, but given that they are "debt like" this is often something investors should adjust for.

Long term liabilities are looked at by investors assessing a company's financial health using ratios such as **interest cover** [p. 176]. Because of **gearing** [p. 157] high debt enhances the benefits of growth.

Like shareholders, the holders of long term debt (i.e. banks and bondholders) are suppliers of funds to a company. They rank higher than shareholders in getting their money back if a company fails and therefore their money is safer, but they do not gain if the company performs better than the minimum necessary to pay back its debt.

LPG (Liquefied Petroleum Gas)

Liquefied Petroleum Gas (LPG) is obtained by extraction from **natural gas** [p. 212] or from refinery processes.

It is stored under pressure, but because this causes it to liquefy it needs less storage space and can be handled more easily than it could be as a gas.

Most LPG is used for fuel, but it is also used as a refrigerant and an aerosol propellant. As a fuel it is used for domestic gas supplies, as an automotive fuel and, to a limited extent, for electricity generation.

Like other oil and gas products, demand for LPG is **cyclical** [p. 84] – but with sustained underlying demand growth significantly higher than that of oil.

M0 (monetary base)

M0 is the narrowest definition of **money supply** [p. 206] in common use.

The definition used in the UK is bank notes and coins in circulation, plus banks' deposits with the Bank of England.

M0 is also known as the monetary base. This term refers to the fact that the money measured by M0 supplies the base on which other forms of money (such as bank deposits) are based.

M1

M1 is one of the narrow measures of **money supply** [p. 206].

The UK definition of M1 is: notes and coins in circulation plus sterling sight deposits by the UK private sector in banks and building societies in the UK.

Sight deposits are sterling deposits that can be withdrawn on demand or have been deposited overnight.

Notes and coins in circulation excludes those held by non-residents, financial institutions and the public sector.

The most important types of money excluded from M1 are: time deposits, foreign currency deposits, non-residents money, public sector holdings and financial institutions' holdings.

M2

M2 is a narrow measure of **money supply** [p. 206]. The UK definition is equivalent to the retail component of **M4** [p. 195]. This is:

Banknotes and coins in circulation plus retail deposits with banks and building societies.

Retail deposits are deposits made at a banks' and building societies' advertised rates. It excludes very large deposits for which banks are willing to negotiate interest rates.

Notes and coins in circulation excludes those held by non-residents, financial institutions and the public sector.

Definitions used in other countries are very similar. It is usually broadly equivalent to **M1** [p. 193] plus savings accounts.

M3

M3 is a broad measure of the **money supply** [p. 206].

M3 has been replaced by M4 in the UK as the main broad money measure. It is still calculated as part of certain European aggregates.

M3 consists of the following:

- notes and coins in circulation (defined as for **M1** [p. 193] and **M2** [p. 194])

- overnight deposits and sight deposits (as for M1)

- other short term deposits (with a maturity of under two years, or withdrawal notice of under three months)

- **money market funds** [p. 206]

- debt securities with a maturity of under two years

- **repos** [p. 274].

Unlike M2, M3 includes public sector and foreign currency deposits.

Definitions in other countries are broadly similar.

The US has also stopped publishing M3 numbers. Unlike the UK, it has not replaced it with another broad money measure.

M4

M4 is the main broad measure of **money supply** [p. 206] in the UK. It is similar to the **M3** [p. 194] measure used in some other countries.

M4 includes everything in **M2** [p. 194] (also called the retail component of M4) plus:

- other deposits with an original maturity of up to five years

- other claims on financial institutions such as **repos** [p. 274] and bank acceptances

- debt instruments issued by financial institutions including **commercial paper** [p. 63] and **bonds** [p. 37] with a maturity of up to five years.

- 95% of the inter-MFI difference.

Major financial institutions (MFI) means banks (including the Bank of England) and building societies. The inter-MFI difference is defined by the Bank of England as "the mismatch in reporting of UK MFIs assets and liabilities with each other". It is the deposits banks have with each other after netting off. 5% of the mismatch is assumed to be due to amounts in transit.

Majority shareholder

A majority shareholder (or group of shareholders) can cast the majority of votes at a general meeting of a company, and therefore controls all important aspects of running the company such as the appointment of directors.

This affects the rights of **minority shareholders** [p. 204] who are effectively deprived of their say in the running of the company.

Mandatory offer

The **City Code** [p. 58] (of the **Takeover Panel** [p. 318]) requires that if a shareholder or a **concert party** [p. 67] acquires more than 30% of a company it must offer to buy the remaining shares on terms as good as its most recent purchases.

The reason for this is that 30%, although not giving a shareholder formal control, is sufficient to give effective control.

When a change of control takes place it may adversely affect the share price. This is because **minority shareholders** [p. 204] are likely to worry that the company will be run to suit the controlling shareholder, and the interests of minorities may be affected. Therefore, it is only fair to allow them to sell out at the price that the new controlling shareholder paid before the change of control.

There are circumstances in which the Takeover Panel may grant a waiver from the requirement to make a mandatory offer – for example, if major shareholders state that they will not accept the mandatory offer.

Margin trading

Margin trading is investing in securities (usually shares) using borrowed money, with the securities used as collateral.

Margin trading is funded by brokers or banks. Banks need the cooperation of the broker through which the trading is done in order to track positions in margin trading portfolios.

Investors generally use margin to increase their purchasing power so that they can own more stock (and make a greater gain) than their own resources allow. Like **derivatives** [p. 96], margin trading exposes investors to the potential for higher losses as well.

The lender usually agrees to lend an amount that can only fund a fixed proportion of the portfolio. The remainder will be funded by the investor to provide a buffer against the value of the portfolio falling below the value of the debt it secures.

When the value of a portfolio falls so low that the debt exceeds that fixed proportion the lender is willing to fund, then a margin call will be made. This means that the investor must either pay down the debt (putting more of their own money into the portfolio), selling securities, if necessary, to do so – or the broker will sell on their behalf.

Margin traders pay interest on the debt, which reduces net returns.

Margins

See **profit margin** [p. 253].

Market capitalisation

Market capitalisation (market cap) is the total value of the shares of a company, sector or market.

If a company has only one type of share its market cap is simply the share price multiplied by the number of shares. If a company has more than one class of share then the market cap is the sum of the market caps of the different types of shares. In either case it is the value of the company at current share prices, or alternatively the cost of buying the company at current prices.

Market caps are also calculated for sectors and stock markets in order to compare sizes and as part of the process of calculating indices.

Market cap is not the only measure of the size of a company. Its most obvious weakness is that it only looks at the value of **equity** [p. 123], whereas in reality the debt holders have a claim on the company that needs to be taken into account. This means that investors often find **enterprise value** [p. 121], and related **valuation ratios** [p. 334], to be more relevant.

Measures of size based on sales or **value added** [p. 335] can also be useful.

Market capitalisation/sales

See **price/sales** [p. 250].

Market maker

A market maker is a dealer who receives privileges in share dealing in return for providing **liquidity** [p. 190]. This generally means that market makers are required to always quote firm **bid** [p. 35] and **offer** [p. 222] prices for at least a minimum quantity of each security they are a market maker in (the minimum varies from security to security).

The **London Stock Exchange's** [p. 192] SEAQ system requires that all deals are done with a market maker. In return for providing liquidity by maintaining constant quotes, market maker's profit from their **bid-offer spread** [p. 35].

London, and some other markets also use hybrid systems which mix market makers with an **order driven system** [p. 198] in order to guarantee liquidity while reducing spreads.

The responsibilities and the privileges of a market maker vary. The key principle of special privileges in return for maintaining liquidity and an orderly market remains the same. In some US markets the term specialist is used, but this tends to be where the market operates in quite a different way from the British model of market making.

Market order

A market, or "at best" order is an order to buy or sell a quantity of securities at the best price currently available in the market.

Not specifying a maximum or minimum price may seem risky, but most trading systems have safeguards to protect investors against unreasonable or unexpected prices.

- Investors can find out what the current market price is before placing an order.

- Some **trading systems** [p. 24] will only trade market orders within certain limits relative to either existing **limit orders** [p. 189] or the last traded price.

- Some trading systems allow the investor placing a market order a few seconds in which to confirm that the price is acceptable.

Market orders are the order type most often used by private investors in the UK. They almost always have a chance to confirm the price before the order executes. Depending on the security and circumstances these orders may match against another order, or a **market maker's** [p. 197] quote.

Market PE

See **sector PE** [p. 289].

Market penetration

Market penetration is the proportion of a potential market who actually buy a product or service.

Market penetration is a key issue in assessing the growth prospects for an industry. It is usually fairly straightforward to assess the potential market for a product: the number of sales it could make if everyone who could reasonably buy it, did. What proportion of those people actually become paying customers of an industry is another matter.

Over optimistic estimates of eventual market penetration is a common trap for **growth investors** [p. 161]. Some products do achieve very high penetration in a fairly short time (as mobile phones have done, for example), but others never do – as seems to be the case for PDAs (handheld computers/personal organisers).

Matched bargain

Matched bargain trading systems are order driven, rather than quote driven as **market maker** [p. 197] based systems are. Investors' offers to buy and sell securities are directly matched with each other. This contrasts with a market maker driven system where investors buy and sell to market makers.

The disadvantage of a matched bargain system is that it can not guarantee **liquidity** [p. 190]. With a market maker system the market makers are required to provide liquidity, so that investors are always able to buy or sell shares. This does not apply to large quantities.

For shares that are in any case very liquid, a market maker system is not needed to ensure liquidity, which is why the London Stock Exchange uses a matched bargain system for the most liquid shares (e.g. **FTSE 100** [p. 150] shares), a market maker system for moderately liquid stocks and a matched bargain system for the most illiquid shares (which are so illiquid as to make market making too risky and impractical).

MBO

A management buy-out (MBO) is the **acquisition** [p. 5] of a business by its existing management.

If the owners (the existing shareholders) of a business want to sell, the existing management are often the people in the best position buy them out take the business forward. They know the business and are therefore in a strong position both to value it (to decide if it is worth buying) and subsequently run it. One may also take the view that they will work harder for themselves than for other people.

MBOs are often carried out by a consortium of the current management and external backers. MBOs generally require more capital than a start-up and often are financed by **venture capital** [p. 338] or **private equity** [p. 252] firms.

If a business is under-performing due to bad management, a management buy-in may be preferable. This is the purchase of a business by new shareholders who include new management.

Mboe (Millions of barrels of oil equivalent)

See **barrels of oil equivalent** [p. 37].

Mechanical investing

A mechanical investment strategy is one that follows a fixed set of rules to make buy and sell decisions. Mechanical strategies exclude any exercise of human judgement, making them less subjective. This also implies excluding the benefits of experience, intuition and common sense.

A simple example of a mechanical strategy is:

1. Invest equal amounts of money in the 10 highest **yield** [p. 107] shares in the **FTSE 100** [p. 150].

2. Adjust the portfolio once a year so that it again has equal amounts in the 10 highest yield shares.

This is an adaptation of the **Dogs of the Dow** [p. 108] strategy. It is a reasonable approach for someone who wants a simple, low cost, conservative **income** [p. 168] portfolio.

More complex mechanical strategies are possible. They may be based on **chartism** [p. 319], automated exploitation of **arbitrage** [p. 18] opportunities or based on complex **financial models** [p. 140].

Simple mechanical stock picking criteria may also be used to produce short lists of securities for further consideration.

Mechanical royalties

Mechanical royalties are royalties that are paid by a person making a new recording of an existing piece of music (most often a cover version of a song).

Mechanical royalties are calculated using either a fixed rate per copy (common practice in the US) or as a percentage of the price of the CD (or other medium) on which the recording is sold. In the latter case it is necessary to adjust for the fact that a CD may contain several other works.

In the UK, mechanical royalties are usually collected by Mechanical Copyright Protection Society which then passes them to the music publisher (usually itself a recorded music company). What the publisher receives is then split between the publisher and the creators of the music.

Mechanical royalties are one of many income streams a music company generates. Others include the sale of music, **synchronisation fees** [p. 315] and performance royalties.

Media convergence

Convergence in the context of media refers to the technology driven unification of different media channels.

For many years different media were clearly separated: broadcast TV, broadcast radio, newspapers, books, video and film, recorded music etc.

The internet and other digital methods of distribution have changed this. A digital connection or physical medium can carry any type of content. Video can be distributed on a mobile phone network or music over the internet.

This not only means that different types of media are converging, but also that media and telecoms are converging.

In addition to convergence at the distribution level there are areas in which the same content can be re-packaged across media: for example, computer games and films use the same content in different ways. This also creates powerful marketing **synergies** [p. 316].

Convergence is part of a much broader change in the media that is being brought about by new technology. Although this has not happened as fast or as profitably as many hoped during the dotcom boom, changes are nonetheless happening.

From an investment point of view the key consequence is the potential impact of the change on established media companies revenue streams.

Media Fragmentation

When terrestrial broadcast TV (with cable being significant in some countries) was the only way of distributing video signals over large geographic areas, the result was that there were (and still are) huge audiences for a small number of channels.

The addition of satellite TV, and an increase in the number of cable channels, means that audiences are now divided between more operators and a far greater number of channels.

Similar changes are affecting other media. Digital radio and podcasts are dividing the audience for audio. Completely new media (like the web) are competing with old media, dividing the audience up further.

This is the fragmentation of the media.

The result has been not just loss of market share for media companies. It has also made advertising more complex. Advertisers need to buy and manage ad space/time over a much greater number of channels. This has created opportunities for media buying businesses.

Median

The median is a type of **average** [p. 25] of a series of numbers.

For an odd number of numbers, the median is the number which is less than exactly half the other numbers (and therefore more than exactly half).

For an even number of numbers there is no one number that would be exactly half way down a list of the numbers ordered by size, so it is defined as halfway between the two middle numbers.

The median is often used to pick the "consensus" from financial forecasts. This is because an arithmetic mean would be distorted by outliers, and there are not enough distinct different forecasts for the mode to be meaningful.

Merger

A merger refers to a combination of two or more companies, usually of not greatly disparate size, into one company. It differs from an **acquisition** [p. 5] in that it is not really true from a business or economic point of view that one company bought the other – although this must be so from a legal or accounting point of view.

A merger is a combination of equals. Therefore it is usual for the board of a merged company not to be dominated by the management of either of its predecessors. As a merger is necessarily an agreed (by the boards) transaction, this is anyway likely as directors are not likely to agree to a merger that would deprive too many of the board of their jobs.

Unlike an acquisition, a merger is not likely to involve a payment of significant premiums to the shareholder of either predecessor company. This makes it less likely to destroy shareholder value. Like acquisitions, the **synergies** [p. 316] that provide the usual rationale for a merger may not actually happen, and integration is almost always difficult and costly.

Some mergers appear to be an attempt by directors to scale up sufficiently to deter acquisitions.

Mergers often require clearance from competition regulators. In some case they are blocked, or only allowed subject to conditions (such as the sale of particular businesses).

Mezzanine finance

Mezzanine finance is used to describe forms of finance that have characteristics of both debt and equity. They are typically used to finance **MBOs** [p. 198] or expansion.

Mezzanine finance often has one or more of these characteristics it:

- ranks after normal debt but before equity in the event a company fails

- pays higher interest rates than other debt

- is convertible into shares

- is repayable after a long term, typically seven to ten years, so it does not drain cash flows on the meantime.

Its exact nature will vary depending on the needs of the business concerned and the suppliers of the mezzanine finance.

It is most often provided in the form of **subordinated debt** [p. 310], **preference shares** [p. 244] or **convertibles** [p. 72].

Mid-cap

A mid-cap company is one that has market capitalisation that is too small for it to be a **blue chip** [p. 36] (or large cap), but which is bigger than a **small cap** [p. 297].

There are no strict rules for identifying a company as a mid-cap. In the UK companies in the **FTSE 250** [p. 151] index are considered mid-cap.

There are some good arguments for paying particular attention to mid-cap shares.

- They are less heavily followed and analysed than large companies, and therefore there is a better chance of finding opportunities the market has missed.

- Being smaller than large companies, mid-caps are more likely to have room for growth within their industry.

- As businesses that have reached a certain scale they tend to be more stable than similar smaller companies.

- They tend to be less complex than large companies, and therefore easier to analyse.

- Analyst coverage and attention from investors is sufficient to ensure that **disclosure** [p. 98] is usually reasonably good. Accounts and reports tend to be more informative than those of small companies.

Mid-price

The mid-price of a security is the average of the its **bid** [p. 35] and **offer** [p. 222] prices.

The mid-price is frequently quoted when it is necessary to provide a single number for a security price. It has the advantage over the last traded price of a constantly updated quote being available for securities that are traded through **market makers** [p. 197].

The main disadvantage of quoting the mid-price is that,for very illiquid securities trading through **matched bargain** [p. 198] systems, the bid or offer price may be unrealistic and distort the mid-price. For these securities, it is preferable to use the last traded price.

Mineral Reserves

This is the economically mineable part of the measured and indicated **mineral resources** [p. 203]. At the time of reporting, extraction should be reasonably likely to be justified. This implies consideration of a range of economic, legal, financial and other factors.

Reserves are further divided into:

- proved reserves

- probable reserves

Probable reserves are known with a lower degree of confidence than proved reserves.

Similar categories of proven and probable are used to classify **oil reserves** [p. 223].

Mineral Resources

A mineral resource is a concentration of a mineral in the ground. Unlike **mineral reserves** [p. 203], resources are not necessarily economically mineable. The classes of mineral resource used in accounts, in decreasing order of confidence, are:

- measured resources

- indicated mineral resources

- inferred mineral resources.

Minority interests

The minority interests line in a company's **consolidated accounts** [p. 68] shows amounts that are deducted from the group's profits because they are attributable to outside shareholders.

Suppose a company makes a post-tax profit £200m from its own operations. It also has a 75% stake in a **subsidiary** [p. 311] that makes a post tax profit of £100m.

The consolidated **P & L** [p. 234] will show a fully consolidated post-tax profit of £300m (£200m from the company itself + £100m for the subsidiary).

Below this will appear a line that shows minority interests of £25m. This is the stake in the subsidiary not held by the company of 25% × £100m profit made by the subsidiary.

Finally, the profit attributable to shareholders will be £275m (£300m consolidated minus £25m attributable to minority interests).

Minority shareholder

Minority shareholders are shareholders who have minority stakes in a company that is controlled by a **majority shareholder** [p. 195].

The majority shareholder is most commonly the company's **parent** [p. 236] but may also be an individual or a group of connected shareholders. This is more common with smaller companies and in **emerging markets** [p. 121].

The value of shares can be depressed by the existence of a majority shareholders (including a group of connected shareholders). Minority shareholders are often effectively deprived of any real say in the running of the company, and they may find that the company is run in a way which benefits the majority at their expense.

Although legal protections exist against the latter danger, they are not always effective. A majority shareholder cannot (at least in any country with an effective legal system) blatantly cheat the minority, but there are more subtle ways in which the majority can favour itself, for example, by preferring to deal with group companies (such as other **subsidiaries** [p. 311] of the parent).

MIRR

Modified internal rate of return (MIRR) is a variant of **IRR** [p. 183] that assumes that cash generated is re-invested at the cost of capital (usually the **WACC** [p. 342]). This is preferable because:

- Any series of cashflows has a single MIRR.

- It takes account of the rate at which cash generated is re-invested.

Consider the returns at the end of the life time of a project, including returns on cash generated and re-invested elsewhere. For the IRR to equal the total return the project has generated at that time, the cash inflows must be re-invested at the same rate as the IRR. This is unrealistic.

The MIRR does suffer from some of the other drawbacks of IRR. Relying on it can lead to an incorrect choice between mutually exclusive investment.

Mode

The mode is the frequently occurring number in a set. The mode of these numbers:

5, 5, 10, 10, 10, 10, 10, 10, 20, 100
is 10,
whereas their **arithmetic mean** [p. 19] is 17.3.

Modified duration

The modified duration is a measure of the sensitivity of a bond price to interest rates:

$$Modified\ duration = D \div (1 + r)$$

where D is the **duration** [p. 113] and
r is the interest rate paid per period: **coupon** [p. 77] payment divided by price.

The percentage change in the price is equal to the change in interest rates multiplied by the modified duration. This is an approximation and becomes less accurate for larger interest rate changes. Interest rate changes are usually small and the approximation is more than good enough.

Modified internal rate of return

See **MIRR** [p. 204].

Modigliani-Miller theory

An alternative name for simple **capital structure irrelevance** [p. 48], derived from the names of the originators of the theory: Franco Modigliani and Merton Miller.

Momentum Investing

Momentum investing is, in essence, a fairly simple **strategy** [p. 179]: buy what is going up, sell what is going down.

It is a strategy that tends to work well at certain times. For example, a sustained **bubble** [p. 41] can make momentum investors a lot of money. It is also a strategy that can go badly wrong and momentum investors tend to take big losses when bubbles burst.

Investors often become momentum investors without really meaning to. There is comfort in buying what is already doing well. There is also pressure on professional investors, such as fund mangers, to pay attention to momentum.

If there is momentum in a share, sector or market and you stay out of it, you lose gains others (and the market) are making. Thus your comparative performance looks worse. During the dotcom bubble some fund managers who had the insight to realise that it was a bubble lost their jobs for underperforming. Going with the herd is a safe option – as long as your own money is not at stake.

Money market fund

A money market fund invests in short term debt instruments such as **commercial paper** [p. 63] and **government bonds** [p. 160] close to expiry (short term **gilts** [p. 158] and **treasury bills** [p. 328]).

Money market funds invest in low **risk** [p. 281] and **liquid** [p. 190] securities. This makes them as much an alternative to bank deposits as to bond funds.

Money supply

The money supply is the amount of money in an economy.

This is superficially straightforward but is complicated by the difficulty of defining what is meant by money.

The simplest possible definition is the actual amount of bank notes and coins in circulation. The problem with this simple definition is that most money exists as bank deposits rather than in physical form.

Even the narrowest of the definitions that are actually useful, **M0** [p. 193], is broader than this as it includes banks' deposits with the Bank of England (or their own central bank in other countries).

The next narrowest definitions of money supply are **M1** [p. 193] and **M2** [p. 194]. These add various types of deposits by the private sector with banks and other financial institutions. These are still regarded as narrow measures. They are sometimes referred to as referred to as narrow money.

The broad money measures (**M3** [p. 194], **M4** [p. 195] and others) add other types of money such as **repos** [p. 274], bank acceptances, **commercial paper** [p. 63] and **bonds** [p. 37]. Some countries (but not the UK) include foreign currency deposits.

Narrow money measures aim to measure the money supply that is actually held for use in transactions. Broad measures also include money that may be held as a store of wealth. **Divisia** [p. 107] aggregates weight different types of money, giving a higher weight to those likely to be used for transactions.

There are various variations on these basic types and the exact definitions vary from country to country. The exact definitions are revised from time to time by the Bank of England (or the appropriate central bank).

Monopoly

A monopoly exists where there is only one supplier of a product or service. This allows the supplier to charge higher prices than if there was competition. There are degrees of monopoly and only the market in a **commodity** [p. 64] is completely free of monopoly pricing power.

What is usually meant by a monopoly is that there is no competition and therefore the supplier has a very high degree of pricing power. If there is no competition, the product being sold should have a price **cross elasticity** [p. 80] close to zero with any other product. As prices change, volumes sold follow the demand curve for the market; if prices rise, buyers either pay up or do without rather than switching to another supplier.

A market that falls short of monopoly but which also falls short of perfect competition is described as having monopolistic competition or imperfect competition.

Monopolies can arise in a number of ways including:

- Legally enforced monopolies on an entire market.

- Patents and copyrights: these create (usually very narrow) legally enforced monopolies on particular products or services.

- Natural monopolies: this includes many utilities where the cost of building a distribution network makes building more than one uneconomic.

- Cartels: agreements by former competitors to cooperate on pricing or market share; illegal in most countries.

- **Network effects** [p. 214]: these can both help create a monopoly and make it difficult to dislodge once established.

- Control of access to a market: e.g. if a retailer can buy up all the best sites for distributing a particular product in a particular area they can choke off the competition's access to customers.

It is clearly beneficial for a suppliers to try to reduce competition to their own products as far as possible, this may through **differentiation** [p. 253] of their products, building **barriers to entry** [p. 30] and deliberately exploiting **network effects** [p. 214].

Most countries have anti-monopoly (often, especially in the US, called antitrust) legislation to control the creation and abuse of monopolies and regulators empowered to enforce these laws. This has been fairly successful at stopping some types of abuses (such as the formation of cartels or the buy-out of competition) but has a more mixed record in dealing with network effects and ensuring access to markets.

Where the monopoly is one of buying rather than supplying, it is a **monopsony** [p. 208].

Monopsony

A monopsony is exists in a market that has only a single buyer. It is similar to a **monopoly** [p. 207].

The pricing power that a monopsonist has is similar to that of a monopolist. Rather than increasing prices above the free market level (which reduces the efficiency of the economy as a whole) it keeps them lower (which also has the effect of reducing the efficiency of the economy).

Monopsony is a less common problem than monopoly (perhaps partly because suppliers are better able to lobby regulators to prevent it than consumers are). It is often alleged to be a problem in markets for products sold to consumers by large retailers (such as supermarkets), but sold to the retailers by significantly smaller suppliers.

Monte-Carlo simulation

Monte-Carlo simulation is a useful technique for financial modelling that uses random inputs to model uncertainty.

When a financial model is used for forecasting there will clearly be a number of inputs into the model that are unknown. One approach is to take a best estimate for each of these inputs. For example suppose we are using a model to forecast a company's sales volumes that is something like this:

$$market\ growth = GDP\ growth \times multiple$$
$$market\ size = current\ market\ size \times (market\ growth + 1)$$
$$market\ share = current\ market\ share + gain$$
$$sales\ volumes = market\ size \times market\ share$$

There are three uncertain inputs here: GDP growth, the relationship between GDP growth and market growth and the increase in market share. The obvious approach is to use the best estimate of each.

Using a probability distribution (for example the normal distribution), rather than using the single best estimate, better reflects reality. Using a probability distribution is not easy. One approach would be to mathematically derive the output of the model as a probability distribution. This is usually very difficult, and often simply not possible.

Mote-Carlo modelling provides an alternative. Monte-Carlo methods do use the probability distributions of the inputs. Rather than using the distributions themselves as inputs, the distributions are used to generate random inputs. The methodology is:

1. Draw a number at random from the probability distribution for each input

2. Calculate and record the outputs given these inputs

3. Repeat from step one as many times as necessary

By doing repeatedly, this it is possible to gradually build up the probability distribution of the outputs.

To apply Monte-Carlo methods to the simple model above we would need to estimate distributions for each of the three inputs. So we may end up doing something like this

1. GDP growth is forecast to be 2%, with a **standard deviation** [p. 305] of the estimate of 1% and **normally distributed** [p. 218]. So we randomly take a number from a normal distribution with a **mean** [p. 25] of 2 and a standard deviation of 1. This gives up the GDP growth percentage, call it x.

2. We have a similar estimate for the multiple that relates GDP growth to market size. Here we draw a random number (call it y) from a normal distribution with a mean of 1.5 and a standard deviation of 0.5

3. We multiply x by y which gives us our market growth estimate. We use this to estimate our forecast market size

4. We have a similar estimate for market share growth. Suppose in this case we draw a number from a normal distribution with a mean of 2% and a standard deviation of 2%

5. We can now calculate sales volumes as above

6. We now record the value we get for sales volumes

7. We now repeat from step one, hundreds of times

8. The recorded values form the output of a Monte-Carlo simulation

We end up with a series of estimates. These can be used to calculate a mean and a **standard deviation** [p. 305] for the sales volumes. This is a far more meaningful number than a single best estimate, as it gives both a better best estimate (the mean) and a measure of its uncertainty (the standard deviation).

Obviously Monte-Carlo methods are very tedious to use with manual calculations. Computers make the use of Monte-Carlo analysis far easier.

In many cases the most significant amount of work comes not from the Monte-Carlo simulation itself, but from the need to make estimates of probability distributions rather than simple point estimates.

Moral hazard

A person or organisation who has insurance cover may be be more prepared to take risks than someone who does not.

For example, someone whose car is insured against theft may be more careless about reducing the chances of theft than they would have been without such insurance.

This is partly why insurance companies require excesses (the amount of a claim paid by the person covered) on most claims, and reduce premiums quite sharply as excesses rise. It is also why insurers are very careful about the valuation of what they insure and why they are not legally required to pay more than the real value of what they cover, even if it has been insured for more.

Moral hazard can also occur outside insurance, although it is less of a concern. Banks and financial institutions often have implicit state guarantees (not formal or legally binding guarantees, but a general expectation that they are too big/important to fail). This creates an incentive for the management and shareholders to take bigger risks as they will benefit from gambles that work, but the state will pay for those that do not. This is similar to the **agency conflict** [p. 11] between shareholders and debt holders.

Moving average

The moving average of a security price is its price over the last x days, where x is the period of the moving average.

For example, the 30 day moving average price of a security is the **mean** [p. 19] of the closing prices over the last thirty days. The 30 day moving average for yesterday is the average of the closing closing prices for the thirty days up to the day before yesterday.

Moving averages have a number of applications in finance. **Chartists** [p. 319] use moving averages heavily and see significance in events such as prices moving above the moving average, or different moving average lines crossing.

There is little empirical evidence of the predictive power of the moving averages of security prices. Most of the evidence supports quite the opposite conclusion.

There is evidence that moving average **volatilities** [p. 340] are good estimates of future volatility, however the evidence also shows that **weighted moving averages** [p. 344] are better still for this purpose.

MSCI (Morgan Stanley Capital International)

MSCI is a publisher of indices, best known for its highly influential emerging markets **indices** [p. 169].

The MSCI **emerging markets** [p. 121] indices are so influential that the inclusion or not of a country in the MSCI indices can have a very significant effect on a country's ability to attract foreign **portfolio investment** [p. 242].

The influence of the emerging market indices reflect their wide acceptance as **benchmarks** [p. 33].

MSCI also provides a wide range of other indices covering major markets including **sector** [p. 288] indices, **small cap** [p. 297] indices, **bond** [p. 37] indices and **hedge fund** [p. 162] indices.

Multi-manager fund

The term multi-manager fund is usually used as a synonym for a fund of funds, although it occasionally has a somewhat broader meaning.

See **fund of funds** [p. 152].

Mutual funds

A common type of **collective investment vehicle** [p. 62]. These are called mutual funds in the US and **unit trusts** [p. 333] in Britain.

MVNO

A mobile virtual network operator (MVNO) is a telecoms company that provides mobile phone telecoms without owning its own network. MVNOs essentially buy capacity in bulk and resell it retail.

From a customer's point of view the MVNO is their mobile phone network operator as they pay the MVNO. The MVNO will usually provide some services, but the calls are actually carried on a network belonging to someone else.

An MVNO does not have the heavy **capex** [p. 46] commitments that owning a network necessitates, on the other hand this also means that **barriers to entry** [p. 30] are low.

Nash equilibrium

In **game theory** [p. 154], a Nash equilibrium exists when no player has an incentive to change their strategy when the game is iterated, provided no other player changes their strategy either.

The name comes from their discoverer, John Nash.

It is common for games to have more than one Nash equilibrium.

A very simple example of a game with Nash equilibria is:

		Player A	
		Choose x	Choose y
Player B	Choose x	5,5	1,0
	Choose y	0,1	10,10

It is fairly obvious that if one player chooses x then so should the other. Similarly, if one player chooses y then so should the other.

If the game is repeated, then each player will be able to form expectations about the other's choices and will follow. Therefore the players will both choose the same one of x or y and stick to their choice. The two Nash equilibria are both players choosing x and both players choosing y.

Nash equilibria occur in economics and finance, for example in some exchange rate theory.

Natural gas

Natural gas is usually found together with oil but the proportion of oil to gas varies and either may be the main product of a field. This is why **boe** [p. 37] is used as a measure of volume.

Like crude oil, it is a mixture of hydrocarbon compounds, mostly methane. Methane (CH_4) is colourless, flammable, and odourless (which causes some safety problems). It is a greenhouse gas.

Natural gas is sold in the form of various extracts such as **dry natural gas** [p. 112] and **LPG** [p. 193].

Natural monopoly

A natural monopoly is a **monopoly** [p. 207] that arises from the nature of an industry. The commonest reason for the existence of a natural monopoly is that it uneconomic to replicate expensive infrastructure.

The most obvious examples of a natural monopolies are utilities such as gas, electricity and water – at least at the level of distribution to consumers.

It is fairly clear that it would not be practical to create a competitive market for water supplies by encouraging several companies to each build its own network of everything from reservoirs to pipes running to customers. It would be far more expensive than having a single system built by a monopoly supplier.

It is not always clear what is a natural monopoly. A few decades ago it would have appeared that telecoms was a natural monopoly. It now appears to merely be susceptible to **network effects** [p. 214]. These have largely been effectively countered (at least in the EU) by requiring inter-operability between networks at regulated prices and giving competitors access to **incumbent telecoms companies** [p. 168] infrastructure.

NAV

The total value of a company's assets less the total value of its liabilities is its net asset value (NAV). For valuation purposes it is common to divide net assets by the number of shares in issue to give the net assets per share. This is the value of the assets that belong to each share, in much the same way that **PE** [p. 237] measures profit per share.

NAV is useful for the valuation of shares in sectors where the value of a company comes from the assets it holds rather than the profit stream generated by the business. The most obvious examples of these are **investment trusts** [p. 180] and property companies. Both of these are largely convenient ways in which investors can buy the **diversified** [p. 103] bundles of assets they hold.

The value of the assets may be taken at market price or at **book value** [p. 38]. Which is used tends to depend on the sector and the circumstances.

The net asset value of a **unit trust** [p. 333], **OEIC** [p. 221] or investment trust is calculated using the market value of assets. The value of the underlying assets will change daily, therefore the NAV will also change daily. For funds it is usual to calculate and publish the NAV per share (or unit) daily.

The unit price of unit trusts is based on their NAV. The price that investors pay to purchase unit trust units is the approximate per unit NAV, plus any fees that the fund imposes at purchase (such as sales loads or purchase fees). The price that investors receive on redemptions is the NAV per unit at redemption, minus any fees that the fund deducts at that time (such as deferred sales loads or redemption fees).

Unlike unit trusts and OEICs, investment trusts have a fixed number of shares available and no mechanism for on-going redemptions or issues of shares. Because of this shares can trade at a substantial discount (or, more rarely, a premium) to NAV.

NAV is also used to value property companies. Property companies, like investment trusts, usually trade at a small discount to their NAV.

While NAV can be computed for any company it is of little relevance in service industries because there is little invested in plant and equipment. Where there is a reasonable component of fixed investment, NAV gives some indication of what underpins a company's share price and is liked by some **value investors** [p. 337].

Net premium written

See **premium written** [p. 246].

Net present value

See **NPV** [p. 220].

Net publisher's share

Net publisher's share is, in the music industry, the amount of royalties received by a music publisher less any amounts of those royalties that have to be paid to writers, performers and anyone else who receives a share of royalties.

Net publisher's share can be useful in valuation as it is an indication of how big a music publisher is. The is similar to valuing a company on a revenue multiple such as **EV/sales** [p. 130].

It is usually preferable to use profit multiples rather than revenue multiples, and net publisher's share is a modified revenue number. It is also not a number that is always **disclosed** [p. 98]. In addition, music publishing is usually part of a larger music business (e.g. recorded music sales).

The royalty streams that a publisher receives include performance royalties, **mechanical royalties** [p. 199] and **synchronisation fees** [p. 315].

Net realisable value

Net realisable value is used to calculate the value of assets (usually **stock** [p. 307]) when cost of purchase cannot be used.

Net realisable value is the amount for which an asset can be sold minus the cost of selling it.

Net realisable value is most often used when it is less than the cost of the asset in question. Then, in accordance with the accounting principle of prudence, the lower value must be used.

When an asset is re-valued at net realisable value, an unrealised loss has been made and this has to be shown in the **P & L** [p. 234], as well as showing the reduced value of the asset in the **balance sheet** [p. 28].

How much of an impact the cost of selling has on the value is likely to vary. Goods that are in a shop and waiting to be bought by customers do not require significant further expenditure. On the other hand, **work in progress** [p. 346] may not be saleable without passing it though the rest of the manufacturing process.

Network effects

Network effects occur when higher sales of a product (or a service) increase its value and therefore fuel further sales. One of the simplest examples is the telephone network. There would be no point in owning the only telephone in the world. If a few hundred people had telephones connected to the same network they would start to become useful. In reality, with well over a billion telephones in the world, they are indispensable.

Similar effects take place in other industries. It is difficult to sell a car that uses a non-conventional fuel as there are a lack of places to re-fuel, but no one will build a distribution system without the demand that would result from substantial number of cars already sold.

Perhaps the most important network effects at the moment are those in IT and media. In IT, this is actually a complex three layered effect where hardware, operating systems and application software all selling each other. Many software companies have successfully exploited network effects. Microsoft's success in using its position in operating systems to sell its office software and vice versa is a superb example of how to exploit network effects. There are many others in the industry.

Network effects in media are best illustrated by looking at formats for recorded media. For example, once VHS video tapes got significantly greater market share than Betamax, the latter disappeared. Similarly minidiscs and digital audio tape failed partly because they failed to gather enough momentum to challenge CDs.

Perhaps the best example of network effects is the internet. It was far more successful than any previous attempt to provide on-line information because its open nature (anyone could connect, anyone could publish using it, anyone could write software that would connect to it etc.) meant that it gathered critical mass that eluded proprietary services (those that required a subscription to a particular supplier who was the only publisher for that network).

In some industries regulators put a lot of effort into minimising network effects. If the dominant players in telecoms would be able to lock out competitors by refusing to allow them to connect to their networks, this would make it nearly impossible for new entrants to break in or for smaller networks to survive at all. Therefore telecoms regulators force networks to allow connections from other networks, and regulate the prices charged for doing so.

Regulators have been less effective at managing network effects in software and media. This may be due to the lack of the specialist regulatory framework that exist for telecoms.

New issue

A new issue of a security is the sale of newly issued securities to investors in order to raise money.

New issues take place at different times, whenever the issuer needs to raise money. Important examples of new issues are **IPOs** [p. 182] and **rights issues** [p. 280].

New issues are economically the most important function of capital markets. They allow issuers to raise capital that they can then can invest in their business or use in some other way.

Without new issues companies could not raise money to expand and borrowing by all organisations would be limited to bank debt.

Nominal interest rates

The actual interest rate without any adjustments. Usually, annual interest payable divided by face value.

The nominal interest rates are used in most financial calculations, but it is often useful to think in terms of **real interest rates** [p. 265].

Nominee

A nominee holds securities on behalf of investors, the latter being the **beneficial owners** [p. 34] of the securities.

In markets where this is common practice (which includes the UK) holding securities through nominees is cheaper. The main reason is that investors do not need their own membership of the **securities depositary** [p. 95] used.

The disadvantage of using a nominee is that shareholders may not have certain rights that shareholders on the register have. The most important of these are:

- the right to vote at an **AGM** [p. 12] or **EGM** [p. 119]

- the right to combine with other shareholders to force an EGM and to propose AGM or EGM resolutions.

Shareholders will not directly lose financially by holding securities through a nominee – entitlements to dividends, **rights issues** [p. 280] etc. are unaffected, although these are received or exercised indirectly by instructing the nominee, rather than by dealing directly with the issuer.

There are certain types of nominee relationships that do allow shareholders to vote. Using these is usually more expensive.

The effective disenfranchisement of most small shareholders has been a matter of considerable controversy and it looks likely that changes to company law in the near future will address this issue.

The role of a nominee is similar to that of a **custodian** [p. 84], however the types and level of services offered by a custodian to large institutional investors are very different from those offered by nominees to small shareholders.

Non-performing assets (NPA)

Non-performing assets, also called non-performing loans, are loans on which repayments or interest payments are not being made on time.

A loan is an asset for a bank as the interest payments and the repayment of the principal create a stream of cash flows. It is from the interest payments than a bank makes its profits.

Banks usually treat assets as non-performing if they are not serviced for some time. If payments are late for a short time a loan is classified as past due.

Once a payment becomes really late (usually 90 days) the loan classified as non-performing.

A high level of non-performing assets compared to similar lenders may be a sign of problems, as may an sudden increase. However this needs to be looked at in the context of the type of lending being done. Some banks lend to higher risk customers than others and therefore tend to have a higher proportion of non-performing debt, but will make up for this by charging borrowers higher interest rates, increasing **spreads** [p. 176]. A mortgage lender will almost certainly have lower non-performing assets than a credit card specialist, but the latter will have higher spreads and may well make a bigger profit on the same assets, even if it eventually has to write off the non-performing loans.

Non-interest income

There are two common measures of the income banks generate from sources other than interest: the non-interest income level and the fee income level.

Different banks have very different sources of income. This in turn means they have different profit drivers.

Interest income is influenced by both the economic cycle and the level of interest rates. Fee income is **cyclical** [p. 84]. Non-interest income other than fees (primarily bank charges) is comparatively **defensive** [p. 84].

Non-interest income level

The non-interest income level is:

non-interest income ÷ operating income

This measures total non-interest income as a proportion of operating income; it shows what proportion of profits come from all sources (including fee income) other than **interest spreads** [p. 176].

Fee income level

The fee income level is:

fee income ÷ operating income

Fee income covers most income which is neither interest income nor bank charges. This includes a wide range of sources of income including fund management fees, loan arrangement fees, fees for advice, trust and **custody** [p. 84] fees, and commission on sales of third party financial products such as insurance.

Advice is a very important source of income for investment banks that make money advising on **mergers** [p. 201] and **acquisitions** [p. 5] and similar transactions.

NOPAT

Net operating profit after tax (NOPAT) measures the **operating profit** [p. 227] made for all investors, both shareholders and debt holders. It (with various adjustments) is often used in **EVA** [p. 131] models.

The justification for this is that a company creates wealth for shareholders by providing returns that are greater than the **cost of capital** [p. 342]. Therefore the management should focus on the actual returns to investors. This is the sum of the returns to shareholders and debt holders; the profit generated for shareholders plus the interest paid on debt. This is the same as the operating profit less tax with certain adjustments. Hence the term NOPAT.

The adjustments made may include: removing the effects of **goodwill** [p. 159] and other non-cash items, treating **R & D expenditure** [p. 261] as an investment (rather than a current expenditure) and treating operating lease rentals as interest.

A serious weakness of NOPAT is that it is distorted by the different tax treatment of debt and equity. The returns to debt and equity holders are calculated after tax, but the level of debt affects the level of tax and this is not corrected.

NOPAT is usually used internally as a target for company's management, rather than externally as a valuation measure by investors.

Normal distribution

The normal distribution, also called the Gaussian distribution, is the commonest of the many probability distributions that describe the pattern of future probabilities of some value.

The normal distribution's "bell shaped" curve is also familiar. It is often used in financial economics, even though it is often a simplifying assumption rather than the most accurate description of the probabilities. This is because it is (comparatively) easy to manipulate mathematically to derive useful results.

The standard normal distribution is the normal distribution with a **arithmetic mean** [p. 19] of zero and a **standard deviation** [p. 305] of one.

The cumulative normal distribution is the area under the curve of the normal distribution up to a particular value. In mathematical terms, the integral of the normal distribution.

The nature of the cumulative standard normal distribution (as used in **Black-Scholes** [p. 36]) should now be self-explanatory.

A number of valuation and risk **models** [p. 140] assume that the future price of a security is normally distributed. This is clearly false as a normal distribution function has a positive value for any value of the future price, whereas the price of a security cannot fall below zero.

A particularly important weakness, in the context of risk models, is that real distributions are fat-tailed. Their extremes are more probable than those of the standard distribution, because of the risk of crashes and booms.

The normal distribution is easy to use and the assumption that prices are normally distributed is sufficiently accurate in many circumstances.

Normal market size

London Stock Exchange sets a normal market size for each **listed security** [p. 190]. It is set at 2.5% of the average daily turnover (i.e. total amount traded) in the security in the previous year.

The main importance of the normal market size is for **market maker** [p. 197] quotes on **quote driven** [p. 261] trading systems, primarily the SEAQ system. A market maker for a SEAQ security is obliged to continually quote **bid** [p. 35] and **offer prices** [p. 222] that are firm for deals up to the normal market size.

It is obviously impossible for market makers to offer quotes that would be firm up to an unlimited size. For a quote driven system to provide the liquidity it should, investors should be able to rely on market makers to take reasonably ordinary (i.e. not unusually large) quantities of a security at the quoted price.

The normal market size is a simple transparent mechanism that reconciles these requirements.

When trading more than the normal market size in a security through a quote driven trading system, the mechanism changes. For most trades, the broker will contract a market maker (or market makers) in order to ask for a quote that is good for the larger quantity. If the quantity is only a little more than the normal market size, the price may not change, but market makers are likely to offer worse prices as the deal size gets bigger.

As the size of the number of securities being bought or sold gets larger it becomes harder to get a good price. Very large blocks may be sold over a period of time rather than in one go, or by finding buyers or sellers outside the trading system.

Notes to accounts

The notes to the accounts are a series of notes that are referred to in the main body of the financial statements.

The notes give further details on the numbers given in the accounts. The importance of these numbers should not be underestimated. The accounts are not complete without the notes. Investors who rely on the main body of the accounts and ignore the notes are likely to find themselves misled.

Typical notes include:

- a reconciliation of operating profit to operating cash flow which can be used to calculate **EBITDA** [p. 116], and **working capital movements** [p. 347]

- a geographic breakdown of sales which can give investors an idea of exposure to different national economies

- details of assets and liabilities.

Because the notes can greatly change one's interpretation of the numbers in the financial statements, a very effective way of understanding a set of financial statements is to read the notes first – to read the accounts from the bottom up.

NPV

A present value is the value now of a stream of future cash flows, negative or positive. The value of each cash flow needs to be adjusted for risk and the **time value of money** [p. 322].

A net present value (NPV) includes all cash flows, such cost of acquisition of an asset, whereas a present value does not. So the net present value of a purchase being considered would include its purchase cost (as a negative cash flow), whereas the present value would not.

A discount rate needs to be used to adjust for risk and time value, and it is applied like this:

$$NPV = CF_0 + \frac{CF_1}{(1+r)} + \frac{CF_2}{(1+r)^2} + \frac{CF_3}{(1+r)^3} + \cdots$$

where CF_1 is the cash flow the investor receives in the first year, CF_2 the cash flow the investor receives in the second year etc.
and r is the discount rate.

Periods other than an year could be used, but the discount rate needs to be adjusted. Assuming we start from an annual discount rate then to adjust to another period we would use, to get a rate i, given annual rate r, for a period x, where x is a fraction (e.g., six months = 0.5) or a multiple of the number of years:

$$i + 1 = (r + 1)^x$$

To use discount rates that vary over time (so r_1 is the rate in the first period, r_2 = rate in the second period etc.) we would have to resort to a more basic form of the calculation:

$$NPV = CF_0 + \frac{CF_1}{1+r_1} + \frac{CF_2}{(1+r_1)(1+r_2)} + \frac{CF_3}{(1+r_1)(1+r_2)(1+r_3)} + \cdots$$

This would be tedious to calculate by hand but is fairly easy to implement in a spreadsheet.

See **DCF** [p. 88] and **CAPM** [p. 50]

OEIC

Open ended investment companies (OEICs) are a form of **collective investment fund** [p. 62]. OEICs are legally similar to **investment trusts** [p. 180] in that they are companies whose sole business is to manage the investments they own. OEICs operate more like **unit trusts** [p. 333] in that investors buy and sells shares in the OEIC from and to the OEIC manager rather than on the open market. This is possible as an OEIC can freely cancel existing shares (when an investor sells) or buy new shares (when an investor buys).

As with unit trusts, there may be initial charges and exit charges. However OEICS, unlike unit trusts, are generally **single priced** [p. 296]. As with any type of fund there will be an annual management fee.

Ofcom

Ofcom, the Office of Communications, is the UK regulator of the broadcasting and telecommunications industries.

Its main duty in telecoms regulation is to ensure the wide provision of services to consumers (e.g., by encouraging the roll-out of new services), license and regulate network operators and promote competition.

In radio and television it is also responsible for the quality of material broadcast, preventing the broadcast of offensive material and preventing unfairness and infringements of privacy.

Media convergence [p. 200] means that the regulation of content imposed on broadcasters will also increasingly apply to some of the operations of telecoms companies. This is why the duties of the former telecoms regulator, Oftel, were combined with those of regulating the media.

The primary importance of Ofcom to investors is the power it has over the telecoms and media companies it regulates. Changes to Ofcom policy can have drastic effects. It both sets the framework in which media and telecoms companies operates and it can impose pricing and other restrictions on individual companies.

Ofcom is also a very useful source of information. It gathers detailed statistics on the industries it regulates which are invaluable to investors. There are other useful sources (such as **Rajar** [p. 263]), but Ofcom publishes more detailed information on its publicly accessible website than any other single source.

Off balance sheet financing

Debt financing that is not shown on the face of the **balance sheet** [p. 28] is called "off balance sheet financing".

Off balance sheet financing allows a company to borrow being without affecting calculations of measures of indebtedness such as **gearing** [p. 157].

The motives may include misleading investors and remaining within the terms of **debt covenants** [p. 90]. It may also sometimes be a side effect of the method of raising capital chosen, but it is probably best to be suspicious of the motives for raising debt in a manner that is not visible to investors.

The scope for off balance sheet financing has reduced over the years as accounting standards have caught up with loopholes that allowed off balance sheet financing. In the past these have included leasing and borrowing through **special purpose vehicles** [p. 304].

For the moment off-balance sheet financing does not seem to be much of a problem but it is likely that creative new ways to borrow off the balance sheet will be found and exploited.

Offer price

The lowest price at which a seller is willing to sell a particular security is the offer price of the security. This is therefore the lowest price at which the security can be bought in the market.

As with the **bid price** [p. 35], the quantity automatically available at this price will be limited. For larger orders it may be necessary to pay more, negotiate prices, or both.

Official List

The Official List is the list of all securities that have been approved by the **UK Listing Authority** [p. 330] for trading on financial exchanges in the UK.

Securities can not trade on a stock exchange in the UK unless they appear on the Official List. Most other countries have similar regulations.

Ofgem

Ofgem is the UK regulator of the gas and electricity industries. Its main roles are to promote competition and to regulate the monopolies of the gas and electricity companies.

Because gas and electricity distribution are **natural monopolies** [p. 212] (it is highly unlikely that anyone will build duplicates of existing distribution systems) these require particularly tight regulation. For example, there are restrictions on the prices that can be charged for electricity transmission. Other markets (such as electricity generation) tend to be regulated with the aim of using competition to drive down prices.

Ofgem's duties go for beyond price regulation. The most important of its other responsibilities are to ensure the security of the UK's energy supplies (which implicitly includes the reliability of transmission networks) and to minimise disconnection of consumers through poverty.

Ofwat

Ofwat is the UK regulator of the water industry. The industry has a strong natural monopoly and provides something that is clearly a necessity, so it has become even more tightly regulated than other utilities.

From an investor's point of view, the most important aspect of Ofwat's work is its regulation of prices. These are set for periods of several years at a time, and there is a period of consultation before they are set. This usually includes a preliminary determination, well before a final decision is made.

This means that water company's revenues are very predictable. Ofwat's regulation also aims to give each water companies a reasonable return on the assets invested in the regulated part of its business. This means that, unless either Ofwat or a water company gets things badly wrong, the regulated parts of water companies are very low risk.

The companies may (and often do) also have other, higher risk, businesses, but it is generally a very safe sector.

Oil reserves

Reserves are the amount of oil or gas that has been discovered and that can be extracted profitably with existing technology under present economic conditions.

Reserves are categorised as being **proven** [p. 256], **probable** [p. 253] or **possible** [p. 243]. There are, unfortunately, no standard definitions for these terms which can vary between companies and countries. The definitions are generally broadly similar.

The lack of definitions does create an opportunity for companies to manipulate the numbers. In the UK, definitions are usually similar to those used by the DTI, but companies have wide discretion. In the US, the SEC imposes definitions on listed companies.

Oligopoly

An oligopoly the domination of a market by a few firms. A **duopoly** [p. 112] is a simple form of oligopoly in which only two firms dominate a market.

Where an oligopoly exists, a few large suppliers dominate the market resulting in a high degree of market concentration; a large percentage of the market is taken by the few leading firms.

An oligopoly usual depends on high **barriers to entry** [p. 30]. It often leads to a lack of price competition (although there may be fierce competition in terms of marketing etc) which is the problem from the point of view of consumers.

Because an oligopoly consists of a few firms, they are usually very much aware of each others' actions (e.g. changes to prices). This can lead to informal collusion as firms match prices to avoid provoking a price war. This has a similar effect to deliberate collusion, but is harder for regulators to control.

This also means that when price cuts do occur, the market tends to have to follow the lead of any one firm.

This leads to each firm experiencing a peculiar demand curve, the so-called kinked demand curve. An oligopolist faces a downward sloping demand curve but its **price elasticity** [p. 247] may depend on the reaction of rivals to changes in price and output. Assuming that firms are attempting to maintain a high level of profits and their market shares.

- Competitors will not follow a price increase by one firm, so a firm that raises prices will lose market share and therefore profits.

- Competitors have to match a price cut by one firm to avoid a loss of market share. That means that if one firm cuts prices, all will have lower profits.

This means that the demand curve for the oligopolist is not straight. It is flatter above the current price, with a sudden change of slope at the current price. This means that an oligopolist usually has little incentive to change its prices. It may cut prices where there are prospects of market share gains (i.e. when its rivals will not follow). It may increase prices if it feels sure that competitors will follow (or when the margin increase is sufficient to make up for the large loss in market share). Prices in an oligopoly therefore tend to be higher and change less than under perfect competition.

Examples of oligopolies may include the markets for petrol in the UK (BP, Shell and a few other firms) and soft drinks (such as Coke, Pepsi, and Cadbury-Schweppes).

The word oligopoly is derived from the Greek oligos, which means few.

Oligopolistic supply, corresponding to a **monopsony** [p. 208], is an oligopsony.

Oligopsony

An oligopsony is the opposite of an **oligopoly** [p. 223].

In an oligopoly a few large suppliers dominate a market, in an oligopsony a few large buyers dominate a market.

A good example are the many media sub-sectors where a few companies (the major media conglomerates) publish records, films and books, but there are many musicians, actors, writers etc. selling to these few companies.

OPEC basket price

OPEC has tied its production management activity to the goal of maintaining the OPEC Basket price which is a simple average price of a "basket" of seven **crude oils** [p. 81], including: Algeria's Saharan Blend, Indonesia's Minas, Nigeria's

Bonny Light, Saudi Arabia's Arab Light, Dubai's Fateh, Venezuela's Tia Juana Light, and Mexico's Isthmus (a non-OPEC crude oil).

OPEC uses the price of this basket to monitor world oil market conditions. Of the major **benchmark** [p. 34] crude oils **West Texas Intermediate** [p. 345] and **Brent** [p. 41] are lighter (see **API gravity** [p. 17]) and sweeter, and therefore more expensive, than the OPEC basket.

Open offer

An open offer is similar to a **rights issue** [p. 280], in that shareholders are entitled to buy newly issued shares in proportion to their existing holdings. Unlike a rights issue, an open offer does not allow shareholders to sell the right to subscribe to shares – the shareholders have an entitlement rather than a tradeable right to subscribe to new shares. For this reason an open offer is sometimes called an entitlement issue.

Any entitlement that is not taken up is simply allowed to lapse.

As with a rights issue, the price of the offer is likely to be at a discount to the current share price and the effect of the open offer on the price is calculated in essentially the same way.

Rights issues are more common as they are just as effective in raising money for the company, but more convenient for those shareholders who do not wish to increase their holding, as they can simply sell the rights.

Open outcry

Open outcry is a method of trading used at stock and commodity exchanges that involves calling out the specific details of a buy or sell order, so that the information is available to all traders. The information is then usually written on boards so all traders can see it.

Open outcry trading requires exciting trading floors with brokers rushing around trying to get their orders on the board. Brokers tend to enjoy open outcry markets, particularly during the euphoria of bull markets.

Open outcry has largely been replaced by **automated trading systems** [p. 24]. These are cheaper, globally accessible, disseminate information perfectly and match orders perfectly.

There is evidence that open outcry trading floors can make for good dissemination of information in other ways. Traders can use cues such as noise levels and the behaviour of other traders to monitor where the important movements in the market are happening.

Operating cash flow

Operating cash flow, usually more formally described in accounts as "cash inflow from operating activities", is the amount of actual cash made by a company's business. It is similar to **operating profit** [p. 115] but without the non-cash items and **accruals** [p. 4].

A reconciliation of operating profit and operating cash flow is always included in the full year results, and usually in half yearly and quarterly results. This is worth looking at as it (hopefully) explains any differences between the profits and cash flow. Profits are ultimately useless unless converted into cash and looking at the reconciliation may highlight problems.

The usual non-cash items are fairly obvious – **depreciation** [p. 95] and **amortisation** [p. 15] and changes in **working capital** [p. 347].

Adding back deprecation and amortisation are the adjustments that are made when calculating **EBITDA** [p. 116] from operating profit. This is why EBITDA is often regarded as a cash flow measure. It is the same as operating cash flow without the working capital adjustments, which are volatile and often obscure trends and changes. EBITDA is also usually calculated before **exceptional items** [p. 132], which again gives a clearer view of underlying trends.

Ultimately, cash flow is what is what matters to investors, however operating cash flow, while important, is only part of this and investors need to look at the cash flow statement as a whole. It is also useful to look at measures of cash returns to investors. Operating cashflow can be a useful measure, as can EBITDA and **free cash flow** [p. 146].

Operating cash flow ratio

The operating cash flow ratio measures a company's ability to pay its short term liabilities. It is:

$$\frac{operating\ cashflow[\text{p. }225]}{current\ liabilities}$$

If the operating cash flow ratio is less than one, it means that the company has generated less cash over the year than it needs to pay off short term liabilities as at the year end. This may signal a need to raise money to meet liabilities.

As a refinement, one could deduct the value of **deferred income** [p. 92] from the current liabilities.

The operating cashflow ratio can be used to compare companies across a sector, and to look at changes over time. Generally, a higher ratio is preferred, but as with all liquidity ratios, sector norms and the peculiarities of each business need to be taken into account.

The **current asset ratio** [p. 83] and others based on **balance sheet** [p. 28] numbers gauge liquidity as at the balance sheet date, whereas the operating cashflow ratio uses the cash generated over an accounting period.

Operating margin

Operating margin is simply the **profit margin** [p. 253] calculated using **operating profit** [p. 227]:

$$\frac{operating\ profit}{sales}\ \text{as a percentage}$$

It is often calculated using **adjusted operating profit** [p. 8].
Operating margin may help:

- Show how much of a change in operating profit comes from the change in margins, as opposed to the change in sales.

- Compare the margins of different companies in the same business.

- Estimate how much potential a company has to increase profits through margin expansion, or, conversely, how much profits may be threatened by price competition.

- **Model** [p. 140] future profits.

Operating profit

Profit generated by a company's operations before interest payments and tax is called operating profit.

Operating profit is closely related to **EBIT** [p. 115], and is usually the same.

There may be a difference between EBIT and operating profit. It is almost always small. It comes from the exclusion from operating profit of certain profits or losses that are not part of the operations of a business – such as profits on the sale of businesses.

Although the definition of **trading profit** [p. 327] can vary it is usually very similar to operating profit or **adjusted operating profit** [p. 8].

Operational gearing

Operational gearing is the effect of **fixed costs** [p. 143] on the relationship between sales and **operating profits** [p. 115]. If a company has no operational gearing, then operating profit would rise at the same rate as sales growth (assuming nothing else changed).

Operational gearing is simple and important – and often neglected.

High fixed costs increase operational gearing. Consider two companies with different cost structures but the same profits.

	Company A	Company B
Sales	1,000,000	1,000,000
Variable Costs [p. 338]	700,000	800,000
Fixed Costs [p. 143]	200,000	100,000
Operating profit	100,000	100,000

At this point both companies have the same sales and the same costs, and therefore the same operating profit.

Now suppose both companies increase sales by 50%

	Company A	Company B
Sales	1,500,000	1,500,000
Variable Costs [p. 338]	1,050,000	1,200,000
Fixed Costs [p. 143]	200,000	100,000
Operating profit	250,000	200,000

The company with the higher operational gearing, A, makes 2.5× as much profit as it did before the 50% increase in sales, whereas B has only doubled its profits.

Operational gearing is this effect on operating profit. There is a further similar effect on pre-tax profit as a result of the level of interest a company has to pay (another fixed cost), this is financial **gearing** [p. 157].

Option

An option gives its holder the right to buy or sell an asset at a price that is either fixed or calculated according to a pre-arranged formula.

The buyer of an option is not obliged to either buy or sell the **underlying asset** [p. 331]. The originator of an option, called the **option writer** [p. 229], is obliged to carry out their side of the transaction, should the holder of the option want them to.

The underlying asset is most commonly a financial security (e.g. shares or bonds), a commodity (e.g. a fixed quantity of a metal) or linked to a financial index.

An option which gives the buyer the right to buy an asset is a call option. An option which gives the buyer the right to sell an asset is a put option. The asset the option is called the underlying asset. The price at which the underlying security is to be bought or sold is called the strike price or **exercise price** [p. 135].

Options are closely related to futures contracts, but they give a holder the upside without the downside risk. Because this means that the writer takes the risk but foregoes the opportunity to profit. This means the writer needs to be comensated for taking the risk, and they are worth more to the holder.

Most options traded on exchanges are not settled by delivery (actually transferring the underlying asset) but by a payment of the value of the option at expiry. This value is either zero (if the option is **at-the-money** [p. 23] or **out-of-the-money** [p. 232]) or the amount by which the option is **in-the-money** [p. 167].

Other securities may, in effect, incorporate an option, this is called an **embedded option** [p. 120]. An example of this is a **convertible bond** [p. 72], which effectively combines a **bond** [p. 37] with a call option.

Option value may also exist outside financial instruments, intrinsic in contracts or businesses. These are called **real options** [p. 265].

The most common types of option are the simple **American** [p. 14] and **European options** [p. 128] which have fixed strike prices and expiry dates. **Asian options** [p. 20] are somewhat less common and have strike prices based on the average price of the underlying over a pre-determined period. More complex types of options are hugely varied and are collectively referred to as **exotic options** [p. 135].

Option valuation

The valuation of an option requires the use of more complex **models** [p. 140] than the underlying securities. The value can be regarded as broken down into **intrinsic value** [p. 179] and **option value** [p. 229] – the latter being what is hard to value. The commonest way of valuing options is the **Black-Scholes** [p. 36] formula.

Option value

The difference between the **intrinsic value** [p. 179] of an **option** [p. 228] and its actual value is called the option value. It is called option value because it is the additional value that comes from the option not to exercise if that is a more profitable course.

Option value can be a substantial part of the value of an option. It increases with:

- the **volatility** [p. 340] of the **underlying** [p. 331]

- the time till expiry

- the option moving towards being, or further into being, **out-of-the-money** [p. 232].

It should be obvious that if an option is **at-the-money** [p. 23] or **out-of-the-money** [p. 232], then it only has a positive value because of its option value.

Option value can existing in securities that are not options (see **embedded option** [p. 120]) and in contracts or businesses (see **real options** [p. 265]).

Option writer

Options [p. 228] must originate with a person who creates an option. This is the option writer. The option writer is the first seller of an option, although it may subsequently be traded further.

The option writer takes on a significant risk, due to the potential obligation to buy a security at below its market value (in the case of a **put option** [p. 258]) or sell a security at under its market value (in the case of a **call option** [p. 45]).

This risk can usually be **hedged** [p. 162]. In the case of a call option it can be hedged simply by holding the securities which would have to be delivered if the option is exercised.

Option writers are likely to use strategies that are less expensive than holding enough of a security to be able to settle. **Delta hedging** [p. 93] is a simple example of such a strategy, others can be much more complex.

Order driven trading system

See **matched bargain** [p. 198].

Ordinary shares

Ordinary shares are by far the most common form of **equity** [p. 123] security.

Ordinary shares are equal to other ordinary shares in both entitlement to share in profits and in voting rights.

The equity capital of most **listed companies** [p. 190] is dominated by ordinary shares, sometimes supplemented by **prefs** [p. 244] or **convertibles** [p. 72].

Some companies have other classes of share with greater or less entitlements. These include non-voting shares or shares with extra voting rights. These are disliked by investors and are becoming less common.

Ore grade

Grade is a measurement of the metal content of ore.

The grade of precious metal ore is usually measured in troy ounces per tonne or grams per tonne. The grade of ore bearing other metals is usually a percentage (the weight for weight proportion of metal in the ore).

Mill head grade is the grade of mined ore fed into a mill, as opposed to the grade of the ore mined.

The grade of ore from a mine changes over time. A lower grade will (other things being equal) mean a higher cost per unit weight of extracted metal. Costs are also influenced by other factors such as the costs of the actual mining of ore itself.

The most important factor in the profitability of a mine is usually the price of the metal (or other **commodity** [p. 64]) that it produces.

Organic growth

Organic growth is growth that comes from a company's existing businesses, as opposed to growth that comes from buying new businesses. It may be negative.

Organic growth figures are adjusted for the effects of acquisitions and disposals of businesses. Organic growth does include growth over a period that results from investment in businesses the company owned at the beginning of the period. What it excludes is the boost to growth from **acquisitions** [p. 5], and the decline from sales and closures of whole businesses.

When a company does not **disclose** [p. 98] organic growth numbers, it is usually possible to estimate them by estimating the numbers for acquisitions made in the period being looked at and in the previous year.

It is useful to break down organic sales growth into that coming from market growth and that coming from gains in market share: this makes it easier to see how sustainable growth is.

Orphan Drugs

Some regulators, most importantly the US Food and Drugs Administration (FDA), designate certain drugs orphan drugs.

The company developing the drug needs to apply for this designation and it needs to meet certain criteria – the most important is that the disease should be rare. Once a drug is designated an orphan drug it receives a number of incentives:

- a period of marketing exclusivity – once it is approved, approval of other drugs to treat the same condition will be delayed

- access to grants and tax credits to offset **R & D** [p. 261] costs

- waiving of regulators fees

- faster or simpler **clinical trial** [p. 60] and approval processes.

The exact incentives vary from country to country. The single most important incentive is seven year market exclusivity in the US.

Market exclusivity is a strong incentive because it grants a much stronger **monopoly** [p. 207] that that granted by a patent, albeit for a shorter period. A patent merely stops anyone else from selling the same drug. Marketing exclusivity stops anyone else from selling any drug to treat the same condition. This does not affect sales of existing treatments, only new ones.

From an investment point of view, the consequences of an orphan drug designation are:

- lower costs to get the product to market

- less risk of new competition in the first few years of sales.

The costs are lower and the potential sales volumes and prices are higher than without the orphan drug designation.

OTC drug

An over the counter (OTC) drug is one that can be sold with out a prescription.

The OTC drug market has high volumes, but the drugs are much cheaper. OTC drugs are not designed for the treatment of serious conditions. This limits the advantages any in-patent drugs can offer over **generics** [p. 157]. **Brands** [p. 40] are more important than in the **prescription drug** [p. 246] market, but other aspects of marketing are easier – for example, the need for large sales forces (that sell prescription drugs to prescribers) is reduced.

OTC drugs make up only a small proportion of the sales of the major pharmaceutical companies, but they are more important for some of the smaller specialist pharmaceutical companies. Some are manufactured by companies outside the sector such as Reckitt Benckiser.

Out of the money

An **option** [p. 228] is out of the money (often written "out-of-the-money") if it has a negative **intrinsic value** [p. 179].

A **call option** [p. 45] is out of the money if the **exercise price** [p. 135] is greater than the price of the **underlying asset** [p. 331], vice versa for a **put option** [p. 258].

It is important to remember than an option that is deeply out of the money still has a positive value. An option always has a positive value because its holder can always choose not to exercise. The **option value** [p. 229] is always greater than a negative intrinsic value – unless the **underlying** [p. 331] is worth zero.

Outsourcing

Outsourcing is the contracting out of work, that was previously done within an organisation, to an external provider. There are a number of reasons for outsourcing, the commonest are to enable a business to focus on its core business or to save costs.

Although many people associate outsourcing with the moving of work offshore (to another country, usually one with lower labour costs), outsourcing is far wider than that, and has become extremely common.

While many organisations can both reduce costs and improve management by outsourcing, there are also disadvantages. There is a loss of control involved in outsourcing, as the function outsourced is no longer under direct control. Outsourcing also exposes the organisation doing the outsourcing to the risk that its supplier may fail to deliver, or to deliver satisfactorily.

Outstanding claims reserve

The outstanding claims reserve is the **provision** [p. 256] made in the **balance sheet** [p. 28] of an insurance company for all claims that have been made and for which the insurer is liable, but which had not been settled at the balance sheet date.

Over-the-counter drug

See **OTC drug** [p. 232].

Overhead cost ratio

The overhead cost ratio explains the difference between the **gross margin** [p. 160] and **operating margin** [p. 226].

It shows what proportion of sales is spent on overheads, also called **sales, general and administrative costs** [p. 286]. These are all operating costs other than the **cost of goods sold** [p. 75].

The overhead cost ratio is:

$$\frac{overhead\ costs}{sales}$$

The use of the overhead cost ratio is similar to the use of margins. It is used to compare a company to industry norms and to look for trends. In general, it provides part of the breakdown of why profits are changing.

The overhead cost ratio also forms part of the decomposition of the operating margin:

$$operating\ margin = gross\ margin - overhead\ cost\ ratio$$

Overnight rate

The rate at which money is lent, to be returned the next day, by one bank to another is called an overnight rate.

Banks frequently find that they have surplus or insufficient funds at the end of each day. They settle with other banks by borrowing, and profit on any excess by lending till the next day.

This lending is unsecured and repaid the next morning.

These rates are clearly important to the banks themselves, and they are also used as reference rates to fix **floating interest rates** [p. 144] on certain types of debt. The most important interbank rate is the **LIBOR** [p. 187].

P & L

The profit and loss account (P & L)), called the income statement in the US, shows the profit or loss a company has made over a period of time. It is the most looked at accounting statement. The ratios investors look at most often, such as the **PE** [p. 237] and **yield** [p. 107], are calculated using numbers from the P & L.

Investors should not make the common mistake of thinking that the P & L is all they need to look at. This is not only because the P & L can be manipulated to mislead investors, but also simply because it is important to have a full picture.

The most detailed profit and loss account is given in the annual report, but UK listed companies are required to make annual and half year results announcements as well. The full year results announcement is shorter and covers the same period as the annual report, but it is released earlier.

Many companies make quarterly announcements, as companies in the US and many other countries are required to. Unsurprisingly, UK listed companies that also have a US listing are very likely to report quarterly.

The shortest possible P & L would be: sales less costs = total profit.

In a simple case the profit or loss equals the increase or decrease in the company's assets as shown on the **balance sheet** [p. 28]. This is rarely exactly true and the **statement of total recognised gains and losses** [p. 306] reconciles the P &L to the changes in **equity** [p. 123] shown on the balance sheet

In accordance with the **accrual principle** [p. 4], costs and revenues are matched so that, for example, sales and purchases made on credit during a year, but perhaps not yet paid for, will be included in the P & L for the year.

Most of the detail in the profit and loss account comes from the need to provide detail of costs and, to a lesser extent, revenues. This leads to the general form of a P & L that looks something like this:

Sales	Also called revenues or turnover
Cost of sales [p. 75]	The direct costs of things sold
Gross profit [p. 161]	Sales minus cost of sales
Other operating expenses	Depreciation, admin, marketing etc.
Operating profit [p. 115]	Gross profit less other expenses
Interest costs	Interest payable less receivable
Pre-tax profit	Operating profit less interest
Tax	
Profit after tax	Pre tax profit less tax
Dividends	
Retained profit	Profit after tax less dividends
Earnings per share [p. 122]	

As can be seen, the P & L contains several profit numbers. Each of these gives us different, and useful, information. In addition, the P & L (perhaps together with other information) usually gives us enough information to calculate several other profit numbers such as **EBITDA** [p. 116] and **EBITA** [p. 116]

Many companies will show **exceptionals** [p. 132] separately. If there were any discontinued business, or plans to dispose of a business within a short period, these are also shown separately.

These can give investors a better idea of the underlying business (the justification for doing it). For example, if the company has decided to sell a particular operation and the price has been agreed, shareholders do not really need to worry too much about that operation's performance.

A group balance sheet will need to be **consolidated** [p. 68], which requires extra lines such as those for share or profit in **associates** [p. 23] and **joint ventures** [p. 184], and the deduction of **minority interests** [p. 204].

As well as the valuation ratios, the P & L provides the numbers for measures of the performance and efficiency of the business, such as **margins** [p. 253], **ROCE** [p. 283], and some measures of financial stability such as **interest cover** [p. 176].

The P & L is potential misleading and there are a number of accounting techniques that can shift losses (or gains, although that is rarer) from the P & L to the balance sheet. The P & L should be looked at in conjunction with the **notes** [p. 219] and the **cash flow statement** [p. 54] (which is harder to manipulate).

The P & L is backward looking and investors will need to consider correcting some items such as **amortisation** [p. 15] that are not useful for modeling future cash flows. From an investor's point of view the P & L is essential, but can be misleading and should not be looked at in isolation.

Par value

The par value, or **face value** [p. 137], of a share is the amount that is shown on the face of a share as its value.

The par value is an arbitrary amount that is determined when a company is incorporated. Its only real importance is that (in the UK at least) shares cannot be issued for a payment that is less than their par value.

It is possible to issue shares for a payment that is less than their par value, with shareholders then liable to pay the remainder later. This does not usual with **listed companies'** [p. 190] shares so it is of little importance to most investors.

The par value of a share multiplied by the number of shares is shown in a company's **balance sheet** [p. 28] as its **share capital** [p. 293]. When shares are issued at more than their par value the excess is added to the share premium reserve on the balance sheet.

A company can change the par value of its shares or adjust the amount in the share premium reserve, but it is not able to do so as and when the directors and shareholders wish. These changes require permission from a court and are usually associated with large **returns of capital** [p. 276], **share splits** [p. 294] or **consolidations** [p. 69].

What a company can freely do, is to use the share premium reserve for a **scrip issue** [p. 287].

The par value must not be confused with the net assets (**NAV** [p. 213]) per share. The latter gives investors some information about what a share is worth, the par value does not.

Parent company

A company is the parent company of any subsidiaries it owns or controls.

A parent company is required to publish group accounts that **consolidate** [p. 68] the results of its **subsidiaries** [p. 311] and **associates** [p. 23].

Group structure can also affect taxation, competition regulation and the regulation of **takeovers** [p. 5].

Payback period

The payback period is both conceptually simple and easy to calculate. It is also a seriously flawed method of evaluating investments.

The payback period is the time taken to recover the initial investment. So a £1m investment that will make a profit of £200,000 a year has a payback period of five years. Investments with a shorter payback period are preferred to those with a long period. Most companies using payback period as a criterion will have a maximum acceptable period.

The payback period has a number of serious flaws:

- It attaches no value to **cashflows** [p. 53] after the end of the payback period.

- It makes no adjustments for risk.

- It is not directly related to wealth maximisation as **NPV** [p. 220] is.

- It ignores the **time value of money** [p. 322].

- The "cut off" period is arbitrary.

To compensate for some of these deficiencies, one can adjust the cash flow by discounting the cashflow using the **WACC** [p. 342] and then calculating the payback period. This only really adjusts for the time value of money and it therefore does not address the other deficiencies of the payback period.

One justification for the use of the payback period is that it is conservative, as it values only short term returns which can be foreseen with reasonable certainty. However this argument does not really stand up to scrutiny; the NPV (or **APV** [p. 8]) also adjusts for the uncertainty of future cashflows and does so correctly.

One explanation of the wide use of the payback period is that as a conservative criterion it is preferred by managers who have an **undiversifiable** [p. 102] stake in a company (i.e. their jobs), This makes it preferable to less conservative criteria that might be preferred by shareholders who can diversify.

Payout ratio

The payout ratio is the proportion of bottom line profit that is paid to shareholders as dividends. It is the inverse of **dividend cover** [p. 103]:

$$\frac{dividend\ per\ share}{EPS[\text{p. }122]} \text{ or, equivalently } \frac{dividends}{profit\ attributable\ to\ shareholders}$$

In either case, it is usually expressed as a percentage rather than as a fraction. As its purpose is primarily to asses the sustainability of dividends and the risk of dividend cuts, it should usually be calculated using **pre-exceptional** [p. 132] profits or EPS.

The dividend payout ratio does matter (see **dividend irrelevance** [p. 105] and **dividend cover** [p. 103]), both as a measure of how safe a dividend (low is good) and how willing a company is to pay out cash to shareholders (high is good).

PE ratio

The price/earnings ratio (PE) is the most commonly used valuation measure. It compares the price of a share to the company's **EPS** [p. 122]. It directly relates the price of a share to the proportion of the company's profits that belong to the owner of that share.

One of the reasons for the popularity of the PE ratio is its simplicity. It is:

$$\frac{share\ price}{EPS}$$

Headline or **adjusted EPS** [p. 7] is usually preferable to **basic EPS** [p. 31]. A **diluted EPS** [p. 97] is usually preferable to an undiluted one.

A higher PE means that the same share of a company's profits will cost a prospective shareholder more. There are usually reasons for a higher PE. It may reflect faster expected earnings growth, or lower risk earnings.

As investors are most interested in future cash flows, **prospective PE** [p. 255] and other future PEs are usually more important than **historical PEs** [p. 164].

In order to make fair comparisons of companies with different year ends, and to use the most up to date information, one can use a PE based on the **trailing twelve months earnings** [p. 328].

It is also useful to look at a **relative PE** [p. 273] against a company's **sector** [p. 289] or **market** [p. 289].

PE is the most widely used valuation ratio and has the advantage of being comparatively simple. It is not the only valuation ratio – although many investors, even professionals, appear to think it is – and others are frequently more useful. For example, the closely related **PEG** [p. 238] ratio provides a crude adjustment for growth, while **EV/EBITDA** [p. 129] is not distorted by **capital structure** [p. 48].

DCFs [p. 88] are theoretically the most correct form of valuation, but are harder to do.

PEG

The PE/growth ratio (PEG) attempts to allow meaningful comparison of the prices of companies with different growth rates.

A faster growing company deserves a higher **PE** [p. 237]. The PEG ratio attempts to formalise this by dividing the PE ratio by the percentage annual growth in earnings per share.

The PEG ratio is:

$$\frac{PE}{g}$$

where PE is simply the PE ratio
and g is the percentage growth in **EPS** [p. 122].

It is usual to use **historical PE** [p. 164] and the growth from that to the **prospective PE** [p. 255]. So, if the historical EPS is 200p and the prospective is 210p, then g will be $(210 \div 200) \times 100 = 5$. The use of the prospective PE and the following year's PE instead (i.e., all the numbers one year further forward) is also common.

The problem with this measure is that it only look at the growth rate over one year, whereas with high growth companies it is their long term growth potential that matters. This makes it a rather crude measure that is more useful for screening rather than as a key measure for stock selection.

PEG assumes a linear relationship between growth and value (a company with twice the growth rate should have twice the PE). This is also incorrect, although it is a reasonable approximation when comparing companies with roughly similar growth rates.

Penny shares

The term penny shares is most commonly used by **tip sheets** [p. 323]. It refers to shares that have a low price: a few pence a share as opposed to the more typical tens or hundreds of pence per share.

This idea behind the advocacy of penny shares is that low priced shares have more potential to rise, and therefore investors should do their stock-picking by selecting from among penny shares.

The idea is fundamentally flawed. Looking at price alone, without any indication of what value a share has is not meaningful. A share price can only be said to be too high or low relative to **earnings per share** [p. 122], **NAV** [p. 213], or some such similar measure.

It is not possible to say what a share ought to be worth without properly valuing it. Once a real valuation technique has been used, the fact that it is a penny share is irrelevant.

The falsity of the idea that penny share are in some way special is evident if one considers that a company can decide whether its shares are penny shares are not by consolidating or splitting its shares.

What little value techniques based on the penny share idea have is attributable to the fact that penny shares tend to be those of small companies and those whose price has fallen from more conventional levels. The former are more likely than large companies to have good **growth** [p. 161] prospects. The latter are more likely to be recovery stocks

Investors are better off using the more precise technique of screening by **market cap** [p. 196] to find small companies, and looking at historical data to find recovery stocks.

PIBS (permanent interest bearing shares)

PIBS are permanent interest bearing shares issued by building societies.

They often have a good **yield** [p. 350] but are fairly safe investments with a level of risk comparable with buying a bank's **subordinated debt** [p. 310].

The main risk is interest rate risk, which is high as PIBS are permenant - and therefore not **redeemable** [p. 268]. Most of those that are redeemable, are many years from maturity. Their **duration** [p. 113] is usually very high.

They are **bond** [p. 37] like instruments in that they pay interest. Like other building society investments (including deposits) they make holders members of the building society, with rights with regard to management similar to those of a shareholder in a company.

This means that PIBS also bring the chance of a windfall profit should the building society demutualise. If a building society does demutualise, then PIBS become subordinated debt.

PIBS tend to be somewhat neglected investments, although there is the occasional bit of media coverage to tell investors that they do exist.

Investors in PIBS will usually be looking at them as one of many fixed income securities with a higher yield than **gilts** [p. 158]: others include corporate bonds and **prefs** [p. 244].

Placing

A placing is the issue of new shares, which are sold directly to new shareholders, usually institutions. Unlike a **rights issue** [p. 280] a placing is not an offer to existing shareholders; simply to any suitable buyers who can be found.

The advantage of a placing is that it is a cheap and simple method of raising money. It does not require the paper work and administrative overhead that a rights issue or an **open offer** [p. 225] does. The shares are simply issued to a small number of new shareholders who are willing to buy substantial amounts of the new shares.

Placings can be unfair to existing shareholders by allowing new shareholders to buy shares at a discount to the market price. There are regulatory restrictions on placings that are designed to protect the rights of existing shareholders. However, they are a cheap, fast and simple way of raising money.

PLF (passenger load factor)

The passenger load factor (PLF) of an airline, sometimes simply called the load factor, is a measure of how much of an airline's passenger carrying capacity is used. It is **passenger-kilometres** [p. 285] flown as a percentage of **seat-kilometres available** [p. 20].

This is a measure of capacity utilisation. As airlines frequently have heavy fixed costs and are **capital intensive** [p. 47], the efficiency with which assets are used is crucially important.

This is an important efficiency measure, but it does not consider the pricing and the profitability at which the capacity is sold. It also implicitly assumes that the airline's fleet is fully utilised in terms of the number of kilometres flown.

Plus market

Plus is a specialist British market for small cap shares. Its closest competitor is AIM. It was formerly known as Ofex.

Plus operates two markets: its primary market is **quote driven** [p. 261], while its secondary market is **order driven** [p. 198].

Plus suffers something of a disadvantage in competing with AIM in that it is not part of a large exchange. This means both a lower profile and fewer brokers able to deal in Plus quoted securities.

Plus is a fairly cheap exchange to list on for a company that does not want to raise capital as a **prospectus** [p. 255] is only needed when issuing new shares.

Poison pill

A poison pill is an attempt to discourage an **acquisition** [p. 5] by making it more expensive to acquire a company, or by reducing the value of the acquired business.

A poison pill relies on setting up an essentially destructive mechanism that would be triggered by a **takeover** [p. 5], or by an event likely to be linked to a takeover (e.g., triggered by the purchase of certain proportion of shares by any one person).

Poison pills include:

- issuing **convertibles** [p. 72], with below market **exercise prices** [p. 135], whose conversion is triggered by a takeover

- making employees and directors share options (that would normally be exercisable in the future) immediately exercisable on a takeover

- agreements with customers that include compensation in the event of a takeover (for example, Peoplesoft when subject to a **bid** [p. 317] by Oracle – ostensibly to compensate customers for the risk that a new owner would discontinue products, forcing an expensive migration to new software).

Poison pills are largely designed to protect directors, and are harmful to shareholders. Poison pills are designed to deny them the opportunity of selling to an acquirer (usually at a significant premium to the price without bid interest). Shareholders and regulators have become less tolerant of poison pills, and they have become rarer in most major markets, although Japan appears to be lagging in this respect.

Ponzi scheme

A Ponzi scheme is an investment scam that appears to be actually paying high returns by paying the supposed returns out of victims' own capital.

A typical Ponzi scheme promises investors a high rate of return in a short time. The money that is collected from investors is used to pay the return. This means the scam can run for some time, because investors appear to be making the promised return. Early participants can profit, as they can with a **pyramid scheme** [p. 259].

The easiest way to explain this is with an example. Suppose the scheme promises a return of 10% a month. The scammer simply takes investors' money and returns a tenth of it at the end of every month.

The fact that investors appear to be getting the returns they were promised will encourage more people to put their money in the scheme, and even encourage the original wave of victims to reinvest.

After ten months the fraudster will have returned all the money invested by the very first investors (assuming they did not reinvest), but will have most of the money invested by later investors. At this point the fraudster simply takes the money are disappears.

Common types of Ponzi scheme operate under a variety of names including "high yield investment program" and "high yield debentures". Their common characteristics are very high returns with no clear underlying business to generate them.

More complex forms of Ponzi scheme can be harder to detect. They may well appear to be legitimate investments. They may even be part of an investment that includes both legitimate and Ponzi elements. An example of the latter is an investment or finance company that offers very high returns to depositors, and does lend the money (as a real finance company would) to make returns, but does so knowing that the return on loans will not suffice to cover the interest paid to depositors.

Anything that offers very high returns without correspondingly high risk should be regarded with great suspicion. Any investment sold through unusual channels (spam email or cold calling) or by a business that is not appropriately regulated (e.g., by the **FSA** [p. 149] or another national regulator) is also both suspicious and probably illegal. It is usually possible to check with regulators whether someone selling investments is regulated or not.

Ponzi schemes are named after Carlo Ponzi who ran a huge Ponzi scheme in the US in the 1920s.

Portfolio investment

Portfolio investment is investment made by investors who are not particularly interested in involvement in the management of a company.

The term is often used in the context of foreign investment in a country, which can often be fairly neatly divided between:

- portfolio investors (who buy **debt** [p. 37] and **listed shares** [p. 190])

- direct investors (who set up operations in a country).

Of course the division is not always that neat: a foreign investor who launches a **takeover** [p. 5] of a domestic company may be buying listed securities to do so, but is not a portfolio investor.

Fund managers do sometimes intervene in the management of a company, but any active involvement is short lived: their most common intervention is to change the composition of the board of directors, with the changed board then left to manage the company. Fund managers can therefore almost always be assumed to be portfolio investors.

Private equity [p. 252] funds are an important exception. They usually buy with shares the intention of taking control of a company.

Portfolio mandate

A portfolio mandate sets the parameters within which a portfolio is managed.

A **fund mandate** [p. 151] is a portfolio mandate of a **collective investment vehicles** [p. 62]. The circumstances are significantly different from portfolios that are managed for a particular client.

Where a portfolio is being managed for one client (whether an individual or an organisation) the mandate will be set by the client. This means that clients can tailor such things as **ethical investment** [p. 125] limits and **risk** [p. 281] to their own requirements.

Portfolio theory

Portfolio theory deals with the value and risk of portfolios rather than individual theories. It is often called modern portfolio theory or Markowitz portfolio theory.

The key result in portfolio theory is that the **volatility** [p. 340] of a portfolio is less than the **weighted average** [p. 344] of the volatilities of the securities it contains. The **standard deviation** [p. 305] of the **expected return** [p. 135] on a portfolio is:

$$\sqrt{\Sigma W_i^2 \sigma_i^2 + \Sigma\Sigma W_i W_j Cov_{ij}}$$

where the sums are over all the securities in the portfolio
W_i is the proportion of the portfolio in security i
σ_i is the standard deviation of expected returns of security i
and Cov_{ij} is the covariance of expected returns of securities of i and j.

Assuming that the covariance is less than one (invariably true), this will be less than the weighted average of the standard deviation of the expected returns of the securities. This is why **diversification** [p. 103] reduces risk.

The other important results in the **financial economics** [p. 139] of portfolios are those dealing with the construction of **efficient portfolios** [p. 119].

Possible oil reserves

Possible oil reserves are, as the name implies, oil reserves that have a significant probability of being commercially exploitable, but which can not be said to be probable.

In the UK the DTI defines these as those oil reserves with a less than 50% chance of being technically and commercially producible.

As with **proven** [p. 256] and **probable** [p. 253] reserves the exact definition varies.

Post balance sheet events

Post **balance sheet** [p. 28] events have a significant effect on the values shown in the accounts, and occur after the balance sheet date but prior to the date on which the accounts are approved by the directors.

Some of those events make more information available rather than altering the numbers as such. These are called adjusting events. An example of such

777
77

77

an event is a sale of a **fixed asset** [p. 142] when the sales is agreed during the financial period but the final price is agreed after the end of the period. The final price will be reflected in the balance sheet and the **P & L** [p. 234].

If a post balance sheet event is not an adjusting event but it is material, then it should be **disclosed** [p. 98] separately in the results.

POTS

See **switched telecoms** [p. 314].

Pre-emption rights

Pre-emption rights are the rights of shareholders to be offered any **new issue** [p. 215] of shares before the shares are offered to non-shareholders.

The offer of shares to shareholders is usually required to be pro-rata to their existing shareholding. It most commonly takes place through a **rights issue** [p. 280].

The purpose of pre-emption rights is to ensure that shareholders have an opportunity to prevent their stake being diluted by new issues.

In the UK (and most other countries) pre-emption rights are required for publicly traded companies; by both company law and **listing** [p. 288] rules.

It is possible for shareholders to waive pre-emption rights. This is useful for situations where a rights issue would not be cost effective; it is often cheaper to issue new shares through a **placing** [p. 240].

Pre-emption rights also do not apply to the sale of **treasury shares** [p. 328]: both for obvious practical reasons and because transactions in treasury shares cannot lead to dilution of holdings.

Pre-exceptional

It is common for companies to **disclose** [p. 98] profit numbers adjusted for **exceptional items** [p. 132] in addition to the required **GAAP** [p. 154] or **IFRS** [p. 166] numbers.

The pre-exceptional numbers can give investors a better view of underlying trends, but they are also prone to manipulation as companies have considerable leeway in choosing what to classify as exceptional. Nonetheless, when pre-exceptional numbers are available, they are generally very useful to investors.

Preference shares

Preference shares (prefs) are legally shares, but they are very different from ordinary shares. The economic effect of prefs is more like that of **bonds** [p. 37]. Like **convertibles** [p. 72], they are regarded as hybrids of debt and equity:

- Dividends on preference shares have to be paid before dividends on ordinary shares.

- Preference shareholders have a higher priority if a company is liquidated than ordinary shareholders, although a lower priority than debt holders.

- Dividends on ordinary shares may not be paid unless the fixed dividends on preference shares is paid first.

- In the case of cumulative prefs, if the dividend is not paid in full, the unpaid amount is added to the next dividend due.

- Preference dividends are fixed, so they do not participate in increases in profits as ordinary shareholders do.

The effect of these is to make the income stream from preference shares more similar to that from debt than that from ordinary shares. Most importantly, fixed dividends are similar to interest payments. They are legally shares and are subject to the same tax treatment.

The characteristics of preference shares can vary. Most commonly they may be **cumulative** [p. 83] or **redeemable** [p. 268].

Premium earned

Premium earned is the amount of premiums earned by the risk covered by an insurer during a period. **Premium written** [p. 246] is the amount customers are required to pay for policies written during the year. The two differ because of the timing of premium payments.

For example if:

- An insurance policy that runs from the 1st July 2005 to the 30th June 2006.

- The premium is £1,000.

- The insurance company has a December year end.

Then, as the policy runs for six months of this year and six months of next, half the risk is taken in the current year and half next year. Therefore the premium earned is £500 for 2005 and £500 for 2006.

However as the cover is agreed during 2005, the gross premium written is £1,000 for 2005.

Premium income

The revenues an insurance company receives as premiums paid by customers is its premium income. This excludes other revenue streams, most importantly investment income.

The most important definitions of premium income are **premium earned** [p. 245] and **premium written** [p. 246].

Premium written

The amount of premiums customers are required to pay for insurance policies written during the year. This contrasts with premium earned which is the amount of premiums that a company has earned by providing insurance against various risks during the year.

It may be measured gross (before deduction of **reinsurance** [p. 271] costs) or net (after reinsurance costs). It is a measure of sales.

See **premium earned** [p. 245].

Prepayments

A company may pay for goods or services before they have been received. Any amounts that have been paid for goods and services not received by the end of an accounting period are shown in the **balance sheet** [p. 28] as prepayments. These amounts will not be shown as costs in the **P & L** [p. 234].

When the goods or services are received, then the amounts will be passed through the P & L and deducted from the prepayments section of the balance sheet.

This is necessary in order to **accrue** [p. 4] the costs involved to the correct accounting period.

Prescription drug

A prescription drug may only be sold by a pharmacist when authorised by a written prescription from a medical practitioner. Ethical drug is a synonym for prescription drug that is often favoured by pharmaceutical companies despite being less widely understood.

The law varies from country to country, but a drug that requires prescription in one of the major pharmaceutical markets (the US, Europe and Japan, in order of size) will generally require prescription in all.

The opposite of a prescription drug is an **over-the-counter** [p. 232] drug.

Selling prescription drugs requires a sales force that can successfully reach the necessary prescribers. The number of prescribers to be reached, and therefore the size of the sales force required, depends on who is expected to prescribe a drug. This can vary from a small number of specialists to any GP.

Because of this only the biggest pharmaceutical companies are able to market a wide range of products globally by themselves. Even fairly substantial companies that are nonetheless not giants may do one, or usually more, of the following:

- Specialise in a range of drugs that sell to particular specialists and develop a sales force big enough to reach only those specialists.

- License out drugs in regions where they do not have a sales fore of their own.

- License out some drugs completely.

- Specialise in over-the-counter or **generic** [p. 157] drugs that do not require such a large sales force.

Their large sales forces are a key reason why the major pharmaceutical companies are unlikely to lose their dominance even if their research efforts prove to be less effective than those of smaller companies (a very real risk).

Present value

The present value of a stream of cashflows is its value, adjusted for risk and for the time value of money.

Unlike an **NPV** [p. 220], a present value does not include any initial set up or acquisition costs, and therefore commonly includes only positive cash flows.

See **DCF** [p. 88].

Present value of new business premiums

See **PVNBP** [p. 258].

Price elasticity

Price elasticity of demand

Price elasticity of demand is the proportionate change in the volume of a product that will be bought as a result of a unit change in price. It is:

$$\frac{change\ in\ quantity}{total\ quantity} \bigg/ \frac{change\ in\ price}{price}$$

If the price elasticity is:

- exactly one, then a small increase or decrease in price will result in the value of sales being unchanged because the change in volume will exactly compensate

- less than one, then increase in price will increase the value of sales and a decrease will decrease the value of sales – demand is inelastic

- more than one, then lower prices will mean greater sales in monetary terms – demand is elastic.

Although demand for a good may be inelastic at the level of the total market, in a competitive market prices could still be highly elastic for an individual supplier. Any one firm may find it hard to sell at above the market price, and may gain a lot of sales by undercutting the market price.

Suppliers usually want to maximise their profits, not their sales. While lower prices may increase sales, they will reduce margins, so price elasticity of demand will tend to be significantly greater than one. **Cross elasticities** [p. 80] may be significant.

Price elasticity of supply

Price elasticity of supply is the effect that the price of a good has on the quantity supplied to the market. Its definition is the same as that of price elasticity of demand except that the quantity is that supplied by suppliers rather than that demanded by consumers.

Price sensitive

The classification of information as price sensitive is important because it affects:

- companies' duties to disclose it

- whether or not using the information to trade with constitutes **insider trading** [p. 171]

The regulation of the disclosure and use of price-sensitive information is necessary to ensure that all investors are fairly treated.

Price sensitive information should be disclosed to all investors at the same time, and anyone who has access to it before it becomes public should not be able to profit from it.

Price sensitive information is just that: information that is likely to affect the price of a security. However information is not considered price sensitive unless it is specific and factual.

Other price sensitive information could (depending on circumstances) include:

- financial numbers: profit and sales figures in particular, but almost any part of the accounts should be treated as price sensitive

- information about **takeover bids** [p. 317]

- dealing in a company's securities by its directors (see **Directors dealing** [p. 97])

- large purchases and sales by major shareholders

- **share buybacks** [p. 293], **rights issues** [p. 280], changes to dividend policy and other **corporate actions** [p. 73]

- changes to corporate strategy, new product launches and any substantial changes to the business.

In practice, profit and sales numbers and information about takeover bids are the most likely to be exploited for insider trading. It is these that regulators pay the most attention to.

It is common for takeover bids to be rumoured before they are officially announced. This usually compels the target (and sometimes the bidder) to confirm or deny the rumours, even if only in vague terms.

There is information that does affect the price of shares that is not caught by the definition of price sensitive information. This is usually because the information is not specific or factual, or because the original source of the information is not a company insider.

Price/book value

Price/book is simply:

$$\frac{share\ price}{\textbf{NAV}[\text{p. 213}]}$$

This simply measures the value of a company against the **book value** [p. 38] of its assets (as shown on its **balance sheet** [p. 28]). Because the value of assets shown in the accounts does not necessarily reflect either the market value of its assets, or their value to the company (which depends on what effect they have on future cash flows), this ratio is not widely used.

Asset values shown in the balance sheet are based on the purchase prices of the assets and the principal of **accruing** [p. 4] the costs to the profits they generate.

Price/book value is most often useful with sectors in which the value of a company depends largely on what assets it owns and those assets are accurately recorded in the accounts. In practice this means:

- **investment trusts** [p. 180] (which have no business other than holding assets)

- property companies (whose value is dominated by their assets and who are also required to revalue their main assets).

Price/cashflow

Price/cashflow is simply the share price divided by the **cashflow per share** [p. 53]

Using it obviously requires selecting a **cash flow measure** [p. 53]. Given the comparison to share price one that is post-interest is preferable.

This valuation ratio is not as widely used as its profit based equivalent, the **PE ratio** [p. 237]. Although cash flows are what ultimately matter most to investors there are problems with using cash flow based ratios. Most cash flow numbers are subject to more fluctuation than profits and therefore **EPS** [p. 122] tends to be more sustainable than cash flow per share. The obvious exception to this is **EBITDA** [p. 116] which is a profit measure that is closely related to cash flows, but when EBITDA is used it is preferable to use **EV/EBITDA** [p. 129] for valuation.

Cash flows are, of course, what would be used for a **DCF** [p. 88] valuation, but using them with simple ratios has too many pitfalls to be lightly recommended as a substitute for profit based ratios. They nonetheless make a good additional measure to be used in conjunction with PE and EV/EBITDA

Price/sales

Price/sales and **market capitalisation** [p. 196]/sales are the same ratio calculated in slightly different ways. It measures the share price against a company's sales. Price/sales can be useful when a company is loss making or its **margins** [p. 253] are uncharacteristically low.

Price/sales uses sales as a measure of size. It is in many ways a crude measure of size, but given that this ratio is used when many others can not be used at all, this is acceptable. The ratio is simple to define:

$$share\ price \left/ \frac{sales}{no\ of\ shares\ in\ issue} \right.$$

Or equivalently:

$$\frac{market\ cap}{sales}$$

Comparisons across sectors should probably not be made. The best comparisons using this ratio are with very similar companies in the same sector. **EV/Sales** [p. 130] is in many ways a better alternative as it strips out the effects of debt.

Sales based valuation ratios do have a place as they indicate what a company with (hopefully temporary) abnormal margins would be worth if its margins could be returned to normal. By abnormal, we would normally mean low or negative in circumstances in which investors would expect either a turnaround (i.e. a return to business as usual) or a take-over. The latter as companies that are not profitable enough for their size are obvious targets.

Before resorting to sales based valuations, investors should remember that some profit based valuation ratios (such as **EV/EBITDA** [p. 129]) may be positive when others (such as **PE** [p. 237]) are negative (and therefore not meaningful).

Primary market

The primary market for securities is their initial issue: the sale of securities by issuers to investors as opposed to trading by investors in the **secondary market** [p. 288].

The most common primary market mechanism is an **IPO** [p. 182]. Any new issue of securities to investors takes place in a primary market so **placings** [p. 240] and offers for sale are part of the primary market.

Much of the primary market is intermediated by **underwriters** [p. 331] who relieve the issuer of the risk of the issue failing.

Primary market activities, both underwriting and advising issuers, is, like **mergers** [p. 201] and **acquisitions** [p. 5], an extremely profitable business for investment banks.

Principal

The word principal has two meanings relevant to investment:

1. the amount of a loan excluding **accrued interest** [p. 5] payments

2. a person for whom an agent acts.

The principal of a **bond** [p. 37] or other debt security is the amount shown as its **face value** [p. 137], the nominal value of the bond which is repaid in full on its maturity date.

In the case of a loan, the principal is the amount originally borrowed.

The principal of a bond may be quite different from the amount actually raised by its issue, as the amount the borrower raises will depend on the market value of a bond of that face value, interest rate, terms, and maturity at the time of issue.

The amount raised by issuing a **zero coupon bond** [p. 350] is likely to be lot less than its face value. The amount raised by issuing a bond with a **floating interest rate** [p. 144] is likely to be very similar to its face value.

Private client broking

The services of private client stockbrokers, whose clients are mostly private individuals, are very different from the services of institutional brokers.

The most important difference is that private client stockbrokers often manage a clients portfolio, taking investment decisions on behalf of the client when offering a **discretionary broking** [p. 99] service. This service is more like that of a fund manager (albeit dealing with smaller portfolios) than that of an institutional broker.

A broker providing an **advisory broking** [p. 10] supplies information and advice, but the client makes the investment decisions.

Private clients demand much less research than institutions do. Smaller private client stockbrokers may not even produce any research as such at all, with what little is done being ad hoc and informal.

Discount broking [p. 99] services offer only dealing with no advice or portfolio management.

Institutional investors do sometimes use dealing only services, but they more commonly get broking **bundled** [p. 43] with access to **sell side research** [p. 291]. Even when they do buy broking separate from research, the systems and price structures are very different from those offered to private clients.

Private equity

Private equity covers a range of activities related to making investments in unlisted companies. Private equity investments are often funded by debt, leading either the acquirer or the acquired businesses (or both) to become highly **geared** [p. 157]. The most noticeable private equity activity from the point of view of other investors is the **takeover** [p. 5] of underperforming **listed companies** [p. 190].

Because private equity stakes are fairly large, private equity investors generally have a significant influence over management and much better access to financial information. This is why a troubled or badly-run business is often worth more to private equity investors than as listed companies.

Stock markets are important to private equity investors as they provide a key exit route. The other obvious alternative is a disposal to a trade buyer (someone else in the same industry).

Most large private equity investments are purchases of established but under-performing companies. More adventurous investments in private companies, such as those in start-ups, are called **venture capital** [p. 338].

Pro-forma

Pro-forma accounts are drawn up as though **acquisitions** [p. 5] and disposals that took place during a period had taken place at the start of it. Pro-forma accounts should therefore give a better indication of underlying trends in the business as it is now.

The most looked at (and most often **disclosed** [p. 98]) pro-forma statement is the **P & L** [p. 234], although a pro-forma cash flow statement should also be useful when available. The concept is very similar to that behind **organic growth** [p. 230] numbers.

Probable oil reserves

Probable **oil reserves** [p. 223] are those that are not (yet) **proven reserves** [p. 256], but which are likely to be exploitable.

In the UK, the DTI defines these as those reserves which are estimated to have a better than 50% chance of being technically and commercially producible, but companies have can use their own definitions.

As with **proven oil reserves** [p. 256], the exact definition may vary from company to company.

Product Differentiation

Product differentiation is the opposite of **commoditisation** [p. 63].

Differentiating a product (or service) gives its producer more pricing power and even a degree of **monopoly** [p. 207]. There are a number of ways in which a company can seek to differentiate its products including:

- Improving the product itself by adding features, improving reliability, etc.

- Branding: marketing to make the product appear different to consumers.

- Exploiting **network effects** [p. 214] to increase the value of the product relative to competitors.

- Distribution: making the product more conveniently available than its competition.

Product markets

The term product market is used in order to refer unambiguously to the market for the products a company sells, as opposed to the financial markets its securities trade in. This includes markets for services as well as physical products.

Profit and loss account

See **P & L** [p. 234].

Profit margin

Profit margin is simply profit divided by sales. This means that there are as many measures of profit margin as there are measures of profit. It is usual to be specific and refer to **gross** [p. 161] margin, **EBIT** [p. 115] margin, **operating** [p. 227] margin, **EBITDA** [p. 116] margin, etc.

Profit margins can provide a comparison between companies in the same industry, and can help identify trends in the numbers for a company from year to year. In the latter case it separates the effect on profits of growth or decline in sales from changes related to efficiency and price levels. It does not do this perfectly as margins naturally increase with sales (this is called **operational gearing** [p. 227]), particularly when a company has a high level of fixed costs or high sales growth or decline.

The difference between the gross and operating margins is the **overhead cost ratio** [p. 233].

Proportionate

Mobile telecoms companies frequently **disclose** [p. 98] a substantial amount of information on a proportionate basis.

Proportionate numbers do not **fully consolidate** [p. 68] **subsidiaries'** [p. 311], but instead include each subsidiary's and **associate's** [p. 23] numbers in proportion to the group shareholding in them.

For example, if a group has a total turnover of £100m from fully owned subsidiaries and another £50m from a subsidiary in which it has a 50% stake the group's total proportionate turnover is:

£100m + (£50m × 50%) = £125m

Mobile telecoms companies frequently disclose proportionate turnover, proportionate customer numbers and usually some proportionate profit numbers (proportionate **EBITDA** [p. 116] is common).

This is a very useful in many ways. It simplifies the calculation of **EV/EBITDA** [p. 129] as the EV [p. 121] does not need the usual adjustments for the hypothetical buyout or sale of **minority shareholdings** [p. 204] if proportionate EBITDA is used.

Although there is no reason why proportionate numbers should be only be disclosed by telecoms companies, they are rarely disclosed outside the sector. It has become a standard in the sector because of investor demand for sufficient disclosure to value shares in companies that generate such a high proportion of profits from partly owned subsidiaries and associates.

Proprietary trading

When a financial institution such as an investment bank trades with its own money, deliberately taking risk on its own account, this is called proprietary trading.

Proprietary trading should not be confused with activities such as **market making** [p. 197] and **arbitraging** [p. 18]. These are trading activities and the institution does not deliberately take significant uncovered (**unhedged** [p. 162]) positions relative to the amount of trading.

Proprietary trading can be risky and some institutions have made large losses from it. However, it can also be very profitable.

Its nature is most often similar to the complex strategies used by the likes of **hedge funds** [p. 162].

Some investment banks have taken to proprietary trading with such enthusiasm that critics have described them as "hedge funds with a banking business".

Prospective PE

As investors are primarily interested a company's future profits, it is common to calculate the PE based on forecast earnings.

The PE calculated using the previous financial year's earnings is called the **historical PE** [p. 164]. The PE based on the current financial year's forecast earnings is called the prospective PE.

Both historical and prospective PEs, and PEs based on another year's earnings may be clearly referred to by specifying the year the earnings of which (actual or forecast) are used: by saying something like "12 times 2008 earnings."

Prospectus

A prospectus is a document that is published by a company prior to raising capital.

The most important type of prospectus is that issued prior to an **IPO** [p. 182] as:

- The company is usually trying to raise a substantial amount of capital.

- The company has no track record and has previously published less information than companies that are already listed.

A prospectus is in some ways similar to an **annual report** [p. 16]: it contains a full set of financial statements together with various non-financial information.

IPO prospectuses usually contain more useful information than an annual report. It is usually much easier for an investor with no prior knowledge of a company to analyse it at IPO (relying primarily on the prospectus) than later when there are more, but individually less complete, sources of information.

The level of detail required in a prospectus can make it a very expensive document to produce.

Proven oil reserves

Proven **oil reserves** [p. 223] are those that are known to exist and be exploitable to a high degree of certainty.

In the UK the DTI defines probable reserves as those with a 90% probability of being technically and commercially producible.

The exact definition of proven reserves varies from company to company and from country to country. The numbers disclosed by national governments of a country's reserves are also often manipulated.

Provisions

A provision takes into account an expected liability. A company will create a provision in the current period when the likely liability becomes apparent, thus reducing the reported profit.

As an example, consider a company which sells on credit. At the year end it has debtors of £1,000,000 and, on past experience, expects to fail to recover about 5% of customer's debts. The company will create a provision (provision for doubtful debtors) by reducing this year's profits by £50,000 and reducing the amount of due debtors in the **balance sheet** [p. 28] by £50,000.

Suppose the company has £800,000 worth of debtors the next year. The amount it needs to provide is £40,000 (5% × £800,000). This will increase that year's profit by £100 (while the balance sheet item will reduce from £500 to £400).

One problem with provisions is that they can be used to smooth profits. A company can make make provisions than usual in a good year (reducing that year's profits) and reverse them in a bad year (boosting that year's profits). Accounting standards have been tightened in order to make this harder.

PSTN

See **switched telecoms** [p. 314].

Psychographics

Pschographics essentially segments a market, for marketing purposes, by classifying potential customers by their attitudes and values. It is an alternative to classification by **social grade** [p. 298].

There are a number of ways of doing this and some methods can be quite detailed but the classifications in a very simple (but very convincing) system, devised by ad agency Young and Rubicam illustrate how this works.:

- Succeeders: People who are successful and self confident. They tend not to buy aspirational products and follow they own ideas of what is a good product.

- Reformers: Creative, caring, altruistic, not brand conscious.

- Aspirers: People who want to "get on".

- Mainstreamers: The largest segment, conformists who buy "safe", big brand products.

A few examples from other systems show how else the classifications can work:

- Strivers: status oriented people who seek money, approval and social status. Obvious buyers of "aspirational" goods.

- Explorers: seek novelty and want to try new things. They are likely to be early adopters of completely new products.

- Constrained: they are the resigned and struggling poor.

Obviously no system will be perfect but, especially when combined with income data, this is meaningful classification.

Loyalty cards and other systems that build up a profile of customer's buying habits (such as those of on-line retailers such as Amazon) can be very effective in building this sort of profile of customers.

Purchase method

The purchase method of accounting in current standards is similar to the "acquisition accounting" method used in previous accounting standards. Its use provides some useful safeguards.

Previous accounting standards allowed two methods of accounting for **merger** [p. 201]s and **acquisitions** [p. 5]; merger accounting and acquisition accounting. The former was generally a more favourable treatment in its impact on the **P & L** [p. 234]. The purchase method of accounting is now compulsory in the US, the EU and wherever **IFRS** [p. 166]s have been adopted.

The purchase method of accounting must identify the acquirer (the entity that obtains control over the other entity). Under IFRSs the acquisition must be valued at **fair value** [p. 137]. The difference between the purchase price and the fair value should be recognised as **goodwill** [p. 159].

A company cannot create a restructuring **provision** [p. 256] to provide for future losses or restructuring costs as a result of an acquisition. Such costs must be treated as post acquisition costs. This makes the impact of restructuring costs on profits more visible, and prevents the abuse of provisions to take an exaggerated hit to profits on acquisition and thereafter boost reported profits in subsequent years.

The use of the purchase method improves accounts, but investors are likely to disregard the impact of goodwill, which is the largest change. The elimination of provisions is more useful because of the extra visibility and the prevention of abuses.

Pure play

A pure play is an investment, usually an **equity** [p. 123], that gives investors exposure only to a particular industry or product market.

A typical reason for buying a pure play is that an investor believes that a particular industry will grow. For example, an investor who believes that mobile telecoms will grow at the expense of fixed line telecoms may look for a pure play mobile operator, rather than a telecoms company that owns both fixed and mobile networks.

Although buying pure plays may seems to reduce **diversification** [p. 103], investors should look for diversification in their portfolios as a whole, not at the company level. If anything, pure plays help manage risk by giving investors more control over what they are exposed to.

Put option

An **option** [p. 228] that gives its holder the right to sell the **underlying asset** [p. 331] at a pre-determined price.

The most obvious use of put options is to **hedge** [p. 162] a position in the underlying security. As put options are not available for all securities, investors may also use hedging strategies that rely on options on market **indicies** [p. 169], as well as more complex strategies.

Put options may also be used as part of more complex hedging and **arbitrage** [p. 18]strategies.

PVNBP

Present value of new business premiums (PVNBP) is a measure of sales that forms part of the **European Embedded Value** [p. 127] accounting principles that have been adopted in order to provide uniform measures for all European insurers.

PVNBP is, like **annual premium equivalent (APE)** [p. 16], a way in which the values of **single and regular premium** [p. 296] new business sold during a financial period can be combined to give a single sales number. It is:

value of single premiums + present value of regular premium streams

There are two major differences between PVNBP and APE:

- PVNBP adjusts regular premiums to make them comparable with single premiums, APE does the opposite.

- APE uses a simple adjustment factor, PVNBP uses a more sophisticated **DCF** [p. 88].

The first of these is not of great importance. The APE way of doing things gives a number that is more like the sales number of a trading company and that therefore may be more intuitive.

In using a DCF PVNBP is more correct, but it introduces more uncertainties and more room for manipulation because it requires choosing an appropriate discount rate.

Pyramid scheme

Pyramid schemes are one of the commonest types of investment scam.

The basis of a pyramid scheme is that victims:

- pay to participate in the scheme and,

- are promised a reward for recruiting further "investors" into the scheme.

As with a **Ponzi scheme** [p. 241], this means that early investors often make large profits. However as the scheme needs more and more "investors" to keep joining, it is inevitable that will eventually run out of people willing to join. The result is the that the promoter makes are large profit, people who join early also make profits, and those who join later lose their "investments".

Consider an example to see how it works:

The promoter of a pyramid scheme starts by recruiting a hundred people and charges each of them £100 to join. Each person joining is promised £500 for every 10 people they recruit into the scheme.

All of the first hundred then manage to recruit 10 new members each. At this point the promoter of the scheme has collected £110,000 in fees and paid out £5,000.

The 1,000 investors in the second wave also get 10 recruits each. The promoter has now collected £1,110,000 and paid out £55,000.

The 10,000 investors in the third wave recruit their 10,000, the 100,000 in the fourth wave recruit a million, and the million in the fifth wave recruit 10 million.

With 10 million people trying to recruit new members it becomes very hard to recruit more. The scheme ends here.

At this point the promoter has made £1.1bn and paid out £500m. 1.1m people have made a £400 profit each and £10m will have lost £100 each.

If the 10 million in the sixth wave manage to get some new recruits the promoter will get yet more money, but as few of them are likely to manage to get the 10 required to get the £500, the promoter is likely to pay out little of this extra money.

A lot of money has moved around, but the net result is that the promoter of the scheme gains and most of the "investors" lose. Investing in a pyramid scheme is very similar to gambling, with the promoter playing the part of the bookmaker.

Schemes are likely to be shut down by the authorities long before they get this big. There are cases of pyramid schemes getting big enough to threaten national economies, as in Albania in the 1990s.

Promoters of pyramid schemes are usually very good at disguising their nature. One of the commonest tricks is to claim that a pyramid scheme is a "multi-level marketing" scheme. Another is to use a more complicated scheme than the simple pyramid described above and claim that it is therefore not a pyramid scheme. As a general rule:

- If you have to recruit people into the scheme to make a profit, it is definitely a pyramid scheme.

- If it is marketing scheme that involves recruiting people to sell goods at above normal market prices, it is almost certainly a pyramid scheme.

- If a substantial part of the income it promises comes from recruiting new people into the scheme, it is probably a pyramid scheme.

- If there are any rewards for recruiting people into the scheme, look at it in detail, and check with regulators (the **FSA** [p. 149] in the UK) if you are unsure.

The last step is always a precaution worth taking with any investment that looks suspicious or offers rewards that look to good to be true – there is nothing to be lost by checking.

Qualified audit opinion

A qualified **audit opinion** [p. 25] is given in an audit if the auditor disagrees with the treatment or **disclosure** [p. 98] of information in the financial statements, or if the auditor does not feel that the audit has been too limited in its scope. Except for the qualification of a particular issue, the rest of the financial statements will give a true and fair view.

The accounts of listed companies are rarely qualified and it would seriously undermine confidence in the management if they were.

Quantitative analyst

A quantitative analyst is a specialist in the mathematical techniques of finance.
Uses of quantitative analysis include:

- risk management

- **arbitrage** [p. 18] – particularly in the case of **hedge funds** [p. 162] and **proprietary trading** [p. 254], both of which often use complex arbitrage strategies

- running **tracker funds** [p. 325] – to construct a portfolio that keeps transaction costs down, while having a known high probability of remaining close enough to the index

Slang terms for quantitative analysts include "quants" and "rocket scientists."

Quick assets ratio

One of the problems with the **current assets ratio** [p. 83] is that the assets counted include stocks which may or may not be quickly sellable (or which may only be sellable quickly at a lower price).

The quick assets ratio deducts stocks from the current assets, so it is:

$$\frac{current\ assets - stocks}{current\ liabilities}$$

A quick assets ratio of more than one is usually considered enough, but the same caveats apply as with the current assets ratio.

The quick assets ratio is also known as the acid test ratio. This name is used because it is the most demanding of the commonly used tests of short term financial stability.

Quote driven trading system

A trading system in which orders trade at prices set by **market maker** [p. 197] quotes rather than by being matched against other investor's orders (the opposite of **matched bargain** [p. 198]).

The advantage of quote driven systems is that they improve **liquidity** [p. 190], because investors can be sure that they can at least deal in reasonably small quantities of shares (large parcels are another matter) at the price quoted by a marker maker.

Some trading systems are hybrids of quote driven and order driven systems.

Quoted company

See **listed company** [p. 190].

R & D

Research and development (R & D) is clearly investment that is meant to generate cashflows. This means that the output of R & D meets the definition of an asset. In spite of this, research expenditure is treated as a cost rather than an investment; research expenditure is immediately deducted from **operating profit** [p. 227] rather than being **capitalised** [p. 49]. Development expenditure *is* capitalised and then **amortised** [p. 15].

The reason for the distinction between research expenditure and development expenditure is that development costs create a particular identifiable new asset that can reasonably be expected to either be usable (it will generate cash) or sellable.

An example of development costs are the costs of designing a new product that a company plans to sell. An example of research costs are the large scale screenings of very large numbers of substances by pharmaceutical companies to try to identify those that may have useful properties.

The results of research expenditure are highly uncertain and therefore it is not possible to establish the value of the assets it creates (knowhow, patents etc.) with sufficient certainty to value them on the balance sheet. This can lead to a peculiar situation where assets that have been bought in (e.g. though the purchase of patents) are shown on the balance sheet (and their purchase price is **amortised** [p. 15] rather than being immediately shown as a cost) but very similar assets created in-house are not.

This also means that standard measures of returns on investment such as **RoI** [p. 284] ignore past investment in research and treat current research costs as expenditure. As the effectiveness of R & D is critical for many companies (especially in sectors such as pharmaceuticals and IT) this means that a key measure of efficiency is not being assessed.

One solution is to add back past research expenditure as an asset, adjusting the accounts to capitalise and amortise it. This is not overly difficult to do, although tedious as it would involve collating numbers from several past years.

An easier, and not any necessarily worse, alternative is a more informal look whether a company is generating the fruits of R & D. Does it have a healthy pipeline of new products? Is its technology advancing as fast as that of its competitors?

In many cases, particularly pharmaceuticals, investors can focus on the pipeline of products which are known to be under development, but which have not yet been launched as these are what will drive growth over the next few years. Important though pipelines in these sectors are, it is also important to consider how good a company is likely to be at replenishing it.

Finally, as this is a difficult issue to address from a purely financial viewpoint, getting to know industries and technologies can give an investor a much better idea of what result can be expected from a company's R & D efforts. issues that might help are:

- What reputation do the company's recent technologies enjoy in its industry?

- Is it a place in which people want to do R & D? Do they have a reputation that helps recruit researchers?

- Is its technology well placed to build whatever comes next? A company that is able to build on better versions of already successful products is more likely to be successful than one that has to develop something new and radically different.

None of this gives investors a quick fix as industry and technical knowledge is time consuming. Assessing R & D is difficult but important, especially for long term investors.

RAJAR

Radio Joint Audience Research (RAJAR) collates statistics on radio listening in the UK, covering both the BBC and commercial stations. From an investor's point of view this means that it provides a single, comparable set of performance numbers for all radio broadcasters.

The numbers are an indicator of market share and a leading indicator of **advertising revenues** [p. 7]. The numbers provided need to be interpreted with a little care as the national aggregates do not provide a full picture. The value of an audience also depends on what regions it is drawn from (the London market is particularly valuable, for example) and the composition of the audience (usually measured by **social grade** [p. 298]).

The radio broadcasters **disclose** [p. 98] some RAJAR numbers in their own statements (usually on the day on which RAJAR publishes the results of its quarterly survey). It is worth looking at the full numbers as this allows easy comparison. This also provides fuller information than broadcasters own statements which often quote selectively and incompletely from the RAJAR numbers.

Random walk

A random walk is a description of how securities prices change, if price changes are purely random. Similar processes occur in other fields. The term and the concept originated in physics.

In a perfectly **efficient market** [p. 118], all information available is reflected in the current price of a security. This means that changes in the price result only from the release of new information, which is completely unpredictable.

If future price changes are unpredictable, the path followed by a price over time is that of a purely random process; there are no patterns in price changes.

This is why the efficient markets hypothesis can not be reconciled with **chartism** [p. 319].

The assumption of a random price process is used by many valuation models. For example, the derivation of the **Black-Scholes** [p. 36] assumes that the price of the **underlying security** [p. 331] follows a random walk.

Raw materials

Raw materials are the part of **stocks** [p. 307] that have been purchased for further processing, but on which no work has yet been done.

The valuation of raw materials is more straightforward than that of **work in progress** [p. 346]. There is no question of cost allocation: raw materials cost what the supplier was paid for them, and this is the value used in the balance sheet.

The exception to this occurs when there is reason to believe that raw materials may be worth less than was paid for them, in which case they are valued at **net realisable value** [p. 214] – in the same as other elements of stocks in the same circumstances.

Real estate investment trust

See **REIT** [p. 272].

Re-rating

When the market changes its view of a company sufficiently to make calculation ratios such as **PE** [p. 237] substantially higher or lower, this a re-rating.

Price movements, particularly large ones can be looked at by being broken down into two components:

1. profits

2. rating.

A share price goes up (or down) either because the profits (or cash flows) have increased (or decreased), or because the valuation multiples have become greater (or smaller).

As changes in profits and cash flows usually take longer to happen than changes in rating, correctly predicting how the rating will change will bring high returns.

This means that investors will usually do not only need to consider whether or not they believe a share is undervalued or over valued. They also need to consider what could act as a catalyst for re-rating. This is particularly true when looking at the short term.

Reach

The reach of a broadcast medium (such as a radio or TV station) is the number of people who use it over a given period of time.

Reach is one of a number of statistics that are collected on the broadcast media, the other important numbers being total viewing/listening hours, viewing/listening hours per person (*total hours ÷ reach*), and percentage share of listening hours.

Reach tells you how many people are interested enough in a broadcaster to at least tune in for a few minutes. The statistics usually only include people who listen or view for a minimum time. From an advertiser's point of view, it can be used to estimate how many people are likely to hear or see a broadcast ad that is regularly repeated. Higher reach means greater ad revenues. Listening hours and listening hours per person are equally important metrics.

Advertisers will also be interested in how closely the audience a broadcaster can deliver matches their target market. They will pay more for a more affluent or better targeted audience.

Real interest rates

The interest rates used in calculating payments on almost all debt are **nominal interest rates** [p. 216].

Some bonds and savings products have payments that are linked to an inflation index, and therefore in effect pay a real interest rate. The British government issues such index linked **gilts** [p. 158]. As a government backed inflation proof security these are the ultimate safe investment for a British investor.

For valuation purposes it is sometimes be preferable to strip out the effects of inflation. The commonest approach to a **DCF** [p. 88] is to use financial forecasts that include the affects of inflation and discount using a nominal discount rate. Instead of this, one can forecast in real terms and then discount using real interest rates. This can simplify financial modelling.

For formulae and other details, see **real return** [p. 266].

Real option

A business may enter courses of action that give it extra freedom of action in the future. Opening up alternative courses of action creates value in the same way that **options** [p. 228] do. This is **option value** [p. 229]. For example, a company may launch an unprofitable product because it may put it in a better position to launch another product if and when the market for the second product develops.

This means that a course of action that is apparently unprofitable on a simple **NPV** [p. 220] basis may be worth pursuing because it allows extra freedom of action. It does not require a knowledge of options to see this. What options theory allows us to do is to actually place a value on this freedom of action. Even where the data to calculate the exact value is of not available, understanding that it is option value better can still provide in insight into how much it might be.

Real return

A real return is the return on an investment, less the reduction in its value as a result of inflation.

$$real\ return = \frac{1+r}{1+i} - 1 \approx r - i$$

where r is the nominal return over a period and
i is inflation over the period.

The nominal return is simply the percentage increase measured in currency. The approximation is accurate enough for valuation, except when inflation is very high.

Real rates are important as they tell you what the actual increase in value was, and how much of a return was just the effect of inflation.

Real interest rates [p. 265] are the most widely used type of real return.

Investors rarely think in terms of real returns. There is an obvious advantage in considering inflation for financial planning. There is another good reason to use real rates: for any kind of long term **financial modelling** [p. 140] real numbers are more stable than nominal numbers (see the **Fisher effect** [p. 141] for an example). This means that they are often preferable for long term models such as those used for **NPV valuations** [p. 220].

Real terms

"In real terms" means the change in a financial number after correcting for the effect of inflation.

For example, if a company's revenues have increased 4% over the previous year, but prices were (on average) 2% higher than in the previous year, then its revenues have only increased 2% in real terms.

It can be very significant that positive reported growth numbers are flat or negative in real terms, sales growth numbers in particular. Apart from this, the most important real terms corrections for investors are **real returns** [p. 266] and **real inflation rates** [p. 265].

Real time

A real time system can respond to events with no significant time lag. This is primarily an IT term, but it is often used in the context of financial data and banking and trading systems.

Real time data is data that is supplied with no significant delay.

Given the value of financial data and the importance of timeliness users can usually expect the pricing of access to data to reflect the time taken to deliver it.

For example, one can get share prices with a delay (usually of around 20 minutes) free. Getting access to real time share prices will require a fee. The vendors can thus make more money out of the people who really need the real time numbers.

In IT, the opposite of a real time system is a batch processing system which collects data over a period of time and processes it together.

Batch processing systems usually make more efficient use of computers. They have therefore become less common as computing power has become cheaper. Batch processing is now used only for very large complex processing.

The term hard real time is used to describe systems in which failure to respond within a particular (very short) time is a critical failure (e.g. a car's braking system). Adding real time or hard real time capabilities to software may expand its potential market.

Recession

A recession is a decline in economic activity that lasts long enough to be a significant event. One common definition of a recession is a decline in GDP that lasts for two or more consecutive quarters. Some economists argue that such definitions are arbitrary and that there is no qualitative difference between a recession and a depression.

Recessions are often global as economies are now intertwined. A recession in one economy affects all the countries it buys from, by reducing demand for their products.

Governments can act to help recovery by increasing spending and cutting interest rates. What works and when is a matter of some controversy.

There is also an element of automatic stabilisation that comes from the rise in government expenditure relative to tax revenues when an economy shrinks.

Record date

The record date is the date on which (or, to be more accurate, as at which) a list of the holders of a **registered security** [p. 270] is extracted from the register in order to process a **corporate action** [p. 73].

For example, a dividend will be paid to shareholders who are on the register at the end of day on the record date. Because of the time taken to clear trades this will usually be a few days after the last date on which the shares trade **cum-dividend** [p. 82].

Recovery

In the mining industry, recovery is the amount of metal extracted from ore as a percentage of the actual metal content. The metal content of the ore is measured by **ore grade** [p. 230].

Recovery clearly has a significant impact on profitability. An increase in recovery generally reduces **cash cost** [p. 52]. This is a number that is less directly important to investors than cash cost and is not as frequently **disclosed** [p. 98], so investors are not likely to look at this number unless doing fairly detailed analysis.

Red chip

Red chips the the shares of mainland Chinese companies incorporated outside mainland China and **listed** [p. 190] in Hong Kong. The actual business is based in mainland China and usually controlled by shareholders in mainland China.

The shares of companies registered in China that are listed in Hong Kong are called H shares.

Red chips are a way of buying exposure to the mainland Chinese economy while retaining some of the benefits of Hong Kong's better legal and regulatory environment.

Redemption yield

See **YTM** [p. 350].

Redeemable

The term redeemable may mean:

- That a **security** [p. 291] has a maturity date on which the **principal** [p. 251] will be repaid and the security will be cancelled.

- That a security is redeemable at the option of the holder – the holder can require the issuer to redeem before maturity.

- That the security is redeemable at the option of the issuer – the issuer can choose to redeem before maturity.

The first of these is easily understood.

If a security is redeemable at the option of the holder, this effectively gives the holder a **put option** [p. 258] **written** [p. 229] by the issuer.

If a security is redeemable at the option of the issuer, then the issuer effectively has a **call option** [p. 45] on the security written by the holder. These bonds are therefore sometimes described as callable.

Any security may be redeemed by the issuer purchasing it in the market and then cancelling it. The difference between this and a security redeemable at the option of the issuer is that the issuer can get rid of its liability to the holder of the security at a rate other than the market price.

This means that the valuation of redeemable (in this sense) securities is complicated by the value of the **embedded option** [p. 120]. The option may only be exercisable under certain conditions, which further complicates valuation.

The value of a security redeemable at the option of the issuer is the value the security would have if it were not redeemable, less the value of the call option the issuer holds on it.

The value of a security redeemable at the option of the holder is the value the security would have if not redeemable plus the value of the embedded put option.

Redeemable bonds

When a corporate bond is referred to as redeemable it usually means that it is redeemable at the option of the issuer (callable). The term redeemable is rarely used to simply indicate that a coporate bond has a fixed maturity, because that can usually be assumed.

A callable bond is worth less than any bond (that is the same in other respects) with a fixed maturity date at any point between the earliest date on which it can be called and the latest possible date for repayment.

Because of the existence of perpetual **government bonds** [p. 160] the term redeemable can mean that they have a fixed maturity, however **gilts** [p. 158] redeemable at the option of the issuer also exist, so the reference may be to those.

Redeemable prefs

Redeemable prefs have a fixed life, and will mature like a bond. This means they are even more bond like than other prefs – they pay a fixed amount of interest for a fixed number of years, followed by a repayment of principal.

Reducing balance

The reducing balance method of **depreciation** [p. 95] is an alternative to the commonly used straight line (equal amounts each year) method. It is often used for tax purposes, but less often in published accounts.

Rather than charging a fixed amount every year, a (fixed) percentage of the remaining value of the asset is charged every year. A £10,000 asset depreciated at 25% a year will be depreciated by £2,500 in the first year, but by 25% × (£10,000 - £2,500) in the second year. Compared to the straight line method, depreciation is more heavily weighted towards early years.

Although the reducing balance method usually more closely reflects the actual diminution in the market value of an asset, the straight line method is generally preferred as it better conforms to the **accrual principle** [p. 4]. If an asset provides the same benefit every year, then the best matching is provided by charging the same depreciation every year.

In the UK, writing down allowances (the equivalent to depreciation for tax purposes) on most assets are calculated on a reducing balance basis. The main exceptions are certain buildings, and those assets that are immediately written off in full.

Registered securities

If the ownership of a security is recorded in a register kept by the issuer (or a third party **registrar** [p. 270]) it is a registered security. If its ownership is not recorded it is a **bearer security** [p. 33].

Shares are almost always registered securities but **ADRs** [p. 14] and **eurobonds** [p. 126] are usually bearer securities.

If a register exists, it is then usually the main evidence of ownership of the securities. It is more important than paper certificates. Certificates and other written evidence of ownership may be useful for trading, when tracing fraud or for tax returns.

It is now usual for shares in **listed companies** [p. 190] to exist in **dematerialised** [p. 94] form. No certificates are issued and the shares exist only as ownership registered in **depositary systems** [p. 95] and registers.

It is also common for securities to be held by stockbrokers' **nominee** [p. 216] companies. The broker's clients who bought the securities are the **beneficial owners** [p. 34]. There are problems with this arrangement as these shareholders do not always receive the same rights (particularly to vote at **AGMs** [p. 12] and **EGMs** [p. 119]) as those whose names appear on the register.

Registrar

A registrar provides a service to **listed companies** [p. 190]. The core tasks of a registrar are:

- maintaining a register of holders of shares (and other **registered securities** [p. 270])

- dealing with **corporate actions** [p. 73] such as dividend payments.

These are primarily the responsibility of a **company secretary** [p. 65]. It is usually more cost effective to **outsource** [p. 232] the work to a specialist registrar who is able to invest in the systems and staff to deal with these efficiently. This is a good example of **economies of scale** [p. 117].

Registrars usually also offer other services such as **DRIPs** [p. 110], **treasury share** [p. 328] holding, share dealing services, employee share ownership plans, and broader company secretarial services.

The work of a registrar mirrors that of a **custodian** [p. 84]. Both reduce a client's costs and paperwork that result from the ownership of securities. One does this for issuers, the other for large investors.

Reinsurance

Reinsurance is simply insurance for insurers. It allows them to pass on risks that they cannot, or do not wish, to absorb themselves.

Insurance companies typically insure some (but not all) of the risks that they are exposed to with specialist reinsurers. The insurer can then recover a part of the claims they pay out from the reinsurer. This reduces the risk of the failure of the insurer in the event of a catastrophic event, such as a natural disaster, that may produce a very high level of claims.

Reinsurance companies are usually very large, well funded and have a wide spread of operations.

Risk measures such as **solvency margin** [p. 299] are adjusted for the level of reinsurance cover.

There are two types basic types of reinsurance arrangement, facultative reinsurance and treaty reinsurance.

Facultative Reinsurance

This is the arrangement of separate reinsurance for each risk that the insurer underwrites. This is normally part of an on-going arrangement and the insurer continually offers policies to the reinsurer, and the reinsurer decides whether to accept each or not individually. Obviously this requires a lot of work and is now generally regarded as too expensive in human resources to be practical.

Treaty Reinsurance

Treaty reinsurance is arranged for a block an insurer's underwritten policies. The reinsurer reinsurers a whole large chunk of the insurer's business. This means that the reinsurer does not need to scrutinise each policy individually and the insurer does not have the added workload of providing the reinsurer details of each and every risk it underwrites.

Reinsurance may be agreed on a *pro rata* basis or a stop loss basis:

- *Pro rata* basis: the reinsurer gets a fixed proportion of the premium on the risks covered, and in return pays out a fixed proportion of the claims made.

- Stop loss basis: the insurer will absorb losses up to a limit (the retention), and reinsurer will absorb almost all losses above that limit.

Reinsurnace may also cover only individual risks of above a certain size or losses above a specified excess.

Major reinsurers include Swiss Re, Munich Re, General Re, Berkshire Hathaway and (collectively) **Lloyds** [p. 190] syndicates.

Reinsurance retention ratio

The reinsurance retention ratio is:

$$\frac{net \textbf{ premium written}[\text{p. }246]}{gross\ premium\ written}$$

It is a rough measure of how much of the risk is being carried by an insurer rather than being passed to **reinsurers** [p. 271].

REIT

A real estate investment trust (REIT) is simply a **collective investment vehicle** [p. 62] that allows tax efficient investment in property. Its main purpose is to remove the tax disadvantages of investing in property through a collective vehicle (such as a property company) compared to investing directly in property.

REITs have long been popular in the US and a number of other countries, but are new to the UK and will be introduced from the 1st January 2007. The main characteristics of a UK REIT are that it will be exempt from tax on:

- rental income

- gains on the sale of property.

However it must:

- be a **listed company** [p. 190]

- not have any shareholder with a stake of over 10%

- have investment properties that comprise at least 75% of the value of its assets

- make at least 75% of its income from property rents

- have rental profits that are at least 1.25× interest payments

- distribute (i.e. pay out as dividends) at least 90% of its tax exempt profits.

The distributions of profit made out of the tax exempt profits are paid after the deduction of basic rate tax. Higher rate tax payers will have to pay further tax on the distributions, but they will be treated as UK property income, not as dividend income.

The above is a rough summary of the implications of the expected legislation. Taking an investment decision based on the tax treatment of REITs requires further research or professional advice.

Relative PE

PE comparisons are more meaningful if they are made between similar companies. They are very often used to compare companies in the same sector, which are presumed to have similar long term growth prospects.

Taking this further, the PE can be divided by the average PE for the companies the comparison is being made with. A company PE is often divided by the **sector PE** [p. 289] of its sector, or the **market PE** [p. 289] of its market. This gives a sector or market relative PE.

This gives a measure of how expensive a share is against peers. If it is less than one it is cheaper, if it is more than one it is more expensive. This measure is not useful unless one considers why it is cheaper or more expensive, and how much of a premium or discount is actually deserved.

Relative returns

A relative return, in contrast to an **absolute return** [p. 2], measures how well an investment has performed compared to some other potential investment. It is usual to compare portfolios to market or sector **indices** [p. 169].

Suppose a portfolio makes a gain of 10% over an year, but the market the portfolio is invested in makes a gain of 5%. The absolute return is 10%, but the market relative return is:

$$\frac{1 + 10\%}{1 + 5\%} \approx 10\% - 5\% = 5\%$$

The benchmark against which the relative gain is compared will vary. Sometimes more than one relative gain number may be useful. The performance of a share may be compared to a national market, or to its sector, or to its sub-sector.

Replacement cost profit

Replacement cost profit is a measure often used by oil companies. It is a profit figure that calculated using the cost of supplies at the cost of replacing supplies at current prices, rather than the prices at which they were actually bought. Current prices usually means the average purchase price over a period.

The replacement cost profit is useful because it excludes the profit or loss made by carrying **stock** [p. 307].

If inventory levels have not changed, then replacement cost profit should be the same as profit calculated using **LIFO** [p. 188] costs. If stock levels have changed LIFO based and replacement cost profits will be different. Unless price movements have been extreme or the change in stock levels very large the difference is unlikely to be material.

As replacement cost profit is not an **IFRS** [p. 166] measure (or a **GAAP** [p. 154] measure where that still matters) its exact definition may vary a little from company to company.

Repo

A repurchase agreement (repo) is the sale of securities (usually **government debt** [p. 158]) tied to an agreement to buy the securities back later. A reverse-repo is the purchase of a security tied to an agreement to sell back later.

These agreements can be viewed as loans secured against the security. The effective interest rate is called the **repo rate** [p. 274].

Which transactions are called repos and which are called reverse repos varies between markets. The transaction may be looked at from the point of view of a dealer dealing with a customer or vice verse. What is called a repo in one country may be called a reverse repo in another country.

Generally, whether an agreement is called a repo or reverse repo depends on which party initiates the transaction. In the UK, a repo between a dealer and the Bank of England or between a dealer and an individual investor is looked at from the dealers' perspective. If a retail investor buys securities from a dealer, the transaction is termed a repo as the dealer sells the security with the agreement to buy it back. Similarly the purchase by a dealer from the central bank it is called a reverse repo.

A central bank's repo rate is an important instrument of monetary policy, as the central bank is the lender of last resort. The repo rate in the UK is set by the MPC (Monetary Policy Committee of the Bank of England).

Repo rate

A repo rate is the gain in price between the two trades in a **repo** [p. 274] transaction (i.e. the difference between the sale and repurchase prices) as an annualised percentage of the sale price.

If you regard the transaction as a secured loan and repayment secured against a security (which is the economic effect it has), the repo rate is the **interest rate** [p. 177] on the loan.

Research and development

See **R & D** [p. 261].

Reserve requirement

A reserve requirement is imposed by regulators (usually central banks) on banks. It is a proportion of deposits that must be held by a bank rather than being lent to borrowers.

The reserve requirement is usually held in a bank's account with the central bank.

The main purpose of the reserve requirement is to control growth in the **money supply** [p. 206].

The reason banks increase the money supply is that they lend the money deposited with them, but most of this is then redeposited in the banking system. For example if you deposit money in a current account, your bank can (and will) then lend it. At the same time, you can still write a cheque against it.

Banks can thus create money in the form of bank balances, but the reserve requirement can act as a brake on the process by preventing banks from lending as much as they might. Because of the iterative nature of this process a small change in the reserve requirement can have a large effect on the money supply.

A reserve requirement is usually a single digit percentage, resreve requirements have tended to fall over the years as developments such as the growth of **eurocurrency** [p. 126] markets have made them less effective as a policy tool to control the money supply.

Retail format

The format of a retailer is the overall appearance and feel that it presents to customers, primarily its look and layout, the sort of range it stocks and the approach taken to pricing.

Format is distinct from fascia which, strictly speaking, refers solely to external appearance. Retailers occasionally use it as as a synonym for format.

The format, together with range, pricing and marketing, is one of the key determinants of a retailer's success. Of these, the format is very often the hardest to get right. A good format will both draw in customers (generating **footfall** [p. 144]) and help present products well to generate sales.

Because the format is so important, growth investors can often benefit by identifying smaller retailers who have recently developed formats that are good enough to provide a platform for sustained growth.

Return on capital employed

See **ROCE** [p. 283].

Return on invested capital

See **ROIC** [p. 284].

Return on investment

See **RoI** [p. 284].

Return on operating capital employed

Return on operating capital employed is closely related to **ROCE** [p. 283], but strips out the effect of cash holdings and provisions to measure the returns generated by the actual operations of a company.

It is:

$$\frac{EBIT[\text{p. }115]}{\textit{capital employed} - \textit{investments} - \textit{cash}}$$

Where capital employed is defined as for ROCE.

Returns of capital

Companies that have more money than can be invested at better than market rates, or who can benefit in some way by replacing **equity** [p. 123] financing with debt, should return capital to shareholders. Common methods of doing this include:

- **Special dividends** [p. 301]

- **Share buy backs** [p. 293]

- Capital restructuring

Special dividends are simply dividends that the company calls "special" to make it clear that their payment is not part of the normal dividend stream that the company pays.

Share buy-backs have tax advantages and offer shareholders more flexibility than special dividends.

A company may restructure its share capital or issue **redeemable** [p. 268] securities to return money to shareholders. This can give shareholders a great deal of flexibility in when and how to take their money. A restructuring may include a cash payout, a share **consolidation** [p. 69], exchanging shares for redeemable bonds or prefs, etc.

Substantial share buy backs are often viewed favourably as evidence of a focus by the management on shareholder wealth, rather than on "empire building". The choice of what method to use tends to depend on the amount to be returned and the tax implications for shareholders. The latter, in turn, depend on what sort of shareholders own most of the company.

If shareholders are non-tax payers (e.g. pension funds) a special dividend (which immediately creates an income tax liability) is more likely. If shareholders are largely small shareholders a buy back may be preferable. If the amount to be returned is large then a restructuring may be preferred for maximum flexibility.

Revenue per available lower berth day

Revenue per available lower berth day is a measure of revenue for cruise ships, and is very similar to **revpar** [p. 279]. Like revpar, it measures the revenue generated per unit of available accommodation.

Like revpar, revenue per available lower berth day can be broken down into pricing and occupancy components. Similarly, trends are more important than absolute rates.

Revenue per available lower berth day is sometimes stated net of travel agents' commissions and air transport costs. This is sometimes called net revenue yield.

Revenue per available room

See **revpar** [p. 279].

Revenue recognition

Revenue recognition, the choice of which transactions a company should consider to be part of its sales, can be extremely straightforward. It can also be complex, uncertain and subject to manipulation.

Revenue recognition is very simple for companies that sell goods in single standalone transactions. Customers either pay or are invoiced and become debtors. In both cases the value of the sale is added to the company's revenues.

As terms of payment become more complex, so does deciding when revenue should be recognised.

Examples of such situations include:

1. An advertising company that buys advertising space or airtime on behalf of clients.

2. A software company that sells a customer a license, customisation services and support under a single long term contract.

3. A construction company working on a large project that will take several years to complete.

4. A company that gives the customers interest free credit.

The accounting standards dealing with this (principally IAS 18) use a number of criteria to decide when revenue should be recognised:

- In the case of goods, that ownership has genuinely been transferred; that the economic benefits and risks of ownership lie with the buyer.

- The revenue the seller gains must be measurable.

- The costs of supplying the goods or services can be measured.

- It is probable that the revenue will be received.

- The stage of completion of a partially completed contract for services can be determined.

There are special rules for recognising revenues from interest payments, dividends and royalties, barter and for adjusting revenues for delayed payments. There are also **disclosure** [p. 98] requirements for each type of revenue source. Applying these principals to the examples above:

1. An advertising company should only recognise revenues from the supply of its own services, not for acting as a buying agent for customers (of course the commission or mark-up it receives for this buying is part of its revenues).

2. Revenues should be recognised for the license and each service separately as payment for them becomes probable. This is likely to depend on contract terms that allow a customer to approve, reject or cancel.

3. Revenue can usually be recognised as pre-agreed mileposts in the project are passed.

4. Revenue can be recognised when the sale takes place but the amount recognised may need to be adjusted for the economic value of the interest foregone.

While the rules are complex, investors analysing a particular company do not need to make the judgements accountants do. The notes to the accounts should explain the revenue recognition policy. This should alert investors to any potential over-optimism.

Comparing a company's revenue recognition policy with others in its industry can be useful, but there have been times when almost all companies in a sector adopted weak policies (such as software in the 1990s).

Although new rules have improved the situation, revenues remain one of the most easily manipulated numbers in the accounts. Any manipulation of the revenues will be reflected all the way down the **P & L** [p. 234].

Reverse takeover

A reverse **takeover** [p. 5] is one in which control goes to the shareholders (and usually management) of the company that is legally the one that is bought.

The term reverse takeover is also be applied to the purchase of a **listed company** [p. 190] by an unlisted company, again with the listed company formally (and legally) being the acquirer, but with control passing to the shareholders and management of the unlisted company.

A reverse takeover will almost always take place by way of a pure equity acquisition, also called a share swap.

While a reverse takeover by an unlisted company can be a cost-effective way of acquiring a listing it is not as easy as it may seem at first glance. It is regulated and disclosure requirements are close to those required for an **IPO** [p. 182].

Reverse-repo

See **Repo** [p. 274].

Revpar

Revenue per available room (revpar) is the key indicator of performance for hotels. It reflects occupancy and rates:

$$revpar = occupancy \times average\ room\ rate$$

where occupancy is the percentage of available room-nights occupied.

Trends in revpar are very important. Revpar can be used to compare companies only if they have broadly similar hotels – similar quality in similar locations. This is often possible as most hotels companies give regional breakdowns of revpar and this can be compared.

Revpar only measures the performance of the core business of hotels, letting rooms. Many hotels make much of their revenue from additional services such as food and drink.

Rho

Rho (the Greek letter ρ) is the rate of change of the price of a portfolio or **derivative** [p. 96] with the interest rates. It is the measure of the interest rate sensitivity of a portfolio or security.

It is approximately the percentage change in value that will result from a one percent change in interest rates.

More rigorously:

$$\rho = \frac{\partial P}{\partial r}$$

where P is the price of the security and
r is the risk free rate.

Rho is used in **hedging** [p. 162] strategies in order to hedge against the risk of interest rate changes. It is usually used in hedging bond portfolios as they usually heavily exposed to **interest rate risk** [p. 178].

Rights issue

A rights issue is a way in which a company can sell new shares in order to raise capital. Shares are offered to existing shareholders in proportion to their current shareholding. The price at which the shares are offered is usually at a discount to the current share price, which gives investors an incentive to buy the new shares.

Rights issues are common because, in the UK and most other countries, shareholders have a right of first refusal (**pre-emption rights** [p. 244]) on **new issues** [p. 215] of shares.

The rights are normally a tradeable security themselves (a type of short dated **warrant** [p. 343]). This allows shareholders who do not wish to purchase new shares to sell the rights to someone who does. Whoever holds a right can choose to buy a new share ("exercise the right") by a certain date.

Some shareholders may choose to buy all the rights they are offered in the rights issue. This maintains their proportionate ownership in the expanded company, so that an x% stake before the rights issue remains an x% stake after it. Others may choose to sell their rights, diluting their stake and reducing the value of their holding.

If rights are not taken up the company may (and in practice does) sell them on behalf of the rights holder.

It is possible to sell some rights and exercise the remainder. One possibility is selling enough rights to cover the cost of exercising those that are not sold. This allows a shareholder to maintain the value of a holding without further expense (apart from dealing costs).

As with a **scrip issue** [p. 287], the price before the rights are issued needs to be adjusted for the rights issue. The calculation is a little more complicated as the new shares are paid for. Before comparison with share prices after the rights issue, prices before the shares went **ex-rights** [p. 82] need to be multiplied by:

$$\frac{(m \times y) + (n \times x)}{m \times (x + y)}$$

where x is the number of new shares issued for every y existing shares
m is the closing price on the last day the shares traded cum-rights and
n is the price of the new shares

The same adjustment needs to be made to per share numbers such as **EPS** [p. 122] if they are to remain comparable, for example, when looking looking at growth trends. However, a large rights issue is often associated with other changes that will distort these numbers or change trends such as paying off debt, expansion, etc.

This calculation makes the assumption that all rights will be exercised. This is usually an acceptable assumption as rights issues are usually priced at a discount to the share price to ensure that they will be exercised.

In the interval between the shares going ex-rights and the rights being exercised, if the share price falls low enough for the rights to have significant **option** value [p. 229], then an adjustment may have to be made for this. This happens very rarely.

Risk

In the context of investment, risk may be defined as the statistical distribution that describes the probabilities of various levels of future returns relative to the **expected return** [p. 135]. The **normal distribution** [p. 218] is often assumed – but is invariably a simplification.

A key difference from the use of the word risk in the most other contexts is in an investment context the word risk may also cover the possibility that the actual outcome may be better than expected, as well as worse than expected.

The terms upside risk and downside risk are used to describe the positive and negative risk respectively. An analyst who comments on the upside risk to a share price is talking about the chances of the price rising.

When investors talk of managing risk, it is mainly downside risk that is being minimised. Strategies for reducing downside risk involve trade-offs, so will either reduce the expected return (for example, **hedging** [p. 162] with **options** [p. 228]) or the upside risk (for example, selling a very **volatile** [p. 340] share to buy something more stable).

Risk aversion

Risk aversion is a concept central to financial theory. Many valuation models, including **CAPM** [p. 50], assume that higher risk investments need to be priced to generate higher returns.

A risk averse investor prefers certainty to risk, and low risk to high risk. Consider two investments, one of which will definitely return £100, the other of which has a 50% chance of returning £200 and a 50% chance of returning nothing. Both have an **expected return** [p. 135] of £100.

- A risk averse investor would prefer the certain £100.

- A risk neutral investor would not have any preference.

- A risk seeking investor would prefer the chance of getting the £200.

Whether people actually are risk averse is an interesting question. Investors do seem to act fairly consistently in a risk averse manner. However, there are plenty of examples of people exhibiting risk seeking behaviour – gambling for example.

Investor attitudes to risk and what determines it is one of many questions that are considered by **behavioural finance** [p. 33].

Risk premium

The difference between a rate of return and the **risk free rate of return** [p. 282] is a risk premium. Risk premiums may be calculated for a particular security, a class of securities, or a market.

Market risk premiums in general are important, as they are used by securities valuation models such as **CAPM** [p. 50]. The equity risk premium is particularly important.

The risk premium of a share is usually considered implicitly rather than explicitly. The term $(\beta \times (r_m - r_f))$ used in the CAPM is the equity risk premium of the security being valued. Similarly, it usually easier to think in terms of sector **beta** [p. 34] compared to the market. Sector and security risk premiums are more likely to be explicitly calculated for **bonds** [p. 37] – see **yield spread** [p. 349].

Risk free rate

The risk free rate of return is the best rate that does not involve taking a risk. Both the return of the original capital and the payment of interest are completely certain.

The risk free rate for a given period is taken to be the rate on **government bonds** [p. 160] over the period. This is because a government cannot run out of its own currency, as it is able to create more as necessary.

Any other investment should produce greater returns than the risk free rate. The extra return (the **risk premium** [p. 282]) reflects the extra risk involved.

The risk free rate is used by the **CAPM** [p. 50] and other valuation models.

RNS

Regulatory News Service (RNS) is a news service provided by the London Stock Exchange.

All announcements that London **listed companies** [p. 190] make to investors are carried by RNS. These include all announcements that are required by regulators such as results announcements, announcements of **takeover bids** [p. 317] and **directors dealings** [p. 97]

This means that access to RNS news is essential for investors. RNS stories are carried by a wide range of media ranging from free access websites to expensive and sophisticated data feeds that can be fed into corporate systems.

RNS also offers listed companies a number of other services that can help with regulatory reporting obligations and with investor relations in general.

Most listed companies also carry RNS announcements and on their own websites.

ROCE

Return on capital employed (ROCE) is the rate of return a business is making on the total capital employed in the business. Capital will include all sources of funding (*shareholders funds + debt*). To be consistent with this the return should be taken prior to interest (the return to lenders) and tax. It is therefore:

$$\frac{\textbf{EBIT}[\text{p. 115}]}{\textit{shareholders funds + debt}}$$

RoE [p. 283] is a similar measure which looks only at the returns to share-holders. return on equity (RoE) is normally higher than ROCE and is affected by the level of debt.

Return on operating capital employed [p. 276] is a variant of ROCE that looks at the operations of the business only, ignoring the effects of cash holdings and provisions. It is therefore a better measure of how efficiently the actual business is run and is more comparable across companies.

Comparisons across companies using any measure of return on capital require that numbers for both profit and capital are comparable. This means looking closely at a range of accounting policies and adjusting where necessary. For example, differences in **depreciation** [p. 95] or revaluation policies that change the amount of capital employed.

RoE

Return on equity (RoE) measures the return shareholders' are get on their money. It is used as a general indication of the company's efficiency. It is:

$$\frac{\textit{profit}}{\textbf{Equity}[\text{p. 123}]}$$

While a high RoE is generally good, the profitability is usually reflected in the share price. This limits its usefulness for stock picking. Bargain hunting investors may look for companies with a low ROE compared to others in the same sector, as it may reveal room for profit growth through efficiency improvements.

RoE should not be used to compare companies in different businesses. It is normally lower in **capital intensive** [p. 47] businesses. The comparison can also be distorted by different financial structures: a more heavily indebted company would have a higher RoE for example.

A clear example of this occurs when companies engage in a sale and lease-back of assets (most often property). They are able to **return the capital** [p. 276] raised by selling the assets. This reduces shareholders funds, increasing RoE. However, the company then faces additional fixed costs which both reduce profit and increase **operational gearing** [p. 227].

RoI

Return on investment (RoI) is similar to **ROCE** [p. 283] but is a broader term that can be applied to particular projects or operations, whereas as ROCE refers to returns at the company level.

RoI is the profit an investment generates as a proportion of the value of the assets used to generate it:

$$\frac{\textbf{EBIT}[\text{p. 115}]}{value\ of\ assets}$$

RoI obviously needs to be compared to **cost of capital** [p. 342], but the cost of capital for a particular project may not be the same as that for a company as a whole. If an investment is in line with a company's business as a whole (in terms of risks to cash flows it will generate) then the company's cost of capital may be used, otherwise it needs to be adjusted.

One way of calculating an appropriate cost of capital for a particular investment is to use **CAPM** [p. 50] and to estimate its **beta** [p. 34]. This is often by comparison with listed companies in the same business.

Because RoI uses accounting numbers it reflects accounting conventions in the measurement of profits and the value of assets. For this reason it is often preferable to instead use **ROIC** [p. 284] or **CROIC** [p. 80].

ROIC

Return on invested capital (ROIC) is closely related to **ROCE** [p. 283]. Like ROCE it looks at returns (usually **EBITDA** [p. 116]) free of the effects of **capital structure** [p. 48]. There are a number of definitions of ROIC in use which incorporate various refinements:

- Stripping out assets not used in the business (such as cash and financial investments)

- Stripping out free funding (most often trade creditors)

- Adding back the cost of assets that have been written off (most often goodwill)

- Adjusting for the effect of financial structure on tax paid.

The point of all these is the same: to give investors a better idea of the return the company makes on the money it has invested in the past. ROCE is flattered by writing off assets, ROIC is not. There are a number of definitions of ROIC. A good starting point is:

$$ROIC = \frac{EBITDA}{A - C - X + W}$$

where A is total assets (equivalent to debt plus **equity** [p. 123]),
C is cash holdings,
X is non-interest bearing **current liabilities** [p. 84],

It can sometimes be useful to refine this further by replacing EBITA with $EBITA \times (1 - tax\ rate)$. This shows what the **total return** [p. 325] would be if the company was purely equity funded. This variant is preferable if comparing companies with permanently different tax rates (e.g., operations in different countries). Total assets includes all **fixed assets** [p. 142] and **current assets** [p. 83].

Although some references suggest excluding **goodwill** [p. 159] from ROIC, there is a very strong case of including it. It is an investment that has been made and that requires a return. The cash balance is excluded as it is not invested in the business, the same reason cash is not included when calculating **EV** [p. 121].

Non-interest bearing current liabilities are excluded as they are free sources of funds for the company. If a company is funding a part of its assets by borrowing at no cost (often from trade creditors). By obtaining free funding a company is boosting returns to shareholders and this should be reflected in the ROIC.

ROIC is used to compare the efficiency of companies within a sector. Cross sector comparisons will not be meaningful: an aircraft manufacturer needs more assets than a software company. However, whatever industry the company is in, ROIC must be more than the **WACC** [p. 342] – otherwise the company is destroying rather than creating wealth.

ROIC is not perfect. As described above, it is still subject to the vagaries of asset values shown on the **balance sheet** [p. 28]. These depend on **depreciation** [p. 95] policies and the age of a company's assets. ROIC does nonetheless give investors a useful way of assessing how well run a company has been.

CROIC [p. 80] is similar to ROIC but measures cash returns.

RPK (Revenue Passenger Kilometres)

Revenue passenger kilometres (RPK) is a measure of the volume of passengers carried by an airline

A revenue passenger-kilometre is flown when a revenue passenger is carried one kilometre.

A passenger for whose transportation an air carrier receives commercial remuneration is called a revenue passenger. This excludes passengers travelling under fares available only to airline employees and babies and children who do not have a seat of their own.

The RPK of an airline is the the sum of the products obtained by multiplying the number of revenue passengers carried on each flight stage by the stage distance – it is the total number of kilometres travelled by all passengers.

RPK is a measure of sales volume of passenger traffic.

S,G & A

See **sales general and administrative costs** [p. 286].

SAC

See **subscriber acquisition cost** [p. 310].

Sales Mix

A sales mix is the proportions of sales coming from different products or services. Changes in sales mix often affect profits because different products often have different profit **margins** [p. 253], therefore a change in the sales mix can have an impact on profits even if total revenues are unchanged.

Selling less of a more profitable product but making up the sales with a less profitable product still leaves one with lower profits.

Sales, general and administrative costs

Sales, general and administrative costs (S,G & A), also referred to as overheads or administrative overheads, is one of two elements of operating costs. The other is the **cost of sales** [p. 75].

These costs are often largely **fixed costs** [p. 143], although they do contain some **variable** [p. 338] elements. The fixed costs also contain many discretionary costs (costs that management can easily choose to reduce) such as **R & D** [p. 261].

Same store sales

See **like-for-like** [p. 188].

Scenario planning

Scenario planning is a process that is used by organisations that make long term plans.

It, as the name implies, involves the construction of a number of alternative scenarios. Scenario planning starts with identifying the key driving forces in the area of interest (which might be an industry, a country, or the global economy).

The key driving forces are those that are both important (any changes will have a significant effect) and uncertain.

The scenarios are then drawn up estimating the outcomes of different combinations of the key drivers. These possible scenarios are then used for planning.

Scenario planning was invented by Shell and has been credited with making Shell significantly better prepared than the other major oil companies for the fall in oil prices in the 1980s.

Scenario planning is not often used in investment, although a case could be made for using it more widely. Its strength is taking into account qualitative rather than quantitative changes. This deters most professional investors, who prefer more quantitative methods. It has some similarities to **monte-carlo simulation** [p. 208] which is widely used by investors.

Scrip dividend

A scrip dividend is a **scrip issue** [p. 287] made in lieu of a cash dividend. Shareholders are able to choose whether to receive a cash dividend or shares. This is the difference between a scrip dividend and a scrip issue.

Shareholders who wish to reinvest will prefer a scrip dividend to a **DRIP** [p. 110] as it avoids dealing costs, and the number of shares received is known at the time the election to receive shares rather than cash is made. In the case of a DRIP, the number of shares bought will depend on the share price on the day of the purchase itself.

As with any scrip issue, the shares issued to pay a scrip dividend need to come from the capitalisation of reserves.

Scrip issue

A scrip issue (also called a capitalisation issue or a bonus issue) is the issue of new shares to existing shareholders at no charge, *pro rata* to their existing shareholdings.

The term capitalisation issue is less common but more accurate than the terms scrip or bonus issue. It reflects what happens in the books of the company. The **share capital** [p. 293] (on the **balance sheet** [p. 28]) has to increase by the **par value** [p. 235] of the newly issued shares. This is balanced by an equal decrease in another part of the shareholder's funds, such as retained earnings or a revaluation reserve. This is capitalisation

A scrip issue moves money from one account that belongs to the shareholders to another account that belongs to the shareholders. It is therefore basically a bookkeeping exercise and the value of any shareholding is unchanged by a bonus issue despite the increase in the number of shares held.

Share price charts and other comparisons should be adjusted for the bonus issue. For example, if a 1 for 5 bonus issue has taken place, then prices from before the share went ex-scrip should be adjusted by multiplying by 5/6 in order to make them comparable with the current price.

In spite of being a bookkeeping exercise, a scrip issue can have an impact on the share price for two reasons:

- A scrip issue is a gesture of confidence. The amount available to pay dividends is reduced – therefore it can be inferred that the management of the company is sure that the amount capitalised will not be needed to pay dividends.

- It can improve the liquidity of very high priced shares, if the old share price was so high as to make the trading of small blocks awkward.

Secondary listing

A security may be **listed** [p. 190] in more than one market. It is common for one such listing to be a primary listing and the others secondary listings.

Having multiple listings gives an issuer access to a wider pool of money. Although there are mechanisms that allow multiple primary listings these are more complex and expensive.

Liquidity [p. 190] tends to shift to the market where the primary listing is. Companies also tend to be less committed to the markets in which they have secondary listings: an example of this is the speed with which British companies got rid of the secondary listings in the US when the Sorbanes-Oxley legislation made US listings more expensive.

Secondary listings may be direct listings of the securities concerned, or they may be listings of **GDRs** [p. 159] or **ADRs** [p. 14].

Secondary market

The secondary market is trading in securities after the initial issue; the sale of securities from one investor to another.

The term is needed in order to distinguish such trading from the initial issue of shares. In a **primary market** [p. 251] shares are sold by issuers to investors.

The most important secondary markets are securities exchanges, such as stock exchanges. The secondary markets for some securities may operate through dealers and brokers operating outside exchanges. Regulatory restrictions mean that access to markets other than exchanges is, in most cases, restricted to institutional investors.

Sector

A sector is simply a grouping of companies that have similar businesses. The grouping is done be exchanges or the compilers of **indices** [p. 169].

Most sectors group together companies within a particular industry such as telecoms and oil. Some are more varied. The **FTSE** [p. 150] Support Services sector verges on being a catch-all for companies that do not fit elsewhere.

Sector classifications are useful for several reasons:

- They enable investors to analyse their exposure to different industries. This also means it is easy to analyse exposure to categories of sector, such as **cyclical** [p. 84] sectors.

- Sector indices provide **benchmarks** [p. 33] for specialist funds that only invest in certain sectors.

- Communication: they help funds, analysts and others to describe their speciality in a clear way.

- They provide a peer group with which to compare a company – for example, when comparing a company's **PE** [p. 237] to the **sector PE** [p. 289].

There are a number of different sector classifications, but by far the most widely used in the UK is the FTSE classification. FTSE Sectors are also grouped into industry groups (such as "cyclical services"), and further divided into subsectors.

Sector PE

A sector PE is a **PE ratio** [p. 237] for a whole sector rather than an individual company. A market PE is the same for an entire market. A sector or market PE is:

$$\frac{market\ cap}{profit}$$

where *market cap* is the total **market capitalisation** [p. 196] of all companies in the sector or market and
profit is the total bottom line profit of all companies in the sector or market.

Sector PE is used to compare a company to its sector, a company to market as a whole or a particular sector to the market.

Market PE

A market PE is a sector PE as above, where the "sector" is an entire market

Market PE may be used as a comparison for a company's PE. A sector PE is usually more suitable.

Market PE is also used as a measure of the value of the market as a whole. A market PE may be compared to:

- another market,

- historical market PEs of the same market,

- returns on other types of securities or the risk free rate.

Like any valuation ratio, a higher market PE may be justified by higher growth. The growth rate of the market may be estimated by aggregating the profit forecasts of large companies, or economic growth forecasts may be used as a proxy.

Securities market line

The securities market line (SML) graphs the relationship between risk and return.

The securities market line is a straight line. It touches the **efficient frontier** [p. 118] and passes though the risk free rate of return.

The SML lies above the efficient frontier, except at the one point where it touches. This shows that the availability of a risk free asset improves the returns available for a any given level of risk and vice-versa.

Securitisation

Securitisation is the creation of **asset backed securities** [p. 21]. These are debt securities that are backed by a stream of cash flows.

The borrower issues debt securities that are repaid using only these cash flows. Buyers of these securities have no further recourse against the borrower if the cash flows prove insufficient.

Assets to be securitised are first sold to a **special purpose vehicle (SPV)** [p. 304], thus isolating the ultimate borrower from any claims for repayment. The SPV then issues **bonds** [p. 37] or other debt instruments. The SPV then uses the money raised by issuing the debt securities to pay the ultimate borrower for the assets.

The borrower has raised money without risking assets other than those held by the SPV and it has got a lump sum in return. It has lost some assets or cash flows in return for cash. The debt is also kept off the ultimate borrower's balance sheet (see **off balance sheet financing** [p. 221]). This is quite reasonable given the limited recourse. Securitisation can therefore be seen as a way of selling off a stream of cash flows.

Securitisation also has benefits for investors. It widens their choice of available investments. The asset backed securities created by securitisation may also be easier to analyse as investors need only evaluate the cash flows from a small pool of assets, instead of a whole complex business. The assets most often securitised are loans of one kind or another which are usually (when pooled, not individually) a low risk investment.

The last of these usually also means that, for the issuer, it is often a cheap way of borrowing.

Security

A security is one of:

- An asset that has been pledged to raise a loan – such as a house used to secure a mortgage

- A financial instrument that entitles its owner to some future stream of cash flows.

The second meaning is what matters in an investment context. The purpose of a security is to allow fractional ownership or other rights to be traded. This may be ownership of companies (shares), debt (**bonds** [p. 37]), contractual rights (**derivatives** [p. 96]) or other entitlements to streams of cash flows.

A financial security may give its holder other rights in addition to the stream of cash flows. For example, shareholders are usually entitled to vote at company meetings.

It is possible to create securities from a wide range of cash flow streams other than the traditional repayments of debt, or the distribution of profits. Such creation of a security from such a stream of cash flows is called **securitisation** [p. 290].

SEDOL code

A Stock Exchange Daily Official List (SEDOL) code is one of many codes used to identify UK **listed** [p. 190] securities.

A SEDOL code is a seven digit number. A security's SEDOL is the basis of its **ISIN** [p. 184]. The ISIN is the SEDOL plus the prefix "GB00" with a single check digit suffixed.

SEDOL codes are not memorable, and therefore more commonly used by automated systems than by people. **TIDM** [p. 322] codes are generally easier to remember. The main advantage of SEDOL codes is their simple relationship with ISINs.

Sell side analyst

Sell side analysts (as opposed to **buy side analysts** [p. 44]) are employed (usually) by stockbrokers to write investment research that is circulated to clients. Sell side research is usually detailed. Sell side analysts produce complex **financial models** [p. 140] and forecasts. They usually specialise in a sector or a sub-sector.

The access clients get to research usually depends on how much business they give the brokerage producing the research. It is possible to buy access to some sell side research for a fee, but this is a rarer arrangement as it is usually cheaper to simply switch some business to the broker who produces the research wanted.

Typically, the best clients will be regularly contacted by analysts, updating them on developments and changes in the analysts' views as well. They will also get regular delivery of written research in printed and electronic form. At the other extreme marginal clients will receive a limited amount of published research, have no real access to analysts to ask questions and will have limited (if any) access to other distribution channels such as research web sites.

Sell side research is primarily produced for external users – the brokers clients. It can therefore be widely circulated. It can very influential in changing investors' perceptions and driving share prices.

One of the key problems with sell side research has been its lack of independence. Brokers are usually owned by investment banks which dislike research that upsets clients or potential clients – for example, by criticising a company that may give the bank future advisory work. This is particularly so because part of the traditional function of sell side analysts was to display investment banks' analytical skills and to use their contacts with **listed companies** [p. 190] to get clients for the far more profitable corporate finance departments.

This problem has been ameliorated by regulators and by banks' wish to improve their reputations. However the problem is far from solved and this remains one reason for employing buy side analysts.

Sell side analysts usually have enormous expertise in the companies and sectors they cover. The forecasts are the most important single product of their detailed financial modelling, but sell side research is very useful because of the depth of information it contains.

Semi-variable costs

Semi-variable costs are those that have both **fixed cost** [p. 143] and **variable cost** [p. 338] elements. For example, a manufacturer's electricity bill may include elements that are fixed (such as lighting that is required regardless of the level of production) and elements that are variable (such as the electricity used by machinery directly involved in manufacturing).

Semiconductor

The term semiconductor is used, slightly inaccurately, to mean electronic components such as integrated circuits ("chips") and transistors. Strictly speaking, it refers to the materials out of which these components are made. This is most commonly silicon, although other materials (including germanium, gallium arsenide and indium arsenide) are used for when necessary.

The market for semi-conductors is global and demand is **cyclical** [p. 84]. The actual manufacturing of semi-conductors is dominated by a fairly small number of large companies. These include **fabless semiconductor companies** [p. 136] that do everything other than manufacturing. There are many smaller companies involved in the design and marketing of semiconductors.

Senior debt

Senior debt takes priority over **subordinated debt** [p. 310]. Subordinated debt is only repaid with the funds left over after repaying senior debt.

Senior debt is not necessarily first in line to be paid:

- Bankruptcy law gives priority to tax and certain payments to employees.

- **Secured** [p. 291] debt has the first claim on assets used to secure it.

Senoir debt is lower risk, and should therefore be lower **yield** [p. 350], than junior debt.

Share buy-back

A share buy-back is the purchase by a company of its own shares in the market. These shares are usually then cancelled.

Companies do sometimes retain bought back shares as **treasury shares** [p. 328] in order to be able to re-sell them, or allocate them to fulfil share options or to otherwise avoid issuing new shares.

Large share buy-backs are a way of carrying out a **return of capital** [p. 276] to shareholders. The alternative would be a **special dividend** [p. 301].

The advantage of buy-backs is that, by boosting the share price, they give shareholders **capital gains** [p. 47] rather than income.

Some companies buy back a small number of shares every year. This is an alternative to increasing the dividend. It also does not commit the company to sustaining the payment in the same way the increasing the dividend would and, again, turns the return into a capital gain rather than income.

Another advantage of a share buy-back is that it gives shareholders more flexibility than a dividend as it allows shareholders to choose when, and if, to sell and realise their cash. This can also help minimise tax.

Shareholders can even, by selling the correct proportion of their holding, get exactly the same amount of cash out of the company as would have been paid if a dividend had been paid instead – however the money may be taxed differently and doing this involves paying brokers commissions and other expenses of trading.

Share capital

Share capital is an accounting number that is part of the breakdown of shareholders' **equity** [p. 123] on the **balance sheet** [p. 28].

If a company has issued only **ordinary shares** [p. 230], then the share capital is the **par value** [p. 235] of a share multiplied by the number of shares in issue.

If a company has issued more than one class of share the share capital is the sum of the contributions to share capital (as above) of each class of share.

The total shareholders' equity has some importance for investors. It is the same as the NAV. This is used for valuations based on asset values (e.g. **NAV/share** [p. 213]).

However, the breakdown of shareholders equity into categories such as share capital reflects the history of a company and decisions such as issuing bonus shares (see **scrip issue** [p. 287]). As such it says little that is useful from the point of view of valuation.

One exception to this are the **distributable reserves** [p. 102]. Dividends must be paid out of this. If they fall to nothing (which is rare) dividends cannot be paid without a capital re-organisation.

Share split

A share split is similar to a **scrip issue** [p. 287]. Shareholders are issued with new shares are no cost, but its effect on the **balance sheet** [p. 28] is different from that of a bonus issue.

A split reduces the **par value** [p. 235] of each share, but increases the number of shares by the same proportion. For example, if the par value of shares is reduced from 10p to 5p, then the number of shares will be doubled, and each shareholder will receive two shares to replace each one they currently own.

Because a split does not increase the share capital, it cannot be taken as a gesture of confidence as a bonus issue can. However a split can improve the **liquidity** [p. 190] of very high priced shares.

The number of shares can be reduced by a similar exercise, a reverse split or share **consolidation** [p. 69].

Sharpe ratio

The Sharpe ratio compares the return on a portfolio to the risk. It is:

$$d/\sigma_d \text{ where } d = r_p - r_b$$

where r_p is the return on a portfolio and
r_b is the return on a **benchmark** [p. 33]
d is called the relative return and
σ_d is the **standard deviation** [p. 305] of d.

A very simple case of this is where the benchmark is a **risk free** [p. 282] investment, in which case the Sharpe ratio is the **excess return** [p. 133] on the portfolio divided by the standard deviation of the return on the portfolio.

The Sharpe ratio is interesting because it is a measure of the relationship between risk and return, a concept that is central to financial theory. It can be applied to both ex-ante (expected) returns (to assess an investment) and to ex-poste (historical) returns (to test the relationship between risk and reward).

One useful property of the Sharpe ratio is that the Sharpe ratio of a portfolio does not depend on the time over which it is measured. It will change with time period depending on the actual historic data, but there is no **correlation** [p. 74] between the Sharpe ratio and the length of time period. This is because the return and the standard deviation both increase with time. Sharpe ratios calculated over different periods of time are directly comparable.

Shell company

A shell company is a company that exists but does not actually do any business or have any assets. The most interesting type of shell company (to investors) is one that has a **listing** [p. 190]. This is a listed shell, and is almost always what is meant by a reference to a shell in an investment context.

Given that it takes time and money to obtain a listing, a listed shell has significant value even if it does not have any assets. Listed shells are therefore often the targets of **reverse takeovers** [p. 278].

A listed shell company must have had an active business in the past, or it could not have met the requirements for a listing. Exchanges can take a dim view of shell companies (and even **cash shells** [p. 54]) and may make it difficult for their listings to be maintained indefinitely without acquiring some real business

A shell company can also mean a company that has never had a business (and certainly not a listing). In this context it often means what is also called a shelf company. These are incorporated purely to sell off-the-shelf. This offers a convenient alternative to setting up a company from scratch (the name of the company can be changed, new directors appointed, and possibly shares issued).

If a shell company in this sense has no active business, and has been in that state for some time, it is likely to be considered dormant and may be exempt from many reporting requirements.

Finally, the phrase is also used to describe companies that exist merely as a front for a person or organisation that wishes to hide its identity.

Short position

An investor who has sold a security without owning it (often by borrowing a holding to sell), has a short position in it.

Short selling [p. 296] is a way of profiting from a decline in the market that an investor expects.

Investors may use **derivatives** [p. 96] rather than underlying securities to take a short position: for example, by buying **put options** [p. 228].

Short selling

An investor who expects the price of a security to fall may exploit this to make a profit by selling shares that they do not actually own with the intention of buying them back at a lower price to settle the trade.

Originally this could be done simply by offering securities for sale and buying them before delivery was due. Modern electronic trading systems make this more difficult (as they usually check ownership of shares before accepting orders). It is now usual to borrow shares from an existing share holder (who will charge a fee for doing this), sell these in the market, and buy replacement shares when the borrowed shares are due to be returned.

Shrinkage

Shrinkage is the rate of loss of products (e.g., through shoplifting) from retailers' stocks as a percentage of profit or sales; the value of products lost between supply and sale as a percentage of the total cost of goods sold. The main causes of shrinkage are shoplifting, employee theft, administrative errors and fraud.

The British Retail Consortium estimates the total loses due to shrinkage of £1.96bn in 2003. £1.00bn was due to losses from crime while the remainder was a result of prevention costs.

41% of shrinkage was caused by shoplifting, 28% by staff and the remaining 11% by burglary, fraud, damage and other losses.

The Centre for Retail Research estimates average UK shrinkage to be 1.6% of sales.

The effect of shrinkage on profits can be very significant, especially for retailers with small margins.

Single premium vs regular premium

Single premium insurance policies are those on which the customer pays a single one-off payment. The insurer gets an up front payment for covering a continuing risk over a period of time. This contrasts with regular premiums which give the insurers an income stream in return for covering the risk. General insurance is paid with regular premiums but single premiums are not uncommon in life **assurance** [p. 23].

Annual premium equivalent [p. 16] or **PVNBP** [p. 258] can be used to measure insurers' new business using a single number that combines regular and single premium business.

Single price

A **collective investment vehicle** [p. 62] has a single price if investors can buy and sell stakes in it at exactly the same price.

OEICs [p. 221] and **investment trusts** [p. 180] single priced.

Unit trusts [p. 333] and **ETFs** [p. 124] are dual priced: the buying and selling prices are different.

Single priced vehicles are not necessarily cheaper to buy and sell than those that are dual priced. It is common for OEICs and unit trusts to make an initial charge when you buy (or sometimes an exit charge instead). This often more than makes up for the lack of a **bid-offer spread** [p. 35].

Small cap

Small cap shares are those with a comparatively low **market capitalisation** [p. 196]. Small caps make up the vast majority of **listed companies** [p. 190] by number but only a small part of the market by market cap.

Small caps offer investors the opposite of **blue chips** [p. 36]. They are under-researched but doing research oneself is difficult because the information available to investors is not as good.

In general, compared to large caps, **disclosure** [p. 98] is poor, there is less of an **investor relations** [p. 181] effort and less careful treatment of **price sensitive** [p. 248] information. This puts private investors are at an even greater disadvantage with small caps than they are with larger companies.

Institutional investors (apart from specialist small cap funds) tend to pay little attention to small caps, as do the majority of brokers. There is very little **sell side** [p. 291] research available.

This means that investors who look at small caps do have a good chance of finding opportunities that the market has missed – the market is less likely to be **efficient** [p. 118] with regard to a small cap share than a large or **mid cap** [p. 202].

In addition, there are many growth companies among the small caps. This further increases a small cap investor's chances of out-performing the market. There is fairly good evidence that small caps tend to out-perform the market over the long term.

The downside of this is that there are many people in the business of providing tips on small caps. They are often commented on by **tip sheets** [p. 323]. It is best to be sceptical of any share tipping service – particularly if dramatic results are claimed. The low **liquidity** [p. 190] of small caps means that prices are susceptible to manipulation.

SME (small to medium enterprises)

The term SME is used to describe businesses that are too big to be just small businesses but which are too small to be regarded as big business. The term is usually used as a plural (i.e. SMEs).

The definition of SME will vary in different contexts and the term is often used without a clear definition. Definitions are usually based on the numbers of employees (from a few tens to a few hundreds) and turnover (usually up to a few tens of millions of pounds).

SMEs are more likely to be growth companies than larger companies are. However they are harder to invest in as they are rarely **listed** [p. 190]. Even those that are listed are very small companies by listed company standards and therefore have less liquid shares, are less likely to be well covered by analysts and tend to **disclose** [p. 98] less information to investors than larger companies.

The difficulty investors face in investing in SMEs is unfortunate as SMEs tend to be more innovative and generate more growth than bigger companies. The costs involved in accessing capital markets make this something that is unlikely to change despite the lack of access to capital faced by SMEs.

Social grades

Social grades are a way of classifying people. It is particularly important for media companies, as the composition of their audience affects how much they can charge for advertising. A key metric is the proportion of an audience in the ABC1 grade (those with non-manual occupations). This refers to a system that uses the following categories:

1. A: Higher managerial and professional

2. B: Intermediate managerial and professional

3. C1: Supervisory, clerical, junior managerial

4. C2: Skilled manual workers

5. D: Semi-skilled and unskilled manual workers

6. E: State pensioners, casual workers

There are a number of problems with this classification which reflect how society has changed since it was devised decades ago. These limit its usefulness for marketing and advertising. The worst of these drawbacks are:

- It classifies an entire household on the occupation of a single individual.

- It ignores groups such as wealthy people who do not work and some groups of self-employed people.

- It contains no information about the size or structure of households.

- It is too broad brush: 55% of the British population are ABC1!

This does not mean that this system is useless, it does capture much important information in a simple form, however there are alternatives that can be used when appropriate. Examples include:

- education

- political leanings

- family size and family life cycle – e.g., single person, couple, family children, "empty nest", sole survivor

- type of housing - e.g. affluent suburbs, council estates, agricultural areas, affluent urban areas

- behaviour – brand loyalty, purchasing patterns etc.

- lifestyle and aspirations.

Soft commission

Soft commission is commission given in a non-cash form.

Soft commission frequently raises problems because it is not transparent. This is often a problem in an investment context because investors' money may often be used to pay soft commission in ways that are not apparent to them.

The problem with soft commission is not the commission per se. The soft commission is very often given in a form that clearly helps provides investors a better service (e.g. research, financial data etc.). The problem is the lack of transparency. The **bundling** [p. 43] of services implied by soft commissions can also distort prices and therefore impose extra costs on investors.

The most common example of this is the provision of research to fund managers in return for brokerage business. It is usual for access to **sell-side** [p. 291] research to be given mostly to institutional investors who give the brokerage business, with different levels of access being granted depending on the volume of business.

This leads to a serious problem because the value of the soft commission is shown as a cost of broking (which customers see as a reduction in performance) rather than being shown as a management cost (part of the fund mangers fees).

This means fees can look lower than the real cost to investors of the manager's services.

The fact that broking and sell-side research are almost always bundled together makes the system even less transparent as it is virtually impossible to place a financial value on access to research.

At the time of writing, British regulators are considering how to restrict the use of soft commission by fund managers.

Solvency margin

The solvency margin is a minimum excess on an insurer's assets over its liabilities set by regulators. It can be regarded as similar to **capital adequacy** [p. 45] requirements for banks. It is essentially a minimum level of the **solvency ratio** [p. 300], but regulators usually use a slightly more complex calculation. The current EU requirement is the greatest of:

- 18% of **premium written** [p. 246] up to €50m plus 16% of premiums above €50m.

- 26% of claims up to €35m plus 23% of claims above €35m.

Some other adjustments are also made. Premiums for high risk classes of business are increased for the purpose of this calculation, an adjustment is made for **reinsurance** [p. 271], etc.

This requirement is being replaced by "Solvency II". This is a development that is very similar to the Basel II capital adequacy requirements for banks, as it will mean a move to more complex risk models.

The **free asset ratio** [p. 146] is net assets adjusted for the solvency margin.

Solvency ratio

The solvency ratio of an insurance company is the size of its capital relative to premium written. The solvency ratio is (most often) defined as:

$$\frac{net\ assets}{\textbf{net premium written}[\text{p. }246]}$$

The solvency ratio is a measure of the risk an insurer faces of claims that it cannot absorb. The amount of premium written is a better measure than the total amount insured because the level of premiums is linked to the likelihood of claims.

It is a basic measure of how financially sound an insurer is, but this simple calculation that does not take into account the types of business the company does.

Sovereign debt

Sovereign debt is money borrowed by a government.

If a government borrows in its own currency then it usually does so by issuing **government bonds** [p. 160] or **treasury bills** [p. 328]. These are very different from government borrowing in foreign currency because they are risk free – whereas many governments have defaulted on foreign currency debt.

Sovereign debt in a foreign currency is not intrinsically greatly different from corporate debt. The same systems of **credit ratings** [p. 78] are used, although the assessment of risk is rather different. In particular it is subject to **sovereign risk** [p. 301] and therefore political factors.

The sovereign foreign currency debt of most developed economies is usually low risk. Although it is not safe enough to be treated as **risk free** [p. 282], as a government's borrowings in its own currency are, it is often the next best thing.

The **credit rating** [p. 78] agencies issue credit ratings on governments using the same scale they use for corporate debt.

Sovereign risk

Although government **bonds** [p. 37] in the government's own currency are usually regarded as **risk free** [p. 282] (because governments need never run out of money they issue themselves), there are certain risks involved in dealing with governments.

As a country is a sovereign entity, it is impossible or difficult for someone dealing with a government to enforce repayments of debt (a government can even change the law to avoid repayments, if it wishes to), hence the term sovereign risk. Many governments have defaulted and there is little investors can do about it (whereas with a non-governmental body investors would sue). The risk that this will happen is sovereign risk.

Sovereign risk can also apply to other dealings with governments, such as undertaking government contracts. Its most wide definition is that of all risks arising from the ability to governments (as sovereign bodies) to pass laws and regulations.

The assessment of sovereign risk on government debt is in some ways similar to the assessment of the default risk of corporate debt. It is complicated by the relevance of political issues which may lead a government to default even if it could pay.

Spark spread

Spark spread is the difference between the wholesale price of electricity and the cost of the fuel used to generate it. The wholesale price is the price in the market in which electricity generators sell to distributors.

The price of fuel is important because it is the main **variable cost** [p. 338] in the generation of electricity. This makes spark spread a measure of **contribution** [p. 72] per unit.

Spark spread will vary between plants using different fuels and may vary even between plants using the same fuels. It should be positive for any plant that is actually in current operation (otherwise the there would be a negative contribution, and presumably a shutdown).

In the long term the spark spread should be large enough to provide electricity generation companies (and most individual power plants) with an adequate RoI [p. 284].

Special dividend

A special dividend is a dividend that is stated to be a special dividend when it is declared. The main reason for declaring a dividend special is to make it clear that it is a one-off. This is a signal to investors that it is not part of a sustainable increase in dividends.

Usually, when a company raises its dividend, the market takes this as signalling that the company will keep paying dividends at the new higher level. It may also signal a change in the company's **dividend policy** [p. 106].

Labelling a dividend "special" makes it clear that the company does not wish to signal this.

It is quite usual for a company to pay a special dividend and increase its normal dividend as well. In this case the increase to the normal dividend is a signal and can be taken as indicating the company's current dividend policy. The (usually much bigger) increase due to the special dividend is not.

For this reason the special dividend should not be included in **yield** [p. 107] calculations and has only a a limited effect on valuation.

Special dividends are most often used to **return capital** [p. 276] to shareholders.

Special items

See **exceptional items** [p. 132].

Special purpose vehicle/entity

See **SPV** [p. 304].

Spin-off

See **demerger** [p. 94].

Split capital investment trusts

Split capital **investment trusts** [p. 180] issue multiple classes of shares, most commonly:

- income shares that receive the dividends paid by the trusts' investments. There may be more than one class of income share with different characteristics

- capital shares which do not receive any dividend, but which eventually receive all the capital gains made after paying off any debt and preference shares

- **zeros** [p. 350].

Some funds may have more than one class of share of each type: for example, a higher risk type of "geared" or "ordinary" income share, or "annuity" shares that have a high **yield** [p. 107] but pay back less when the trust is wound up than the price at which the share were issued.

The advantages of a split capital trust are:

- Because investors can get more of their returns as **capital gains** [p. 47] or income, they can choose whichever would give them the more favourable tax treatment.

- **Income investors** [p. 168] get the highest possible income, because they get the dividends paid on a greater amount of capital (the investment made by the holders of capital shares as well as their own) than a non-split income trust would have

- **Growth investors** [p. 161] looking for long term capital gains get greater capital gains as they benefit from the capital gains on the capital invested by the holders of income shares as well as their own.

- The other classes of shares provide variants on the above with different balances of risk and return: for example if there are both ordinary income shares and preference income shares, the holders of the latter get a lower return at a lower risk.

A split capital trust has should not be expected to produce better returns for any type of investor, because it has to compromise between the **growth investing** [p. 161] strategy that would suit the holders of capital shares, the **income investing** [p. 168] strategy that would suit the holders of the income shares and the conservative strategy that would suit holders of zeros.

The added complexity of how returns are distributed can make it harder for investors to assess how much risk they are exposed to than would be the case with a more straightforward fund.

Spot price

A spot price is the price of something with immediate settlement. It is most often used in currency and commodity markets in order to distinguish current prices from **forward prices** [p. 154].

The term spot price is not often used in the context of securities because less forward trading takes place. Investors looking for that type of exposure generally use **derivatives** [p. 96]. Most trading is for delivery as soon as market mechanisms allow.

In **commodity markets** [p. 64] much of the trading is for future delivery. In some markets for it to be usual to quote prices with delivery dates because so much trading is done forward. Under these circumstances it is important to clarify that a quoted price is spot.

Spot prices are used for the settlement of futures and other derivatives in many markets where settlement is by payment rather than delivery.

SPV (SPE)

A special purpose vehicle (SPV) or special purpose entity (SPE) is a company that is created solely for a particular financial transaction or series of transactions. It may sometimes be something other than a company, such as a trust.

SPVs/SPEs are often used to make a transaction tax efficient by choosing the most favourable tax residence for the vehicle. This is commonly done with **eurobonds** [p. 126] so that foreign investors do not have to pay withholding taxes in the borrower's country of residence.

SPVs are used for other transactions including **securitisations** [p. 290] and the issue of **catastrophe bonds** [p. 55].

In addition to reducing tax, SPVs can also remove assets or liabilities from **balance sheets** [p. 28], transfer risk and (in securitisations) allow the effective sale of future cash flows.

The management of an SPV will need to be structured in a way that takes account of accounting standards that require a company controlled by another to be **consolidated** [p. 69] as a **subsidiary** [p. 311]. This is not usually a problem as SPVs require very little in the way of management.

The effect of SPVs on accounts is obviously open to abuse. SPVs have often been used to manipulate published accounts, most notoriously by Enron. Accounting rules have since been tightened to make such abuses harder.

Stag

A stag buys shares though an **IPO** [p. 182], with the intention of selling as soon as dealing starts.

Shares sold through an IPO are normally sold at a discount to the expected market price in order to ensure that the IPO is full subscribed.

This creates a low risk opportunity to make a profit by buying through the IPO process and selling as soon as dealing starts.

Although this is not true **arbitrage** [p. 18], because there is an element of risk, it is a very low risk way of making money.

Stagflation

Stagflation is the combination of **recession** [p. 267] with high **inflation** [p. 171].

Stagflation is not a state that occurs often because recession reduces demand for goods (because people have less money to spend). Low demand usually leads to low inflation.

The word stagflation is a conflation of stagnation and inflation.

Possible causes of stagflation include short supplies of essential **commodities** [p. 64] (such as oil) and too fast a rise in **money supply** [p. 206] (which in turn usually reflects government policy).

Stagflation occurred in the 70s and 80s. Economic theory prior to that time regarded the combination as unlikely, if not impossible.

Once stagflation occurs it is difficult to deal with. The measures a government would usually take to revive an economy in recession (cutting **interest rates** [p. 177] or increasing government spending) will also increase inflation.

Under normal recessionary conditions inflationary policies are acceptable, but given already high inflation, pushing inflation still higher is itself damaging.

Stamp duty

A tax that is charged on the transfer of an asset. It is usually a percentage of the value of the asset.

It can be a significant part of the cost of buying securities and property.

Standard deviation

The standard deviation is a measure of how spread out a set of numbers are.

The standard deviation of a set of numbers is the square root of their variance. Variance is usually denoted by σ^2 and the standard deviation by σ, and:

$$\sigma^2 = \frac{1}{n} \sum_{i=1}^{n} (x_i - \mu)^2$$

where x_i is one of n numbers and
μ is the **arithmetic mean** [p. 19] all n numbers x.

The most common use of the standard deviation in finance is to measure the risk of holding a security or portfolio. We first need the expected price (see **expected return** [p. 135]):

$$E[S] = \sum_{i=1}^{n} S_i p(S_i)$$

where S is a price
and $p(S_i)$ is the probability that S will be the actual price.

Denoting the variance of S, Var(S):

$$\text{Var}(S) = \sum_{i=1}^{n} (S_i - E[S])^2 p(S_i)$$

Var(S) is a measure of **volatility** [p. 340]. Its square root (the standard deviation) is the most widely used measure of volatility.

To use continuous times and prices replace the sums above with integrals.

Statement of total recognised gains and losses

The statement of total recognised gains and losses (STRGL) gives investors a summary of a company's gains and losses regardless of whether or not they were shown in the **P & L** [p. 234] or the **balance sheet** [p. 28].

The STRGL is a primary statement, and should be given the same prominence as the **p & L** [p. 234], the **balance sheet** [p. 28] and the cashflow. It is given this prominence in published accounts, but investors rarely pay much attention

The starting point of the statement of total recognised gains and losses is the profit for the year (profit after tax, before the payment of dividends) and this is followed by other gains and losses – changes in the value of items shown on the balance sheet.

The statement of total recognised gains and losses will typically look something like this:

Profit for the financial year	200
Revaluation of property (unrealised)	20
	220
Currency translation differences	(50)
Total recognised gains (losses) for the year	170
Prior year adjustment	(20)
Total gains and losses recognised since the last year	150

The prior year adjustment is a change in profit in the previous year due either to an error or (more likely) a change in accounting policy (to bring reporting in line with current accounting standards). This prior year adjustment should include the cumulative effect over all prior years.

The gains and losses made for the period do not completely explain all changes in shareholders' **equity** [p. 123]. This is because shareholders funds are also changed by **share buybacks** [p. 293], **new issues** [p. 215] and dividends.

A reconciliation should be provided that will look something like this

Total recognised gains for the year	150
Dividend	(50)
New share capital	200
Net addition to shareholders funds	300

The STRGL helps prevent an important class of manipulations of accounts. By requiring that all changes to the balance sheet are shown, it highlights any attempt to move losses to the balance sheet without passing them through the P & L. It may not provide as much material for analysis as the other primary statements, but it should still be looked at.

Stock

The term stock as two main meanings in a financial context. Firstly it can mean **current assets** [p. 83] held for sale or being processed for future sale. This is a British usage synonymous with the American "inventory" (see below). The word inventory is commonly understood in Britain and sometimes used. The other meaning is "financial security", but what securities it refers to can vary.

The strict meaning of the word stock (when it does mean a security) is a security which is not divided into units, as shares and corporate bonds usually are. Companies usually divide their **equity** [p. 123] capital into shares, and all shares and purchases have to be of quantities that are a number of whole shares – it is possible to buy one share or 100 or 101, but not 100.5 shares. Stock is not divided into shares, and therefore can be traded in as small a unit as the holders wish. In practice trading systems limit the possible sizes of units.

In some countries **government debt** [p. 160] has the characteristics that meet the strict definition of the work stock. However the practicalities of trading systems make is common for there to be some minimum trading unit. For this reason, stock frequently means government and other fixed interest securities (sometimes even those that do not meet the strict definition above).

In the US the word stock is often used to mean ordinary shares, because they are the most common type of security and almost identical to common stock (ordinary equity capital not divided into shares).

The broadest meaning of the word stock is simply any debt or equity security (but not more exotic securities such as **derivatives** [p. 96]). This broad meaning justifies its use in terms such as stock market.

Stock (inventory)

Stocks (called inventory in the US and sometimes in Britain) are current assets held for sale, or for processing and subsequent re-sale.

Stocks should be valued at the lower of:

- Cost (purchase price + the cost of any processing)

- **Net realiseable value** [p. 214]

Socks may consist of:

- goods that will be sold as they are: finished goods for a manufacturer, most stocks for a retailers

- **work in progress** [p. 346]: unfinished goods

- **raw materials** [p. 264].

The cost of stocks of the same type changes with time. It is also neither useful nor practicable to separately track identical items. This means that the cost of stocks has to be appropriately allocated when they are used or sold. How this is done has an impact on both the **balance sheet** [p. 28] and the **P & L** [p. 234]. Most commonly **FIFO** [p. 138] is used which assumes that the first items to be bought are the first to be sold. Other methods such as **LIFO** [p. 188] and **replacement cost** [p. 273] are also used.

The valuation of any goods that have been processed (including work in progress) adds some complications as it is necessary to decide which costs can be allocated to which items.

Stock turnover

Stock turnover measures how well a company coverts **stock** [p. 307] into sales. It is closely similar to **asset turnover** [p. 22] and is also a measure of efficiency. It is:

$$\frac{annual\ sales}{stocks}$$

Stock turnover is more specific than asset turnover. It measures how well the company is making use of the part of its **working capital** [p. 347] that has been invested in stock.

Stock turnover is the main component of asset turnover for companies that have little tied up in fixed assets but hold large amounts of stock, usually trading rather than manufacturing companies. For more **capital intensive** [p. 47] businesses fixed asset turnover becomes more important.

Stock days

Stock days measures the same thing as stock turnover, but is calculated in a way that puts it on a more similar basis to **debtor days** [p. 91] and **creditor days** [p. 79]:

$$\frac{stocks}{\textbf{cost of sales}[\text{p. 75}]} \times 365$$

Sales can be used as a proxy for cost of sales where **gross margins** [p. 253] are low, as with **creditor days** [p. 79].

Stock days is a useful number largely because it makes it easier to see how changes in stock days, debtor days and creditor days combine to change the **working capital ratio** [p. 347].

Stop loss

A stop loss trade is one that is made in order to set a limit to the loss made by an adverse price movement.

For example, an investor who buys a share at 100p may decide to sell if the price falls below 80p so that the maximum loss will be 20p per share (or 20% of the amount invested) plus trading costs.

It is possible to enter limit orders that execute when the price reaches certain levels, thus automating the stop loss process. An investor then does not have to keep checking security prices, merely choose a stop loss price and enter a limit order.

One problem is that there is no guarantee that it will be possible to sell at the stop loss level. If a share price collapses suddenly it may only be possible to find buyers well below the stop loss price.

A stop loss transaction need not be a sale as **short selling** [p. 296] losses can be limited by a stop buy.

Market crashes can be exacerbated by the widespread use of stop loss strategies, in particularly where the trades are automated.

Straight through processing

Straight through processing (STP) is the processing of orders for dealing in securities purely through electronic systems with no paperwork involved and little human intervention.

This means that a fund manager can place an order on the systems run by a fund management company. This is then electronically passed on to a broker and execution takes place through an **automated trading system** [p. 24] with no manual intervention. Settlement then also takes place through automated systems.

Straight through processing is something that has yet to be achieved but the required technology and systems are under active development. STP is perfectly achievable. An important part of this are standards such as the FIX financial messaging standard that allow different systems to work together.

Strike price

See **exercise price** [p. 135].

Strips

Strips are securities created by separating the payments (each interest payment and the repayment of the **principal** [p. 251]) of a **bond** [p. 37]. Each cashflow is **securitised** [p. 290] to create a separate **zero coupon bond** [p. 350].

Strips are most often derived from **government bonds** [p. 160]. In many countries, including the US and the UK, there is official support for creating strips.

The use of strips offers investors more flexibility. The resulting availability of a broader range of zero coupon bonds makes it easier to construct portfolios that manage **interest rate risk** [p. 178].

Structured notes

Structured notes are **bonds** [p. 37] that contain embedded derivatives, usually some type of **embedded option** [p. 120].

If the embedded derivative is an option, then either issuer or the holder may be the **option writer** [p. 229].

There are a number of ways in which the derivatives are embedded. It is not possible to list all the possibilities (which are endless) but examples include:

- interest rates linked to an equity **index** [p. 169] or the price of a **commodity** [p. 64]

- repayment in a different currency

- an interest rate that is a multiple of a benchmark rate, rather than being a fixed premium above it as a **floating rate** [p. 144] would be

- an interest rate that rises when a benchmark rate falls and vice-versa (this is called an inverse floater).

- a repayment of the principal that is linked to the performance of some index.

Certain types of structured notes are purchased by financial institutions and repackaged into investments more suitable for retail investors. Many products that offer exposure to equity markets, but with a limit on losses, are based on structured notes. As consumers (or even the advisers available to consumers) are rarely able to value these accurately, this can be a very profitable business.

Subordinated debt

Subordinated debt (also called junior debt) is debt that takes a lower priority than other debt.

Debt that takes higher priority is called **senior debt** [p. 293].

If an issuer goes bankrupt then subordinated debt holders will only be paid after senior debt has been fully paid.

This makes junior debt much more risky and this is reflected in its price. It should have a higher **yield** [p. 350] (in many cases a significantly higher yield) than senior debt from the same issuer.

Subordinated debt may, but need not, be publicly traded **bonds** [p. 37].

Subscriber acquisition cost

Subscriber acquisition cost (SAC) is the average cost of signing up a new customer. It is most frequently used by mobile telecoms companies.

The customer acquisition cost of mobile companies is complicated by the number of costs involved. Mobile telecoms companies frequently pay incentives to retailers who bring in customers for their networks. They also usually subsidise the costs of mobile phones (heavily so in the case of contract customers).

The SAC of contract connections is usually far higher than that of prepay connections because of the greater incentives and subsidies. This is more than outweighed by the greater value to the networks of contract customers who are committed to minimum expenditure levels.

Subscription revenues

Media companies' subscription revenues are generally more stable than advertising revenues, or revenues from selling one-off items (e.g. newsstand, book and CD sales etc.). There are exceptions, for example even the subscription revenues of financial information providers such as Reuters are cyclical because they are selling to a highly cyclical industry.

Not only are subscription revenues less **cyclical** [p. 84], they are also more visible and predictable because customers often need to make a positive decision to discontinue a service rather than a positive decision to buy, which makes them more stable. Subscription services, whether for business or domestic use, also tend to become things that customers are used to having and dislike doing without. Customers do subscribe and unsubscribe so it is important to monitor **churn** [p. 57].

Subsidiary

A company is the subsidiary of another, if the latter either owns a controlling stake (usually 50% or more of ordinary shares) or has control of it through other means (such as a management contract that gives it complete control).

The company that has the controlling interest is called the parent company.

When the parent has an interest that falls short of giving it control, but which does give it substantial influence, the company is regarded as an **associate** [p. 23] rather than a subsidiary.

The group accounts required of the parent company must **consolidate** [p. 68] subsidiaries.

Apart from accounting, the status of a company as a subsidiary or not may affect taxation and have regulatory implications.

Sum of parts valuation

A company may have businesses that are too varied for the application of a single valuation method or ratio to all its businesses to be useful. This means, for example, that applying **EV/EBITDA** [p. 129] to total **EBITDA** [p. 116], or using a **DCF** [p. 88] with a single discount rate may be not be the right approach.

The solution is to value the different parts of the business separately and add the values of the different parts of the business together. This is a sum of parts valuation.

A sum of parts valuation may be used to adjust a valuation method to suit different parts of a business. For example, a company may have a growth business that deserves a high **PE** [p. 237] and a mature business that deserves a low PE. A cyclical business may require a higher discount rate when doing a DCF.

A sum of parts valuation also allows different valuation methods to be used for different parts. Consider a company that has three businesses:

1. a **subsidiary** [p. 311] in which it owns a 50% stake and which is separately **listed** [p. 190],

2. a new business in which it has invested heavily but which is not expected to become profitable for several years,

3. a mature, stable, **defensive** [p. 84] business that produces dependable cash flows.

Applying a single PE or EV/EBITDA to this business would be difficult. A possible approach using a sum of parts would be:

1. Value the separately listed subsidiary using the market value of its shares, possibly with a premium for the fact that it is a controlling interest.

2. Use a **DCF** [p. 88] for the new start-up.

3. Use an **EV/EBITDA** [p. 129] for the stable business

Depending on how this is applied this will give you three numbers that can be added together to give an **enterprise value** [p. 121] for the whole company.

It may be necessary to adjust the total (usually by applying a smallish discount) for the effect of the fact that the businesses are in fact combined.

Sunk costs

Sunk costs are sums that have already been spent and can not be recovered.

The concept is important because sunk costs are irrelevant to financial decisions. Many people tend to feel instinctively that because an investment has been made it is necessary to get a return on it. This can lead to people rejecting one course of action in favour of another that actually generates smaller cash flows. This can happen to business, portfolio investment and personal decisions.

Suppose a hotel has calculated that their cost for providing a room is £100 per night, of which £50 covers their rental of the building (i.e. the cost of the rental divided the number of rooms) and £20 covers their other fixed costs (such as staff) and £30 covers the costs that result from having an extra guest (e.g. electricity, laundry, food included in the price etc.)

Now suppose the market rate for hotel rooms goes down and they are only able to charge £50 per night. The hotel is committed to remaining open. It appears that the hotel will make a £50 loss on each night per guest so they should not accept bookings until prices rise. Of course this is wrong as the rent and other fixed costs are already committed to and have to be paid anyway. The hotel should accept bookings at any price it can get above £30, as these make a positive **contribution** [p. 72].

A common mistake made by investors is reluctance to sell securities at a loss. It does not matter what you paid for shares, if the market price has fallen you have already made that loss. It is a sunk cost and should be forgotten about. What matters is whether the shares are worth holding or not at the current market price. A key question is whether the shares would still be worth buying at current prices. If not, they are probably not worth holding.

Survivorship bias

When returns from a class of classes of investment are measured, it is common to look at what investments in that class are available and how they have performed.

Suppose we were looking at global returns on equities in the very long term (often done in the context of **equity risk premiums** [p. 123]). The obvious approach is to look at the world's equity markets and look at what returns an investor who invested in those markets at some past date would have made.

The flaw in this approach is that it only considers those markets that exist today. An investor who actually invested in the past may also have invested in markets that have since ceased to exist. If we look at returns over the course of the 20th century all the Eastern European markets, and some Asian ones, closed in countries that became communist. Investors lost all money invested in those markets. This exaggerates returns significantly as the worst performers are eliminated. This is survivorship bias.

Survivorship bias can also distort calculations of returns on stock markets in much the same way, and a similar effect can distort returns on companies in an **index** [p. 169] (through changes in the companies included and excluded). The importance of the effect in the last case is arguable as the reason for most index changes is to keep indices representative of their markets.

Swaps

A swap is an agreement to exchange one stream of cashflows for another. Swaps are most commonly used to:

- switch financing in one currency for financing in another

- to replace a **floating interest rate** [p. 144] with a fixed interest rate (or vice versa).

Swap transactions are usually large.

Currency swaps

Currency swaps may be used where a borrower can get a better rate in one currency, but where the borrowing is linked to assets or cashflows in another and therefore a **currency rate risk** [p. 133] can be eliminated by borrowing in the latter currency.

A company in this position can do is to borrow in the currency in which they get the better rate (often the company's home country), and then enter into an agreement with another party (usually a bank) , in which the counterparty pays the original debt in exchange for a stream of (fixed) payments in the other currency. For example:

Company A needs Yen to fund its new Japanese operation, but as it is not well known in Japan it finds it hard to raise debt there.

It borrows in Euros, on which it is able to get a good rate. It sells the Euros for Yen which provides the funding, but this leaves its Japanese operation, which will earn Yen, with a Euro debt.

A therefore enters into an agreement with a bank whereby the bank pays the Euro debt off (as it falls due) in exchange for payments in Yen, the amounts of all payments being fixed at the start of the agreement. This effectively leaves the Japanese operation with a liability in Yen, matched to its revenues.

Interest rates swaps

Interest rates swaps involve exchanging one set of interest payments for another, which may be in the same currency. A common motivation for this is to swap a floating interest rate for a fixed interest rate.

Commodity and other swaps

A wider range of other swaps are possible. One common example are swaps of **commodity** [p. 64] **futures** [p. 154]. More complex swaps may also be created to meet particular needs.

Switched telecoms

Switched telecoms systems are older voice telecoms systems that are sometimes also called public switched telecoms network (PSTN) and plain old telecoms service (POTS). They are being replaced by internet protocol (IP) networks.

Switched telecoms systems use electronic switching systems to connect telephone calls. Historically, the first telecoms networks actually used mechanical switches. Although the technology has advanced, the underlying architecture has not and PSTN works in much the same way it always did.

Leased lines provide a constant connection between fixed points, they are therefore not switched because there is no need for switching.

Both leased lines and switched telecoms are now being replaced by internet protocol (IP). This technology, which was originally developed for the internet, carries data divided into packets, which are routed to their destinations by software rather than electronic switching.

Most telecoms companies moving to pure IP networks, so that even customers who subscribe to what appear to be PSTN networks will actually have their calls carried (in part) by IP networks. This allows telecoms companies to make savings by replacing separate voice (PSTN) and data networks with a single IP network.

The emergence of consumer **VOIP** [p. 340] technologies means that calls can now be carried over an IP network end-to-end.

Synchronisation fees

Synchronisation fees are royalties that are paid for the use of music as part of another work, for example as background music in a film or an ad.

Synchronisation fees are one of many cash flow streams that are generated by music companies, and one that seems likely to grow (especially compared to retail sales of music).

Like **mechanical royalties** [p. 199], synchronisation fees are usually collected by bodies that act for all major music publishers, giving them an effective monopoly on the collection of such royalties. In the UK this is the Mechanical Copyright Protection Society.

Syndicate

In an investment context, syndicates usually exist in order to spread risk.

Any financial institution (such as an investment bank) has a limited capacity to take risk. If it takes on too much risk, not only does it expose its shareholders to excessive risk, but because of the nature of its business, it also exposes its customers and counterparties (see **counterparty risk** [p. 76]) to risk.

Large financial institutions may also create **systemic risk** [p. 316] by taking on too much risk. Because of this, and to protect depositors, regulators set limits on the exposure any one bank has to a single risk.

This means that risks that are two large for any one institution to take on by itself need to be spread out through syndication.

A simple example of syndication is when it occurs with bank loans. A major borrower may find it hard to raise a large loan from a single bank. If a group of banks form a syndicate the risk is spread over several banks. Usually, one bank will act as the lead manager of the the loan and handle most of the work involved.

The **underwriting** [p. 331] of large **IPOs** [p. 182] can also be too large a risk for a single institution to take. The arrangements are usually similar to a syndicated loan with a lead underwriter doing most of the work.

Insurance may also be undertaken by a syndicate. This is common practice in the **Lloyd's** [p. 190] market.

Synergy

A synergy is a combination that has a greater effect than the combined parts. In an investment context, the word is most commonly used to justify **acquisitions** [p. 5] and mergers.

This most common synergies are:

- cost synergies – savings, generally through economies of scale

- Sales synergies – better reach through a larger sales force or expanded customer base, cross selling one product to buyers of another etc.

Companies may also sometimes generate (or claim to) synergies in other ways, for example, through combining technologies. Cost synergies may come from internal economies of scale or through purchasing (i.e. the better bargaining power of a larger entity).

It is generally advisable to be sceptical about claimed synergies as they often need to be *very* large enough to be worth the costs of the acquisitions that they supposedly justify. Most acquisitions leave the shareholders of the acquiring company worse off because the synergies (and other claimed benefits) are not big enough to justify the cost of the acquisition.

It is also worth considering whether there are any **diseconomies of scale** [p. 100] or other disadvantages to large size (a larger company may have more layers of management, be less nimble, etc.)

Despite sounding like yet another unnecessary management neologism the word does encompass a useful concept. It is respectably derived from the Greek συνεργι (*sunergi*), which means cooperation.

Systemic risk

Systemic risk is risk that is posed to the financial system or the economy, as opposed to risk that is faced by an investor or a portfolio.

Systemic risk is most commonly discussed in relation to the risks posed by banks and financial institutions. The failure of a major financial institution can have serious consequences. If a bank fails, not only will its depositors lose money, but it is also likely to renege on obligations to other financial institutions. Both the depositors and the other institutions are then likely to be under financial pressure, which can lead to further failures of both banks and other businesses.

The resulting ripple effect can bring down an economy. Controlling systemic risk is a major concern for regulators, particularly given that consolidation in banking has lead to the creation of some extremely large banks. Even though governments would probably bail out those banks that are "too big to fail", the cost of doing so would have its own effects.

T-bill

See **treasury bill** [p. 328].

Take private

A **listed company** [p. 190] is said to have been taken private when it is bought by someone other than another listed company, and its listing is cancelled.

Companies are most often taken private by directors, founders and **private equity** [p. 252] companies.

The rationale for taking a company private is that the buyer feels that they can run the company better without the need to justify their decisions to other shareholders. In the case of founders, one often also suspects a sentimental attachment to the business they created.

There are a number of reasons why someone might feel that they can run a company better as a private company. They may find it difficult to convince other shareholders of the benefits of the strategy they want to follow. They may also simply feel that the costs of a listing and the management time it takes are simply not worth it.

Takeover

See **acquisition** [p. 5].

Takeover bid

A takeover bid is an offer to buy a company outright (see **acquisition** [p. 5]).

If a takeover bid has the the support of the directors of the company to be taken over (the "target" or "offeree") it is called an **agreed takeover bid** [p. 13]. If they oppose it is called a **hostile takeover bid** [p. 165].

Takeover bids are most commonly made by:

- other companies in the same industry

- **private equity** [p. 252] companies

- major shareholders or directors who wish to **take a company private** [p. 317].

Takeover bids usually create conflicts of interest between directors (who may lose their jobs) and shareholders (who are likely to be able to sell shares at above the market value before the bid was announced). Takeovers can also lead to situations in which **minority shareholders** [p. 204] can be unfairly treated.

Because of this, takeover bids are subject to regulation in most markets. The main British regulation is the **City Code Code on Takeovers and Mergers** [p. 58].

Takeover Panel

The Panel on Takeovers and Mergers, often called the Takeover Panel, the City Panel, over even simply the Panel, is the UK's main regulator of issues connected to mergers and **acquisitions** [p. 5]. The Panel's main objective is simple: to ensure that all shareholders are treated equally during **takeover bids** [p. 317].

The Panel's rules, the **City Code on Takeovers and Mergers** [p. 58], regulate the takeover process.

For most of its history the Panel was not a statutory body and had no actual legal powers. It functioned very effectively through industry agreement. In accordance with an EU directive, it is now a statutory body with powers to order compensation. It can also ask the courts and the **FSA** [p. 149] to enforce its rulings.

In the past, the Panel ensured compliance with the Code through discussions, by censure (private and public). With the only punishment of offenders being "cold shouldering" for a breach of the code. A cold shouldered firm would find others refusing to deal with them in order to support the authority of the Panel. This would seriously impedes the offender's ability to do business.

This system was a rather nice example of how the old fashioned British way in which the city functioned could work. The Panel intends to follow the approach used in the past, but has accepted its new powers and will presumably use them if all other measures fail.

Tangible assets

Assets that have a physical existence, or give the holders definite set of financial rights are classified as tangible assets, as opposed to **intangible assets** [p. 173] such as patents and **goodwill** [p. 159]. Examples of tangible assets include land, machinery, bank deposits and investments.

The distinction between tangible and intangible assets is made on the balance sheet, where a breakdown of **fixed assets** [p. 142] as tangible or intangible is provided.

There is also a slight difference in the treatment and terminology used to describe the matching of the cost of an asset to its useful life. Tangible assets are **depreciated** [p. 95] or (more rarely) **depleted** [p. 94]. An intangible asset is **amortised** [p. 15].

Both tangible and intangible assets may be **impaired** [p. 166], but intangible assets are more likely to be regularly reviewed (this is required for goodwill).

Techmark

The Techmark is a grouping of companies listed on the **London Stock Exchange** [p. 192]. It was originally launched in 1999 to cash in on the dot-com boom.

The Techmark has survived largely as a way of identifying a wide range of technology companies. It includes not just IT companies, but those from a wide range of sectors such pharmaceuticals, engineering and telecoms.

There are three **FTSE** [p. 150] indices covering Techmark companies. The Techmark All-share includes all Techmark companies. The Techmark 100 covers small and medium sized companies. The Techmark Mediscience covers small and medium sized pharmaceutical and healthcare companies.

Techmark is a grouping and does not change how companies' securities trade. It is not a sector in itself and Techmark companies are also grouped into the usual sectors. It is usually obvious that a company is a technology company – so what is the point of the Techmark grouping? To a large extent, it serves the same purposes as sector classifications:

- It allows investors to measure their exposure to technology companies in the same way that they can use sector classifications to measure exposure to a particular sector (or to, for example, **cyclical** [p. 84] sectors in general).

- It allows funds to define their mandate with more clarity. "Invest in Techmark companies" is a lot more definite than "invest in technology companies".

- The Techmark indices provide benchmarks for technology funds that invest in multiple sectors (as most do).

Technical analysis

Technical analysis is the rather solid sounding name given to what is also called chartism: the attempt to predict financial markets purely by looking at past financial data (securities prices, indices and other trading data). Its practitioners are sometimes called chartists.

This flies in the face of the **efficient markets hypothesis** [p. 118]. Even the weak form of efficient markets requires that all information in historical prices is reflected in current prices.

Technical analysis may appear to be given some justification by **behavioural finance** [p. 33] but it does not use the results of the latter. The details of some techniques have their own self-evident justifications, however it still lacks sufficient theoretical underpinnings to be credible.

The most serious objection to technical analysis/chartism is that if it works, it should be possible to use it to set up purely automatic trading strategies. These could be **back-tested** [p. 26]. If technical analysis worked, it would be possible to produce evidence that it worked. The chartists have so far failed to produce much evidence.

Many advocates who accept the objections to technical analysis, suggest that it is used in conjunction with fundamental analysis. This is most commonly done by using fundamentals to pick stocks and technical analysis to decide on timing. However, even this implies rejection of even the weak form of efficient markets.

A better use of price data lies in more conventional measures such as **volatility** [p. 340], **beta** [p. 34] and **correlations** [p. 74].

Technical reserves

Technical reserves are the amounts insurance companies set aside from profits to cover claims. Technical reserves include the unearned premium reserve and the **outstanding claims reserve** [p. 233]. The latter is the amount of **premium written** [p. 246] but not earned (see **premium earned** [p. 245]).

Any reinsurance receivables will be deducted from the technical reserves, as will deferred acquisition costs (the acquisition or marketing costs relating to policies which have not expired by the year end).

Technical reserves may also include the **unexpired risk reserve** [p. 332] and the **claims equalisation reserve** [p. 58] if such reserves have been created.

Term structure

The term structure of **interest rates** [p. 177] is the variation of interest rates with time – for example it is usual for a government **bond** [p. 37] with 10 years to run till maturity to have a different **YTM** [p. 350] from one which is only one year from maturity. The term structure, especially when depicted as a graph, is also called the yield curve.

It is usual for interest rates to increase with time; the longer the time till maturity of a zero coupon bond the higher the rate of return on it. When the term structure shows this behaviour, the yield curve, when drawn as a graph, slopes upward.

A yield curve that is downward sloping is called an inverted yield curve.

There are a number of explanations for the upward sloping yield curve. The most important is liquidity preference, that investors need compensation for the potentially lower liquidity of long term bonds. Another explanation is that higher **duration** [p. 113] means greater exposures to **interest rate risk** [p. 178] and inflation risk.

The **Fisher hypothesis** [p. 141] suggests that inflation and interest rates move together, so the risks are linked.

Terminal value

It is not practical to forecast cash flows for an infinite number of future years. It is usual to end the cashflow used in a **DCF** [p. 88] with a terminal value as the final year cash flow. This is the value of all cashflows after the final year. A rough estimate suffices because cash flows that are very far off in the future are less important: the the **time value of money** [p. 322] means there is an exponential loss of value with time.

The terminal value may be calculated using a valuation ratio, or by assuming a constant growth rate and using:

$$PV = \frac{CF}{r - g}$$

where PV is the **present value** [p. 247] as at the terminal date (it will have to be further discounted in the DCF itself),
CF is the actual final year cash flow,
g is the growth rate after the final year and
r is the discount rate.

Incorporating the above into the DCF formula, it becomes:

$$PV = \frac{CF_1}{1+r} + \frac{CF_2}{(1+r)^2} + \frac{CF_3}{(1+r)^3} + \cdots + \frac{CF_n}{(1+r)^n} + \frac{CF_n}{(r-g)(1+r)^n}$$

where PV is the present value,
CF_i is the cash flow received in year i,
n is the number of years till the last year of the DCF
r and g are as above.

Termination rates

A phone call between subscribers to two different networks usually means that both networks require a payment for carrying the call.

The commonest arrangement for this globally is calling party pays. This means that the originator of the call pays the full cost. The network from which the call originates is charged by the network on which the call terminates. This charge is the termination charge.

As the termination charge is not likely to be something that people take into account when choosing a network, the level of termination charges is not really subject to competition. For this reason, termination rates are regulated in Europe and elsewhere.

Historically, termination rates have been high and therefore generated high revenues at high **margins** [p. 253]. Changes to termination rates (by regulators) have a significant impact on telecoms companies' profits.

Theta

Theta (the Greek letter Θ) is a measure of the rate of change of the value of a derivative or portfolio with time. Mathematically:

$$\Theta = \frac{\partial P}{\partial t}$$

where P is the price of a security and
t is time.

The price of most options tends to decay with time. This is because **option value** [p. 229] increases with time till expiry.

Tick

Security prices on most exchanges move in units of a minimum size.

For example, London **listed shares** [p. 190] will usually have prices that are multiples of 0.25p. So a share can have a price of 10.25p or 10.50p, but not, for example 10.3p.

This applies to **bid** [p. 35], **offer** [p. 222] and last traded prices. **Mid-prices** [p. 203] and other averages, such as **VWAP** [p. 341] prices are not restricted by the tick.

TIDM

TIDM codes are used to identify UK **listed securities** [p. 190]. They were previously called EPIC codes.

TIDMs are short and are usually based on an abbreviation of the name of the company. For example, the TIDM for Glaxosmithkline ordinary shares is GSK and the TIDM for Vodafone ordinary shares is VOD. They are memorable enough for people to remember, and are commonly used to enter orders into trading systems and to call up quotes and other information related to a security.

The disadvantage of TIDM codes is that they are a UK only system. Although equivalents exist in most markets, there is no co-ordination or standardisation. Therefore systems that must cope with global trading generally use **ISIN** [p. 184] codes.

There are some codes that combine TIDM codes (and their equivalents elsewhere) with a country identifier in order to combine the memorability of TIDM codes with guaranteed global uniqueness (like ISIN codes). The most important of these are Reuters and Bloomberg codes. Both add a country code suffix. The Reuters code for Glaxosmithkline is GSK.L and the Bloomberg code GSK LN.

Time value of money

The time value of money is one the fundamental concepts of financial theory. It is a very simple idea: a given amount of money now is worth more than the certainty of receiving the same amount of money at some time in the future. Furthermore, a given amount of money to be received at a given future date is worth more than the same amount of money to be received at a date further in the future. This is fairly self evident: receiving £1,000 right now is better than a reliable promise £1,000 at the end of next year, which in turn is better than £1,000 the following year.

This leave the question of how much more a given amount of money on a future date is worth than cash now. There is a market rate that can be used to determine this. When investors buy **government bonds** [p. 160] they are exchanging cash now for a certain amount of money on a future date. Therefore the **risk free rate of return** [p. 282] can be used to calculate the **present value** [p. 220] of a certain future payment.

If a future payment is not certain its value needs to be adjusted for risk as well as time value. Its present value needs to be calculated using a discount rate that reflects both time value and risk, such as those calculated using **CAPM** [p. 50].

Tip sheet

A tip sheet is a newsletter that offers investors advice on stocks. Tip sheets tend to be looked down on by sophisticated investors.

In the UK, tip sheets are regulated by the FSA. This means that there are rules in place to control malpractice. It is not, in itself, any reason to regard tip sheets are useful.

Investment research published by stockbrokers and investment banks tends to be more balanced and have greater substance, although, as a general rule, no investment research should be taken as perfect.

Investors should read research from more than one source and preferably do research for themselves as well.

It is probably wise to be very sceptical about tip sheets. They do not have the resources or the depth of talent that the major brokers and fund managers have, and yet many of them produce marketing material that implies that following their tips will lead to huge market out-performance.

It is usually best to be very sceptical about any investor's or tipper's ability to reliably produce positive **alpha** [p. 14].

To make things worse, it is much harder to assess the historical performance of a tip sheet than, for example, that of a **collective investment vehicle** [p. 62].

Tobin's Q

Tobin's Q compares the market value of a companies' to the replacement value of their tangible assets:

$$Q = \frac{market\ value}{replacement\ value}$$

The market value of a company is the total market value of its debt and **equity** [p. 123]. Economist James Tobin hypothesised that the combined market values of **listed companies** [p. 190] should approximately equal their combined replacement cost.

A Tobin's Q of more than one means that the market value of assets (as reflected in share prices) is greater than their replacement cost. This means it is likely that capex will create wealth for shareholders. This means companies should increase capex, raising more money to do so if necessary, but should not make acquisitions. This should reduce share prices and increase asset prices, pushing Q towards one.

A Tobin's Q of less than one suggests that the market value of the assets is less than replacement cost, making **acquisitions** [p. 5] cheaper than **capex** [p. 46]; buying cheaper than setting up from scratch. This should increase share prices and reduce asset prices, again pushing Q towards one.

The validity of Tobin's Q at the level of individual companies is, at best, questionable. There are better ways of valuing companies. It is more interesting at market level.

Top down investment

Top down investors start from the highest level decisions such as deciding how much to invest in different classes of investments (such as equities and bonds) and in which geographic regions (globally). Next, they look at which sectors to invest in. Picking individual securities is the last step.

Top down investing tends to lead to good **diversification** [p. 103]. It tends to encourage investors to be conservative. Many top down portfolios are close to being closet trackers.

Investors who look primarily at individual securities are using a **bottom up** [p. 39] approach.

Total billings

Advertising agencies charge their clients an amount that includes charges for advertising space. This amount clients are charged are an ad agency's "billings". An ad agency's billings form part of its turnover but are not generally **recognised as part of its revenues** [p. 277].

When ad agencies retain part of the charges for buying media space as a commission (from the seller of the space) this *is* recognised as part of its revenues. Traditionally, ad agencies retained a commission of around 15%. This has been changing and negotiated fees paid are becoming commoner.

Total billings are an indicator of how much business an agency is handling. Numbers for total billings are often announced in trading statements before turnover numbers for the same period are **disclosed** [p. 98]. They are often the earliest performance measure available to investors.

Total billings numbers are disclosed by media buying companies as well as ad agencies.

Total return

The total return on an investment is the total cash gains that come from it. This usually means both **capital gains** [p. 47] and income.

For example, the total return to the holder of a share will be the increase in the share price since purchase plus any dividends paid since purchase. The former could well be negative and therefore the total return could be negative as well.

The exact calculation that should be used for total return varies a bit depending on the circumstances.

Total return **indices** [p. 169] will usually assume that income (such as dividends) will be reinvested in the constituents of the index. Given that it is perfectly possible to do this with many securities (and even cost effective for many **equities** [p. 123] thanks to **DRIPs** [p. 110]), it is generally the most correct calculation.

It also makes them better **benchmark indices** [p. 33] for portfolios that reinvest income.

In other contexts, reinvestment is not always chosen (or cost-effective or even possible). An investor may choose to assume reinvestment elsewhere – typically either the market, in bank deposits, or at the **risk free rate** [p. 282].

The problem with this approach is that the total return on the investment will now come from two cash flow streams with different **volatilities** [p. 340] and **betas** [p. 34], making valuation a little more complicated.

Tracker fund

An index tracker fund is a **collective investment vehicle** [p. 62] that is designed to follow the performance of a particular index.

The simplest way to track an index would be to buy every share in the index at exactly its weight in the index, and re-balance as companies are deleted from or added to the index. The problem with this naive approach is that buying hundreds of shares adds to transaction costs.

What tracker funds actually do is to use sophisticated statistical techniques, the work of **quantitative analysts** [p. 260], to construct a portfolio that has a smaller number of holdings but that has a very low risk of deviating from market performance.

The key advantage of index trackers is that they are very cheap. Charges are well below those of actively managed funds. The disadvantage is that they provide little chance of out-performance, but then, necessarily, neither the average active fund manger or the average private investor outperforms either.

Private investors primarily need to reduce the **volatility** [p. 340] of their investments so a tracker fund need not be significantly lower risk than a well **diversified** [p. 103] portfolio.

Active fund managers very often place a significant proportion of the money they manage into a **closet tracker** [p. 61].

Tracking stock

Tracking **stocks** [p. 306] are securities that are designed to have a value that reflects the value of a division of a company. Issuing a tracker is an alternative to a **demerger** [p. 94] or partial demerger.

A separate listing for a subsidiary should cause the market to separately value that subsidiary. This often increases the **sum of parts valuations** [p. 311] of the the parent company.

The problem with this is that the parent company loses some degree of control. The management of the subsidiary become accountable to the minority shareholders in the subsidiary as well as to the partent. If a large enough stake is sold (to raise more money) the parent could even lose outright control. It also scales down the size of the parent, which is not something that is likely to appeal to its management.

A tracking stock allows a company to both retain full control and have the benefits of the separate valuation of a division. A security is created that shares in the profits of a division, but that has reduced or no voting rights.

The end result of issuing a tracker is not dissimilar to selling non-voting shares in a subsidiary. It has the same drawbacks from the point of view of investors. Like a separately **listed** [p. 190] subsidiary, a division that has a tracking stock will report its financial results separately from the parent company and the tracking stock will trade separately from the parent company's ordinary shares.

While there are sometimes arguments in favour of tracking stocks, such as synergies between the division and the company as a whole, it is often difficult to understand the benefit to shareholders of issuing a tracking stock rather than selling ordinary shares in a subsidiary – or even demerging it completely.

One common justification is cheaper access to debt. The benefit of a parent company's good **credit rating** [p. 78] can be retained. This should adversely affect the parent company (by increasing its debt burden) so it is often difficult to be sure that there is a net benefit to shareholders.

Tracker stocks were very popular during the dot com boom, as companies used tracker stocks to exploit the high valuations that internet arms of large businesses could achieve. There is evidence that this partly represented a failure of **market efficiency** [p. 118]. They have since become less popular.

Trade buyer

In the context of a **takeover** [p. 5], a trade buyer is a bidder who is in the same industry as the target.

Trade buyers are by far the most common type of takeover bidder, because they can hope to gain from **synergies** [p. 316], **economies of scale** [p. 117] or **monopoly** [p. 207] or **monopsony** [p. 208] pricing power.

The other common types of bidders are **private equity** [p. 252] companies and directors or founders of the target.

Traded option

A traded option is an option that can be traded through one or more securities markets. It is one of the most important types of **derivative** [p. 96].

Traded options require standardised contract terms (i.e. **strike price** [p. 135] and expiry date), in order to create **fungible** [p. 153] securities with reasonable **liquidity** [p. 190].

Traded options are usually settled by payment of cash, rather than by delivery of the actual security.

Trading profit

Trading profit is closely related to **operating profit** [p. 227] and **EBIT** [p. 115]. The definition of trading profit can vary. It is usually excludes certain items, in order to give a better view of the underlying results. The excluded items typically include:

- one-off items such as restructuring charges and profits on the sale of businesses

- **impairments** [p. 166] and other non-cash items

- changes in the **fair value of financial securities** [p. 137]

- profits from **associates** [p. 23] and **joint ventures** [p. 184].

Trading profit is rarely very different from **adjusted operating profit** [p. 8].

trailing twelve months

See **TTM** [p. 328].

Treasury bill

A treasury bill is a short term (less than one year) government **zero coupon bond** [p. 350].

As they are zero coupon bonds, treasury bills do not pay interest. They are instead issued at a discount to their **face value** [p. 137].

Treasury bill prices are used to determine short term **risk free rates** [p. 282]. Short term rates are useful in themselves. They are also used to adjust for the value of intervening interest payments when calculating longer term rates.

Like other **government bonds** [p. 160], there is very little risk attached to investing in treasury bills. Default risk on a government's borrowings in its own currency is low enough to be regarded as zero. Because these are very low **duration** [p. 113] bonds, their price is not very sensitive to interest rate changes either.

Treasury shares

Treasury share are shares held by the company that issued them. A company acquires treasury shares by buying them in the market.

In the UK, Treasury shares can be cancelled, sold, or used in employee share (or share option) schemes. Companies are required to **disclose** [p. 98] their holding of treasury shares and any sales, cancellations or transfers.

The commonest use of treasury share among UK **listed companies** [p. 190] seems to be to hold shares for employee share schemes.

Treasury shares do not receive dividends or **rights** [p. 280] and they cannot be used to vote at or attend company meetings. They are shown on the **balance sheet** [p. 28], but they are deducted from share capital.

Treasury shares are disregarded in calculating undiluted **EPS** [p. 122].

Treatment and refining costs

In the mining sector, treatment and refining costs are the main costs of extracting metal from ore.

Treatments costs are those of the smelting process which uses heat to melt metal in order to extract it mechanically from the ore.

Refining costs are those of **electro-refining** [p. 56] processes, the output of which is metal that is pure enough to be sold for most purposes.

Treatment and refining costs are an important component of the **cash cost** [p. 52].

TTM

Direct comparison of **valuation ratios** [p. 334] of companies with different year ends can be misleading.

Consider two companies, one with a March year end, the other with a December year end. In February they both have a **historical PE** [p. 164] of 15×. The company with the March year end is cheaper because it reached the level of earnings on which the 15× PE is based sooner.

If quarterly **EPS** [p. 122] numbers (actual or estimates) are available for both companies, then it is relatively simple to calculate a directly comparable PE. This is done simply by using the sum of the EPS numbers for the last four quarters as the EPS number. This is the trailing twelve months (TTM) EPS.

If a company only discloses half yearly EPS the sum of the last two half years would have to be used. This is not quite as good as it often means that there can still be a difference of one quarter between the periods being compared. It is still an improvement on using the financial years.

The same method can be applied to EPS forecasts (using estimates for the next four quarters). It can also be applied to other valuation ratios.

In many cases (e.g., low growth companies, year ends in successive quarters, large differences in PE) it is not be worth bothering to calculate TTM numbers as the adjustment makes an insignificant difference. This is especially true for investors who are looking for large gains – and therefore comparatively very cheap ratings.

Turnover

Turnover is a broad measure of a company's sales. In **consolidated accounts** [p. 68] the turnover number in the **P & L** [p. 234] usually includes all sales made by a company and its **subsidiaries** [p. 311] – the sales of **associates** [p. 23] and **joint ventures** [p. 184] will be shown on a separate line.

For many companies the value of sales is perfectly straightforward and it does not matter whether the term used is turnover, revenue or sales. There are circumstances when they can be very different.

Examples include:

- Advertising companies which often include money paid to then by customers for buying adspace and airtime in turnover (or **total billings** [p. 324]) but never in revenues.

- Tobacco companies which often report a gross turnover number that includes excise duties (in effect a tax the company collects and passes on to governments), which are not part of the companies' own revenues.

For more on the definition of revenues, see **revenue recognition** [p. 277].

Uberrimae fides

Uberrimae fides means "utmost good faith" in Latin. Insurance is agreed *uberrimae fides*.

Buyers of insurance do not only need to answer the questions that the insurer asks honestly. They must also disclose certain facts unasked. These are those that may cause a "reasonable insurer" not to **underwrite** [p. 331] the risk, or to underwrite it on different terms. Failure to do this can invalidate insurance.

The reason insurance contracts are agreed *uberrimae fides* is that it helps to reduce **adverse selection** [p. 9]. If insurance contracts were agreed *caveat emptor* (buyer beware) like most other contracts, then the slightest omission from insurance proposal documents would attract significant numbers of people who could exploit the loophole.

The contrast of *uberrimae fides* with *caveat emptor* is legally correct, in that contract law in itself imposes no duties on either party to act fairly. However there are often other protections in place – particularly for consumers. Most transactions are covered by laws (such as the Sale of Goods Act), regulators and implied terms of contract.

UKLA (UK Listing Authority)

The **FSA** [p. 149], is the competent authority for the **listing** [p. 190] of companies for trading on UK stock exchanges. When acting in this role it is called the UK Listing Authority.

Its main role is to maintain the **Official List** [p. 222]. This is simply a list of all securities it has approved for trading on exchanges in the UK. It also maintains a list of the issuers of those securities.

The UKLA also sets the requirements for listing and the rules for procedures and documents related to listing, such as **IPO** [p. 182] **prospectuses** [p. 255].

The reason for referring to the FSA as the UKLA in this context is that, in theory, the role could be passed (or delegated) to another body that would then become the UKLA.

Unconditional offer

In the course of a **takeover bid** [p. 317], once the bidder has received sufficient **acceptances** [p. 2] from the shareholders of the target company, the bid becomes "unconditional as to acceptances".

This essentially means that the shareholders of the target company have agreed to sell to the bidder.

There may be some shareholders who still refuse to sell. The level at which a bid becomes unconditional as to acceptances is usually set high enough to allow them to be compelled to sell (a **compulsory acquisition** [p. 67]).

The bidder may choose to declare the bid unconditional as to acceptances before the original required level of acceptances has been reached. Even in this case, an offer may not become unconditional before acceptances are sufficient (together with the bidder's existing stake) to give the bidder a 50% stake in the target.

Even after an offer has become unconditional as to acceptances, there may remain other conditions that have to be met. The commonest examples of these are approval from competition regulators and approval from the bidder's shareholders.

Once all conditions are met, the offer becomes "unconditional in all respects" and the takeover is certain to go ahead. The **City Code** [p. 58] sets deadlines by which the offer must be declared unconditional as to acceptances and unconditional in all respects.

Uncovered interest arbitrage

Uncovered interest arbitrage is a similar strategy to **covered interest arbitrage** [p. 77]. The difference is that the currency risk is not **hedged** [p. 162], so it is not a true **arbitrage** [p. 18] strategy.

The strategy is simple:

Suppose the **risk free rate** [p. 282] for currency B is higher than that for currency A, and that the difference in interest rates is greater than the expected depreciation of currency B against currency A (both over the same period).

1. Sell currency A and buy B.

2. Invest the amount of B bought is risk free securities.

3. When the securities mature convert the holding of B back to A.

This can be used to derive an **interest rate parity** [p. 177] relationship.

Although this is not true arbitrage, it is a strategy that should usually make a profit over the risk free rate, provided the *average* error in the forecasts is small.

Underlying asset

An underlying asset is the asset on which the price of a **derivative** [p. 96] depends. Most traded derivatives (i.e. those traded on exchanges) are settled for cash, not by actual delivery of the underlying.

Some derivatives, such as **CFDs** [p. 71], do not actually involve even a possible trade in an underlying security. They are simply a contract to exchange cash depending on the underlying. This means that they can use an underlying that cannot itself be delivered (such as an index value, weather conditions etc.)

Underwriter

An underwriter is someone who takes a financial risk (relieving another party of it) in return for a fee.

The most familiar underwriters are are insurance companies, whose entire business is the underwriting of a wide range of risk.

Some **new issues** [p. 215], most importantly **IPOs** [p. 182], of securities are underwritten, usually by investment banks. The underwriter agrees to buy any securities that unwanted by the market. If the offer is not as successful as expected the underwriter may make a loss.

The underwriter does not usually take as large a risk as may appear. New issues, especially large ones, are priced low enough to make it likely that the issue will be fully subscribed. This is why **stags** [p. 304] usually make a gain on IPOs.

The underwriter of an issue of a security may be a single investment bank or, especially in the case of a large IPO, a **syndicate** [p. 315] of banks.

Underwriting is very lucrative, and there has been a long running controversy over whether this is an indication that investment banks are colluding on pricing (see **cartel** [p. 51]).

Unearned premium reserve

The unearned premium reserve is an item that appears on insurers **balance sheets** [p. 28]. It shows the total amount of premiums written but not yet earned (see **premium earned** [p. 245]). The **unexpired risk reserve** [p. 332] is very similar to the unearned premium reserve.

Unexpired risk reserve

If an insurer considers its **unearned premium reserve** [p. 332] to be too small, then it may create an unexpired risk reserve in addition to it. The unearned premium reserve is required, unexpired risk reserves are created at companies' discretion

Unit cost averaging

Unit cost averaging is a method of timing purchases to reduce the exposure to fluctuations in the price of the security being purchased. It is also called pound cost averaging, dollar cost averaging etc.

An investor using cost averaging splits a purchase of a security into several tranches which are bought at different times. This has the benefit of smoothing out the effects of short term fluctuations in the share price.

The price that is finally paid will tend to be closer to the bottom end of the range in which purchases were made than to the top end. To see the reason for this consider a simple example.

An investor spends £2,000 buying shares in two tranches of £1,000. The first purchase of 1,000 shares at 100p. The price then falls and the next purchase is of 2,000 shares at 50p. The average price paid is £2,000 ÷ 3,000 = 67p. This is less than the average of 100p and 50p.

Unless the price is likely to fluctuate wildly, any gains from cost averaging are likely to be outweighed by the additional costs of trading this way.

Unit Trust

A unit trust is a **collective investment vehicle** [p. 62] that allows investors to pool money. It is open ended like an **OEIC** [p. 221] so the size of the fund grows or shrinks as investors add money to it or withdraw money from it.

Unit trusts always have an annual management charge. There may also be initial or exit charges. There is also a difference between the buying and selling prices, which are set by the manager of the unit trust.

The cheapest way to buy unit trusts is through a discount broker or a "money supermarket", as the initial charge is eliminated or greatly reduced. This is because the initial charge is commonly used to pay sales commissions. The low cost sales channels refund the commission they receive to customers.

Unpaid dividend

An unpaid dividend is one that has been declared by a company (the company has announced the amount of the dividend), but which has not been paid. An unpaid dividend is shown as a liability in the balance sheet.

Assuming the shares are not yet trading **ex-dividend** [p. 82], then investors may meed to adjust their analysis of the company for this. The simplest adjust-ment is to deduct the value of the dividend from the share price.

Unqualified audit opinion

If the statement that "in our opinion the financial statements give a true and fair view" is given as an **audit opinion** [p. 25] then the audit is unqualified. This is what should happen.

The accounts of **listed companies** [p. 190] are almost always given an un-qualified opinion on the audit report. Potential problems will be identified and dealt with ahead of the release of the financial statements.

Upstream

The oil and gas industry can be divided into two types of operation: upstream and **downstream** [p. 110]:

- Upstream operations are concerned with the production of crude oil and natural gas. They also include exploration and transportation.

- Downstream operations include refining and distribution of refined oil.

The major oil companies such as BP and Shell usually have both upstream and downstream activities. These are called integrated oil companies.

Smaller companies tend to be specialised: there are several London listed upstream companies such as Premier Oil and Burren Energy.

Upstream companies are heavily exposed to the risk of changes in **crude oil** [p. 81] prices. The risk goes both ways (profits will rise if the oil price does, as well as fall if the oil price falls). Changes in prices for downstream companies' supplies are usually passed on to customers. Their profits are less effected by changes in oil prices.

Utility

The concept of utility is central to the economic analysis of the behaviour of individuals. It is usually defined as the satisfaction that individuals gain from buying products (whether goods or services).

The assumption is that individuals will make choices that maximise their utility. It is not unreasonable to define utility as what individuals are attempting to maximise through the economic choices they make.

The utility of money is important in **financial economics** [p. 139]. It is usually assumed that the utility of an individual's wealth increases at a declining rate – that an extra pound means more to a poor person than to a rich one. In mathematical terms, the first derivative of the function relating utility to an amount of money is always positive and its second derivative is always negative. This assumption is used to derive the **CAPM** [p. 50].

Other assumptions may be made. These include using money as a measure of utility so, by definition, the utility of wealth increases at a fixed rate as wealth increases.

Utility is an important and useful concept, but it is difficult to define in an objective way. Some economic models avoid defining utility as a measurable of numerical quantity, and instead rely on consumer choices between possible baskets of purchases.

Utility curve

A utility curve is the relationship between **utility** [p. 334] and the supply of something that increases utility, or the graphical representation of that relationship.

This is a key concept in economics. In **financial economics** [p. 139] the important utility curve is the one that describes the utility of wealth.

Valuation ratios

A valuation ratio is a measure of how cheap or expensive a security (or business) is, compared to some measure of profit or value. A valuation ratio is calculated by dividing a measure of price by a measure of value, or vice-versa.

The point of a valuation ratio is to compare the cost of a security (or a company, or a business) to the benefits of owning it.

The most widely used valuation ratio is the **PE ratio** [p. 237] which compares the cost of a share to the profits made for shareholders per share.

The **EV/EBITDA** [p. 129] also compares price to profits, but in a somewhat more complex manner. It compares the cost of buying the businesses of a company free of debt, to profits. Because someone buying a company free of debt would no longer have to pay interest, the profit measure used changes to profit before interest. It is also adjusted for non-cash items.

Price/book value [p. 249] compares a share price to the value of a company's assets. This ratio is generally only important for certain sectors, such as property holding companies and **investment trusts** [p. 180]. This is because investors buy shares for the **cash flows** [p. 53] they will generate, and because asset values shown in the accounts usually reflect the **accrual principle** [p. 4] rather than real economic value.

The most theoretically correct way in which to value securities is to use a **DCF** [p. 88]. So why do investors rely so much on valuation ratios? One advantage of valuation ratios is that they are a lot simpler. The uncertainties around the numbers used for a discounted cash flow means that it may not be any better in practice.

It is also possible to regard valuation ratios as a quick equivalent to a discounted cash flow. Suppose one is comparing companies in the same sector, and they are broadly similar businesses with very similar risks and the same expected rates of cash flow growth. In that case a **price/FCF** [p. 250] will show the same same companies as being relatively cheap and expensive as a **free cash flow** [p. 146] DCF valuation will.

Value added

Value added is the amount by which the value of goods or services are increased by each stage in its production. It is the difference between the value of all the inputs (raw materials, purchased services) and the price at which the product is sold.

A company's value added is the total amount of value added by all a company's activities. It is:

sales − payments to suppliers

Value added can be decomposed into three components:

1. employees emoluments

2. taxation

3. returns to providers of capital (interest and dividends).

Money that is retained by a company is part of the return to providers of capital as it is still owned by the shareholders.

Value added is used as a basis for taxation: i.e. VAT.

Value added is used as a measure of the size of national economies, **GDP** [p. 156] is the sum of value added of all firms in an economy. Value added can similarly be used as a measure of the size of a company. As a measure of size it is rarely of interest to investors as it can not be related to valuation measures – **EV** [p. 121] and **market cap** [p. 196] are more relevant. It does give a more meaningful answer to the question "how big is this company?" than turnover or profits because it is not distorted by the amount of **vertical integration** [p. 339] or by low **margins** [p. 253].

Value added statement

An accounting statement based on the concept of value added, the value added statement, shows:

- sales

- amounts paid to suppliers

- the distribution of value added; its division between tax, employees and returns on capital.

The value added statement has enjoyed periods of popularity in several countries, but has never really established itself. It is often seen as a form of social reporting and its **disclosure** [p. 98] is often aimed at groups other than investors – for example, it can be a way of demonstrating to workers how large a share goes to them.

It can often be illuminating from the point of view of investors, even if it is not as important as the major accounting statements.

Value at risk

Value at Risk (VaR) is a measure of the risk of a portfolio. It is closely related to its **volatility** [p. 340].

The Value at Risk is the largest amount that a portfolio risks losing with a given level of confidence.

If a portfolio has a VaR of x with 99% confidence over one week, this means that there is only a 1% chance that a portfolio will lose more than x in the next week.

VaR is particularly useful for managing complex combinations of risk over short time periods. It is therefore often used by banks and other financial institutions to measure the risk of their trading positions. It allows them measure the combined risk of a large number of different positions that may be held at any one time. It does this in a form that can be related to their ability to absorb that risk

Value at risk is usually used as a measure of short term risk: often as little as a day or a week. It is difficult to apply to longer term risk as the probability distributions of the future value of securities deviate further from the **normal distribution** [p. 218]. The chances of very large movements in the market (such as a crash) are often much larger than would be the case with a normal distribution: the actual distribution is "fat tailed" compared to the normal distribution. This makes the calculation of an accurate VaR harder

Value investing

Value investing is a style of investing based on picking shares that have low valuations relative to their current profits, cash flows and **dividend yield** [p. 107]. It is one of the two main approaches to stock picking, the other being **growth investing** [p. 161].

Value investing is generally regarded as lower risk than growth investing. Unlike growth investing, which is only suitable for investors looking far capital gains, value investing strategies can be used by investors looking for either capital gains or income – although an **income investor** [p. 168] is likely to use a different value strategy to one who wants capital gains.

Value investors look for low valuations on current earnings rather than for higher valuations that may be justified by future growth. A value investor is more likely than a **growth investor** [p. 161] to prefer a share with a low valuation and stable earnings to one that has a higher valuation and growing earnings.

Value investing is less likely than growth investing to interest investors who are looking for dramatic results, however there are a number of value investors who have been very successful.

Exactly what measures a value investor will look at varies. **PE** [p. 237] and **dividend yield** [p. 107] are obviously easy and are widely used but **EV/EBITDA** [p. 129] is also useful and the most successful growth investors seem to pay a lot of attention to cash flows. The last is, after all, theoretically the most correct approach.

Investors who emphasise yield should also look at earnings and cashflows, if only to ensure sufficient **dividend cover** [p. 103].

There is usually a reason for low valuations. Investors should know why a stock is cheap before buying it. For example, if the historical or prospective PE (or yield, price/cashflow etc.) is very low, there may be a risk of a significant deterioration.

VaR

See **value at risk** [p. 336].

Variable costs

Costs that change in proportion to sales are variable costs. Common variable costs include raw materials, shipping and depletion.

The opposite of variable costs are **fixed costs** [p. 143]. In between are **semi-variable costs** [p. 292] that have fixed and variable elements.

A high level of variable costs means a low level of **operational gearing** [p. 227].

Variance

See **standard deviation** [p. 305].

Vega

Vega is a term (for which varying symbols are used) for the rate of change of the price of a derivative or portfolio with the **volatility** [p. 340] of an underlying security. It is:

$$\frac{\partial P}{\partial \sigma}$$

Unlike most related terms, it is not a Greek letter. It is, nonetheless, one of the **greeks** [p. 160].

Venture capital

Venture capital companies and funds invest in start-ups, or in the expansion of the existing operations of private companies.

Venture capital investments are high risk, but the risk is usually well **diversified** [p. 103]. Any one venture capital company makes a wide range of investments and only expects some to succeed. The returns on venture capital investments can be very high, but the failure rate of early stage companies is also very high.

Venture capital investors usually have real influence over the management of the companies they invest in. This is quite natural as they are likely to be a major shareholders. They often have expertise that can be useful in managing companies better. The level of involvement they seek can also lead to conflicts with the founders of a business.

Venture capital companies are wary of investing in very early stage companies. They are also frequently reluctant to make small investments (usually, much less than a million pounds) because of the time needed to actively manage a large number of separate investments.

As many start-ups need small amounts, and venture capital companies are reluctant to provide it, the gap has increasingly been filled by **angel investors** [p. 15].

Venture capital is only part of the broader **private equity** [p. 252] industry.

Vertical integration

Vertical integration is integration along a supply chain. For example, if a retailer starts manufacturing the products it sells, it is increasing its level of vertical integration. Vertical integration may be **backward integration** [p. 27] or **forward integration** [p. 145].

The advantages of vertical integration include the ability to secure supplies and future orders. This can also mean that the parts of the business sheltered from competition can become less efficient as they are no longer subject to the discipline of competing in an open market. Vertical integration is most often justifiable where it leads to either operational efficiencies or some other source of strategic advantage.

Businesses have increasingly moved to **outsourcing** [p. 232] many functions. This is often a significant move away from vertical integration – for example the separation of design and marketing from manufacturing that has occurred in electronics.

Businesses may also choose to **integrate horizontally** [p. 165].

Vertical markets

Vertical markets are those defined by the type of customer (often by type of industry) rather than by the type of product.

For example, it is possible to divide the market for computer software for business use by the type of software: e.g. accounting software, **CRM software** [p. 80], office productivity software, operating systems etc.

Alternatively, it is possible to divide up the market by the type of buyer. For example the telecoms, healthcare, banking and utilities industries are all important buyers of software. If each of these industries is regarded as a separate market, then each is a vertical market.

There are a number of reasons why it may be important to think in terms of vertical markets, and why companies may organise themselves to address vertical markets:

- The growth drivers will generally differ in different vertical markets. For example telecoms is **cyclical** [p. 84], utilities are not.

- The needs of customers may vary between vertical markets. Therefore it may be possible to design or modify products to address those needs better.

- Business units specialising in a vertical market can develop a better understanding of customers' needs.

Specialising in vertical markets can be an important way of **differentiating** [p. 253] products and services. A strong position in a vertical market can erect a high **barrier to entry** [p. 30]. It can reduce **economies of scale** [p. 117] because addressing vertical markets requires smaller specialist business units rather than larger generalist divisions.

VOIP

Voice over internet protocol (VOIP) technology is the use of internet protocol (IP) networks (data networks of the type developed for the internet) to carry voice phone calls.

The most obvious use of VOIP for consumers is to use internet connections to make voice phone calls through a computer. This is usually cheaper, but less reliable, than the use of a standard phone line.

More important, although much less visible, is the move by telecoms companies from networks that handled voice and data separately (demanding two separate networks) to unified IP networks that handle both. These networks, unlike consumer VOIP technology, can guarantee the quality of voice calls. They reduce costs by allowing telecoms companies to move to a single network, rather than maintaining separate voice and data networks.

VOIP is also being built into telephones and many corporate internal networks are already using VOIP, for much the same reasons as the telecoms companies. Ultimately all voice calls are expected to be carried over IP networks end-to-end.

Volatility

The volatility of the price of a security is a statistical measure of the risk of holding it.

The volatility is the **standard deviation** [p. 305] of **expected return** [p. 135] on a security. The volatility therefore changes with the period of times over which it is measured.

Beta [p. 34] is a slightly more sophisticated measure of risk, based on both relative volatility and the **correlation** [p. 74] between movements in the price of a security and the market are a whole. Although beta is useful for valuation, volatility is a better measure of the risk an investor takes. It is the basis of measures such as **value at risk** [p. 336].

The problem with volatility is that it can only be measured with certainty for the past, but what matters to investors is the volatility now – over time periods starting from the current time and ending at some future time. There are two simple approaches:

1. Assume that the volatility is unchanged in the long run and therefore use the average volatility over a past period.

2. Use the **implied volatility** [p. 167].

More complex models can be used. Approaches such as using a **weighted average** [p. 25] of past volatilities (with more recent data getting a higher weighting) have proved successful.

Methods for estimating volatilities do usually have the advantage of being well suited to **back-testing** [p. 26].

VWAP

A volume weighted average price (VWAP) is used as the published closing price of a security.

The obvious closing price is the last price at which a security traded before trading stopped for the day. The problem with this is that a small transaction at the end of the day can change the closing price. This means that the closing price can reflect freakish trades (e.g., one resulting from the accidental entry of a buy at a very high price of a sell at a very low price). Even worse, it can open the way to deliberate distortion of the price through the placing of orders at very high or low prices just before trading closes.

Using VWAP solves this problem. It the average price at which a security traded over a period prior to the close of trading. The period runs for a fixed time ending with either the close of trading or at the time of the last trade in the security. The exact method used to calculated a VWAP will depend on the trading rules of the market in question.

The VWAP is the value of trading in the period, divided by the number of shares traded in the period.

Of course the VWAP does not solve the problem completely for very **illiquid** [p. 190] securities, whose prices remain easily manipulated, but it does make it much harder to manipulate closing prices for a wide range of moderately liquid securities.

There are a number of motives for manipulating closing prices. Closing prices of **underlying** [p. 331] securities are used to calculate the settlement values of **derivatives** [p. 96]. Closing prices are also used for formal statements of the value of a portfolio (e.g., in a company's annual report). They are sometimes used to calculate directors' remuneration. They will have an impact on an **index** [p. 169] and therefore on the prices of index derivatives.

An alternative way in which markets can provide a hard to manipulate closing price is through holding a closing **call auction** [p. 44]. This has the disadvantage of requiring the use of a particular trading mechanism, whereas VWAP requires only an extra (automated) calculation.

WACC

Weighted average cost of capital (WACC) is the return that the providers of a company's capital require. Calculating it requires knowing the rates of return required for each source of capital

This is generally straightforward for bank debt. The rate of return is the interest rate charged. For traded debt, such as bonds, the rate of return needs to be corrected for the price at which the debt trades, so one would use the **yield to maturity** [p. 350].

The cost of capital for equity is the rate of return used for calculating the value of a company to shareholders using a **discounted cash flow** [p. 88]. It can be calculated from the **beta** [p. 34] of shares, market returns and the **risk free rate of return** [p. 282] using **CAPM** [p. 50]. If a company has more than one class of share, then a rate of return needs to be calculated for each.

For other forms of capital, such as **convertible bonds** [p. 72], it becomes more complicated.

The cost of capital will be different for each of the different types of capital a company has, reflecting the different risks. The WACC is the **weighted average** [p. 344] of the costs of each of the different types of capital. The weights are proportion of the company's capital that comes from each source. In a simple case:

$$WACC = \frac{D}{D+E}i + \frac{E}{D+E}r$$

where i is the interest rate,
r is the required return on equity,
D is the amount of debt capital,
and E is the amount of equity capital.

This is not complete. WACC unifies the costs of sources of capital that are subject to different tax treatments. This needs to be adjusted for. It is particularly important to adjust the cost of debt capital (usually tax deductible) to put it on the same basis as equity capital.

To do this we need to adjust the tax deductible costs by correcting the cost of debt for the tax savings made. This means the calculation becomes:

$$WACC = \frac{D}{D+E}\frac{1}{1-t}i + \frac{E}{D+E}r$$

where t is the tax rate.

This may need to be adjusted further where there is more than one type of debt or equity capital. To take a common example supposedly debt D is actually split into **senior debt** [p. 293] and **subordinated debt** [p. 310], then:

$$WACC = \frac{D_1}{D+E}\frac{1}{1-t}i_1 + \frac{D_2}{D+E}\frac{1}{1-t}i_2 + \frac{E}{D+E}r$$

where D_1 is the amount of senior debt,
D_2 is the amount of subordinated debt,
i_2 is the YTM of the senior debt and
i_2 is the YTM of the subordinated debt.

More complex forms of capital such as convertible debt would require considerably more complex adjustments.

Walled garden

In media and telecoms, a walled garden exists when a communications service provides access to content that is restricted to a communications providers' own content. It does not allow customers to access content from third parties unless they have made an arrangement with the provider (usually paying for the privilege). Walled gardens are the opposite of open networks such as the internet.

The internet killed many walled garden services. A few internet service providers have a limited amount of success in directing subscribers to their own services. Most attempts to set up walled garden services in this space after the advent of the internet have failed.

Walled gardens continue to flourish in television (e.g. satellite and cable services), albeit subject to regulatory control. They also survive in high value niches such as financial data (e.g., Reuters and Bloomberg terminals).

Telecoms companies (both mobile and fixed) are attempting to set up walled garden services for the delivery of multimedia content (films and music in particular). History suggests that they will fail, and trying to sell such services to customers now accustomed to the free access the internet gives them can only be more difficult than in the past. However, much depends on the attitudes of regulators.

Warrants

A warrant is a security very similar to a **call option** [p. 45]. A warrant is issued by the company whose shares are the underlying security. If it is exercised, the shares are not delivered by a transfer of existing shares. The company insstead issues new shares at the **exercise price** [p. 135].

This means that, unlike options, warrants can cause dilution of earnings and therefore affect the value of the underlying security. This is not usually significant, but some companies have large numbers of warrants or equivalent securities (such as **convertible bonds** [p. 72]) which would have a significant impact if exercised.

Warrants are often sold together with bonds or other debt instruments. The effect of this is similar to a convertible bond issue, with the advantage that the option and pure bond elements can be sold separately. If debt holders keep the warrants, they **hedges** [p. 162] the risks of changes that benefit shareholders at the expense of debt holders. There mere existence of the hedge reduces the incentive shareholders have to do so.

It is common for warrants to have a term of years, whereas options have a shorter life.

Warrant premium

A warrant premium is the amount by which the cost of buying and exercising a **warrant** [p. 343] exceeds the cost of buying the underlying shares directly.

A warrant premium is the **option value** [p. 229] of a warrant. It is calculated the same way: price less **intrinsic value** [p. 179].

Weighted average

A weighted **average** [p. 25] is more heavily influenced by some of the numbers it is calculated from than others.

It is calculated by:

1. multiplying each number by a weight

2. adding the results together

3. dividing the total by the sum of the weights.

Stock market **indices** [p. 169] are based on weighted averages of share prices. The weights are the **market caps** [p. 196] of the companies in the index. More complex variants on this are often used.

Weighted average cost of capital

See **WACC** [p. 342].

Weighted moving average

A weighted moving average is simply a **moving average** [p. 210] that is weighted (see **weighted average** [p. 344]) so that more recent values are more heavily weighted than values further in the past.

The commonest type of weighted moving average is exponential smoothing. The calculation is quite simple:

$$P_0 + \alpha P_1 + \alpha^2 P_2 + \alpha^3 P_3 + \cdots + \alpha^n P_n + \cdots$$

where α, the smoothing factor, is more than zero and less than one, P_0 is the latest value on which the moving average is being calculated and P_i is the value i periods previously (usually i days ago).

It is not necessary to sum the entire infinite series, just enough of it to give an accurate estimate.

There is evidence that the use of weighted moving averages gives better **volatility** [p. 340] estimates than simple moving averages do.

West Texas Intermediate

West Texas Intermediate (WTI) is the most important US benchmark **crude oil** [p. 81]. WTI crude oil is of high quality and can produce a high proportion of petrol. A light (see **API gravity** [p. 17]) sweet oil.

White knight

A white knight is a bidder who makes an **agreed takeover bid** [p. 13] as an alternative to a **hostile takeover bid** [p. 165] that is already in progress.

There are a number of reasons why the directors of the target company may prefer the white knight. It may be that the white knight offers a better deal for shareholders. It may also be that the white knight offers a better deal to the directors.

While directors have a legal duty to make recommendations on the basis of shareholder's interests, there are often clear conflicts of interest when takeovers occur. See **hostile takeover bid** [p. 165].

Wi-Fi

Wi-fi is a set of standards for technology allowing computers and other devices to communicate using radio connections instead of cables. It was originally intended to allow the replacement of the cables which commonly connect computer networks on a single site with more convenient radio links. It has proved to be useful well beyond this limited role.

Wi-fi is also known as WLAN, because it is a wireless type of local area network (LAN).

One particularly important application is the use of wi-fi for mobile internet access. Its main competitor in this role are 3G mobile phone networks. In comparison to them:

- Mobile networks provide extensive coverage, covering whole countries. Wi-fi provides coverage in "hot spots" and even city wide coverage is only now becoming common.

- Wi-fi requires much cheaper infrastructure. It is so cheap that some cities are building free wi-fi networks and cafs and airports offer free hotspots. Even some private individuals provide free internet access through a single hotspot.

- Wi-fi uses unregulated spectrum (radio frequencies) so the **barriers to entry** [p. 30] are much lower.

- Mobile networks can provide uninterrupted connections to moving equipment.

Because of its low cost and the increasingly wide availability of equipment (such as laptop computers) that can use wi-fi, it is a serious threat to mobile phone networks' **data revenues** [p. 85].

WIP

Work in progress (WIP) is the part of **stocks** [p. 307] that is currently being worked on.

WIP is no longer **raw materials** [p. 264] because it has undergone some processing. It is also not yet finished goods because more work has to be done to put it into the state in which it would normally be sold.

Like any other stock, WIP is valued at the lower of:

- Cost: this is the cost of the raw materials and the processing.

- **Net realisable value** [p. 214]: the price for which it could be sold less costs involved in selling.

The value of WIP includes the cost of processing in order to match costs with revenues in accordance with the **accrual** [p. 4] principle.

If the value of stocks falls, an unrealised loss has been made and this needs to be reflected in the accounts.

The valuation of work in progress does depend on the methods of costing employed by a company: companies have a lot of discretion about which costs are allocated to the cost of goods they make, and which are simply taken as expenses in the period.

The rules for calculating WIP for tax purposes are (for obvious reasons) more rigid than those for financial reporting purposes.

WLAN

See **Wi-fi** [p. 345].

Work in progress

See **WIP** [p. 346].

Working capital

Working capital is the amount of money that a company has tied up in funding its day to day operations.

A company has to tie up money to fund its stocks, credit sales and other **current assets** [p. 83], but this is offset by its ability to fund this from **current liabilities** [p. 84] liabilities such as purchases on credit. If a company buys on credit it does not have to tie up (as much) money in its stocks. In some businesses (such as grocery retail) working capital can even be negative. A business that buys on credit and sells for cash is being partly funded by its suppliers.

The most common definitions of working capital are:

- *current assets − current liabilities*

- *stocks + trade debtors − trade creditors*

The advantage of the second definition is that it focuses on the most important parts of working capital from the point of view of judging the efficiency of a business's operations. It avoids some short term liabilities (such as overdrafts) which reflect the financing of the business rather than the capital requirements of its operations.

It is worth looking at trends in working capital, and in particular the reasons for increases or decreases. For example, if working capital is growing faster than sales it could mean that the company is offering over generous credit terms to get sales, or that it is over-stocking. These are just two of many possibilities. Either of these would also slow the conversion of profits into cashflow.

Working capital, particularly when defined as current assets minus current liabilities, is closely related to key measures of financial stability such as the **current assets ratio** [p. 83] and the **quick assets ratio** [p. 261] .

Working capital ratio

The working capital ratio is an indicator of the efficiency of a company's management of stocks, debtors and creditors, it is:

$$\frac{stocks + trade\ debtors - trade\ creditors}{sales}$$

If the working capital ratio is 0.2, this means the company needs 20p of working capital for every £1 of annual sales. If annual sales increase by £100,000 of then the company will have to invest £20,000 in working capital to be able to meet this.

Changes in the working capital ratio can be further analysed by decomposing them into changes in **debtor days** [p. 91], **creditor days** [p. 79] and **stock days** [p. 308].

Written down value

See **Book value** [p. 38].

Yankee bond

A Yankee bond is a US dollar denominated **bond** [p. 37] issued in the US by a foreign issuer.

The reasons for issuing a yankee bond are much the same as for **eurobonds** [p. 126] in general but:

- The size of the US bond market makes it attractive to borrowers who wish to raise very large amounts. These include countries issuing **sovereign debt** [p. 300].

- The size of the US economy and the common use of the dollar in international trade means that many companies have dollar income streams with which to pay dollar debt.

Issuing and trading bonds in the US makes the issuer subject to US regulation. Complying with this is very expensive. This is one reason for the issue of, and trading in, US dollar bonds off-shore.

Yellow strip

Certain **London Stock Exchange** [p. 192] trading screens show **market makers'** [p. 197] quotes in two columns. One column shows bid prices, the other column shows offer prices. Both columns show the best quotes (highest bid and lowest offer) at the top.

A yellow strip runs through the top line of both columns, highlighting the best **bid** [p. 35] and **offer** [p. 222] prices. The best bid and offer prices are therefore known as "yellow strip" prices.

Yield

The most common meanings of the word "yield" in an investment context are:

- **dividend yield** [p. 107]

- **yield to maturity** [p. 350]

- **flat yield** [p. 144].

Although they are superficially similar measures, there are important differences between them.

The first is that yield to maturity is a measure of **total return** [p. 325] on an investment. On the other hand **flat yield** [p. 144] and dividend yield are measures of the income at a point in time relative to the price.

Dividends are a very different income stream from interest. Bond yields are usually either fixed or floating and will be paid unless the issuer is in serious financial difficulty.

Dividend yields depend on company profits and dividend policy. This usually means that dividend will grow. It also means that they tend to be far more risky than interest payments on bonds. This is why a **yield gap** [p. 349] exists.

Yield curve

See **term structure** [p. 320].

Yield gap

The yield gap is the difference between the average dividend yields in a market and the bond yields in the same market.

By "market" we would usually mean either a national market or the global markets for shares and bonds.

The yield gap is a useful measure of the valuation of a stock market and can be an indicator that a market is over or under valued. An unusual yield gap can be justified by higher or lower growth expectations.

The yield gap is also changes over time in response to changing conditions. For example, if companies commonly choose to increase share-buy backs rather than dividends, the yield on shares will fall. There are a number of reasons why companies might choose to do this, including tax structures, and the widespread tying of directors remuneration to share prices.

Yield spread

The yield spread is the difference between the **yield** [p. 350] on a **bond** [p. 37] and the yield on a similar risk free debt instrument. It is the amount by which the yield on a bond exceeds the **risk free rate** [p. 282] for the same cash flows.

This means that the yield spread represents the **risk premium** [p. 282] a particular instrument pays.

It therefore reflects the **credit risk** [p. 79] taken.

Yield spreads can also sometimes usefully be calculated for a sector, or between a particular bond and a basket of other bonds such as its sector.

YTM (Yield to maturity)

The yield to maturity (YTM) of a bond is the **IRR** [p. 183] that a buyer would receive if they purchased the bond at the current market price. This is also called the redemption yield.

It does not provide a perfect comparison of bond values, even leaving aside issues such as risk. Interest rates may vary over the life of the bond so that a bond with a lower YTM may be a better buy because the timing of payments may mean it provides a better return compared to market rates. It is, nonetheless, generally a much better measure than **flat yield** [p. 144].

Zero (zero dividend preference share)

Zero dividend preference shares, often called zeros, are simply **preference shares** [p. 244] that do not pay an annual dividend. They instead simply redeemed for a lump sum at a fixed date.

Zeros are similar to **zero coupon bonds** [p. 350]. They are more risky because they are shares and therefore rank lower than bonds for repayment if a company becomes bankrupt or is otherwise wound up.

To look at this another way, consider how the **present value** [p. 220] of a zero will change if the risk changes. With a single payment a long way off in the future, even a small change in the discount rate will have a large impact on the value. Therefore a small change in the **risk premium** [p. 282] will mean a large change in the value.

Zeros gained something of a bad reputation due to problems at a number of British **split capital investment trusts** [p. 302] that come to light in 2002. This was due to the way in which those particular trusts were managed, and does not say much about the intrinsic qualities of zeros – except perhaps highlighting a need for transparency to allow proper valuation of different classes of share.

Zero coupon bond

A zero **coupon** [p. 77] bond is one which does not pay interest. It is instead issued at a discount to its **face value** [p. 137] (which is what the holder will receive at maturity). Instead of interest payments, the holder receives a **capital gain** [p. 47] at maturity.

The **duration** [p. 113] of a zero coupon bond is clearly longer than that of an otherwise similar bond that pays interest and it will be more sensitive to changes in interest rates. This is best understood by looking at how the **present values** [p. 220] of a zero coupon and an interest paying bond will be affected by changes in interest rates.

The UK, and many other countries, treat some of the capital gain on a zero coupon bond as income for tax purposes.

Zero sum game

A zero sum **game** [p. 154] is one in which the total pay-offs are the same for all possible combinations of players' strategies. This means that each player can only gain at the expense of others; any player's loss is balanced by an equal gain (or gains) made by other players.

It does not actually matter much whether the sum of the pay-offs is zero (the strict requirement for the zero sum game) or another number, as long as the total is the same for all possible outcomes. For this reason, zero sum games are often called constant sum games.

A real life example of a zero sum game is gambling. If one player wins, other players (including the house, if any) must have lost the same amount.

Printed in the United States
71697LV00004BA/83